LITTLE JOE SUPERSTAR

THE FILMS OF JOE DALLESANDRO

MICHAEL FERGUSON

companion
★ P ★ R ★ E ★ S ★ S ★

Laguna Hills, California

ALL RIGHTS RESERVED

No part of this book may be reproduced or utilized in any form or by any means, electronic or mechanical, including photocopying, recording or by any information retrieval system, without permission in writing from Companion Press, PO Box 2575, Laguna Hills, California 92654.

Neither the publishers nor the editors assume, and hereby specifically disclaim, any liability to any party for any loss or damage caused by errors or omissions in *LITTLE JOE, SUPERSTAR—The Films Of Joe Dallesandro* whether such errors or omissions result from negligence, accident or any other cause.

Copyright © 1998 by Michael Ferguson

Companion Press, PO Box 2575, Laguna Hills, California 92654

Printed in Canada

First Printing 1998

Library of Congress Catalog Card Number 98-70584

ISBN: 1-889138-09-6

Cover photo courtesy Joe Dallesandro

For Joe

Courtesy Joe Dallesandro

Photo by Kenn Duncan/Courtesy Joe Dallesandro

contents

acknowledgements	6
foreword by joe dallesandro	8
little joe, superstar: a biography	11

the films

an undress rehearsal (1965)	35
the loves of ondine (1967)	41
lonesome cowboys (1968)	52
san diego surf (1968)	64
flesh (1968)	70
trash (1970)	89
heat (1972)	104
the gardener (1974)	116
flesh for frankenstein (1974)	119
blood for dracula (1974)	130
donna e bello (1974)	139
il tempo degli assassini (1975)	141
l' ambizioso (1975)	144
black moon (1975)	146
calore in provincia (1975)	150
fango bollente (1975)	151
je t'aime moi non plus (1975)	152
la marge (1976)	157
l'ultima volta (1976)	160
un cuore semplice (1977)	162
merry-go-round (1978/83)	163
suor omicidio (1978)	165
queen lear (1978)	167
6000 km di paura (1979)	169
vacanze per un massacro (1979)	172
tapage nocturne (1979)	175
the cotton club (1984)	176
critical condition (1987)	179
sunset (1988)	180
double revenge (1989)	182
private war (1990)	184
cry-baby (1990)	187
almost an angel (1990)	191
guncrazy (1992)	192
bad love (1992)	195
wild orchid II: two shades of blue (1992)	196
sugar hill (1994)	198
theodore rex (1996)	200
pacino is missing (1998)	202

joe-pourri

documentaries	205
short films/music videos	206
television appearances	209
renters', buyers' & screeners' guide	211
about the author	213

acknowledgements

In late 1969, you could have rented Joe Dallesandro for $4,500 a week. Now, now—get your mind out of the gutter. You see, Andy Warhol was offering to rent out his Superstars for roughly that amount as examples of living art. "People only want art so they can talk about it," he told *Esquire*. "This way, they can take the art home, have a party for it, show it to their friends, take Polaroids of it (which I will sign), make tape-recordings. And after the week is over, they'll still have anecdotes."

The offer made for a suitably quirky publicity stunt, complete with Superstars on leashes and even one of them mounted on the wall, but as with many of the bizarre things Warhol said and did, it also touched upon a deeper truth.

There were plenty of us who would have liked to take one of his Superstars home with us and many would have put Joe at the top of the wish list.

The next best thing to having him around to help with the dishes, though, was the comparatively easy task of claiming his Image, the same way you could claim John Wayne's or Clint Eastwood's. To hell with shelling out $4-5,000. For a couple of bucks, you could always see one of his movies and take him home in your mind.

That is, if you could find one of his movies. In the sixties and early seventies, Warhol's flicks weren't exactly reaching small town America. They were the artsy stuff relegated to the big city specialty houses, and in America, at least, Joe was a decidedly urban underground sex symbol.

Then came video and a new generation of enlightened and culturally inquisitive film fans. Joe Dallesandro was about to be re-discovered.

What no book about films can do is replace the experience of actually seeing the movies themselves. Filmgoing is such an intensely subjective experience, even when you're surrounded by hundreds of other moviegoers, that seeing for yourself truly is believing for yourself.

Unfortunately, many of the films of Joe Dallesandro are still not easily found at your local video store. His early work for Andy Warhol is among a 4,000 reel catalog of the artist's films largely unavailable to the general public and only relatively recently undergoing the arduous process of preservation. Even the classic trilogy Joe made for Paul Morrissey—**Flesh**, **Trash** and **Heat**, all part of the first phase of his career—has disappeared from distribution after less than a decade of availability on video; less from lack of interest, I'm convinced, than from lack of proper marketing, and something that I hope will be redressed in the very near future.

The Video Age in which we live has a conspicuously Jekyll/Hyde duality. On the one hand, it has given us access to a world of cinema never before available to the home viewer; on the other, the sheer number of titles and a predictable numbing to the technology have caused information age apathy. People don't know it's out there after it's left the "New Releases" shelf.

The curious thing about the Warhol/Morrissey films' relative obscurity is that they already have a built-in audience: a growing number of people interested in the late Pop Artist, the sixties counterculture scene, and the rise of the underground film. Both gay and straight audiences are eager to have access, but have no place to turn. Even **Andy Warhol's Frankenstein** and **Dracula**, the two titles most easily stumbled across, exist in highly-varied prints from an assortment of video companies that claimed distribution rights at one time or another, most of which offer edited versions of the films that suffer from murky transfers.

One of the goals of this book is to encourage the re-distribution of the Warhol/Morrissey films on videotape and laserdisc so that they can be enjoyed by an audience that just might get their first glimpse reading about them here.

The second phase of Joe Dallesandro's career took place in Europe, where he made at least 18 films from 1974-1979, very few of which have made the trip across the Atlantic.

The third and presently ongoing phase of his career was marked by his return to the American movie screen in 1984. Many of the films of this phase are available on video or laserdisc, but only hint at what his fascinating career has given us over the past three decades.

In an era in which the word "icon" is so frequently assigned that it has nearly lost its power and associated meaning, it would not be an overstatement to say that Joe Dallesandro was an icon when it still meant something: he was a potent sexual image to gay men all over the world looking for open and positive expressions at the time of Stonewall. He was and is more than that, of course, but simplicity is essential to all this icon-business, so it might as well be acknowledged here and now before we take a closer look at him over the next couple of hundred pages.

My deepest gratitude to Joe Dallesandro for providing the hours and hours and hours of his time for interviews and follow-up questions for this book, as well as for providing a wealth of rare photos from his private collection. (He didn't have to do any of this, after all. He's already given us the films and will continue to do so.)

For granting interviews and providing valuable input, sincere thanks to Paul Morrissey and Holly Woodlawn, as well as Callie Angell of the Andy Warhol Film Project at the Whitney Museum of American Art.

For much appreciated assistance in locating resources, screening films, and sharing from their own collections, thanks to Eileen Clancy of the Andy Warhol Foundation for the Visual Arts, Inc., Matt Wrbican of the Archives Study Center and Greg Pierce of the Film and Video Department at The Andy Warhol Museum in Pittsburgh, Buddy Barnett of *Cult Movies* magazine and Cinema Collectors, the staff of the Margaret Herrick Library at the Academy of Motion Picture Arts and Sciences, Wayne Stanley of the Athletic Model Guild, Fred Frey of Luminous Film & Video Wurks, Craig Ledbetter of European Trash Cinema, Video Search of Miami, Doug Aitken, Curtis Brown, Jim Chambos, John Guzman, Steve R., Thea Roessler (for translation services), and Francesco Scavullo. Thanks also to Johnathan Murad for his exceptional copyediting skills, and to my publisher, Steve Stewart, for providing me the opportunity.

Special thanks to Wenzel Roessler, Jr., a good friend and inspiration to this book, also to my sister, Denice Ferguson, as well as Robert Lentz, Michael Crouch, and Christopher Carr for their advice, encouragement and support.

And to my family, for knowing I could do it.

foreword

Over the years I've been approached by many writers, whether they were friends, strangers, or even pizza delivery men, in the prospect of putting together an autobiography, a filmography of my work, or a combination of sorts. I've always said "no," mainly because those who approached me in the past had no real knowledge of my work. They associated me with the Warhol "pop star" scene and they had difficulty separating me from my movie persona (image). I was tired of repetitive questions, like "How did you meet Andy Warhol?" Or ignorant ones, like "What was Edie Sedgwick like?" Questions like those would piss me off and leave me cold and uninterested. These aspiring "authors" obviously never did their homework, usually asking me about people who weren't even there during my period at the Factory.

Although it was a great opportunity to "Star" in Warhol's films and it made me famous, it was also hard to be taken seriously later in my acting career; due to such a strong identification with Warhol, it was like I had done nothing else. So let me tell you, it was really refreshing to meet Michael Ferguson, who immediately impressed me with his knowledge of the scene.

I was first approached by Michael via phone from Chicago. He wanted to interview me for an edition of a magazine called *Cult Movies* and he asked if he were to fly out to Los Angeles would I grant him some time to talk to me? I said sure. I'd had calls like this in the past and I wasn't overly anxious, to be honest, because many times—thank God—these people would never be heard from again.

A few days later Michael showed up at my door, hands full with tape-recorder, photos, a briefcase full of notes and press articles—finally, I met a man who does his homework. His sister dropped him off and wanted to know when she should come back to pick him up. I wanted to tell her to come back in an hour, but suggested to Michael that we call her when the interview began winding down. And so we were off.

From his notes, Michael knew I had been unhappy with some past interviews, especially one I did years ago with Rex Reed. There had been this silly mix-up in our conversation that made me angry and managed to upset my dad, as well. Michael wanted to know what I had really meant to say. His immediate concern and integrity, and even more impressive, *the amount of work he had done before meeting me* kept me engrossed and comfortable enough to pull an all-nighter, with Michael sorting out photos, getting dates right and stories straight. We worked up until the last minute when his sister showed up the following day to whisk him back to the plane to Chicago. (And we've logged quite a few hours since in preparation for the book you now hold in your hands.)

Little Joe, Superstar: The Films of Joe Dallesandro is the first book to deal with my body of work alone, not as part of a Warhol retrospective or as a part of the works of Paul Morrissey, but of *my* work. It is also the first book *anywhere* that I have participated in and endorsed.

To my real fans, and you know who you are, I hope *Little Joe, Superstar* adds another notch to a love affair that's been like a house on fire since I first started hearing from you. Those of you who know me from the very early shots of the Athletic Model Guild to **Loves of Ondine** to **Flesh** and **Trash** and so on, we need no introduction. Just make sure, as always, to leave your donation on the way out. For those of you who may just be discovering me here, I hope you like what you see and that maybe you'll feel inspired enough to demand that more of my early films be made available for the home market. (A residual couldn't hurt now and again.) To the rest of you scum, we've all got to pay our dues. Little Joe never once gave it away, but I do work cheap, which has been both a blessing and a curse. I've been acting for over thirty years now. My room here in Hollywood doesn't quite compare with Paul Morrissey's Montauk Haute, and certainly pales in comparison to Andy's homes or to Calvin Klein's, for that matter, but I've paid my dues. I think we can all agree on that.

I offer nothing more than my work, and like I said, I work cheap. I'm not one to drop names, so I won't, but if you care to read further, I think it will remain quite clear that I shouldn't have to …

Love,
JoeBoy

Photo by Jack Robinson/Courtesy *Vogue*, Copyright © 1971 by The Condé Nast Publications Inc.

little joe superstar: a biography

"When people ask me how do I feel about being in the movies, about having my pictures in the movie ads every day, I don't like to say I don't feel anything, because sure, I do. But it's not like a lot of people probably think I should feel. I don't want to sound conceited. I mean—I'm just Little Joe—and I hope people like me."

—*Joe Dallesandro, age 20, July, 1969*

Writing a "biography" when you're technically not writing a biography presents a unique challenge. For example, I did not conduct corroborating interviews with all who are mentioned in the following sketch of the life of Joe Dallesandro. However, I did have rare access to the subject himself, a man who used to tell interviewers: "whatever isn't in there, just make it up." That was a catchy credo developed during the earliest days of his fame, when he learned that any exposure was better than no exposure at all.

Dallesandro, though, has not been a frequent interviewee over the years, less from lack of media interest than from the savvy combination of a calculated desire to cultivate a mystique, an honest aversion to yapping replies to the same old questions over and over again, and a persistently guarded posture designed to avoid allowing the press to turn him into something he never was.

Then there's the not-so-insignificant matter of bringing his family into focus.

"One of the first interviews that I'd done really set me off," he explains. "It was with Rex Reed. He'd done this interview and he wrote this shit, picking up on some of the stuff I had said, but then getting it confused. He elaborated on these little things I'd said, and I could really have cared less, but he was off on his facts and he wrote that my father had been married one more time than he was, or something similar, and it really upset my dad. That it upset my father, it upset me, and it made me really hate Rex for years. It also made me kind of shy about how I did my interviews, because something could be read the wrong way, misconstrued—or if it was my fault and I didn't get the facts exactly right, people could get offended."

He then takes the time to both name and count the number of wives his father had over the course of his life. 1, 2, 3, uh, 4.

"That was four, not five—that's not bad. He gets mad if I get the facts wrong. Even though he's gone. [Joe's father passed away in 1993.] I'm sure he'd get pissed off if I said five and there were only four."

The first time I met Joe Dallesandro I expected him to be disquietingly quiet, perhaps so low-key that I'd have to duct-tape my tape-recorder to his chin just to register a reply.

So much for being smart enough not to confuse the movie image with the actor who provides it.

Joe, in fact, can be quite the lively conversationalist. True to his urban roots, he talks like the inner city kid he still harbors inside, casually dispersing his "fucks" throughout normal conversation and tending to lapse in and out of first-person present-tense dialogues when recalling conversations and events from his distant past.

Photo by Kenn Duncan/Courtesy Joe Dallesandro

"All this stuff is true," he reassures me. "Because," he adds, "when you make up shit about your life it's too hard to remember."

And yet, with almost Warholian counter-logic, he is still fond of telling reporters to wing it. He rarely reads the finished product.

It's because, I think, he's the real thing.

Twenty-five years ago, for the hell of it, Norman Mailer socked a silent Joe in the arm at a party and was happily and unexpectedly the recipient of a return blow to the stomach, causing the writer to proclaim loudly to the rest of the crowd that he'd found the only real man in the whole place.

Not schooled in the studio-bred refineries of giving good PR, his voice, his word-choice, and his manner come directly from a life lived on hard streets and in hard times. He's just a kid from the neighborhood who's found himself in the creepy realm of celebrity where unnatural significance is assigned to every ordinary thing a guy does.

His earliest interviews capture a charming naiveté, an inability to be much other than himself—though perhaps with a tendency toward exaggerating the cocky, rough-and-tumble sort of scrapper he wanted others to see. This has caused some writers to comment on his simplicity and others to come away seriously mistaken about his intellect.

Viewing Joe through elitist eyes is a mistake, however, for two reasons. First, he's a good storyteller if you get him going and he holds nothing back when it comes to offering an opinion on person, place or thing. Secondly, he seems as largely devoid of ego when talking about his career and the famous people whom he's encountered as you'd hope a regular Joe like Joe would be. He's not even a name-dropper. You have to *ask* him about the rich and famous people he's rubbed up against.

So what happens when Joe Dallesandro speaks, when an appealingly enigmatic Superstar of the underground film movement of the sixties and seventies at long last decides to talk *in detail* about his life and his career? (And more may follow, since Joe has been working on and off again on an autobiography for years.)

Well, honestly, for me, there's the fear of demystifying a potent mystery. Maybe I don't want to know what Joe was thinking when he did that scene in **Flesh**. Maybe it'll spoil it if I find out that "he" has a different attitude than "him." Or just maybe I'll discover that even Joe doesn't know who that "other" Joe is or what he can possibly mean to his fans. After all, once committed to film, the actor no longer owns the image; the image belongs to the audience.

In a sense, the actor belongs to us, too.

Joseph Angelo D'Alessandro III was born December 31, 1948, in Pensacola, Florida. His father was an 18-year old Italian-American sailor, stationed at the local Naval base, who had married 14-year old Thelma Testman. Joe, Sr. had been trained as an electrical engineer, and his occupation would often take him between New York City and his Florida homebase. Joey had been born when Thelma was just 16.

It was in New York, almost exactly one year later, on December 28, 1949, that Thelma gave birth to the couple's second son, Robert. There was trouble ahead for the D'Alessandros, however, even beyond the challenge of having children when the mother was so young. Sandy, as Thelma was now nicknamed in an abbreviation of D'Alessandro, ran into some major trouble when she was arrested back down in Florida for interstate auto theft and subsequently convicted and sentenced to five years in a Federal penitentiary.

Joe, Sr. maintained custody of their children in the separation and divorce that was to follow, and took the boys up to New York with him. But maintaining full responsibility over his sons was something he felt he couldn't do. Apparently, it was something of which no one in the family felt capable, either. Even with other family in the area, including a grandmother, the boys ended up at Angel Guardian Home awaiting foster care. They were not housed together, however, since Bob wasn't yet potty-trained and was kept separate from those who were.

The facility was in the inner city and populated largely with minority children. The separation from family had to be devastating to the boys, but much of what Joe remembers about his time there comes from things he's been told years later. For instance, things such as racial prioritizing. Being white was an advantage.

"I'd walk up to the glass window and say, 'Will you be my mommy?'" Joe recalls. "And, of course, a white person looking down at the only white person in this institution in Harlem wasn't going to say, 'No, I'll take the black boy over there.' So pretty much I had the choice of any white person who walked in there. It was just a matter of deciding which one I was going to say, 'Will you be my Mommy?' to, and it was hard. I didn't want to say it. So, you see, events in my life prepared me to be the kind of actor who could just come in off the streets and do it. I was taught to deliver lines when I was very young."

Not only did this impact the psyche of a little boy of three or four now suddenly surrounded by strangers and vaguely aware that he was being looked at by people who might want to take him away, but it also made him afraid that such a decision would mean he would go alone, leaving his little brother Bob behind, signifying its own kind of abandonment unavoidably understood as no one's fault but his own.

Fortunately, when a foster family did step forward and make the choice, they decided not to split up the brothers. Joey and Bobby D'Alessandro went out as a parcel to a couple who already had two kids of their own and lived in Brooklyn. The boys began what would become a full decade of their formative years in the foster care setting.

Joe went to Catholic school in Brooklyn until the second grade, when the family moved to Long Island where the curriculum wasn't as tough. The school had to shuffle him back and forth a grade or two to find out where he belonged.

Joe, Sr. would come and visit approximately once a month.

The visits, as welcome as they were, also were double-edged. Joe says, "You know, when your father comes to visit you once a month, or at least tries to, he's the greatest dad in the world. For one day out of the fucking month it's easy to be the best person in the world. And so the people who kept us in foster care, they became the evil ones because they kept me from seeing my father all of the time. Every time I'd come back, I wouldn't want to come back. You want to stay with your real dad."

The moving around and the sense of not really belonging to anybody promised trouble. And trouble was something Joe soon found. He claims that he was consistent in school, if not outstanding—until he hit puberty, when a combination of hormones, rebellion, competition, and a growing sense of resentment over his family situation began to stew. Singing in the school choir and participating in extracurricular sports didn't help.

"I started getting bad around 12 or 13," he says. By the time he saw **West Side Story** (1961), he was positively set on his life as a tough guy. The movie musical sang to his pre-teen heart about belonging and brotherhood and all he wanted to do was join a gang.

Feeling quite like an outsider among his peers, he was also aware that his body wasn't growing the way many of the other kids' were. He remained short while other boys shot up, and because he had no idea when or if he'd ever get that growth spurt, his self-consciousness and timidity became self-defensiveness and aggression. He might not be the biggest guy in school, but Joe D'Alessandro was sure as hell going to be the toughest and meanest little fucker you'd never want to mess with.

He was getting quite the nasty reputation both on and off school grounds. His foster folks started putting pressure on Joe, Sr. "When my Dad would take me home, I promised not to get in trouble," he says. He had started a scheme of running away from his foster home to force his father's hand. The resentment and pain were building and he was acting on it.

"All these people that were around never offered to take care of my father's two kids, me and my brother. My grandmother couldn't do it. My father couldn't do it. And as wonderful as my grandparents would be, you know that one visit a month? I really was always kind of upset that they never brought my brother and me home to live with them. I mean, we'd be in school—not home—for eight hours a day, or however long kids go to school. And we could join extra things after school even. They'd only see us for a couple of hours before we'd go to bed. That really upset me that they didn't make more of an effort."

Help was too little and too late in coming. "The first time I saw a social worker to deal with my problems was when I was a teenager and had been running away from home. You've been ignoring this problem and now you're going to send help, I thought? It's a bit late. I needed help all along. Now you want to know what's wrong with me? Well, what's wrong with me was that there was nobody there to find out what was going on from day one. The social worker threatened to move me to another foster home and after spending over ten years with one family, you're not going to be able to successfully move a kid to another one."

Joe shows me a photo of himself taken for his First Communion and laughs that you "can see the Devil in those eyes," and he's right. Something lurks behind the smirk and the squint, something altogether missing from the photo of his brother taken at Bobby's otherwise-identical religious milestone. Tellingly, one of Joe's memories from that pre-adolescent period includes his foster folks segregating him and his brother at a tiny kid's table for dinners while the parents and their two children ate together at a table that sure as hell looked like it could have fit two more little guys.

So, Joe started his own family. His "gang" consisted of himself and a couple of friends named Joel and Eddie. Joel got arrested so many times that the cops wouldn't put him in prison, they'd put him in the crazy house. He'd be in school during the week and on weekends he'd break out of the hospital and hit the town with his partners in crime.

The crimes Joe and his buddies perpetrated ran the gamut from petty to not-so-petty. Joe fed on the power and the sense of having a specific role to play being a neighborhood bad-ass gave him. He'd hang out at the candy store where he and his cohorts demonstrated their bravado by snubbing out cigarettes and lit cigars with their forearms, playing a version of "chicken" in which you had to see how long you could keep your arm still after having a fiery ember dropped on it. Too young to drink in bars in his own neighborhood, he'd head over to Jersey and belt them down at black pubs where nobody carded you so long as you had the cash.

He was also a chronic runaway. After an impromptu trip to Philadelphia with his brother, Bob, their dad had to come get the boys. Social services placed Joe in another foster home. This second family Joe likens to Dickens' *Oliver Twist*, complete with a Fagin teaching his wards how to commit crimes. A new development was going up nearby and so Joe and company (all the other foster kids) were entreated to rob old buildings by pilfering them of their toilets or windows and bringing the stuff back for use in their own neighborhood.

Joe and his brother were separated for about a month's time during all this, but then Joe, Sr. intervened and Bob joined his brother at the second foster home.

Things got bad enough that Joe finally insisted that his father "take me home or you put me into a military institution; not realizing, of course, that my Dad couldn't afford military school. He had to take me home. He had little other choice, so he did.

"When I finally did go home, it was the same as the other house. It had all the rules and regulations. My father was not the most wonderful guy all the time. But to his credit, he was more insistent on me getting a great education than anyone, because my father continued to go to school all the time. He'd be going to some kind of night classes for engineering, because they'd always be updating and changing stuff. He was the oldest student I'd ever seen. As a kid, it never made sense to me. I used to ask him, 'Don't you ever get smart enough?'" (Up until his early twenties, Joe used to tell interviewers that he had read only one complete book in his entire lifetime, *Andrew Carnegie and the Age of Steel*, and that was only because a passing English grade depended on it.)

Home for the 14-year old was now in Queens, living with his dad at Joe's grandparents' house. His sense of self had been disrupted again. Surrounded by inner city kids and facing a whole new round of having to establish identity and stake out territory, he took it all in macho stride. "These were tough guys, these were little gangsters," he remembers thinking. "But I only saw them as kids who hadn't had a good meal. They weren't healthy. They were just skinny little guys. Out on Long Island, all we had was fresh air and everybody was on the fucking football team, so when I went to the inner city and these tough guys tried to get tough with me, well, I just got into a thing where I'd beat up people all the time. It made me the leader of the school for a short while. There was nobody tougher than me."

But Joe's feelings of bitterness and, even moreso, restlessness, grew. The timing of his move back in with his dad was neither good nor bad, it was just that Joe, Jr. was now a teenager and a kid who found himself getting into trouble, like it or not. "It was as if I was standing in line when they were handing out cowboy clothes and I just happened to get the black hat," he says. "I wanted to play the good guy, but it never worked out that way for some reason." Trouble had a way of finding him.

One such altercation clinched his entire educational career. Joe had a habit of walking around his school in Queens wearing a girl's kerchief tied around his neck—a long black kerchief perfect to wrap around the tender young throats of hall monitors.

"I got in trouble that day for doing one of the hall monitors, and so they had me down in the principal's office with the gym teacher on one side of me and the English teacher on the other." The usual litany of authoritative threats was thrown out and then the principal made the mistake of mentioning that Joe's behavior was somehow his father's fault.

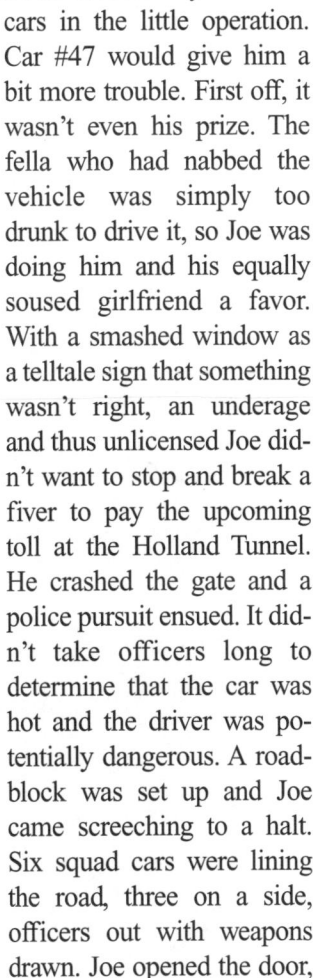

"I dived across the desk. I didn't mean to hit him. All I was actually trying to do was push him ... but my hand was closed." The principal's nose was broken with a resounding crunch and Joe was pinned and subsequently booted from the school. Expelled. Permanently.

Not long after, there came another decisive bit of bad luck. Though he's quick to point out that he and his buddies "weren't the type of criminals who were doing the kind of violence you see today," they were getting fairly proficient at what they were doing. There would be the occasional bout with a few construction workers just for kicks, but basically they were procurers of property, not thugs who beat up little old ladies for their pocketbook. (They did not, however, shy away from stomping a complete stranger if the mood struck them.)

Since about the age of 15, Joe and his cronies had been stealing cars in New Jersey and driving them across the state line into New York. There they'd try and sell them for the bucket-seats or the mag wheels, but more often than not would end up either abandoning or creatively junking them by sending them dramatically off the proverbial "Suicide Hill," an entertaining thirty foot drop sure to blow all four tires. "That was only because it was going on in the neighborhood with the older guys," explains Joe of his car-theft exploits. "Anything that went on with the older guys, I would pretty much get into that."

He was, admittedly, a miserable criminal when he set his sights on being one. He rarely got much in the way of cash for his efforts; more likely, he'd get a slap upside the head from his prospective buyer for being such a "stupid kid."

He recalls, however, that he had successfully stolen 46 cars in the little operation. Car #47 would give him a bit more trouble. First off, it wasn't even his prize. The fella who had nabbed the vehicle was simply too drunk to drive it, so Joe was doing him and his equally soused girlfriend a favor. With a smashed window as a telltale sign that something wasn't right, an underage and thus unlicensed Joe didn't want to stop and break a fiver to pay the upcoming toll at the Holland Tunnel. He crashed the gate and a police pursuit ensued. It didn't take officers long to determine that the car was hot and the driver was potentially dangerous. A roadblock was set up and Joe came screeching to a halt. Six squad cars were lining the road, three on a side, officers out with weapons drawn. Joe opened the door, stuck one foot out, and then one officer opened fire. The rest joined in. Joe slammed the door, ducked, put the car in gear and went straight at them.

The car's exterior was riddled with holes. There was one in Joe, too, just above the kneecap in his right leg. "They started shooting," he says, "because they claimed later on that they thought I was coming out with a gun. From the other side of the car, they said I was armed. Well, no, not

Pin-Up Boy/Photo by Bruce Bellas

exactly. What I was armed with was a motor vehicle."

He miraculously escaped the cops, sunk the car in the Hudson River, and made off with another car, but he was inescapably wounded. His first idea was to wait and see if he could take the slug out himself, but there was no way. When he showed up at his dad's and explained what happened, his father took him to the hospital and it was there that he was charged and arrested as a juvenile.

"I had a bullet in my leg. That gets taken care of and then I've got to go to court. So when I got out of the hospital, they sent me to Bellevue for observation to see if I was crazy or not." As part of his evaluation, Joe somehow ended up on the 7th floor ward for the "criminally insane" instead of the children's ward. He claims he "never would have gotten out of there except for this dumbbell, a little Spanish guy about 5' tall who called himself Lucky Luciano, that I gave a box of gumdrops and a pack of cigarettes to in exchange for answers on their psycho test. You see, they were asking me the wrong questions. Actually, they were asking me the right questions, but the answers I was giving were those of a child and they were looking for the answers of an adult."

When Joe was certified "sane," he told his Spanish inmate that Lucky Luciano was Italian. "Yeah?" came the clueless response. As in "so?" (This wouldn't be the last time the gangster's namesake would help Joe out of a jam. In 1983, after returning from Europe, Joe was cast in his first big-budget Hollywood film in the role of Luciano for Francis Ford Coppola's **The Cotton Club**.)

"Remember, my father had always impressed upon me how important school was," Joe says. "It's the most important thing in your life. But they weren't going to accept me back into the school system." His options were few. Joe still thought military school was the way to go, but a farm, of sorts, is what was mandated to avoid any sort of more structured penal institutionalization. There was, after all, a crime to pay for.

"I could have gotten into a lot more trouble than I did, " Joe says, "because the cops were shooting crossfire into the car and they could have killed each other."

Joe was naive enough to believe that he was actually going to go to a farm, to a place that had a school and a church. "And the farm turned out not be a farm. I thought I was going to go milk fucking cows. Instead, the first month they gave me pots and shit to scrub."

"They" was the Camp Cass Rehabilitation Center for Boys in the Catskills. Joe's tour of duty: four months.

"After the first month, you go into forestry and you go and cut trees down for fifty cents a day. But back then, fifty cents could buy you five candy bars and two packs of cigarettes."

Wards of Camp Cass, a sprawling farm that prided itself on setting kids straight, weren't supposed to be over the age of 16, but the truth was that there were plenty of much older kids there. The camp was a repository for juvenile offenders and lost souls. There was also a white minority. The few whites that were there were kids from places like Albany who had been sent by hard-nosed parents and teachers for chronic truancy or adolescent vandalism. The camp was a place where a white boy could get a dose of discipline in a hurry. Joe was about the only inner city white kid there serving time for a serious offense.

Camp Cass ran itself in a surprisingly open manner, allowing the kids to roam free within its confines, even make a run for it if they so desired. Few desired, however, because few escaped that way. Psychological warfare was waged against these adolescent minds and it kept things running pretty smoothly. If a kid walked off the place, the "counselors" would throw a bunch of kids into a truck and off they'd go to hunt down the escapee. If they caught you, and they often did, you were treated to a merciless beating by your fellow "inmates" all the way back home in the back of the truck. On top of that, you knew that the entire camp would lose its privileges just from your attempt to run, so there was plenty of peer incentive to stay in line.

One day, Joe and some of the fellas were fooling around with homemade tattoos. Several of the kids had been doing them and it quickly became all the rage. Joe decided it was time he had one, too. His choice: his nickname, "Little Joe," with the "Little" done in scroll-work over the "Joe" on his upper right arm.

A fellow inmate drew the design on him with a pen, because Joe is right-handed and couldn't have done it well upside down or sideways with his left hand.

"You take a piece of thread, wrap it around a needle, just leaving a small point on it, and then you dip it in India ink," he explains. "Everyone was doing their own tattoos, but they were all getting infected, so I was going to be more careful. When the guy was doing mine, it was hurting too much, so I took a piece of wood and I laid my arm on the wood to flatten it out and I did it myself over and over again—about six times—so it came out thick."

The famous "Little Joe" tattoo was born. Ever since its first appearance on film, it has been used to identify Joe Dallesandro by nudie film collectors and cineastes alike. With those large letters and the scroll-like design, the marking is both an emblem and an obstacle. Like movie buffs out to catch Hitchcock's appearance in each of his films, Joe's fans look for his tattoo each and every time out—often enjoying how a director chooses to work creatively around it.

"The problem is that it can never be removed now. You

can't even cover it up or laser it out, because it's so deep and so dark that besides being color, it's also scar."

Does he ever regret having done it?

Occasionally. "Only because in certain period films you can't have a tattoo." Not to mention a tattoo of a man's name on a man's arm. Either he must forever play characters named Joe (which I've always thought would have been a brilliant career gimmick) or there has got to be some "other" reason why a guy's name is there. In any case, he says that from his eyes' vantage point the tattoo looks cool, but when he sees it in photographs the "J" tends to look a bit too much like a "T," and thus he's also "Little Toe."

Life at Camp Cass after a few months was beginning to wear thin for Little Joe. It was time to get the hell out. So one day not-so-in-particular, he walked.

"All you had to do was stay away from the roads long enough, stay in the woods, and when you got far enough away, you go out on the highway and hitchhike." Joe stayed in those woods for three days, subsisting on whatever he could find and laying real low. Once out on the road, he went and saw his Dad, who had a job coming up in Florida loading and unloading wine casks, so he tagged along with him.

The job wasn't much to their liking, so father and son headed back up to the city. By this time, Dad had a new girlfriend and was essentially taking care of Bob. Joe had already decided, at age 16, he wanted to be out on his own.

The authorities had sent a "dishonorable parole" to Joe's grandmother's house, which is where his father and brother were staying, stating that if he were busted before his 21st birthday, he would do the time he was to have done at Camp Cass plus whatever he'd get for being busted. He knew he had to stay out of trouble. He also knew it was time to get out of town, and to do that he had to pull off one last crime. He needed the cash.

A gay friend was the manager of the RKO theatre in Brooklyn. He wasn't the first guy who looked twice when he saw Joe walking down the street. D'Alessandro had

Photo by Kenn Duncan/Courtesy Joe Dallesandro

bloomed in puberty and was in good physical condition, despite never working out to keep himself that way. His natural beauty and precocious, streetwise charm worked wonders on just about anybody he encountered.

The theatre manager liked Joe. He also knew Joe needed cash, and one night when he was closing, he half-jokingly said: "If this money were mine, I'd give it all to you." So when his back was turned, Joe grabbed two stacks out of the wall-safe and stuffed it in his shirt. When he hit the street, he ran like crazy.

He went to a friend, Stanley, whose parents were threatening to put him in an institution because he had chased his father around the house with a hammer—apparently because his father had beaten him once too often and he'd had enough. Joe told him, "You're not crazy, man, it's a normal thing to do. C'mon, let's get the fuck out of here."

Having to get out of town was nerve-wracking, but the pair decided that they should head to Mexico to escape any possible recriminations from the U.S. police. They stopped in Philadelphia first where Joe gave half the cash to his dad. Then the pair jumped on a bus headed for Dallas.

They outfitted themselves for the trip in "puke yellow mustard-colored sports jackets" and told people they were in a band. "They were the most horrific jackets," Joe recalls with a grimace. "But this was Philly where we were buying. We weren't doing the best clothes shopping, you know."

With a surprising amount of their bounty spent at reststop pinball machines on the long and boring trip down, they bailed in El Paso and walked across the border to Ciudad Jùarez, where they lived in a glorified hole in the ground—a cave really—just on the border of town.

"We had milk crates, a blanket and candles, and that's where we lived. We stayed there, it could have been as long as three weeks, but it was probably only two and it seemed like forever."

Joe found work in town, much to the delight of locals, who were amused to see an American white boy with a New York accent and spiffy cowboy boots who had endured a hellish trip from the Big Apple only to bus tables and wash dishes in a Mexican cafe for breakfast, lunch, and cigarettes. What little other money the boys had quickly was spent on sodas. When the fellas decided they'd see what they could get by reselling their shitkickers, they were amazed that the boot dealer came out with a little gadget that measured how much had been worn off the sole and paid them accordingly.

The duo managed to hitch a ride with a guy in a trailer who was heading all the way up to Los Angeles, which was fine with the boys. The gentleman dropped them off at the bus station in L.A. where they encountered another gentleman who had "other" interests in them beyond the purely charitable.

He was a black man and Joe admits they tried to put the hustle on him to find a place to camp out, so he took them home ... to Watts. "He was the nicest guy and he took us to his apartment and it had a swimming pool. I couldn't believe it. This was a ghetto and they had a swimming pool? This was luxury!"

Stanley was 15 and wanted to drive their new friend's car. The teenager's chumminess was sending out wrong signals. Joe could see where this new friendship was heading and told the guy that Stanley had nothing against gays, but the kid wasn't interested. "So forget about it."

"Are you interested?"

"Yeah," said Joe, "but not with a black man—which is what I told him just to put him off. But the more I put him down, the more he was attracted to me. I told him, 'As long as I've got a place to sleep, man, I'm fine.' So then the guy decided he was going to befriend us and not come after me."

Joe hadn't made any concrete

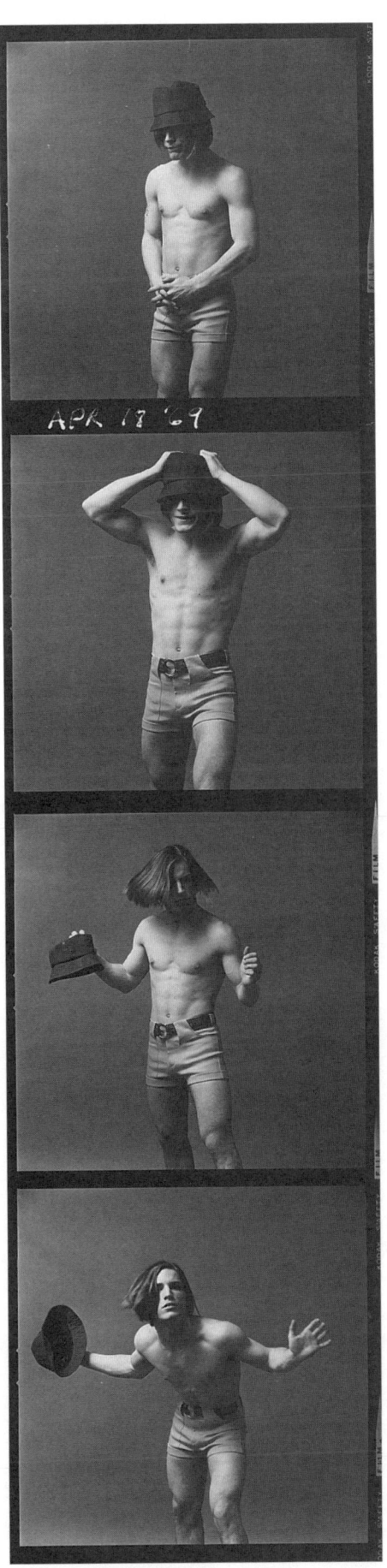

Photos by Kenn Duncan/
Courtesy Joe Dallesandro

decisions about his sexuality at this stage, but he was open to the supernatural powers of persuasion that sexual attraction could command. Certain men were obviously more than just interested in this strapping young Italian. They were also the more likely to come up and make a play, because women (to whom Joe was himself attracted) still tended to see him as a kid. On the streets, the sexual power plays were all controlled by men; men with desires for boys like Joe. The luckier kids, naturally, were the ones able to keep their wits about them.

"I'd come from New York where I'd seen people do the hustle," says Joe, "and I knew that people could get away with anything if they just knew what to say. My hustle was about getting anything I could for nothing."

While hanging out at the bus station, a popular place to get what you want for little or nothing, he was approached by a man who asked him if he'd be interested in doing some modeling. Believe it or not, that kind of thing happens every day, even today. In Joe's case, however, that little modeling gig was the start of an unimagined career as nude pin-up and erotic underground icon. The straight boy had just found his queer destiny.

During the three months he spent in L.A. in 1965, Joe was shuffled back and forth between several photographers doing nudie shots for their muscle mail-order skin magazines. The market was burgeoning in sunny Southern Cal and the pay was decent, too. He also landed a job at a pizza joint, where he says he taught them how to make dough and everything else he knew about making a decent pie, but he quit when they wouldn't let him cook, only do dishes.

His West Coast sabbatical ended, however, following a lively skirmish. The teenager got into an argument during which the other fella broke a beer bottle and came after him. Joe ended up smashing his attacker's face into the broken glass. He was arrested for assault and held at the Spotford House, but the judge didn't feel the teenager's case merited any sort of trial. Joe essentially told the judge that all he was doing was trying to survive. The judge decided that it was best Joe do his kind of surviving anywhere but in California. The court bought him a plane ticket and sent his ass back to New York, ostensibly a return flight to his family.

Instead, Joe hung out with the denizens of Times Square, experimenting with drugs and finessing a life on the streets. Eventually, he managed to get a job working in a pizza parlor in Queens. (Even when he became famous through the Warhol films, Joe told interviewers that his dream was to own and operate his own pizza house.)

Joe's father was living in Jersey at this time with his new ladyfriend and her two daughters. One of the girls, Leslie, was pregnant and spent much of the time with her friends in Brooklyn. Eager to get his life in order and achieve even a modicum of normalcy, and perhaps eager for some responsibility, too, Joe decided to marry Leslie in a little church in New York. By then, she had already had her baby daughter (Kim) and was now pregnant again (with her son, Joe's eldest boy, Michael).

The couple lived for a short time in Jersey, but Leslie was restless. "We were living in a terrible place," recalls Joe. "But the place she wanted to go live in Brooklyn was no better. Or not much better. She found a place in Brooklyn right across the street from where she grew up. Her aunt also lived there. And all the rest of these friends of hers, who would be playing hooky from school, now had a place to come stay.

"She was young. She was a kid. And now they had a clubhouse. I'm trying to be an adult, to be the parent, to play grown-up, and working towards one day having the picket fence."

And so Joe chased away all of his new wife's friends. She was not happy. They were not happy.

According to Joe, Leslie's aunt sent her own boyfriend over one day to read him the riot act and put him in his place. The threat backfired and Joe walked, telling Leslie that the apartment was hers, as well as everything in it. "I'm gone," Joe remembers telling the boyfriend. "I'm not packing anything. I'm not taking anything, but she'll never see me again."

He got a crummy little apartment on 10th Street. For the first and really the only time, Joe says, he and his father had harsh words and came close to blows over the situation with Leslie. Joe's dad didn't want his son marrying the girl in the first place, though eventually Joe Sr. ended up marrying Leslie's mother and had Leslie's daughter's last name legally changed to D'Alessandro.

Joe made it a point, he tells me, of sharing everything with his father at that time. "From street life, to my gay encounters, to everything that ever happened in my life then, I shared it with him. Because I wanted my father to know who I was and what I was about. And how much I loved him and wanted him to be a part of my life; how much I needed his love. And that was how he was able to share with me, for the first time, that he loved me, how he cared about me. Your parents are your blood. The best they can do is love you the way they love you. The best you can do is try and do better than them and try to love them back."

One legendary day in 1967, at the tender age of 18, Joe and a buddy went to visit a friend at a Greenwich Village apartment complex and happened upon an apartment where some peculiar people were making a movie. Artist Andy Warhol and filmmaker Paul Morrissey were shooting a flick and a good-looking stray like Joe was simply too much to resist. Incredulous though he was, he agreed to participate for the afternoon, and underground film history registered a new biographical entry. Joe Dallesandro (as his name was now Americanized) became the centerpiece of all advertising for **The Loves of Ondine** (1967), a rambling splutter of film stock meant as part of a planned 24-hour experimental film entitled ****. Due to slightly less than a reel's screen time, this tough little kid from the neighborhood began a life as an underground film sensation, and all he had to do was show up for it.

His father could hardly believe it. Joe, quite frankly, didn't think much of the whole experience, particularly since the circumstances were so strange that any concept of this thing actually playing in a real movie theatre was beyond him.

Of course, it did play.

Joe now had a job as a cutter in a bookbindery. Even with the daytime preoccupation, he found himself increasingly aware of the city's gay subculture. Or vice versa.

His sensibility about homosexuality seemed born from a uniquely mature understanding for a teenager in those times, but undoubtedly also from a need for acceptance and companionship. Perhaps, as it has been suggested, he was looking for a father figure out there on the streets.

"My introduction to the gay world did two things," he says. "One, saved me from life in prison for murder, which is probably where I would have wound up. How? Because the gay world showed me that you didn't have to beat up every man you saw or hurt people to make a point. It gave me a whole other attitude, a calmer attitude. Two, it taught me never to be homophobic, even before there was such a term. I think it was because I grew up in a period, especially later on, when the people I looked up to were people like David Bowie. All of those characters were my heroes. You know, people would adore Mick Jagger, both male and female, for a look or an attitude, and that's what I liked about the period I grew up in, that a man could say he liked both, that he appreciated both the look of a man and the look of a woman without being stereotyped."

For a young man with Joe's intense good looks, familiarity bred understanding, compassion and brotherhood. "At 16, I had this gay friend that I lived with. He must have been in his early forties and he owned a club down on Columbus and 76th or 78th Street. It was an after hours club that I ran for him. It catered basically to the bartenders of the gay bars and so they all came to our club at the end of their shift. We were open from 2 a.m. to 6 in the morning. I did that for about six months before I ever met the Andy Warhol people."

That is, before he was introduced to a world rife with flamboyant homosexuals, drag queens, drug addicts, actors, musicians, and the habitually misplaced.

For a long, long time, Joe wouldn't even talk to interviewers about these associations. The reasons aren't particularly difficult to comprehend. Interviewers would simply play the one-note association for all its tabloid glory. (The press became that much more persistent when his first starring role was playing a hustler in Paul Morrissey's **Flesh**. He told *Newsday* in 1970 that he never was a hustler, "but when you're young and beautiful, you do get a lot of propositions.")

In social circles, as he became more and more well known via the Warhol films, every Tom, Dick and Harry loved to name him as a former lover. He'd meet a lot of people for the first time who claimed to have had a roll with him in his heyday. What price beauty?

Of course, it was Joe's alleged reputation that later led to his inclusion as "Little Joe" in the Lou Reed song "Walk on the Wild Side," whose famous lyric seems to indicate a young man who made everybody pay. Without the proper context, the lyric sounds critical, even biting. But Joe hears it differently.

"I always said it wasn't about a hustle," Joe tells me. "It was about how you got people who wanted to be a part of your life. The pay was that they became a part of your life, even for a short time. The lyrics have been misinterpreted, but I'm sure that Lou knew what I was talking about."

So what was his reaction the first time he heard the song?

"I thought it was right on, because when you take all the stories in "Walk on the Wild Side," they're about people discovering who they are. Everybody is making a discovery. For me, it wasn't about money. Everybody just came away with, 'Oh, Joe's a hustler.' They didn't get the whole point of the lyric. It was about what I wanted. New York was the place I came to get what I needed."

"But, Joe," I point out, "you 'never once gave it away, everybody had to pay and pay,' doesn't that ..."

"Well, in a manner of speaking, Paul (Morrissey) was paying," he insists. "I came back to New York City. Didn't I become a part of that whole Warhol group and didn't they want to keep me there? Weren't they then paying me by giving me a profession? So the hustle never stopped."

At the time, Joe probably thought he'd heard the last of the Warhol people after his underwear stint in **Ondine**, but then they called him back and asked him if he'd be willing to fly to Arizona and appear in their latest effort, **Lonesome Cowboys**. Joe figured what the hell, gave them some terms, which included matching the salary he was making at his job, and off he went for the weekend shoot.

That appearance was followed by a part in **San Diego Surf**, an aborted project that nevertheless showed the neophyte young actor that these people were truly interested in using him; particularly Paul Morrissey, Andy Warhol's right-hand man and the emerging force behind all of the film projects.

Joe was eventually to do eight films under the Warhol banner, but in order to star in his very next outing, something awful had to happen.

On June 3, 1968 Andy Warhol was nearly killed. Valerie Solanas, an angry young woman who desired to have one of her plays produced by the Pop Artist, went nuts that day and showed up at the Factory—Warhol's famed workplace at 33 Union Square West—to blast the celebrity "yes" man into tomorrow's headlines. She succeeded in doing that, where she, too, shared headlines which described her as one of Andy's actresses gone off the deep end. When she turned herself in to police later that night, she showed no signs of remorse and was, in fact, more than outspoken about her right to emancipate herself from the controlling Warhol. Delusionally, she had made Andy the target of her rage. Her extreme feminist ideologies and famed manifesto for an imaginary group called S.C.U.M. (Society for Cutting Up Men) also made her a twisted cause célèbre for some extremist factions of the Women's Lib movement. (Her manifesto is today accessible on the Internet and her "story" became the 1996 independent film hit **I Shot Andy Warhol**, with a gutsy performance by Lili Taylor.)

Though the incident was quickly overshadowed in the news by Robert Kennedy's assassination, the attempt on

Andy Warhol's life was of seminal impact. Warhol nearly died from the wounds, the .32 caliber bullets had ricocheted throughout his innards and done significant damage. His eventual recovery was nothing short of miraculous. On the day of the event, doctors were sure he would die.

For some, the horrific event was a logical extension of the bohemian life the artist allowed to flourish around him almost uncontrolled. It wouldn't be the last time that charges were made against Warhol of engendering a climate of unabated bizarre behavior.

By deciding to call his unknown "actors," transvestites, artistes, fey performance artists, etc., by the term "Superstars," Andy Warhol was both bestowing legitimacy and robbing Show Business proper of its elitist assignations of pomp and circumstance. America's royalty was its Cult of Celebrity, and Andy Warhol's down-and-dirty, glam-trashy coterie was no less worthy of the titles than those endowed by Hollywood. In the very same manner in which he had challenged the art world, he defied the mainstream entertainment media—by joining them. The emulation may not have been exact, but the ideology was. What's more, who was anyone to say that his stars weren't precisely what he called them?

"Andy's idea of making anybody a star would have been okay if the people hadn't completely lost their mind and taken it to a place where they wanted to do harm to him," says Joe. "A woman like Valerie Solanas comes along and wants to shoot Andy, but who's never made anything with Andy. She's basically a person who in her delusion thought Andy was stealing something of hers. But he wasn't. Yet she wants to physically hurt him because she thinks so."

Ironically, part of what became the new security force at the Factory was to have been put in place the very day of the event, at least the way Joe tells it. Paul Morrissey, clearly interested in using the young man in future films, had invited Joe to the Factory, ostensibly to work as an employee.

"When I went to work there," says Joe, "I showed up thinking I was going to be the bodyguard. I could be a little hot-tempered and I could do damage, because I'm dangerous for just a little guy. I prided myself not on my acting ability, because I didn't know anything about that, but on the way I was able to fight. And on my first day they were taking Andy out on a stretcher and I went up to Paul and said, 'Well, I guess I don't have a job.'"

During their crime scene work at the premises, investigating police officers reportedly lingered over stills from **Lonesome Cowboys**, as well as a stash of nude photos

At work at the Factory/Courtesy Joe Dallesandro

from Joe's physique magazine sessions that Warhol now had on file.

With Andy recuperating in the hospital, and **Midnight Cowboy** in production (featuring a "parody" sequence at the Factory), it was Paul Morrissey who took the reins for the Factory's next film. He knew precisely who he wanted as its emblematic star: Joe Dallesandro.

Flesh (1968), the first in what was to become a famed trilogy of cult classics starring Joe, not only beat **Midnight Cowboy** to the movie screens, thus becoming the first explicit cinematic look at the life of a male prostitute, but also launched a kid from the 'hood in Queens to an international career of singular fame and adoration. Fame sent Joe on a voyage in his early twenties to see all of Europe, to be celebrated by German audiences (in particular), but also to be celebrated in Italy and France and the United Kingdom, as well as here in the United States, where the subsequent successes of **Trash** (1970) and **Heat** (1972) granted him increasing exposure and even a taste of Hollywood enthusiasm.

Interestingly, though not surprisingly, because of the manner in which these films were made (that is, unscripted and improvised), audiences had a unique sense that the people they saw up on screen were in fact the people they were portraying. Joe was "Joe" in each of the trilogy. The assumption, therefore, was that Joe Dallesandro must not only be a hustler (**Flesh**), but also a rampant drug user (**Trash**).

Truth was, Joe had dabbled with drugs, and he would face a monstrous battle with booze and drugs in the coming decade, but at the time he made the Warhol films, he tells me, he was kept both dry and un-high.

He had moved into a four-unit brownstone owned by his mentor, Paul Morrissey, where he was supervised in pretty much the same way a father supervises a son. It was a controlling and disciplined lifestyle as Joe worked by day to help with restoration of the brownstone, and also put in partial days down at the Factory. There he did any number of odd jobs, from answering phones to providing security (standing guard next to a stuffed Great Dane), from sending prints of Warhol films out to college campuses and then retrieving them to running night-time projection of the films. He also operated the elevator for house events.

As for Andy's equally celebrated and castigated art, Joe admits he's not much of a fan. "It's worth something to somebody who thinks it's worth something." Of course, Warhol is now notoriously famous for the mechanically-processed silk screens he often had others do for him (and even sign). But a young Joe still felt bad when he put his hand through a freshly minted Elvis painting.

"Don't worry," Andy told him. "We'll make another one."

"Everybody was doing the paintings—even I pushed fucking paint through the screen. It was nothing. It was a fucking joke. Realize that I've seen some of the greatest art in the greatest museums all over the world and so when I looked at Andy's work, I said, that isn't art. *I* did it. How can that be art?"

Warhol had offered the actor some pieces over the years, but Joe says he didn't take him up on it because, frankly, it wasn't anything he'd be interested in hanging up.

"The only way I like Andy's art," he says, "is when you see it in a show. When you see thirty or forty pieces together, it looks beautiful. But for a person to hang one piece on the wall, it looks idiotic."

The legendary party scene so synonymous with the Warhol gang was something in which Joe rarely indulged. In fact, he always thought of himself as an outsider. He didn't live at the Factory, he didn't breathe the artifice, he didn't buy into the hype.

"I never was one of the gang," he says. "I think Andy liked me, but he couldn't talk to me like he talked to the other people. I'm a person that doesn't make chit-chat and doesn't *like* to make chit-chat, so I'm not going to sit there and ramble on while he tape-recorded me. I didn't go to any of their parties. It wasn't that I wasn't social, it was just that I didn't feel comfortable with them. I thought they were too phony. They didn't talk about anything that was real."

At least part of his resistance came from the fact that he was treated as an adolescent who was told quite explicitly what he could and couldn't do in public ... and at parties. For instance, no drinking.

"So in other words, they took over my being an adult. They became my parents, which included not providing contracts for me on the films until I insisted on them. Hell, when I was 16, I was an adult. By the time I was 18, I was a child again."

At the brownstone, too, Joe was kept in check and Paul Morrissey had his hands full.

"Paul in those days would say, 'Joe, you're an alcoholic,' and back then I didn't know ... I didn't understand what the fuck he was talking about. 'You can't drink,' he'd tell me, 'because when you drink you lose control.' So whenever I went out, was seen in public, I wasn't allowed to drink. And whatever Paul told me to do, I did. He worked real hard on me. I told you I was violent as a kid, and if you called me a fag, I'd chase you down and want to kill you. Not because I was homophobic, but because I was angry at what you were saying to me, how you were using it, to belittle me. If you'd thrown it at me in any other way, hey, I'm fine with it. But if you throw it at me to put me down, then I want to hurt you.

"And Paul would say, 'it doesn't matter how they mean it or what they say, it shouldn't make you want to chase a person down and hurt them.' And he knew all the buttons to push in me to set me off and he would do it on a regular basis. We were restoring the brownstone on the Lower East Side and he would say things to dig at me, to set me off, just so I would learn not to get pushed. He'd do it and he'd run behind a door and I'd come crashing through. Then he'd run behind the next door and I'd come running and crash through that one, too. By the time he got to the bathroom door, I realized I'd broken two doors, so now I'm going to have to fix them. Then I'd calm down and say, okay, I can talk now."

Between lessons, Joe had also met Theresa, or Terry, as he would call her. She was a teenage girl of Sicilian heritage, "mature beyond her years," according to Joe. They eventually married (after her pregnancy), and the two of them stayed at the brownstone together.

"The first three years of our relationship she was with me 24-hours a day," says Joe. " I really loved this woman. She was real special." Terry doted on Joe and he loved the attention. She would come down to the Factory during the day when he worked, then go out with him and the boys at night.

Terry was interested in having a family and Joe says that they seriously considered foster care first, because he wasn't interested in populating the world with his children. He also thought that he'd be at the top of the list as a likely candidate because he'd been raised in the system and knew what to look out for.

Even after Terry got pregnant, Joe was still interested in foster parenting, but his wife was not. His second son, Joe, Jr. was born on November 14, 1970, during a particularly difficult delivery. Just weeks later, photographer Annie Leibovitz shot father and son together for the cover of *Rolling Stone*. The photo is odd, however, in that Joe's features seem strangely disproportionate.

"When my son, Joe Jr., was born, he was brought out with forceps," Joe explains. "So his head was ... you know, when you're taken out with forceps, your head sometimes gets a little deformed. It's only a temporary thing, but his head got elongated. I was frightened that it was going to stay that way, but they said, no, it'll go down. So when Annie wanted to do this picture, I said please don't make my baby look terrible. She said, 'no, I'm going to use this fish-eye lens.' So, she made it the worst picture ever taken of *me*—because," he chuckles, "I'm noted for my beauty."

Detailing his shockingly normal and domestic life as daddy while noting that he was still playing nude hustlers and drug addicts on screen for the Factory, *Coast FM and Fine Arts* magazine threw him on the cover and declared him a "closet bourgeois." And *Vogue* gave Joe a full page photo, too, in 1971; the real beauty that's reprinted at the beginning of this chapter, with his tattoo showing prominently in backward reflection as he gazes at himself in the mirror *a la* Narcissus. The accompanying text glowingly refers to him as "the first really big star to come out of the New York film underground." It goes on to say: "short, with pimples, deadpan bordering on rigor mortis, Dallesandro has an endearing way of ducking his head and delivering his nowhere lines into his chest. His blond, blank-faced ways draw comparisons to Dietrich and Garbo, but his is a new uni-sexed glamour ... Dallesandro's attraction is much like that of Charlie Chaplin's Little Tramp: the winning, superior charm of a David against all the Goliaths, the triumph of an effortless innocence over a society that leans too hard on the little guys."

With such characteristically ambivalent praise, young Joe Dallesandro was beginning to break through the barriers of his Factory fame. There were talks of up and coming projects, there were trips back to Europe where he was fêted as the deliberately taciturn star of great social comedies, and with all this came interest from Hollywood.

Just how much interest from Hollywood has been debated, as well as just what Hollywood would have done with him.

"It's not to say that it was going to happen, but there was a possibility. The reason they were looking at Al Pacino and the reason they were looking at me was because of two movies. Al Pacino because he had done this movie called **Panic in Needle Park** and me because I had done this movie called **Trash**—two drug movies. They were far, far apart, but they were both interesting as portrayals, and even why these two characters ... I don't know, but these were the performances they were looking at. And for my people to put me down that way was really upsetting."

Joe Dallesandro is talking about a time in the early seventies when Hollywood came knocking on his Factory door. As the gorgeous star of increasingly visible underground movie hits, he could no longer go unnoticed by the big boys out west. At the very least, Francis Ford Coppola wanted him to screen test for the role of Michael Corleone in **The Godfather**. [Warhol told *Time Out* in February of 1971: "Oh, you know, they are really thinking of using Joe for **The Godfather**, but the uhhh director wants uhh someone like James Caine (sic) or somebody."]

His dark Italian good looks and urban edge particularly suited him to the material; whether he could play a dramatic role under studio conditions needed to be determined. Yet at the very height of his career, he never really even got the chance to give it a shot.

When I ask Paul Morrissey whether there's any truth to the notion that both he and Warhol were determined to keep their hands on their star—that Dallesandro was considered Factory property—and that subsequently he and Andy told the Hollywood suitors that Joe wasn't really an actor, that he couldn't handle a script, and maybe even that he had some drug problems, the director tells me (with

(Right) © Francesco Scavullo. Reprinted with permission.

annoyance registering at the suggestion) that the scenario I've provided is "garbage." Both he and Andy, he adds, would have been thrilled had Joe been able to get a role in a major motion picture.

"There was no interest from Hollywood agents or producers," Morrissey told me, "because they regarded Joe as being from outer space, just as they regarded the rest of us. There was no such thing as independent cinema then. Today, you've got a Sundance Film Festival and all that shit. People don't remember the period. Back then it was Hollywood and that was it. They didn't know what category to put us in; God knows what their perceptions of us were. I said, 'you know, Joe, you should connect with an agent in Italy, because I think there you could find much more work.' And that turned out to be true. That's the only advice I recall giving him."

Joe sees it differently. He says that the Warhol folks made no bones about cooling off outside opportunities for their leading actor. Had Warhol or Morrissey been able to land their own Hollywood film, which they attempted to do by courting studios from time to time and even trying to put together a television show for a local New York station, Joe would have no doubt continued to be their star attraction. But would they let him go out on his own? Leave the nest? After all, he was their box-office moneymaker.

In a 1974 interview, done while he was living in Italy, he remarked, "I was in the United States for six years (as an actor) and I never got an offer to do any films except by Andy Warhol's people. In America, they identified me too much with Warhol. And in America they don't take Warhol too seriously." Ten years later he would tell Robert Osborne in *The Hollywood Reporter* that because of Factory "badmouthing, it got so I had to leave the family."

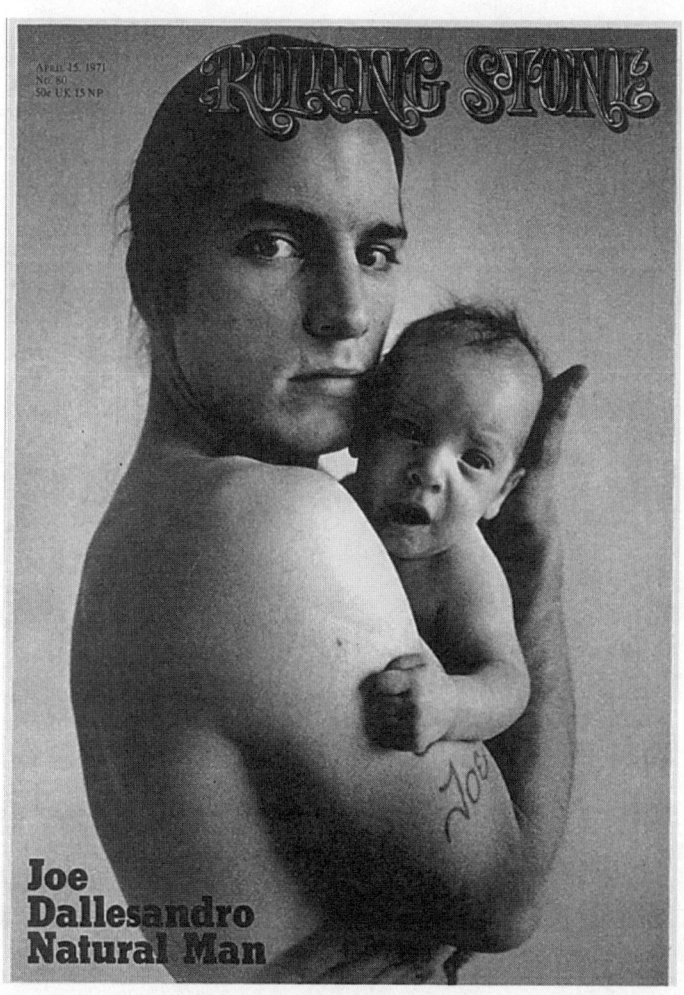

April 15, 1971

He tells me, "For them to do this kind of stuff was real sabotage to me. I made them a lot, a *lot* of money, and I didn't make it to be a greedy pig, because I always felt they were giving me a career."

Further frustrated by a deal that was made unbeknownst to him with Italian producer Carlo Ponti to make a duo of films in Italy in which he would star, Joe reluctantly made the trip, filmed what were to become **Andy Warhol's Frankenstein** and **Dracula**, and then immediately went to work for other film companies anxious to use him.

In fact, he decided to stay in Italy and forge himself a career that he hoped would take him above and beyond what he had done with the Warhol clan. He was looking for opportunities to play roles different from those he was playing for Morrissey. His wife Terry was with him at first, but when he decided to stay on, she didn't. The marriage was strained and Joe decided they should separate, but not divorce. He said that he would make sure she got half of whatever he was making; on at least one occasion she smuggled the money out of the country under her skirt.

While Terry and Joe, Jr. moved back to New York, Joe was enjoying a whirlwind, breathless romance with actress Stefania Casini, his co-star in **Dracula** and a beautiful, intellectually outspoken and provocative woman. Whether vacationing on the isle of Lesbos or appearing naked in each other's arms for a steamy layout in *Oui* magazine while Joe was still officially married, they were a couple steeped in romance, alcohol, political and intellectual differences, and undeniable passion.

"It was difficult, because when I left the United States, people there didn't look at the Andy Warhol stuff as legit, so it was real hard trying to move from what I was doing with them over to what was being done in Hollywood.

26

Whereas when I came to Europe, they really liked my work. They were very appreciative of it. And in Italy, the opposite was true, because my films had been banned there for a long time—the trilogy—and so it was a great thing for me to go do my films in Italy, not having an audience there that I had to live up to what I had already done. I could do something completely different and people could appreciate me for that. So I wasn't fighting an image. I was developing an altogether new image. Of course, the people of importance, directors and critics, had seen the trilogy in other countries, so they knew who I was."

Managing to work regularly in both Italy and France during his European stay, he also tried to maintain as best he could his family relationships. His movie career allowed him to fly his father and his Sicilian wife over to vacation in their homeland, with trips to both Sicily and Venice (Joe's family originated from Tropani, a small town about thirty miles outside of Palermo). He flew his foster mother and her Sicilian husband over for a holiday. He also brought his brother Bob over to Italy. Bob stayed for about a year, during which time he talked about wanting to go to Russia to become a clown or a mime.

Joe was amazed by his brother's lack of direction. "What you want to do," he tells me he told Bob, "is to go to Bangladesh to see starving people, because there's so much else you can do with your life. I wouldn't be doing what I'm doing except that it was a gift to me."

Joe wanted to send his brother to school to learn Italian so that he could justify paying him a salary. Joe didn't speak Italian at the time. But Bob didn't want to do it, so Joe figured it was time to send him back home to decide what it was he really wanted to do with his life.

When Bob contacted his brother from back in New York around Christmas time in 1977, he was asking for money. Joe now suspects that Bob may have been asking for extra cash for presents for the foster kids, but at the time, he didn't know. He thought his brother was "pretending to be broke," and so he said "no." It was to be the first year that Joe wouldn't be flying back to the States to spend Christmas with the family. He'd never spent the holidays with Stefania, so he decided to do so.

When the call came from his father that last day of December, he thought it was because it was his birthday. It may have seemed unlikely—even wishful thinking—on Joe's part. As it turned out, what his father had to tell him didn't involve a sentimental memory of birth, it was a message of death.

When he heard his father's voice say the words, he thought it was a joke. "A sick joke. And then came the realization that it wasn't a joke." His brother Bob was dead; an apparent suicide who took his life on his own birthday, some three days before his body was discovered.

Within nine hours of getting the call, Joe was there to identify the body, which had decomposed to such a degree that Joe's grim task was simply to suppose that who he was shown was indeed who the police surmised it to be. His father either wouldn't or couldn't identify the remains. The combination of shock and guilt was devastating, and would only increase.

"So this was the first holiday that I wasn't going home. I was going to spend it with her. I don't send money. He dies. It was a total catastrophe all around."

Though their relationship hadn't always been physically close, the brothers shared a powerful bond, an almost mystical fraternity borne out of lives built among strangers, without family.

"I always admired him," says Joe. "I thought he was the intelligent one between the two of us. He was the smart one. And yet, how can I call him the smart one for doing something as silly as ..." His voice trails off.

Bob worked for a time at the Warhol Factory and spent five years employed as Andy's chauffeur.

Understandably, Joe's voice softens and his mood darkens a bit when talking about the frustrating and tragic end of his brother's life. He has a series of gorgeously photographed stills of him and his brother that were shot by photographer Jack Mitchell and used for a piece in *After Dark*, but just a few years ago a fan walked off with some of them and copies started showing up for sale at local memorabilia stores. The problem wasn't the content of the photos—I'm happy to include one in this book—but the context. Joe may have been willing to become a commodity, but his brother wasn't for sale. The memories these shots evoke are too precious to be marketed merely as celebrity beefcake.

Joe claims that he and his brother used to "plane from our bodies." It began, apparently, when they were quite young, before they ever took any mind-altering drugs, but Bob became even better at it when he smoked marijuana, his particular drug of choice.

"When we both lived in the Village, we sometimes talked to each other on LSD ... from different rooms," says Joe. "We had such a bond."

The exact circumstances surrounding Bob's death are particularly difficult for Joe to come to grips with even twenty years later. "He wrote this thing called 'Magic Trick,'" he explains matter-of-factly. "He put this little string around his neck. He was into this thing—I had done it for a little bit—you know, lovemaking with asphyxiation. So he put this little string around his neck and he sat down on the couch like this, and he could have sat up at

27

Courtesy Joe Dallesandro

any time, but he didn't. He choked to death. That's how they found him. All he had to do was sit up.

"Anyway, next to the table was 'magic trick.' It was written on a piece of paper and all I could think was that he did it on purpose. That he smoked enough, that he kept calm enough, that he didn't sit back up. Because normally, if your body is choking, there's a reflex. You have to have some will or no will whatsoever not to move. I don't think anybody hated him to murder him, so it had to be something he did himself. And it had to be drug-related. How else could he have done it? The police claim 'accidental death' because of the fact that he could have sat up.

"Why write 'magic trick,' though? He knows what magic trick connotes to me, because we used to do it all the time. When we planed, when we left our bodies, that was magic to us; to float up above our bodies and look down and see ourselves, that was real magic. When it happened to me for the first time, I was fearful of it. I didn't want to do it over and over again, because it was kind of a frightening thing. But it was a great thing for him. He wanted to do it all the time. So, yeah, I knew what 'magic trick' meant. He was planing. He was leaving his body and going to different places. Only this time he left himself hung up. He didn't get back in time."

For Bob's funeral, his foster mother, a strong-willed Irish woman who suffered from a blood disorder and was hospitalized at the time, insisted on coming. Joe was the one who brought her to the services. "Then she went back to the hospital. It had taken so much out of her."

Of course, she wasn't alone. Joe's father dealt with the death in his own way, withdrawing to the basement of his home and obsessing over a train set he'd been building.

"I know that the hardest thing in the world is for a parent to lose a child," Joe says. "Because I watched my father and he was just ... gone. He did this train set for four years down in the basement. That's all he could do was play with his trains. It was an enormous set, a beautiful set, but he couldn't do anything else. He just fell apart. I felt bad. There was nothing I could do to bring him out of it. It wasn't like he lost his mind, he just lost his desire to participate in anything else outside of his space and his trains."

Joe flew to Los Angeles while he was stateside to talk about his career with some European directors who made American co-productions. Even with his personal strife, he felt it was a good opportunity to keep his mind pre-occupied. Besides, if things worked out with these guys, he could continue to live in Italy while they landed him work from back in Hollywood. Less than a week after his brother's death, he got a call saying that his foster mother had taken a turn for the worse. He got on a plane before any professional contracts were signed and landed in New York to learn that she had died while he was en route.

Joe's return to Europe was clouded by their deaths. Quite naturally, the senseless loss of his brother haunts him to this day. "They wind up killing a person they never knew," he says of people who take their own lives.

Shortly after his brother's death, Terry served him the divorce papers he didn't even know she filed. She got her divorce on grounds of abandonment.

"My re-entry into the drug world was basically because I didn't deal with the deaths very well," admits Joe. His bouts with alcohol and drug use in the past were already legendary among friends. They even surface in the *Warhol Diaries,* when Andy reports Joe calling from Paris on February 26, 1979, and admitting to drinking a bottle of whiskey a day.

The major reason his relationship with Stefania was falling apart, according to Joe, was because she'd had enough of the ups and downs. "Basically, she had seen me as a stronger person through other people's pain (including the loss of her own father near the beginning of their relationship) and she couldn't understand why I wasn't dealing with mine very well. And so that pretty much ended the relationship. She thought I should go back to America, but I told her I'm not going back, because there's nothing to go back for now."

They split, he says, "supposedly because I was a mean guy. Who knows? I tried to commit suicide in our home. I tried to hang myself or something pitifully stupid. It was in a drunken stupor. It should have never happened, and I don't even know if I was trying to do it or not, maybe I was just looking for some attention. In any case, I didn't hurt myself. The only thing that happened was that I had gagged myself to dizziness and to the point of crapping myself. And she woke up to that."

It was past time for Joe to make a move. He was drowning in drugs and drink and the hospitals in Europe couldn't provide the kind of treatment he needed with English-speaking one-on-one intervention. The only way he was going to have a real chance at drying out and saving his life was returning to America, so in 1980 he moved back to New York and in with his father, who had a unique way of trying to flush his son into sobriety.

"My father's way of detoxing me would be to put me on booze. He'd feed me a case of booze a day, as much booze as I could do until I would fall down. I'd be so drunk that I'd never feel any pain from detoxing off whatever drug I was doing."

But winter was coming to the Big Apple, and though he'd been raised there, Joe says there must be something to the fact that he was born in Florida, "because my little body craved the warmth."

A decade before, in the early 70's and at the height of his Warhol fame, Joe made efforts to contact his real mother by following up leads based on her maiden name. He had located his grandmother who was living in Pensacola and it was she who made the call to California to tell her daughter that Joey had been in touch and had left a New York number.

Now re-married, Sandy Hoyt had absolutely no idea that her son was the underground star of the Warhol films. Her husband had made the connection when he ran across a newspaper ad for **Flesh** and showed it to his wife, telling her that the boy in the photo resembled her. But she didn't take it seriously.

"There were a lot of apprehensions associated with contacting her," admits Joe, "because you never know what people want, and my feelings were: I want no amends, no apologies, I just want the moment now. Whatever moment you can give me now is what I desire."

When she and Joe finally talked on the phone and then Joe and Bob came out to Sacramento to see her, she learned that her husband had been right after all. Joe keeps a newspaper article about their reunion in his scrapbook. "Long-Lost Son Is X-Rated Star Of Warhol Films," declares the headline of The Saturday Morning *Sacramento Bee*, October 13, 1973.

"I was embarrassed when I first learned about Joe's movie activity," his mom told the paper. "I'm far from a prude but I had never seen a porny movie and I didn't know what kind of movie it would be. I hadn't the vaguest idea—really—about what he was doing. But I read the reviews and I gathered from the reviews what was going on."

Joe reportedly requested that his mom not go to see **Trash**, the most recent film and the one she had heard about. A month after Joe left, however, she and her husband traveled to San Francisco to see it. The paper says she was shocked, but that she also began cutting out all the newspaper reviews and enjoyed charting the film's box-office in *Variety*.

"All I know is that my son is in the films and I'll go and see them," she said. An accompanying photo shows her holding glossies of her long-haired, shirtless boy.

"And does it bother her that her son plays roles that exploit his attractiveness to both men and women?" the paper asked.

"I don't have any objection," she replied. "I could accept it if he was a homosexual because he is my son ... If this is Joe's way of making a living, then fine. It's a job like anything else, really."

The times and circumstances were better for Joe and his estranged mother in the 1970's. They enjoyed the opportunity to reunite and Joe and Bob visited her from time to time. She was so proud of Joe and his wife and her grandson, Joe, Jr. But in 1980, things had taken a turn for the worse. Joe needed help and his mom did, too. She called him in New York because she heard he was back from Europe. She wanted to move from Seattle back down to

California to be near her two children from the second marriage.

Joe went out to lend a hand. He'd help pack her things up and move down to Oakland. They traveled in a trailer together, drinking their troubles into oblivion.

"I think we were doing about a half gallon of vodka per day," Joe says. "And that was just for the afternoon. Later on we'd have another half gallon to try and finish for the evening."

The situation was bad, on the brink of growing worse, and Joe decided he needed to move out. He called up a friend of Andy Warhol's and Paul Morrissey's who was living in Los Angeles (later murdered by the Billionaire Boys Club) and asked him to find him a roommate, maybe even a fan, "preferably someone with a pool and a large liquor cabinet."

Teddy was a well-known hairdresser in L.A. and the two shared a place, unexpectedly becoming friends in the process. It was good for Joe, despite his continuing near-fatal addiction to booze and drugs.

"It was a long struggle to finally get me to an AA meeting," he says. "I did fine in Europe. I had a wonderful time and lived a pretty good life, but I drank enormous amounts of liquor ... at times."

Within a year of being back in the states, and after a hard knocks course in the trials and tribulations of understanding who you are and what you're doing to yourself—a process illuminated by 12-step programs and personal sponsors—Joe was sober again in 1981, though one might almost be tempted to say for the very first time. He was 33.

"Yeah, Jesus Christ's age," he smiles. In the coming year, his life would change dramatically, though he rebuffed any suggestions that he augment his treatment with therapy.

"I've seen therapists who weren't all together," he winces. "I've dated them. Besides, if I'm not uncomfortable with it, then it's got to be right for me. To make myself uncomfortable about something that I've always been comfortable with is wrong. That means I'm trying to look at myself through your eyes, to judge myself by the way other people think. And, of course, then I'm always going to be ill in comparison. I was just born to be that way ... to be way sicker than others.

"For the first time in my life, really, I'd experienced a year without having to take a drink or have any substance in order to change my mood. And I thought that was wonderful. I'd never really experienced that in my life. I'd always had to have something. Then I finally resolved that this was going to have to be life one day at a time. I can go through this for the rest of my life, but one day at a time. Because who knows how long my life will be? And with that came a big sigh of relief and a big grin of total surrender to the fact that I'm going to be okay. I'm looking at my reflection in the windows as I'm walking down the street and tears are coming from my eyes and I'm saying, 'I'm okay.'"

Half a lifetime before that point, he had seen someone completely different reflected in those windows. "My attitude was if there was something in the front window of a store that I wanted, I'd break the window and take it. And as brazen as I was, then I'd wear the same shirt the next day and walk down the avenue right past the store. It was stupid stuff. It was like catch me and punish me and make me well, because I'm lost. The stealing of the cars when I was a kid was simply my not realizing that I would get all that I needed in my time."

And yet, addiction being the complex disease that it is, he would also be open with his sons when he was finally reunited with them in the '80s. He told them that knowing his own proclivity, "If you drink, you may drink obsessively, because it's in your genes. If you pick it up, you may have a hard time putting it down, so the best thing to do is not to pick it up."

His first job in Los Angeles came to him for very practical reasons, outside of needing money. Feeling that he didn't have a chance at an opportunity in an office setting (because, "what was I qualified to do?"), he figured he needed a car to get around to potential meetings should he decide to refocus on getting his acting career up and running again. "I knew I could drive, so that's what I got a job doing. And I really wasn't qualified to do that, because I didn't really know the roads here."

But, as fairy tales go, the person in charge of the driver's application process was a fan. Joe passed the test the second time around "with a little help from some fellow cabbies." Ironically, while taking the test, he had a couple of other fellows from the program sitting drunk in his car out in the parking lot waiting for him to take them back to the hospital.

Before long, he was approached by a gentleman to work for a sedan-limo service, a classier job that he enjoyed doing very much. Occasionally he'd motor a celebrity or two—and a couple of times he was recognized by surprised, bug-eyed passengers.

With fresh-faced head shots, Joe Dallesandro was also about to reignite his acting career ... in style.

He had been cast to play legendary mobster Charles "Lucky" Luciano, a small but nice role, in the latest extravaganza from Francis Ford Coppola: **The Cotton Club** (1984). A stream of other film roles began to come his way on a nearly regular basis, as well as a key supporting part in a short-lived television series.

Joe married again in 1988, to an artist and songwriter

named Kim. The ceremony took place at the beautiful home they shared in Los Angeles, with Joe decked out in black T-shirt, as promised, to assuage fears his father-in-law had about the affair being too fancy.

This marriage, too, was to have its ups and downs (like all marriages), but hopes that the maturity of both parties would prevail—in contrast to Joe's previous marriages to teenagers—were unfortunately not borne out. After seven years, the two separated and divorced.

In 1993, Joe's father died. Their relationship, too, had its requisite ups and downs over the years, but the love they had for one another became stronger and stronger as the years went by. His dad's own father had died when Joe Sr. was a very young man (his mother re-marrying to a widower and having another son by him) and so the two shared a generational fissure which continued with Joe's sons, but which both men tried to close during their lives.

"I never put him through a guilt trip," says Joe. "I always told my father that he was the best father that he could be. For years, I used to say, 'you were the best father in the world because for one day out of the month you could be the best.' But the facts are, Dad, you're not too great in the Pop's department. You don't know how to do that work. And yet, that's a pretty hard fucking job and you've always been the best by me. You've always pointed me in the right direction. If I didn't follow all of your advice, then shame on me. It had nothing to do with you."

Happily, his father's last marriage to Phyllis was long-lasting and nurturing. "It's nice to know that he had at least twenty good years," says Joe with a smile. "He would always say you keep trying until you get it right."

The platitude seems especially true for Joe, who feels strongly that his life has been played out in repetitious seven year cycles. Each time, even at his lowest, he manages to find ways to move on.

It may be true that his work on film since his return to the United States in the early 1980's has not been as frequent as he would like, but all in all, not bad for a kid who never figured how far a guy could get in this business just by peeling down to his jockey shorts—pre-Calvin Klein, of course.

What's more, he's a survivor. The list of Warhol-associated casualties is long indeed.

Though he continues to remain ambivalent about his association with them, Joe is also quite sincere in his appreciation for the direction Morrissey and Warhol gave his life.

He says, "What I got from the Warhol people was—I had no designs or desires to be an actor, knew nothing about the field—and they gave me a trade. They worked with me and they gave me a career. Paul told me early on that there are going to be a lot of people who are going to want to interview you, Joe, and they're going to say all sorts of things about you, but if you fall into the trap of believing what they're saying, then you'll lose yourself. And I watched a lot of people who completely lost it. I think what happened to the other people, the ones that didn't make it, is that instead of just working, they began to believe in their fame and they never did anything else for themselves. They wanted to recognize what they got out of it as what got printed in the paper the next day... and that's not what it was about at all. I recognized what I got out of it."

At the make-up mirror preparing for **Black Moon**, one of his few art films while living in Europe. Photo by Sveeva Vigeveno/Courtesy Joe Dallesandro

Recognized, yes, but not without a certain degree of persistent "embarrassment" over a cult fame sustained by movies he made almost three decades ago.

"The embarrassment comes from having done so

Joe and Bob Dallesandro. Photographed by Jack Mitchell/Courtesy Joe Dallesandro

much other work. Having put in five, maybe six years with the Andy Warhol people, I've done so much other work. Thirty years I've put into the film industry."

When Andy Warhol checked out of this world in 1987, he did so in a manner strangely befitting the eccentric Pop Star whose image had become bigger than his artwork. Somehow it seems sadly appropriate that this man—who famously surrounded himself with an entourage of offbeat characters, who had been pronounced dead two decades before after bullets from an assassin ricocheted in his guts, but who survived and recovered—would die all by his lonesome in a hospital bed after routine gallbladder surgery. Andy's death was the *Death and Disaster* painting he never got around to doing, but should have. In the series, he depicted horrific images of car crash victims and plane crash headlines ripped from newspapers with a kind of detached, alienated starkness that challenged the image into commonality. Death was commodified by its objectification as artless art presented as art.

Andy's celebrity shooting screamed headlines that would have made a nice addition to the series, complete with Jack Smith's photo of Warhol—only his pale white mouth and chin on view, as the officer holding his stretcher blocks the upper half of his head—being loaded into the ambulance. That was America at the end of the '60s.

But America in the '80s provided a different canvas. Had it been rendered, we would have seen the ghostly image of a frightened little man confined to his hospital bed, bathed in the dark loneliness of night, slowly poisoning himself to death ... because somebody wasn't paying attention to the tubes and the monitors.

"All the books came out after Andy passed," recalls Joe. "They all became authorities."

He's not listed as a source in a single book of the near dozen that have been published in the wake of Andy Warhol's death. He hasn't read them, nor cares to ever do so. He does, however, mention Holly Woodlawn's *A Low Life in High Heels* (1991) and Mary Woronov's *Swimming Underground: My Years in the Warhol Factory* (1995).

"Those are the only two books that deserve all of their success," he says with genuine admiration. "And Holly's deserves to be made into a movie, because it wasn't somebody making up shit about the Warhol days. It was Holly talking about her life and her situation."

That is precisely the sense you get talking to Joe Dallesandro, who, for years, recoiled at the prospect of yakking to the media about what it was like working with Andy Warhol, mostly because they all came with the same ten questions and none had an inkling who they were talking to beyond a few misguided key words: Warhol, Underground, Naked, Drugs.

Joe Sr. and Joe Jr./Courtesy Joe Dallesandro

Today, some three decades after happenstance made a New York cult star, Joe still struggles with his unique place in movie history. He figures he'd reconsider if asked again, but at the time Madonna's people approached him to do a cameo in her music video for "Deeper and Deeper," a retro-homage to the New York '60s club scene, he turned them down. She wanted the Joe of yesteryear, he figured, and he wanted to be the Joe of here and now.

He's looking ahead. And even though he might still find it hard to believe that people watch his old stuff and actually like it, he's damned appreciative of his fans and the loyal following he's enjoyed all these years.

As to his career, he sees it in the same terms as any other serious actor: "I haven't done the great performance yet. I've done some things that I appreciate, but I've not done all that I can."

He continues to seek roles, and to find them, while occasionally wrestling a bit with putting his famed past in proper perspective.

His cult of admirers has already done so. For Joe Dallesandro fans, I think, it's less important he's given leads than it is he still shows up somewhere, anywhere—that this kid from the streets still makes movies.

the films

Courtesy Joe Dallesandro

an undress

rehearsal

(1965)

"AMG was the genesis of beefcake photography. With Sharon Stone showing her pussy on the big screen and Jeff Stryker's member available on video, the public is getting numbed to explicit nudity. I think people are finding eroticism again in the kinds of subtle fetishes Mizer made famous."
—*Christopher Makos*

On the often long and sometimes torturous route to making it as an actor, more often than not a guy has to learn to swallow his ego and carry the goddamned spear if he wants to get his foot in the soundstage door. If, on the other hand, being an actor is the furthest thing from your mind, it's still quite possible you'll become one. Just ask Joe Dallesandro.

Preparing for a career as a male sex symbol in underground films wasn't the intention, but, in a sense, that's what happened. Joe's first accidental foray into a "film" career didn't *directly* lead to any of his subsequent Andy Warhol fame, but it has certainly become a significant part of the legend.

How do you make a little extra bread when you're a fugitive teenager on the loose in Los Angeles? You chat up the dirty old men at the bus station. You make calculated decisions about whether you can trust them or not, whether you can take them or not, whether you can knock them on their ass and run faster than them if you need to.

In 1965, Joe showed remarkable street savvy, but he also got lucky. For the promise of a few bucks, he hooked up with a fella who knew a photographer in town who would pay $50 for a good-looking young guy to pose for him. No funny stuff. Just some nudie shots and maybe even a loop if he liked you.

For nearly half a century, Bob Mizer photographed and filmed near-naked and completely naked men showing off their toned, glistening bodies on his property at 1834 W 11th Street in Los Angeles. Starting as a photography referral service in 1945, his Athletic Model Guild would become legendary as both portrait studio and film production house, making boy-next-door models available by mail order to gay men of the Eisenhower era and beyond. Through the publication of *Physique Pictorial* magazine, begun in 1951, AMG became the "Playboy" of the American closet, stressing an aesthetic interest in the male physique as a thing of beauty, as a form to be refined, built up, and displayed with pride. In 1967, for less than $6.00 a year, you could receive four issues (at least half of them coming a little to a lot late) featuring an inspiring potpourri of men in various states of undress. A different guy on each page, too, with details on how you could order sets of black and white 5" x 7" prints and even a home movie of your favorite model.

When Joe posed for Bob Mizer's camera, he was just one of an estimated 6000 young men the photographer had shot. He did only the single session with Mizer, although the photographer liked him and wanted him back. There was "an altercation" between Joe and the fella who brought him to AMG, however, and so Mizer subsequently refused a second session. No matter, in one session with Joe, Mizer managed 86 nudes and even an 8mm posing film. The photos would become hot collector's properties as Joe developed a following in the Warhol films; they remain highly-sought and much-reproduced to this day. Fans regularly send Joe copies from his AMG shoot looking for an autograph and for the longest time they were the only pictures he didn't sign. Not because he was ashamed of them, mind you, it was just that it somehow seemed inappropriate and perhaps a bit too much of an uncomfortable memory of where he was in his life at that period, of why he did the pictures in the first place.

In the last couple of years, Joe slowly has been changing his mind about that. Today, he can look back at the nudes he did with a certain degree of pride, of detached appreciation for a strapping young man showing off his body. Besides, "that little fucker is me."

Joe's first appearance in *Physique Pictorial* came in Volume 16, Number 3, September, 1967. Tellingly noting that Joe "gave his age to us as being 19," the magazine hedges its bet that he's not really 19 without having to own up to it. So long as he says he's 19—well, then, if he's not and someone raises a stink we can always say the kid must have lied to us. A few years later, while running another photo of him, the magazine reports that he claimed 19, but he was actually 18. The truth is nowhere in between.

Note the bullet wound scar above his right knee

Joe's inaugural photo comes in the last of *Physique Pictorial*'s non-frontal issues, the end of an era in which all that the guys could bare completely were their hind-ends. Posing straps and denim jeans were the rage next to the bare bottom pics.

Joe is pictured sitting on a pedestal, demurely reaching an arm toward the ankle of one of his strategically upraised legs. His skin is luminous, his body oiled and well-lit against a black background, showing off his tremendous abdominals and classically cut form. His hair has been lubed with greasy kid's stuff, though immaculately combed and parted on the side. His eyes appear closed, foretelling his eventual fame as a sexual object on display. Unlike other models who stare directly into the camera or pose with a poser's stare off into the distance, Joe could just as well be a statue.

The biography tells us his name is "Joe Angelo Dallesandro." He's listed as 5'6", 140 pounds. "Has worked as a cook and hopes to own his own restaurant."

Joe's next appearance would come in the January, 1969, Vol 17, combined issues 2-4 installment. *Physique Pictorial*, it was easy to see, had by now decided to go full-frontal, with better paper and even some color photos, thus the jump from .35 an issue to a whopping $2 (all back issues going for .47 a piece). By now, Joe had made a name for himself in New York with his appearances in **The Loves of Ondine** and **Flesh**. Mizer and his crew probably weren't all that aware of what he'd done, just that he'd

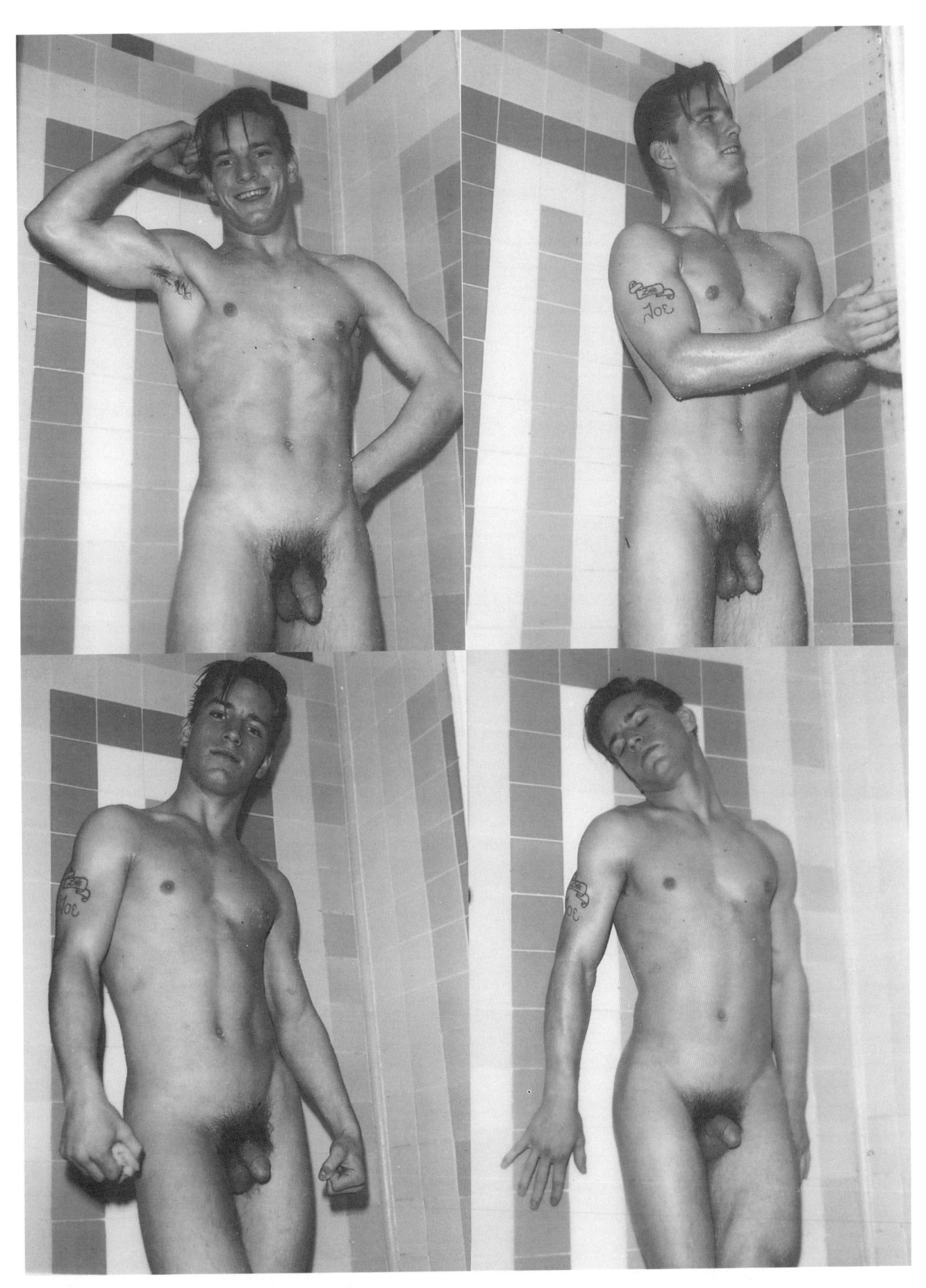

Athletic Model Guild/Photographed by Bob Mizer

worked for Warhol. Alongside his first published frontal—another statuesque pose—the text explains that Joe D'Allesandro "recently did a film for Andy Warhol called 'The Couch' but in many places where it was shown, the police immediately confiscated it." (Warhol did do a film called **Couch** back in 1964, but that was pre-Joe.)

Complete with inadvertent double entendre—something Mizer rarely indulged in considering his (sober) attitude toward his work—the text goes on to say that Joe was "active in gymnastics and football, and has also done hard construction work laying pipe. His regular occupation is a short-order cook, has done dish washing, and hopes some day to open his own Italian restaurant."

A full decade after they shot him, and even after he'd made his last film for Warhol, AMG ran another frontal of Joe in Volume 27, the July, 1975 issue of *Physique Pictorial*, which was trimmed down a bit and back to black-and-white layout for a $1.00 cover price. The text unwittingly betrays his true age at the time of the photos when it repeats that he said he was 19, but was actually only 18, "having given his birthdate as December 31, 1946."

The shot, with Joe looking straight into the camera, his hands in fists awkwardly posed at his sides to tense up his torso, also comes complete with a Mizer trademark missing from their prior Joe coverage: an inch by inch rundown of his physique, save, of course, the appendage one simply cannot "build." It must be remembered that *Physique Pictorial* was for all practical (and legal) reasons a magazine devoted to bodybuilding. Purely for the record, then, here are Little Joe's measurements, which were "all made by the writer, so can vouch for their accuracy, if anyone cares."

"Waist: 29.5 (pulled in to 27.5); Biceps: 13.5; Forearm: 11.75; Wrist: 7.12; Neck: 15.6; Chest: 39 normal (expanded to 40); Hips: 36.6; Thighs: 21; Calf: 14.12; Ankle: 9.4; Shoulders: 47; Leg length to floor: 30.5; Tit-to-tit: 8.75; Tit to navel: 9.75; Head circumference at temples: 22.5." So there you have it guys and gals, go run out and make him a suit.

Physique Pictorial may have officially featured Joe in only three of its issues, as well as presenting him as one of its monthly studs in the AMG 1969 pocket-size calendar, but his photos gained popularity and distinction when he emerged as one of the few young guys in its stock to become even marginally famous. The magazine also photographed Ed Fury and Richard Harrison (no, not that one), both of whom had bit parts in Hollywood films and then went to Italy and had careers in action pictures. Dennis Cole, Glenn Corbett and Gary Conway also made appearances before AMG's cameras. (Of course, Steve Reeves, Arnold Schwarzenegger, and even Sean Connery owe at least some of their professional career treks to the beefcake portraits they posed for, though none posed at AMG.)

Photo sets of the "athletes" went for $3.00 for six or two different sets for $5.00. In addition, Joe fans could purchase a black-and-white 8mm film of their fave for just 10 smackers, though that's pretty hefty 1960's cash considering the film runs only 3 1/2 minutes (it was edited from a 20-minute reel). With the advent of video, Joe's loop appeared in **AMG's Nude Posing Video Potpourri #26**, which could be purchased for $125 (it featured 16 other models) and then traded in on a new tape for just $33. The company actually encouraged clientele to copy their tapes and send the original back for the trade-in.

AMG Film #D-48 begins with a close-up of Joe's face and chest as he holds a placard with his name in white letters in front of him. He manages an awkward smile and puts the sign down as the camera pulls back and reveals him oiled and shining against a black background. He pumps his arms for bicep action, then leans back on a table and tenses his stomach to display his phenomenal "six-pack," smiling and shaking his head. He gets up and moves the table out of the way, then continues to pose and flex.

He seems entirely oblivious to the fact that he is completely naked. While shadow-boxing, he actually appears to be dodging his imaginary opponent, weaving and bobbing and waiting to get in his best shot, so much so that he even waves the "guy" off at the end. Next, he pitches imaginary baseballs, then he runs and dances in place, then he performs a spectacular series of high-kicks in profile. After facing us again and pointing at the camera, he does a complete flip right at us, nearly losing balance, then smiles a charming adolescent grin and wipes his forehead in movie actor's "fatigue." He lies down on the floor, but has some difficulty deciding how to arrange his legs because of the awkwardness of needing to have his genitalia remain on display. He finally chooses a resting posture and the camera slowly pans across his oiled and sleepy physique; a formal black and white study of a dozing Adonis. The lights go out.

Far from the creepy spectacle described by writer Dotson Rader, who was shown the AMG photos and film by Andy Warhol and who sought to read into them a subtext of "being demeaned" in his 1971 *Rolling Stone* cover story on Joe, the film has an almost surreal charm about it. Joe's serious flexing displays, betrayed by smiles all but forbidden from him in the Warhol work, serve as an interesting glimpse—a test reel, if you will—of what he was destined to become. Could he be demeaned, could a teenage kid be taken advantage of? Yes, and it did happen. But, to some degree, Joe Dallesandro worked with AMG

Athletic Model Guild/Photographed by Bob Mizer

on his own terms. (Admittedly, there may be some wishful thinking involved in such a justification, primarily due to Joe having finally come to terms with the photos. An argument that there was no exploitation of this teenager by AMG would, of course, be completely dishonest.)

A 30-second snippet of Joe's loop appears in the low-budget 1990 documentary **AMG: The Fantasy Factory**, itself an entertaining primer to the unabashed good fun that was Mizer's movie studio.

It's really too bad that Joe didn't do more work for Mizer, though that may seem a strange thing to say. It's so easy to see him taking his place among the "stars" in Mizer's film stable. And they did have followings, too; particularly the darkly handsome Brian Idol, the sculpted William Schaller and Joe Leitel, and the boyishly good-looking Forrester Millard and Jim Paris. Joe would have fit right in, ripe and right for dozens of roles as streetpunk, frat pledge or sailor-boy. His innate sense for playing along with an unscripted situation, which is precisely what he would exercise in the Warhol films, could even have been rehearsed here.

AMG wasn't the only studio who photographed him either. He did some work for photographers when he returned to New York that has recently been rediscovered and is making the rounds. But much more "explicit" shots were done while he was still in L.A. by photographer Bruce Bellas, aka Bruce of Los Angeles (and later—Kensington Road Studios). As late as the mid-1980's, Kensington was offering its color photosets of Joe.

Bellas also made the most of his shoot with Dallesandro, offsetting the standard poses he shot with more arty tableaux: e.g., Joe draped with or holding a fisherman's netting. But the big news was that Bob Bellas was shooting hard-ons. Mizer wouldn't venture into that territory for some time to come, but Bellas didn't hold back, particularly if he could manage a pose in which the tumescence of the subject's penis was open to some interpretation. For example, by having a model lie back, an erection could be camouflaged as simply a large penis resting against the owner's belly, a gravitational law arguably still very much within the law. Joe's full-color session of erection shots is among the most highly sought by collectors of his entire nudie photo beginnings.

But these shots are also among the few items the actor refuses to autograph. The reason he doesn't sign them has nothing to do at all with prudery. "Part of not signing photos that 'stand up' is not legitimizing them," he says. "You know, 'yeah, it was wonderful doing that...I'll even sign it for you.' Well, it wasn't."

Bellas published two full-page color (including the back cover) and two full-page black-and-whites of Joe (sans boner) in *The Male Figure Review, No. 1* (1969), which sold for $5. The more explicit poses were available by mail order only.

The irony of Joe Dallesandro's initiation into the world of photographing his flesh, of allowing himself to become an object of male sexual voyeurism even before he met Andy Warhol, is certainly not lost here.

Athletic Model Guild/Photographed by Bob Mizer

When a particularly ugly and well-publicized double murder occurred in my small midwestern hometown several years back, the suspect was a handsome high school quarterback. He miraculously escaped the scene of the crime and evaded police for the next few years, but when his pick-up truck was located in Hollywood, rumors began circulating that he'd probably hit the streets as a male prostitute. Authorities were concerned that if he'd gotten himself into the urban underworld, they'd lose him for good. Truth is, a good-looking face buys privilege. Who wouldn't give the time of day to a sexy young man who was asking for help? Who wouldn't help a good-looking kid set himself up with new ID and a phony Social Security card? Beauty buys favors, too.

Even as a teenager, Joe was wise enough to know what being a beauty could do for you. Bob Mizer and Bruce Bellas paid him for it in what amounts to a prescient undress rehearsal for a career as a thing of beauty. The casting couch chase was caught on film. It is we who were being hustled.

And Joe Dallesandro's career as a naked pin-up boy hadn't ended, it had only just begun.

the loves of ondine (1967)

"This boy, Joe Dallesandro, is good-looking and natural-acting enough to have a showbiz career beyond Warhol."   —*Variety* (8/21/68)

With **JOE DALLESANDRO AS COLLEGE WRESTLER**, Bob "Ondine" Olivo (Ondine), Viva (Girl in Bed), Angelina "Pepper" Davis (Girl on Love Seat), Ivy Nicholson (Girl on Chair), Brigid Polk (Wife to Ondine), Waldo Diaz Balart, Juan Downey, Manuel Peña, Rolando Peña, Katrina Toland. Directed by Andy Warhol/Paul Morrissey. **86 minutes**

Andy Warhol's latest film, titled simply ****, began unspooling at the New Cinema Playhouse at 8:30 p.m. on Friday, December 15, 1967. The projector went off sometime around 9:30 p.m. On Saturday, December 16, 1967. "People bought one ticket and they went in and out all day," says Joe. "The projectionist was the luckiest guy in the world because he got golden time and double golden time and triple golden time. He ended up making more money than it cost to make the movie."

Welcome to the film world of Andy Warhol, America's resident Pop Artist and presumed ringleader of a 24-hour freak-for-all at his silver-coated studio, The Factory, on East 47th Street in New York (the first of three locations for his businessman's circus).

The cultural phenomenon of Andy Warhol, boiled down to fractured images and sound bytes in the 90s, is of soup cans, Polaroids, silver hair, and "everybody will be famous for 15 minutes." A sickly child of Czechoslovakian immigrants, he waged through the travails of his poverty-stricken and isolated childhood (his doting mother always by his side, he spent much of his down time reading and drawing in bed) and ended up studying design at the Carnegie Institute of Technology.

In 1949, the strange boy whose spasmodic nervous breakdowns were later attributed to a condition known as St. Vitus' Dance moved to New York City and made the rounds of advertising agencies with his portfolio in tow. Soon he was doing illustrations of shoes for *Glamour* magazine. A career gave way to a successful streak of doing what he loved doing—and doing it for money. The adage about having to be dead to be appreciated as an artist is something the newly adopted Andy Warhol—he was born Andrew Warhola—was meant to redress.

Commercial art was the big "no-no" of the serious art world, and at the risk of reducing the man's work to generalities, Warhol's open defiance of the art world establishment brought him negative criticism and early dismissals.

"It's sometimes said that Andy Warhol brought a new artificiality into art," wrote Jack Kroll in *Newsweek* after the artist's death. "Actually, he restored art as a natural process, something that came out of the culture rather than out of the private workings of the artist's psyche."

Warhol turned to the kitschy world of commercial advertising and pop culture for his artistic regurgitations. The concept was (and is) brilliant, but how many people want to look at a guy regurgitating?

From canvases reproducing half-finished comic-strip cells to colorful silk-screened images of movie stars and politicians reproduced in multiple assembly-line images on a single canvas—each face a fingerprint of flaws distinguishing it from the last, from paintings of newspaper ads, Coca Cola bottles, and dollar bills, to the ubiquitous Campbell's Soup Cans, Warhol gave the Rauschenbergs and Jasper Johns of the Abstract Expressionist era a run for their money.

The soup cans. There were lots of them. 200 on one canvas. But it was the 32 individual Campbell's Soup cans, 20" x 16" each, that went on display at the Ferus Gallery in Los Angeles in the summer of 1962 that figure most conveniently as the paradigm of this little art history diversion. The asking price was $100 each (though the gallery eventually decided not to break up the lot). In protest, a rival gallery put real Campbell's Soup cans in their window and posted a sign: "Buy them cheaper here—five cans for a dollar."

It was in 1963 that Warhol started making films. He would often venture out to see screenings of independently made movies on 8mm and 16mm stock. The era's cutting edge filmmakers were people such as Jack Smith, Gregory Markopoulos, Kenneth Anger, and Stan Brakhage, all of whom made deeply personal explorations through a series of images caught in a little box and then projected on a wall. And so it had been since Edison and the Lumieres, but the medium now had an established vocabulary and a rich source of shared imagery and iconography (semiotics) from which to draw, giving sway to a "camp" sensibility when some of these filmmakers turned to Hollywood kitsch for inspiration and send-up.

That Warhol was homosexual attracted him, in part, to filmmaking. Making a movie was glamorous, no matter what the scale, and so was the idea of luring people to be filmed. Neither glamour nor voyeuristic tendencies are strictly gay predilections, but much of what Warhol saw at the time was bewitchingly uncloseted. Jack Smith's watershed **Flaming Creatures** (1962), with its tawdry take on Tinsel Town hetero-drag, was surely an inspiration, but so was Kenneth Anger's powerfully homoerotic **Fireworks** (1947), a teenaged incantation of sexual expression which made headlines when the San Francisco police nabbed it for obscenity at a 1960 screening. (Warhol's **Lonesome Cowboys** would nearly suffer the same fate nine years later.) Likewise, Anger's **Inauguration of the Pleasure Dome** (1954) and **Scorpio Rising** (1962) provided creative catalysts.

His first films were silent black-and-whites, noted for their singularity of purpose and their single-mindedness. **Kiss** (1963) was officially his first, though it was a serial combined with three minute reel after three minute reel pasted together with leaders and tails and all. His epic **Sleep** (1963), in which he filmed a slumbering John Giorno in the act from various angles for several hours, was as controversially audacious as his still art.

As Warhol film curator Callie Angell writes: "The utter stillness of this image, immobilized within the stationary frame of the film screen, makes the film equivalent in physical presence to a painting on the wall."

Sleep certainly wasn't commercial filmmaking, but it succeeded in reinforcing the central theme of all of Andy's work: Who's to say this isn't art, too? By challenging the very definition of a lexical abstraction—the word and associated meaning of "art"—Warhol rattled the delicate sensibilities of people who took art seriously and illuminated the narrow ideological chasm between that which an artist does and that which my kid can do with a flick of his watercolors or a scrawl of his crayon. This was particularly resonant in a time when the predominant expression was psychological.

Sleep effectively challenged the popular notion of cinema, as well; strangely, by returning to film's Edisonian roots. The film was silent, the subject was ordinary, and the framing remained static. He lit the subject, framed the subject, and then turned on the camera and just let it run. For **Sleep**, as well as on his other silents, he also distended time, action, and movement by projecting his films 8 frames slower than the speed at which he shot them.

With a running time of five hours and twenty-one minutes, **Sleep** opened in New York in 1964 as part of the nomadic Filmmakers' Co-Operative, a haven for a new generation of experimental filmmakers, also dubbed "underground" filmmakers. Most of the critics were horrified.

By this time, Andy had already shot shorter films, but the message was just the same. **Eat** (1964) chronicles a man consuming a single mushroom for 39 minutes; there's the 27 minute **Haircut** (No.1; 1963); and most brilliant of all, there's **Blow Job** (1964). It's easy to imagine the titillation the audience must have felt going to see this one. Good Lord, what's Andy done now? That pervert!

And so, with expectations high and hormones surging in the name of art, the audience sits and watches for 41 min-

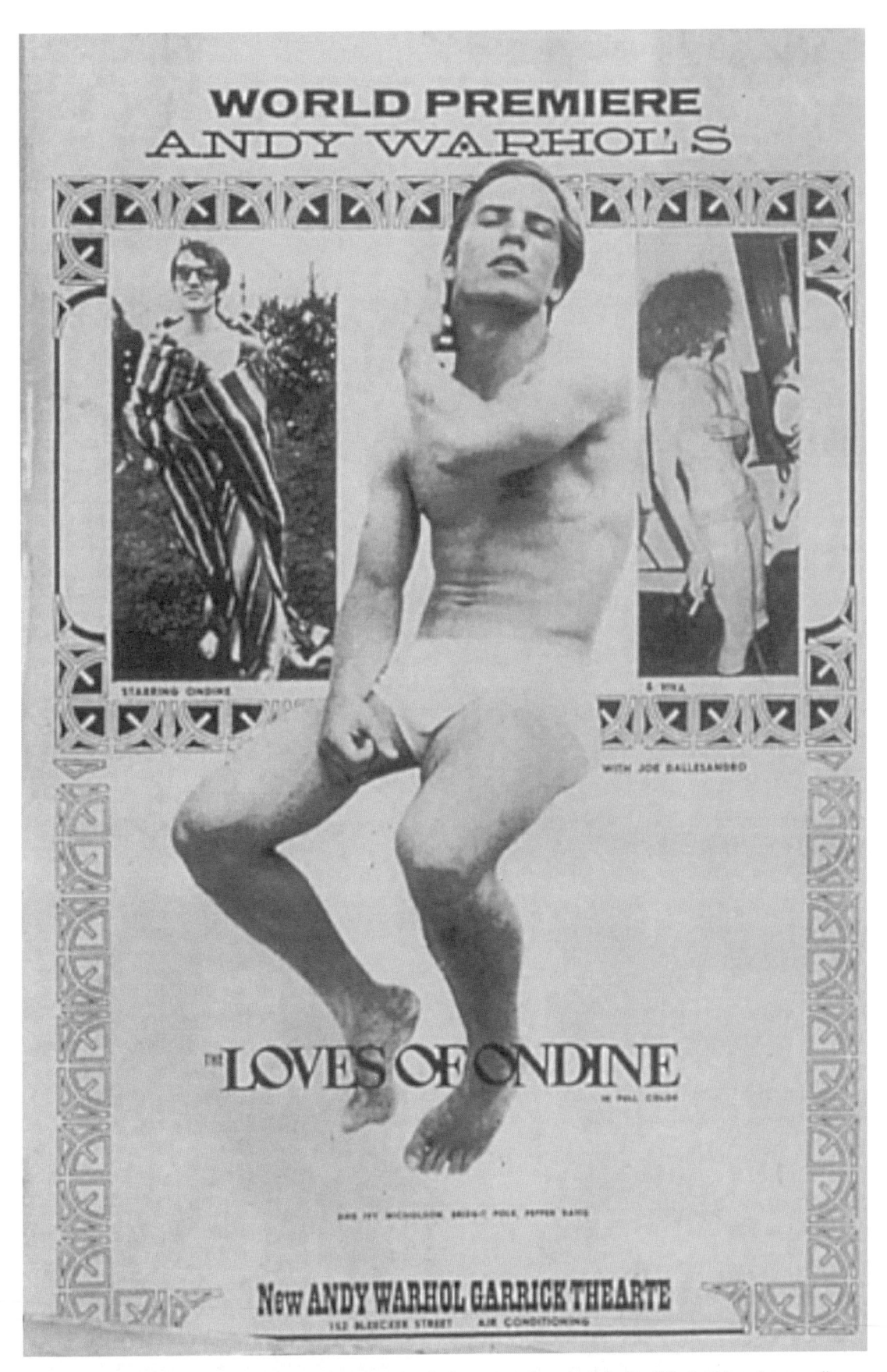

More than suggesting his ascent to the status of male Superstar, the ad run in the *Village Voice* places walk-in Joe Dallesandro at the center of attention/The Archives of the Andy Warhol Museum, Pittsburgh; Founding Collection, Contribution The Andy Warhol Foundation for the Visual Arts, Inc.

utes as a handsome young man is fellated before their very eyes and Andy's camera never once drops below the belt. For 41 long and sexually surreal minutes, we watch the facial expressions of a young man leaning up against a brick wall while supposedly getting blown.

Andy Warhol had seemingly reached his zenith. The dirty movie his title promised filmgoers was a dirty movie they were forced to play out in their own heads.

Thus we arrive at the conceptual beauty of Warhol's early works: you didn't even have to see them to love or hate them. Never was that more toweringly exemplified than by his 8-hour, five-and-a-half-minute **Empire** (1964), an insistently static shot (taken from the 44th floor of the Time Life Building) of the Empire State Building, man's biggest self-erection, chronicling dusk to dawn. Warhol would later say, "**Empire** is a—uh—pornographic movie. When the light goes on in the Empire State Building, it's supposed to represent …"

Filmmaking was intoxicatingly easy for Andy. You just turn it on and walk away, he was fond of telling interviewers. It was easier than painting. He bought himself a new 16mm Auricon camera and began filming 100' reels of just about anybody who walked into his studio, the famed Factory. The space quickly became a hang-out for artists, actors, musicians, and a cornucopia of fringe dwellers, including the requisite druggies, transvestites, hustlers and counterculture deviants.

The Factory was the physical locale for an idea of an entire time and place that has been amusingly fabled as the 60's freak era. With the free flow of colorful humanity came the idea of the "Superstar," another of Andy's contested credits. After replacing Madonna With Child with Campbell's Soup Cans, and answering Hollywood (though he loved Hollywood) with copious footage of slumber, Andy began to turn his camera on subjects who animated the dormant frame by sheer force of personality.

His "actors" came from everywhere and anywhere, from alleyways in Brooklyn to opulent cattle ranches in California. All of them were a little lost and, at the Factory, many felt they were a little found. If Hollywood had "stars," then Warhol's stars would have to be "superstars." Following thematic suit, Warhol challenged the very notion of "stars" by allowing everyone to be one. Along with writer-friend Ronald Tavel, Warhol began his "sound" films featuring an Andy favorite: transvestite superstars.

In the still-silent **Mario Banana** (1964), Mario Montez (a drag performer who also appeared in **Flaming Creatures**) eats a banana for four minutes, then graduated to starring in a 66-minute feature cryptically evoking "Jean Harlow" in Andy's bananarama version **Harlot** (1964).

Among the other original "superstars" who played regularly in front of Warhol's primitive camera—or irregularly, depending on your point of view—were Baby Jane Holzer, Taylor Mead, Gerard Malanga, and troubled spirit Edie Sedgwick, whose tragic slide from slightly disturbed and filthy rich to seriously disturbed and drug-addicted was depicted in the 1982 bestseller *Edie: An American Biography*, an oral history of tragic dimensions. (Madonna once seriously considered bringing Sedgwick's story to the big screen.)

In one of the (at least eleven) films she made for Andy, **Kitchen** (1965), a high-life Sedgwick manages to make an impression despite having to share an increasingly cramped box of space in a bright white kitchen where all sorts of unintelligible events occur.

Norman Mailer, in an interview with Vincent Canby in the *New York Times*, said: "Warhol's **Kitchen** may really be the best film made about the twentieth century and is almost unendurable to watch. The camera is locked into position at an irritating middle distance. Edie Sedgwick and some other people are sitting around the table. Edie has the sniffles and keeps blowing her nose and this other guy keeps opening and closing the door of the refrigerator. They talk and you can't understand a word. You almost can't bear it, but … when in the future they want to know about the riots in our cities, this may be the movie that tells them."

Mainstream critics were less knowing. The faint praise of arty indulgence and camp sensibility used as polite tolerance of his movies was wearing thin.

But what about the audiences?

Vogue asked Andy in 1970, "Isn't it a cop-out, an evasion of responsibility, to characterize as an 'experiment' films that are commercially exhibited?"

"In that case," answered Andy, "the paying customers are the experiment."

The Chelsea Girls (1966) proved him right. At an estimated cost of $3,000 for almost seven hours of film, which he then split-screened into 3 hours and 24 minutes of running time, Warhol's first certified epic about people was also his first to move from the "underground" traveling shows to the "legitimate" New York movie houses. It grossed somewhere in the neighborhood of $130,000. (Warhol liked to say that the film cost $1,500 and grossed over half a million.)

"At its best, **The Chelsea Girls** is a travelogue of hell," said the *New York Times*, "—a grotesque menagerie of lost souls whimpering in a psychedelic moonscape of neon red and fluorescent blue. At its worst it is a bunch of home movies in which Mr. Warhol's friends, asked to do something for the camera, can think of nothing much to do."

Anyone in the least bit interested in a roll call of Andy's superstars will find them in this film. Here we have the statuesque model Nico (who became a part of the Velvet Underground under the auspices of Paul Morrissey), Gerard Malanga (poet, painter, and male star of several Warhol films, including **Vinyl**—a whip-snapping take on **A Clockwork Orange**, pre-Kubrick), Brigid Berlin (daughter of the president of the Hearst Corporation, who nicknamed herself Brigid Polk because of her passion for poking herself with drug injections), actor/speed-freak Robert "Ondine" Olivo, hairdresser/dancer/waiter Eric Emerson, Susan Bottomley (aka International Velvet), Marie Menken, Ed Hood, Mary Woronov, and Ingrid Superstar.

Shocked and amazed audiences watched reel after reel, both black-and-white and color with the soundtrack alternating seemingly at random from one side of the split screen's imagery to the other. They watched these reels unspool the freaky and frightening rants, raves, and bizarre speeches of people supposedly occupying various rooms of The Chelsea Hotel in New York City. A visual paean to the sixties counterculture—political, sexual, and drug-enhanced—paraded before them: from an ornery display of Brigid's poking techniques and phone manners to a bit of bondage sexplay; to the infamous amphetamine-induced explosion of violence from Ondine (who is playing "Pope" and repeatedly slaps an unsuspecting young woman while berating her) to Emerson tripping poetically into a neon-lit free-flow detailing—among other things—the tasty and erotic properties of sweat and the free-love concept of swinging both ways without having to be necessarily queer.

The Chelsea Girls' relative success at the box-office had more than a little something to do with the fact that Warhol's camera was at last trained on more than just a skyscraper and was more than just the filmed record of an act of minimalist execution (eating a mushroom, for example). **The Chelsea Girls** brought the fringe world of dawning hippie culture to the culture at large, where it seemed to be enjoyed as both freakshow and a relevant document of the frayed and fractured times. It was an indictment of the Sixties suggesting what was going either right or wrong with us; it confirmed a degenerate society. There was still plenty of Warhol's minimalist technique, but the frame was coming alive in a way that spoke viscerally to audiences.

The cast of characters Warhol captured seemed to be playing themselves and that was a key ingredient to the growing interest in popularity of and later derision of his films. When Ondine strikes out at Rona Page and slaps her hard, we have to deal with our shock at the force and reality of the slap, and then he slaps her again and again. She need only run out of the frame (which she eventually does), but the initial blows are so shocking and frighteningly real that they stun her as well. That very tangible sense of danger and her guarded and futile attempt to get her attacker to let up is akin to the profound immediacy of documentary filmmaking and it's what made Warhol's films fascinating, uninhibited spectacles for the audience.

Warhol was continuing to eavesdrop on his "friends," but now they were saying things and doing things that audiences found interesting in a strikingly vicarious way. These weren't just actors, they were real live weirdos.

Once the audience connected on that kind of level, the incessant talk, talk, talk (which Andy loved) began to transcend uninteresting jabber.

"They did get a lot of jabbering!" according to Joe. "It wasn't like Andy created great shit. He didn't. It was like old maids chit-chatting on the phone."

A trip to a Greenwich Village apartment complex in 1967 to visit friends—he told me he used to tell interviewers it was to score dope just to jazz up the story a bit—finally lead Joe D'Alessandro to the one man behind a camera whose interest in photographing people meant a shot at being famous, at the very least for fifteen minutes.

The apartment belonged to journalist John Wilcock. Joe poked his head in to watch the filming in progress.

While working on reconstructing ****, Callie Angell, curator of the Andy Warhol Film Project at the Whitney Museum (in partnership with the Museum of Modern Art and the Andy Warhol Foundation for the Visual Arts, Inc.), told me she has seen footage of Joe and his friends wandering into John Wilcock's apartment, effectively capturing on celluloid his inaugural step into cult movie history. How many actors do you know that can lay claim to their first entrance really being their first entrance?

Somehow the idea of Joe's legendary and quite serendipitous arrival being caught on film and kept in an archive somewhere seems an appropriate footnote to the Warholian concept of filming everyday experiences and transforming them into meaningful events simply by projecting them back at us. Even if **Ondine** was originally conceived as only an 8-hour movie, Joe's historic entry while Andy's camera was still turning evokes a 24-hour movie methodology and brings his surveillance-"video" thesis into focus. (Sure wish Joe would have walked off the set of **Andy Warhol's Dracula** while the camera was still rolling so we could have brought this idea full-circle.)

Joe recalls the camera being aimed in the direction of the doorway to the apartment, so he says "it's entirely possible that they did catch me on film when I poked my head in there."

"We finished the first reel and we both realized that it was pretty boring," Morrissey told me. "Nothing had happened and we weren't going to get anything. And Andy, who didn't want to waste time—he didn't care about wasting film—said, 'Well, do you think it's worth another 30-

minute reel?' I said, 'Well, we're here. I think we can do another reel, but we're going to have to change it. There was that young kid who came in with that group. I'll ask him to come into the scene.' So I went next door and I said, 'You, can you stay around and be in this sequence?' I don't know, the others probably left or something. And he did."

Paul Morrissey, complicated film director and friend to whom Joe often refers as his "mentor," was raised in New York City under the strict tutelage of Jesuits. He went to Fordham University, and while working jobs in insurance and then for New York City's Department of Social Services (in Spanish Harlem), began dabbling in 16mm filmmaking as a logical offshoot of a lifelong obsession with the movies. He says he'd seen about an hour's worth of **Sleep** at a theatre—his introduction to Andy's work—and has long since been credited with the very first movement of Andy Warhol's camera in an Andy Warhol film, reportedly due to the suggestion he made while visiting the filming of Edie Sedgwick in **Space** (1965) and the story that Warhol took his advice and panned. (This is pure myth, by the way, but it has taken on a media life of its own because of the erroneous notion that Warhol never zoomed or panned in any of his early films.)

Morrissey, a fiercely opinionated figure whose politics and Catholicism were rigorously held and espoused, seemed a wholly unlikable and unlikely candidate for the mythological mix that was Warhol and the Factory, but he stayed on and gained increasing authority and power, allegedly much to the vocal chagrin of some of the Factory's "elders." He was responsible for the early promotion of the Velvet Underground, including the choice of Nico to front for them, and he produced their first album. He would eventually become Warhol's right-hand man, for a time handling business decisions, founding and then acting as co-editor of Warhol's *inter/View* magazine, and making the movies, as well.

Morrissey's earliest film work, a collection of silents apparently unavailable for viewing today, include shorts made in 1961 (one involves a priest booting an altar boy off a cliff), a 1963 piece entitled **Taylor Mead Dances** that stars early Warhol regular Mead, as well as Roberts Blossom (the scary character actor who decades later sold Arnie **Christine** and was the snow shovel "killer" in **Home Alone**), and a 70-minute feature, **Sleep Walk** (1964), that featured Jennifer Salt (later of DePalma's **Sisters**). The filmmaker showed these in an empty store he rented at 36 East 4th Street as "Experimental Films," but police pulled the dowser within a few short months because he was unlicensed.

"I think I'm one of the few, except for some of his earliest friends, that have seen his first works, that can appreciate the talent that went into doing those kinds of films,"
says Joe. "To shoot a silent movie, especially in that period when there was no interest in silent movies at all, and then be able to capture somebody's interest, especially a younger person who doesn't know for silent movies, like myself—to capture me as an audience—was extraordinary." One of Joe's particular favorites is **All Aboard The Dreamland Choo-Choo** (1965).

Morrissey and Warhol's first major collaboration came on the sound black-and-white feature **My Hustler** (1965), where he essentially directed the actors and made other decisions while Andy was stationed behind the camera. Basically, according to Morrissey, all of the post-1965 films in the Warhol oeuvre, with the exception of **Blue Movie** (1968) and **Andy Warhol's Bad** (1976), were "directed" by him, including **The Chelsea Girls** (1966, in which actors address "Paul" off-screen, not "Andy"), **I, A Man** (1967), **Bike Boy** (1967), and **The Loves of Ondine**.

Truth be told, Joe D'Alessandro probably never would have become a Warhol star if it weren't for Paul Morrissey's keen eye and the new aesthetic he brought to the Warhol film factory. "His eye for casting was phenomenal," says Joe. Morrissey must have sensed a certain quiet ambiguity in this 18-year old beauty. The director always had a thing for faces and Joe's indisputably fit the bill. It *demanded* to be photographed.

Andy liked loud, boisterous, campy eccentrics who loved to talk, tell lurid personal stories, dress up, be outrageous and flamboyant. Most were women, several were transvestites. Joe was neither. Joe was this quiet kid on the sidelines, thoroughly uninterested in the limelight. He'd prefer just standing silently in the corner or sweeping the floor and running the elevator than getting in front of the camera and acting. Paul Morrissey couldn't have been happier. Andy should have been, too, because in Joe he had found his most enduring and most popular male superstar.

Though **The Loves of Ondine** saw various edits even throughout its 1968 run as a feature (it went from 110 minutes to 86 in the first few weeks of release), in the archivally-preserved cut, Joe shows up about 53 minutes into the film.

He's smoking and drinking coffee and strips his sweater off while making curious small-talk with Ondine in the apartment bedroom; curious, because the two of them are speaking in such a way that it seems they know each other. They're discussing some sort of happening at "Katrina's house" in which Joe says he wasn't sure what to do, but Ondine said he handled himself beautifully in the situation.

I've asked Joe about the dialogue and all he could do was confirm that he had never met Ondine before and doesn't recollect any particular incident to which they might be referring. He adds that he knew a Katrina (Toland—she's in the film) from that neighborhood and speculates that maybe Ondine knew her as well.

In any event, a shirtless Joe inspires Ondine to comment, "Next to your chest, your tattoo is dreary." In pointed contrast to the way in which he handles all of the women in the film—starting out charming and friendly and then suddenly, inexplicably turning mean and bitchy and insulting them, Ondine is clearly enamored of the half-naked "Little Joe" in front of him. He is very reassuring when the young man admits to being a little nervous. "I can't get relaxed," Joe says, then yells to his buddies waiting in the next room for him: "I'll be there in a minute!"

As Ondine suggests, "I wonder what they think we're doing in here?"

The two begin their famed wrestling encounter with a round of arm-wrestling. "What are the rules?" asks Ondine.

"That I have to win, first of all," answers Joe with charm, smiling and cute as all hell. When Ondine breathes a heavy sigh into the shy teenager's chest, Joe playfully covers one of his nipples with his hand; an actor's instinct already evident.

Joe says he's worried that he "can't think of anything to say, anything to speak about," that it'll be boring, and "I don't want to talk about nothing, because nothing doesn't excite me."

Ondine decides to have the young man teach him a thing or two about college wrestling, so off come Joe's shoes and then his pants. (A close-up of his belly-button brings to mind the body-part close-ups in **Flesh**.)

Joe is actually quite talkative during the wrestling set-up as he directs Ondine (the bottom) on how to counter moves from the top. Individual cuts show Joe holding Ondine's head in a vise-grip between his legs, something Ondine is clearly enjoying, and it isn't long before the two of them are doing fellatio-type poses with Ondine's face in Joe's crotch.

A reversed print—his tattoo has "disappeared"

Just when things get interesting, Brigid Polk loudly receives her cue and comes storming in as Ondine's wife, breaking up the pairing and sending Joe slinking for his pants. He's introduced as "Joseph," but a disapproving Brigid isn't supposed to like him so she pins him beneath her and sits on him for a moment's punishment. Demonstrating a trademark of his ensuing career for Warhol and Morrissey, as soon as Brigid comes in and there's competition of any sort from a "talker," Joe clams up and practically becomes one of the audience, sitting on the sidelines and finally putting his pants back on at the 72-minute mark.

He's provided with one other opportunity for center-screen attention while posing—still bare-chested—in dreamy recline, but with even more actors having now come into the scene, he finally grabs his sweater and heads for the door approximately 23 minutes after his arrival.

"Will I see you again?" asks Ondine.

"Maybe," mutters Joe. And out he goes into the next room to see if either of his friends are still hanging around waiting for him.

Warhol relates in his book *Popism* that Morrissey was very enthused by what he saw when they screened Joe's reel. What particularly interested him was Joe's on-screen ambivalence, his ability to reach both men and women, as Brando or Dean could do.

In many ways, Joe Dallesandro is precisely the kind of male movie star Andy Warhol should have had: silent, pretty, street-wise, slightly punk-ish, smolderingly sexual, and as energized as a three-toed tree sloth. Joe was Image pure and simply complex; a man-boy who spoke volumes without so much as a grunt. And yet it's unlikely that back then Andy could have realized that Joe was his man, and had Warhol not been near-fatally shot in 1968 and then relinquished the directorial duties for his films to Morrissey, one might speculate whether or not Joe would have graduated from working in a pizza parlor in Queens to becoming something of an international cult legend. After all, it was at Morrissey's suggestion that Andy had this lovely boy who had wandered into the apartment strip down to his undies to appear in the impromptu wrestling match with the film's star.

"Andy was in one corner of the room with the camera, sitting on a stool and reading a newspaper," Joe recalls. "The camera was facing one direction and he was facing the other direction, not looking through the camera at all, just reading his newspaper, and every once in a while he'd hit the on-off switch. And that was him directing this movie. People were doing a whole bunch of yelling and screaming at each other and I guess when Andy overheard somebody he liked, he turned the camera on."

Joe wasn't a screamer. However, he was a damned good-looking kid and that kind of a scream doesn't have to be heard to be noticed. Andy liked boys in their underwear.

"Brigid and Ondine play this couple and the wife was calling in this boy—me—to teach her husband how to defend himself with wrestling and stuff like that. So it was supposed to be like college wrestling and I figured I should be wearing gym shorts or something and they decided, 'just do it in your underwear.'"

Did he find that request at all weird?

"No. See, I had already done male modeling—nude modeling—so there was nothing that bothered me about wearing my jockey shorts in a wrestling scene. I certainly wasn't homophobic in any way, so there was nothing that disturbed me about that either. I saw the humor in it. I was sophisticated enough in that sort of way, even though I didn't even really know why I was there."

His sophistication ended when he figured that nothing would ever come of his afternoon tussle in his skivvies. Certainly this couldn't be a "real" movie that people would pay to see in a theatre.

When Morrissey asked him to sign a release form for his work, Joe says, "I couldn't believe it. The first thing I did when they asked me to sign a release was ask, 'Why?' I just didn't believe that people would actually go and see this stuff. To me, it was just a joke. But then more people showed up to see this movie than any movie they'd ever done. What would I know? I didn't have enough life experience to know what people would find interesting."

"I always told people who did our early films never to sign a release before they went in front of the camera," says Morrissey. "Only after. Because then if they did anything that they didn't want to be seen, we wouldn't show it. The films were, after all, only experiments, and that's all they were ever intended to be."

At least some of this footage was first screened as part of the marathon ****, aka **The Twenty-Four Hour Movie** or **Four Stars**, which was actually 50 hours folded in half to 25 hours of split-screened images and sounds. Andy was obsessed with the fractured quality of television, telling an interviewer that "a television day is like a twenty-four hour movie. The commercials don't really break up the continuity. The programs change yet somehow remain the same."

The concept was that it didn't really matter what you did and didn't see if you attended the **** screening, because the non-existent stories kept changing all the time. You were supposedly just as likely to get involved in whatever you were watching when you came back after going out for dinner as in whatever you watched before you left. In its full 94-reel, 25-hour glory, **** was projected only once.

Though it officially marked his film debut, and by virtue of its appearance in the full-length and shortened versions of the 25-hour movie was his earliest screened, by the time the ads showed up in *The Village Voice* in 1968, Joe was already an employee of the Factory, **Lonesome Cowboys** was already in the can, and **Flesh** was about to begin production.

The Loves of Ondine, titled by Morrissey because Ondine liked opera and there was an Italian film floating around called **Loves of Bellini**, was released as its own feature on August 1, 1968, possibly in a move to capitalize on the headlines Andy had received from his shooting two months before and his subsequent release from the hospital during the last week of July, though **Bike Boy** was still running locally. The venue was The Garrick Theatre at 152 Bleecker Street, a 199-seat movie house that could be had for $2,700 a week and had been operating under the alias "The New Andy Warhol Garrick Theatre." (Pay the rent, name the place after yourself.)

The film was billed as a "World Premiere," but, incredibly, some of the local press recognized it from its original screening as part of the 25-hour movie of the Christmas before. *The Village Voice*'s James Stoller, who mentions that the theatre's new pseudonym sounded like a memorial and that it should more correctly be dubbed "The Valerie Solanas Theatre," didn't have much nice to say about the 16mm presentation on a day when the advertised air-conditioning was on the fritz, but did manage: "**Loves of Ondine**, incidentally, is far from being an unrelieved chronicle of degeneracy or something like that; Joe Dallesandro, in particular, comes across as one of the more exemplary of Warhol's 'innocents.'"

Lita Eliscu, writing elsewhere, found the film particularly notable for two reasons: The first, Viva's "indefinable" quality; the second, "Joe Dallesandro, who is 19 and one of the more lasting male mini-superstars, is totally beautiful and will be in **Lonesome Cowboy** (sic) when it is released

… You may never have believed college wrestling could be so much fun.

"It is a great subject for summertime's lazy thinking," Eliscu continues. "Where do they come from, why do they stay—and how are they chosen—this mythic superstar species of people. The truth is simple, and it is this basic realization that fundamentally structures Warhol movies. They come from a need, a desire to have them exist. They are what the audience wants or even thinks they need: these beautiful, amoral, self-loving people whose humanity and compassion extends most often to, 'To thine own self be true!' They exist because they are true metaphors for this society, illustrating most frankly, through sex rather than politics, the same conclusions as Godard: the decay of one way of life, the rise of another."

Ondine, variously happy and then unhappy with the Warhol people and then banned from showing up because of his temper (Joe told me that Ondine was one of the people he was told not to allow into the Factory), went on record praising the genius of Warhol's approach to film—particularly in capturing his infamous and violent rant as "Pope" in **The Chelsea Girls**—but apparently had a love/hate relationship with the movie that bore his name. That's probably because much of it is filled with "extraneous" material, particularly the lengthy sequence involving a band of naked young Latin American men throwing food at each other, smearing it all over their bodies, and then sitting around talking. The actor usually pointed the finger of blame at Paul Morrissey, an increasingly easy target for the first generation of Warhol actors who were displeased that the films began to evolve and the direction, conception, and focus of the films began to change with the transition from Andy to Paul.

"He's taken the art out of Warhol," Ondine has been quoted as saying of Morrissey. "Which is something you can't do."

From Morrissey's point of view, Ondine "became self-conscious after **Chelsea Girls**, and when we would do other experiments with him, he felt an obligation to come up with something wild. He was very intelligent, but he was just never able to be very interesting again."

The transition from the old stable of superstars to the new stable of superstars couldn't have been more perfectly exemplified than by Joe's 23-minute scene in this film. Quiet beauty wrestles with brash melodrama queen and the beauty silences the beast hands down. Tom Waugh, while examining the influences of hardcore and softcore porn on Warhol's film aesthetic in his *Pop Out* essay "Cockteaser," notes "Little Dallesandro's great wrestling scene (in) **The Loves of Ondine** where his steel innerthigh headlock on the eponymous star ensures the only moment of silence in all of Ondine's performances."

"People who wanted to be in front of the camera, like Ondine, they wanted it too much, and then it didn't work," says Morrissey.

The passage from one era to the next was also apparent in the film's famous advertising campaign which featured Joe Dallesandro, the supporting player, prominently situated centerstage in his white undies, easily twice as large as the photos of Ondine and Viva that flanked him.

"Paul sent the paper the photo," Joe says. "And with that, a lot of people came to see the movie." Imagine that ... sex sells. Even the hint of sex sells. That's the awesome, frustrating beauty of the erotic: you don't even have to deliver to get them to plunk down the money, all you've got to do is get their hopes up.

The ads for the movie sold Joe Dallesandro as beefcake. Who was Ondine? Who cares? Because if this guy in his underwear is Ondine, I sure would like to see who he loves. And if he isn't Ondine, I'm sure he must be one of the loves, so either way, I'm there, baby.

Outside of Joe's scene, the balance of the film consists of barely connected reels of the acerbic ex-Pope's encounters with a variety of women. One reel marks the bright and funny debut by Viva (nee Susan Hoffmann) as a hooker who tells him that he'll have to pay her for every item of clothing he wants her to remove. Much to his surprise and delight, when her shirt comes off, she reveals Band-Aids on her nipples. He pays her with pantomime money to remove the adhesive on her left breast, but says he has no interest in the other one. She wittily tries to entice him by suggesting that "it might be another color." (Warhol was positively smitten with the actress because of her Band-Aid ingenuity.)

Then there's the bunch of naked guys raiding a refrigerator and throwing and mashing the food on one another that was filmed as part of **** at the home of Waldo Diaz Balart, exiled Cuban and ex-brother-in-law of Fidel Castro. The group of young men, known as "The Bananas," start off the oral portion of their presentation promisingly enough with a weird tale that begins, "When I was four years old, I was raped by a colored woman in my house—she was very nice," but things quickly disintegrate into boring jabber eventually augmented by a visiting Ondine.

"Dull, rambling Andy Warhol comedy about a homosexual half-trying to go straight," reported *Variety*.

"Scholars" who have reviewed the film in the context of Warhol's oeuvre have had little nice to say about it. Stephen Koch, in his book *Stargazer: The Life, World & Films of Andy Warhol*, concludes, "The film is indefensible." What Koch doesn't take into account, however, is the lingering interest over Joe Dallesandro's debut, an event he not only doesn't comment upon, but completely overlooks

Photo used for advertising **The Loves of Ondine** in the *New York Times*/Courtesy Joe Dallesandro

in his description of the film's contents.

It has recently been salvaged by the Andy Warhol Foundation, but there seems little impetus in making it available for the home market. Hopefully that will change over the next few years as more and more of Warhol's earlier works find outlets at film festivals and the cult of interest in the enormous output of Warhol's movie-camera cranking grows. (An output encompassing, at last reckoning, in excess of 4,000 reels of film from which only 24 titles have officially been "preserved.") The identification and cataloguing of the footage is an enormous task.

For Joe Dallesandro fans, an eventual release will finally satiate an interest in how it all began. Of course, Warhol maintained right up to the end that his films "are better talked about than seen," but I think something remarkable will occur, adding to the mythmaking "genius" of the late Pop Artist. This largely unseen work, documented for years by those few who saw it, and analyzed and dissected by those who tell us that the concept of an Andy Warhol movie is as potent as the movie itself, will more than likely find acceptance and fascination for that very reason. I can't imagine a Warhol film, even the most banal, failing to live up to its concept.

Gary Indiana, writing in *The Village Voice* (May 5, 1987), thinks "It's bizarre that Warhol's films have been out of circulation so long ... Who will ever forget Ondine, with his face buried in Joe D'Allesandro's underpants? ... I haven't seen these films in 20 years, and I remember every frame. I've already forgotten **E.T.**"

Another reason these films demand release is that we now have a context into which they can be placed. It was only in 1996 that a volume of criticism and analysis, *Pop Out: Queer Warhol,* emerged examining Warhol's work from the perspective of his homosexuality. Themes and subtexts in Warhol's films that have been available only to a select handful of film scholars and art historians who have had access to the prints are just waiting to be explored by a larger audience.

Indiana, again: "When Ondine's about to get into Little Joe's BVD's, the bathroom door flies open and in walks Brigid Polk, demanding to know what that cheap little hustler is doing with her husband. Sexual pleasure is imminent in the Warhol movies, a possibility; but pornographic fulfillment is always shown as a deluded ambition. Real people are too complicated."

It was real people doing "unreal" things that Morrissey saw as the future of Warhol's films. The key to engaging an audience and thereby making money (both goals he shamelessly desired) was to give them strong characters to watch. That was even more important than the story in which they were placed.

"Andy and I talk over ideas for a movie," Morrissey told the *New York Times* in 1973, "but what films really come down to is the people in them. Brando, James Dean, all the naturalistic stars in the fifties have influenced me. Elia Kazan, who did five of the best films ever made, all in a row, between 1950 and 1955 ... emphasized the contribution of the actor as a dominating thing. People don't realize we do this, too."

Believe it or not, Joe Dallesandro was intended to be Paul Morrissey's John Wayne, or even his Alan Ladd.

"They knew they wanted to work with me more from the very day that I showed up for that film," says Joe.

And how.

lonesome cowboys (1968)

"The new film **Lonesome Cowboys**—it's the first one to really tell a story. It's about a group of brothers in the West. We shot it out there. They aren't really brothers, they're, well, sleeping together, or whatever, but they say they're brothers so people won't talk."

—*Paul Morrissey to After Dark magazine*

With **JOE DALLESANDRO AS LITTLE JOE**, Viva (Ramona D'Alvarez), Taylor Mead (Nurse), Louis Waldon (Mickey), Eric Emerson (Eric), Julian Burroughs (Brother), Alan Midgette (Alan), Tom Hompertz (Julian), Francis Francine (Sheriff). Directed by Andy Warhol / Paul Morrissey. 109 minutes

Joe Dallesandro was living with his dad in Jersey when he got the call from those people who'd filmed him wearing his drawers a couple of months ago. "They called me back and asked me if I wanted to go to Arizona," remembers Joe. "I was working in this bookbinding factory and I said all they had to do was make sure that I got my salary—you know, whatever I was making—so that I wouldn't lose that. So basically, I was the only one who got paid anything." (Everybody else received a daily stipend beginning at about $10 and including room and board.)

Andy Warhol, Paul Morrissey, and several other members of their entourage flew—and some drove—to Old Tucson in the last week of January, 1968, to film a Western scenario called **Ramona and Julian**, loosely based on *Romeo and Juliet*. Morrissey has said he was the one who came up with the idea, and he may have, but Joe remembers a treatment being put together by young Julian Burroughs, who Warhol says "claimed he was William Burroughs' son," and who appears as an actor in the film.

"It was sunny in Arizona," Andy recalled for *Rolling Stone* in 1971. "It was so wonderful. Even when it rained … everybody looked so beautiful in their cowboy clothes … Joe was shy. He didn't say anything. He didn't say much at all. He is so quiet."

The concept of doing a Western was an appealing diversion to Andy and Paul and originally there were to be several other Warhol regulars in the cast, but apparently Brigid Berlin, who was to play the head of the rival family of cowpokes, and Ondine, who was to play a dope-addicted Padre Lawrence, didn't want to make the trip into the desert—thus leaving Viva, Louis Waldon and Taylor Mead the only recognizable Factory faces. Viva plays Ramona, the one woman in an apparently "all-fag cowboy town" (quoting Andy again). The original idea of a twist on Shakespeare quickly had turned into an improvisation of an entirely different bent. (The project was variously titled **The Unwanted Cowboy**, **In Old Arizona**, **Lonesome Cowboy**, and even **The Glory of the Fuck**.)

Ramona is the madame/ranch owner of a veritable ghost town; her companion is her effeminate male Nurse, played with stoned gusto by comedian Mead. Gone now were most of the other first generation Warhol superstars, at least with regard to getting in front of the camera. The age of Edie Sedgwick and Gerard Malanga was over.

Warhol and Morrissey brought ten 35-minute reels of 16mm film with them to Arizona to shoot their first location epic. Art critic (and later Warhol biographer) David Bourdon was along for the trip on an assignment for *Life*. His day by day account of the five day shoot in his mammoth book *Warhol* (Harry N. Abrams, Inc., New York, 1989) provides an entertaining behind-the-scenes look at the haphazard production, but not much appreciation for the final result.

Lonesome Cowboys begins as Bob Goldstein's title song plays on the soundtrack and a very cute, curly-haired young man opens Viva's blouse, exposing her blazing white New York tits. She reciprocates, exposing his gorgeously tanned San Diego tits. The young man is Tom Hompertz, an art student whom Andy met while giving a lecture the year before at a California art school. He seems a bit tentative about what he's doing here and when he climbs on top of Viva it also seems that his pants were once split and hastily sewn together and that they are likely to split again. There are tight, out-of-focus close-ups of his bare back and sides, but it is difficult to distinguish anything clearly. Then suddenly Viva calls the proceedings to a halt and tells him, "Maybe we should put it off until tomorrow ... no, on second thought, if I don't do it now, I'll never do it." The music swells and off they go again, but he's noticeably delaying the removal of his pants. Finally, she has to tell him to take them off and he does. His handsomely tanned leg and white, dimpled buttock conveniently block our view as she reaches down to tug at his groin. The day is nearly spent. The light for shooting an exterior is just about gone.

Time for the opening credits.

(Or not, depending on when you saw the film. The first reel, as it has been preserved by the Andy Warhol Foundation for the Visual Arts, Inc., has no credits. There's also no song, and during Tom and Viva's lovemaking you can hear all sorts of extraneous little sounds. It's not certain when the opening reel was re-dubbed—my guess is that it was done when they did the 35mm blow-up—but when Vincent Canby reviewed the film in May of 1969, he reported that "the soundtrack clicks and sputters as if the microphone had been dragged through a gravel pit.")

Appearing with a staff and seeming to be a chorus of some sort, a clumsy Taylor Mead addresses us: "Hello people ... people? ... there are no people. Oh well, the silence is one of the best audiences."

Ramona, outfitted in black jodhpurs and carrying a riding crop, and her Nurse (Mr. Mead), are seen walking down the middle of the dusty street in their abandoned town discussing in unmatched voice-over how they've just come from church looking for a little companionship.

"Even an altar boy would have done," Ramona says.

"For either of us," adds Nurse.

They both become panicky when a herd of young bucks on horseback mosey toward them. Ramona wonders if they are "real men" and seems frightened and/or excited by that possibility. Nurse half-gallantly, half-about-to-swoon, says he'll protect her.

When the boys ride up, all Ramona and Nurse can do is make cracks about their looks, about how the leader seems to be wearing mascara and false eyelashes. Ramona wonders where he got them.

"I heard that fucking retort!" hollers Mickey (Louis Waldon), the eldest of the troupe, in a voice that sounds almost John Wayne-ish. He confronts the woman and suggests that "my boys" are also his brothers and he doesn't want any problems.

Nurse pleads with the town Sheriff to protect them from these wandering cowboys who have bulges in their pants and openly use hashish. Mickey counter-charges against these "perverts," these "creeps."

"Ramona's not a creep," Nurse says defensively, "I am." (All of the preceding dialogue is not on the original 16mm soundtrack reel, where Viva and Nurse amble in silence and the sounds of jets flying over and the buzz of cables crisscrossing can be heard.)

Typical of Andy's camerawork, he misses the sudden flood of piss from one of the frightened horses, which prompts Viva's commenting, "That horse has some sort of kidney problem" to a film audience oblivious to what just took place below-frame.

Mickey shouts a warning to this upstart dame: "If you make eyes at my brothers, I'm gonna kick your ... (the actor pauses for a second before he decides on a word) ... cunt!"

Ramona makes it clear that she'd rather have the horses than any of Mickey's boys. "Look at them. Not one of them has hair long enough to warrant a second look."

Among the boys, of course, is Little Joe, outfitted in a black leather jacket, black cowboy hat, and striking red kerchief around his neck. (On the original soundtrack for the first reel, there's lots of behind-the-camera muttering and at one point Morrissey yells, "Don't ride out, Joe!" when all the rest of the brothers head down the street.)

"Eric, take Little Joe to the barbershop," orders Mickey. "And don't let 'em spend too much time on the lower half of his body, more time on the upper half." That's improvisation for you.

And so we move to the first of Little Joe's scenes in **Lonesome Cowboys**. He stands beside a hitching post as Eric Emerson begins a famous verbal assault on the relative newcomer. The loose improvisational style is evident right from the start when Eric suggests to Joe that they just rap and see what happens, "beins' that we have some time to waste."

Well, friends, Joe is not a rapper.

Emerson tramples Joe with questions and comments about his appearance, including the suggestion that he not use greasy kid's stuff in his hair, that they both share the burden of high foreheads, and that he really should get his hair cut and styled, maybe parted in the middle. During the whole time Eric fluffs up Joe's hair and messes about with it, the camera is on Joe, whose face registers a slightly nervous expression of "I'll play along here, but I don't really know what you want me to do." It's a sweet face of confusion, made that much sweeter by his initial response to Eric's asking if Eric should get a haircut, too: "I don't know, I kind of like it the way it is, man. (He reaches out and touches it.) I don't think you need a haircut." He then adds, "sounds great," when Eric seems to have talked him into changing his mind. Eric hasn't, but Joe doesn't really know what else to say.

"Where'd you get that sexy jacket? You look butch in it," continues Emerson. After pulling a knife from Joe's pocket and replacing it, he adds, "In another year or so, you'll be able to get a gun." Joe manages to sneak in, "Can't wait." We are then treated to an impressive routine in which Eric performs ballet pliés using the hitching post and then does splits, insisting that Joe do these exercises daily because it will put "meat on the buns" and give him something to hold up his holster when he gets one.

What's particularly funny about this scene, even beyond its camp appeal today, is how absolutely consistent it is with the rest of the Warhol/Morrissey oeuvre in which no matter what the setting, the period, or the circumstance, people are obsessed with appearances, style, make-up, and all the other glamorously cheeky preoccupations of the society pages.

Looking good, having an image, is an all-importantly absurd propriety, even among cowboys.

And looking good is precisely what Tom Hompertz, as young Julian, does better than anything else. A golden statue of Endymion, he is as clueless and beautiful as Joe would be accused of being in the later Warhol/Morrissey films. Clearly a stranger in a strange land, he stands at the center of the tale and yet can't muster a response to all the weirdness around him.

Knowing that he's lost actually makes watching him all the more entertaining, especially when the other actors try so desperately hard to rouse him into dialogue.

"Please answer me," Taylor Mead begs while chatting him up in an early scene. He's trying to entice the lad to wear all his leather duds and come up to the ranch and visit Ramona. "You seem indifferent," Mead profoundly comments to the silent boy sitting indifferently on his horse and just watching as Mead goes into his weird Lupé Velez Twist song and dance ("You jiggle and you jangle, but you seldom wrangle"), spooking the horses to the point where one snaps his reins while Tom tries to tie it to the hitching post.

Later, after Mickey is roused from the bedwrap he shares with young Julian and gets up to take an on-screen piss ("Ooooh, get up. Look, we're having a christening!" chimes in a clearly amused Eric), actor Louis Waldon painfully tries to get the kid to talk to him while the camera is rolling. It's a gorgeously obvious attempt on the part of one actor to engage in unscripted dialogue with a fellow actor who doesn't have any lines and Waldon improvises himself into generic nonsense, finally evoking a response from the kid: "What do you mean?"

Waldon actually says, "Help me, somebody help me" at one point, then when he fails in a second attempt, he pauses long enough to add aloud, "I've become silent in my own thinking."

Getting absolutely nowhere, he manages to sum up his fellow non-actor's ultimate role in this movie by telling him, "You're so beautiful." He then adds, "How do you feel?" in a final attempt to force a response by asking a question.

"I feel good."

When Eric interrupts the scene by offering Waldon a beer, the actor vocalizes his distress, telling Emerson to "Get over here, you sweetheart. Give me some conversation."

"Tom Hompertz is an art student. He's a beautiful boy but he never speaks," said Paul Morrissey to *After Dark* magazine. "Never ever. He just doesn't speak. Which makes him hard to work with. He's great with Viva, because she talks enough for both, but with anybody else ... If you ask him a direct question, he'll answer, but otherwise he isn't disposed to speak."

Hompertz's scenes with Viva, the first of which forms the opening of the film, the latter of which makes for a lengthy seduction sequence towards the end of the film, are classic examples of the unwilling trying to resist the willing simply by not paying attention.

Andy and Paul were determined to film a sequence in which Viva seduces and gets it on with young Tom, fulfilling the voyeuristic and prurient instincts to watch pretty boys with beautiful bodies get naked and have sex for the camera. Andy's interest in seeing such was the rumored staple of any sexual life he may have had. He always thought the actual sex act was too silly and too messy and preferred the joys of just wanting to have it to having it. Moreover, watching others have it saved all the inherent embarrassment and was an awful lot of fun, too.

The problem was that Mr. Hompertz wasn't exactly prepared for this kind of moviemaking, and therein lies some of the joy of watching the film today. Warhol is capturing actors who aren't trained actors; some try to act, some don't. Some are natural hams hogging the screen and happy to parade and cavort. Some just want to get it over with and seem to be anxiously waiting for the buzz of the camera to cease. What makes an Andy Warhol film even more enjoyable than its Hollywood low-budget brethren is that there are always at least two levels to watching the people in front of his camera: there's the character the "actor" is playing, and there's also the "documentary" of an actor who's not an actor trying to get away with something, something that you can very often read on his or her face.

Warhol told *Jaguar*, a men's magazine, that "Tom was diametrically opposed to the kind of person Viva was. We figured that instead of getting somebody who would fight with her verbally in the film, we'd use him because he was turned off by her."

Knowing that Tom was uncomfortable makes every effort on Viva's part seem that much funnier. Her growing frustrations, which were actually voiced to Morrissey and Warhol off-camera and in front of Hompertz (sometimes while beneath him), only deflated the possibilities further.

Viva was a proven master of witty improvisation and she had a particular specialty in mixing arcane subject matter with the more practical task at hand. In this film, while lying outdoors with Tom, whom we are supposed to believe she has stolen from Mickey, she begins a sermon encompassing martyrdom, her early Catholic instruction, and a smattering of Eastern mysticism while he sits shirtless and utterly oblivious next to her. (The scene foreshadows Joe's role as a silent and indifferent naked stud in **Flesh,** and a sequence in which an elderly artist pontificates about aestheticism and classical "body worship" in sculpture.)

She then begins to sing, and in a ludicrous attempt to involve her bored partner, she asks him if he knows the words to the Catholic benediction song she's singing. She continues chanting and explaining various church rites and the meaning of "Amen" while reaching over and undoing his pants. She finally cajoles him out of them, but she'd really like him to shuck his boxer shorts, too. He doesn't seem willing to budge.

"Look at that rabbit, does he have pants on?" she asks in an inspired bit of improvisation while pointing at a presumably real bunny out of frame. "No. Do the birds wear pants? No. (She's on a roll; theatrically:) Do the lilies of the field who toil and spin worry about their clothing or what they will eat for dinner? No. Yet I take care of them. That's what it's all about. That's what it's all about. Don't listen to what anyone else tells you. I know what it's all about, because I have been visited by angels. And I know."

After a sudden jump cut, the still oblivious and innocently defiant Hompertz is now standing beside her in his boxers and she has clearly lost her patience. With a terse and demanding clap of her hands, she orders, "Now let's get down to business! Take off your pants!" He finally does. She tells him to lie down. He says, no, you lie down. She says, no, you lie down!, and slaps his thigh. She's irritated; he's bewildered and naked and nervous. Warhol zooms in on Tom's beautiful white buns as he lies on top of her.

Arguably, the kid's best scene in the whole film comes during a silent passage in which he's shown shirtless, washing up at an outdoor washtub, soaping his hands, washing under his arms, around his neck and chest, and then toweling off his face, armpits, and chest while Warhol's lens observes in tranquil awe. The camera lovingly photographs his nicely cut physique, the shadowed curvature of his lats, the tight, healthy elasticity of a young body in perfect shape and physical harmony.

This simple act of washing up and toweling off references the filmed studies of routine behaviors made famous in early Warhol outings, but it also takes its place in a thematic lineage of showering male displays in both Warhol's and Morrissey's work. Andy Warhol was, if nothing else, a consummate voyeur. In **My Hustler** (1965), the first feature worked on by Morrissey, we watch statuesque Paul America shower and then towel off for an eternity while talking to a hustler-friend who repeatedly applies deodorant in the claustrophobic bathroom they share. **Bike Boy** (1967) opens with a lengthy sequence in which brunette Joe Spencer, a nomadic visitor to the Factory who made only this one film, is seen uneasily staring into the camera as he soaps himself up and the camera cuts to close-ups of various body parts (lots of pubes, but no studies of his genitalia). **Flesh** (1968), too, was originally planned to include a shower scene. And **Trash** (1970) does include one in which a talkative young socialite tells dirty stories while sitting on the closed toilet and watching Joe wash himself and shave.

Tom Hompertz's wash-up in **Lonesome Cowboys** is clearly about the intrinsic beauty of the male body. The film's preternaturally casual observance of such a mundane activity finds us caught up in the contemplation of the allure and classical symmetries of the male form. Once again, Warhol/Morrissey's camera seems to be doing one thing—and doing it unspectacularly—when it's actually inspiring us on a whole other level.

The wash-up is that much sexier because the subject appears to be completely unaware of the sexual vocabulary he communicates with each seemingly routine motion. He's doing something that he does every day without the least bit of sensuous intent, but the fact that we're watching him do it, and that he's "letting" us watch him, and that he hasn't any idea what it is we're thinking, elicits a palpable erotic charge. It's his flesh that's talking to us, and his flesh is talking in a way he would only be able to recognize if he were to see a man or woman he thought beautiful doing the same extraordinarily ordinary thing. Since it's his own all-too-familiar body he's attending to, and he's shown no sign of narcissism, he's altogether oblivious of his powers over us. And that's just the kind of potent sexual subterfuge that would become Joe Dallesandro's trademark in the Morrissey trilogy yet to come.

In round two of the Eric and Joe dialogues, Eric wakes Joe from a nap and fires questions about this new guy—supposed to be Julian—but whom he refers to as "Mick," then "Tom." Eric is pretending to be jealous because he was supposed to share a sleeping bag with his brother Mickey last night.

Shirtless and clearly unprepared for this improvised assault, Joe answers with a little ornery whine that he doesn't care what Mickey does. Eric brushes an invisible fleck from Joe's nipple, and follows with the observation that, "You're getting flakes on your chest. Instead of hair, you have dandruff." He then laughs.

Joe doesn't find it funny and mutters a "Shut up."

"Shut up? No. We're supposed to talk a bit."

Emerson has just followed Andy Warhol's dictum that his movies like to call attention to themselves as "being" movies. The mechanics of movie-making call for dialogue in this scene. Joe doesn't want to talk. Eric says they're "supposed to."

He continues to besiege Joe with questions about time he's spent back East, asking him what he's learned, making fun of his kerchief, and answering Joe's defensive inquiry about money by saying he doesn't need money because, "I have a cock in my pants."

"Well, what does that do for you?" Joe asks back.

"Money can't buy you a little rub of a tit. (Eric reaches out and lightly pinches one of Joe's nipples.) It can, but the same feeling isn't there ... Money is for people that don't have any character, who can't get any fucks without it. I get all the feeling I want being broke." He feels his own chest.

During this little repartee, in which Eric pulls back Joe's blanket to reveal his jockey shorts (something Eric can "go for" from a fashion aesthetic), Joe finally discovers that the best way to counter the attack is to simply ask the motor-mouth to explain himself, and thus talk more.

"What feeling? Tell me about the feeling you have," Joe asks.

It's all Eric needs. He explains his concept of self-love, of loving yourself so much that you can't love anybody else, and that "It's the greatest feeling in the world to be lonesome."

In what amounts to a unique documentary profile of a natural actor in the making, it's rather easy to chart Joe's strategies for survival in this new medium, particularly when up against a guy as liberated on camera as Emerson. It's revealing to see the confidence he builds as a result of each successive scene. You can actually *see* the guy getting better right before your very eyes.

Joe says, "It was hard for me to do **Lonesome Cowboys**, because it was an Andy movie and Paul was trying to help Andy put a storyline to it and it ended up a free-for-all. Whoever could talk the loudest and the fastest was the star of the movie. I couldn't compete with that."

Actually, Joe acquits himself rather nicely. I think it was the street survivor in him. There was plenty of competition and he may have felt overwhelmed at first, but all he had to do was learn how to adapt, learn how to make himself fit into the groove, and before you know it he was gettin' cocky.

It starts with a very silly wrestling match brought on by—guess who?—troublemaker Eric Emerson, who's a little drunk and acting a little pissed after confronting his elder brother Mickey about not being able to bed down with him. A silly exchange of words and jealousies turns into a spitting back and forth of beer.

Even after he admits to Mickey that last night "I did what you told me, I slept with my other brother," he's still giggling and looking for a fight.

Little Joe gets thrown into the fray when Eric insists he's going to give Joe a haircut. Joe flips Eric cartwheel fashion up and over and onto his head. Eric manages to do the exact same thing to Joe while Mickey, sensing a fight, warns the boys to watch out for the cactus.

"You're a brother, right?" Eric taunts Joe.

"Yeah."

"So why don't you look like the rest of us?"

"I don't have to look like you," is Little Joe's improvised and perfectly adolescent response to the challenge. Before you know it, the brothers are shirtless (Joe keeps on his red kerchief), Mickey has joined in, and all three of these overgrown boys strain for pinning holds on the desert floor.

It's a funny scene, perfectly juvenile and ever-so-male; they fight each other for the pure pleasure of fighting each other, and the cries of "Brand him, brand him" from the sidelines nicely add to the joke.

This is where Joe has his epiphany, his moment of coming into his own in an Andy Warhol movie. It's as brilliant a moment as could be imagined and it's so natural and unexpected and well-timed and well-delivered that you know a future star has been born.

After the lengthy, silly tussle on the ground, during which Eric cries out in strain and pain as Joe and Mickey stretch his arms back in a submission hold, Joe heaves an exhausted sigh, slaps Eric firmly on the chest and tells him definitively:

"I'm still not gettin' no haircut."

Joe's beautifully instinctive return to an improvised bit of inconsequential storyline—Eric's desire to see him get shorn (Emerson was a hairdresser for awhile in real life)—transcends the diversionary antics of the last couple of minutes in front of Andy's rolling camera. It not only reminds us that's what Joe was thinking about during the fight, but that he is as capable of thinking on his feet and remembering he's a character in a movie as the most lucid, witty, and talkative of Andy's superstars.

Of course, that may not occur to him to be much of a revelation, but that's unmistakably why he lasted in Warhol/Morrissey films where other beauties fell by the wayside. He was a natural actor, capable of taking a hell of a lot, but also capable of giving it back when necessary.

In Joe's very next scene, in which a very likely stoned Taylor Mead encounters the cowboys (humorously commenting that "even your horses are horny") and tries to dissuade them from bothering Ramona, Mead ends up on Joe's mount and says, "If that horse bites my precious ass..."

To which Joe, newly confident on film, contributes:

Courtesy Joe Dallesandro

"What ass? That's not an ass. That's a thing. A thing that's not worth anything to anybody."

"It once was."

"Was it? How long ago? Fifty-six years ago?" (The randomness of the insult makes it that much funnier.)

"No," says Mead laconically. "Twelve years ago."

With Joe now as vocally a part of the gang as he earlier was physically, he's in attendance for one of the film's most notorious scenes.

Viva, as Ramona, sits uneasily on her horse and orders the boys off her ranch. A particularly feisty Eric Emerson succeeds in spooking her horse, doesn't desist even when she smacks his hand repeatedly with her crop, and at last gets her to come down off the animal. With a scary macho cry of "get her," the boys descend upon her like hyenas, knocking her to the ground and ripping off her shirt.

"You're hurting me ... please," she pleads, obviously talking to people both in the scene and outside of the scene.

Unfortunately, the band of surly males descend upon her again, holding her down and stripping off her panties in an orgiastic revel uncomfortable to watch because the actors seem to have forgotten they're actors.

Viva is even heard screaming out on-screen, "ooooh, make them stop! Oh, Andy!" as they continue to paw at her and mock hump her. (Louis Waldon, meanwhile, is dry-humping Nurse, much to Mead's delight.)

When the nasty and degrading display ceases and Ramona calls all of them "fags," Eric walks up to her and begins to lower his pants. She knees him, then rights herself, still sitting on the dusty ground, frazzled and mussed.

"Disgusting pigs!" she yells. "Look at all those children shocked out of their minds." Viva is actually referring to a gathering of tourist onlookers, some of whom had kids with them, who were standing across the street as witnesses during the filming of her completely improvised "rape."

57

Courtesy Joe Dallesandro

Bedraggled, but ever sharp, she manages to compose herself for one last inspired line: "One more impertinence out of you and the fuck is off!"

"I don't even think they let me play in that scene," whines Joe like a little kid when discussing it today. "They kept pushing me aside because I was the younger boy. I think I had too much acne for them to let me play. But, hey, I don't go in for that rough stuff and if I thought for a moment that she was serious ... I was the tough guy, remember. I may have been the smallest one out there, but I was the toughest one there. I could turn into a psychopath and when my eyes crossed you knew it was time to call it quits. So they all knew that as young as Joe may be, he was the meanest, baddest guy there. Yeah, we can push him around because that was his little role to do, but if I thought she was getting hurt in any way, it would have stopped. Same with Paul. He'd lose it if he thought ..., but Paul in certain ways didn't show Viva any respect. He showed respect for her education, but he didn't show her any respect for her femininity. That's because she walked around like a tough bull dyke, and she wasn't."

Later, when brother Alan Midgette talks to Little Joe in the movie about the rape, he is appalled at what occurred, at how they all turned into animals.

"Aww, we aren't animals," Joe answers him. "It was fun. We're out for fun, aren't we?"

Midgette extemporizes a humorous speech directly to the camera after Joe leaves in which he asks for "a little prayer and discipline" because, "Ladies and gentlemen, kids are getting their own horses too soon and riding out on the range alone," and it's only with the aid of a big brother figure that we can all end up "happier children." This is Midgette's sole "big" scene in the film, but it's a fun little glimpse at the actor whom Warhol and Morrissey chose to impersonate Andy in a successful series of paid college campus appearances where he fooled and frustrated students by standing before them in a talcum-powdered wig and answering their inquisitive questions employing Andy's trademark "um's" and "ah's" and "I don't know's." The ruse was eventually uncovered.

Part of the joy of any improvised film, no matter how adept the cast, is watching the less-adept or completely inept fail. Francis (**Flaming Creatures**) Francine, a carnival performer in his boyhood, plays the effeminate sheriff, according to Little Joe in the movie, "a spineless mutha'," who happens also to be a drag performer. Francine is so excruciatingly bad at improvising dialogue, even simple responses to direct questions, that it's funny just watching him try.

If there's a central plot to **Lonesome Cowboys**, and I think one can be distinguished, it's about the desire of a traveling troupe of cowboys to spend some time in Old Tucson without letting their family fall to pieces. The primary threats are the ambivalent bitchiness and desire of the sole woman in town towards the boys, and the jealousies brought about by Mickey's love for young Julian given the fact that Ramona apparently wants to fuck him, too. So are the brothers incestuous queers?

Well, by late in the film, Joe has surprisingly struck a "romantic" chord with Nurse; we first see them together while Joe is playfully choking the screaming nellie in the upper bedroom window of the ranch house, then later hanging on the old "girl" and participating in bawdy pantomimed gyrations with both Nursie and his own brother Eric. During the latter coupling, Mickey explains that "Little Joe was once an altar boy and we all know what happens to altar boys when they grow up!"

"My brothers love each other!" Mickey declares as Joe and Eric hump and twirl each other. "And remember, ladies," he adds by way of explanation of the on-screen sexual frolic, "what you've seen here tonight, this is a cowboy's fantasy out on the range."

Joe's increasing ease with being on screen, and the accompanying confidence in him that Morrissey and Warhol apparently felt, is evidenced when they contrive a dialogue between the two young "silent" beauties: Joe and Tom.

"Yeah, I hear you get rashes from horses," says Joe, referring to something behind-the-scenes that we're not privy to, though author David Bourdon says a reel of film was being saved for a Hompertz monologue. When he told Andy and Paul he didn't have anything to say, they suggested he talk about how he was allergic to the horses and had developed a nasty rash. Turns out he couldn't even talk about that, at least not by himself.

"Yeah, I got one today," Tom says with a smile.

"Got one today?" Joe repeats. Then finding himself in the rare position of having to be the talker, adds: "Yeah, those beasts, they're ugly little things aren't they? I hate them muthas." The seemingly inexplicable comment, coming as it does from a cowboy, is hilarious precisely for that reason.

Joe's got this idea about going to California. "If you'd like to go, man, I'd dig going with you. If you don't want to go, I'm not going to force you into it. I know you dig Mickey and all that. I mean, that's what I hear ... Do you?"

"Mickey?"

"Yeah."

"He's a good friend," is all an uninspired Tom can manage.

To which Joe is left with: "Yeah, he's kind of good that way." Little Joe wants to split from his tiresome brothers and go to California where there are "lots of women ... lots of beautiful men. Oh, it's great. You can find anything you want there. I think you'd dig it."

Joe's speech about California and his emergent role as more than just a pretty face in the Warhol films received unexpected praise from Warhol critic Peter Gidal: "A break from campiness is seen in much of Joe D'Allesandro's 'acting' because as a person, in Warhol's films, he means what he says, with little awareness of the intellectually discernible humorous possibilities. 'I wish I could go to the beach, away from the bunch ... lots of women and beautiful men ...' Coming from Viva this would be camp innuendo, on account of the complete control she exercises over what she says; in that sense, camp has to do with (self-) consciousness. When D'Allesandro says it, the disarmingly truthful way in which it is said (style) negates the camp interpretation. It isn't just funny. He wants to go away; he wants to be with beautiful women. And he wants to be with beautiful men."

Ostensibly, Andy "directed" the film, and he was certainly behind the camera, but Paul Morrissey was calling almost all of the shots. The attempted formality of giving the film a story shows his considerable influence.

"Before **Lonesome Cowboys**, Andy just wanted people to do whatever they wanted," says Joe. "By the time I came in, Paul was trying to convince Andy that it was important to have a story. Andy was still hung up on this idea where the films were kind of like television in the sense that you'd flip a channel and never watch more than two minutes of anything anyway, so a coherent story wasn't important. You'd just flip around. And that was Andy's movies."

Viva reportedly grew increasingly irritated at Morrissey during the shoot because of all the attention he was giving the boys and all of the much-too-specific (for her tastes) direction he was giving the actors. She could feel boundaries being set up around the creative freedom she enjoyed before Warhol's benign camera. The Superstar concept allowed the actors to create the moments, to infuse the static camera with life, to decide in which directions the story would go. Morrissey brought structure and a semblance of form, threatening to change the Warhol films from an actor's medium to a director's vision. At least that was a potential result.

The random deconstruction of period and place (one character mentions eventually having to face WWI, while several speak in 60's colloquialisms, share new twist-top beers, make mention of all the ozone in the air, and jive to "Magical Mystery Tour") leaves room for the actors failing to remember their character's names later in the film. "Julian" becomes Tom and "Mickey" becomes Louis. Even in an early scene in which Taylor Mead asks Hompertz if he's Julian—the part he's *supposed* to be playing—the clueless actor shakes his head no.

Classic film director George Cukor, a major supporter and fan of Warhol and Morrissey's work, remarked that "**Lonesome Cowboys** finishes the Western. I love the swank of it all—not bothering about details, the dégagé act of taking a Western street, not redressing it, letting tourists walk about in the background." This does indeed happen in one scene while the boys ride aimlessly up and down the street shouting for Ramona. Author-critic David Bourdon notes that Warhol also "succeeded in making the first western without a saloon brawl or a gun duel."

Some of the film was shot at the Rancho Linda Guest Ranch at Oracle, but the Old Tucson set rented by Warhol had been used by Hollywood for westerns since the late 1930s. It was often visited by tourists who came to watch the shooting of television shows, such as the episode of *Death Valley Days* starring Robert Taylor that was being shot simultaneous with the Warhol production.

The local press had a field day attempting to interview the freaky band of Eastern invaders. The day-to-day antics, however, left the locals who gathered to watch stupefied by the queer ways of them there folks from the Big Rotten Apple. Taylor Mead is said to have created a snit in a local restaurant which resulted in the group being followed by cars when they left the establishment. (Driven, it turned out, by some curious high school kids; some equally curious college students from one of the universities were also reported to have visited the set and filmed Warhol and gang for a documentary. Anybody know where this footage is?)

Apparent drug use, "pansy" types, hollered cries of "fuck" and "cunt," the improvised rape, and all of the other sexual shenanigans resulted in local law enforcement officials checking out the site, a buzz-by from a surveillance helicopter, and a contingent of men surveying the shoot using binoculars. Eventually, an official complaint was filed against the troupe and the Federal Bureau of Investigation was called in, but Andy had shot all he was going to shoot and had already high-tailed it back to New York. There he faced the task of trying to figure out how to whittle his film down to two hours length.

The F.B.I. snooping was no publicity hoax, as Margia Kramer relates in photocopied detail in her book *Andy Warhol et al: The FBI File on Andy Warhol* (1988), for which she obtained 38 of the original 71 pages of documentation under the Freedom of Information Act. Warhol was being very seriously investigated for the possible transportation of obscene materials over state lines. Agency monies were spent to identify the actors in the film and the flight they took back to New York and to interview local witnesses following a "complaint received that on 1/27/68 they made an obscene film."

When the movie opened as part of the 1968 San Francisco Film Festival in November, where it won Best Film, agents were in attendance at the midnight showing and later filed a 3-page account of its contents, which reads like

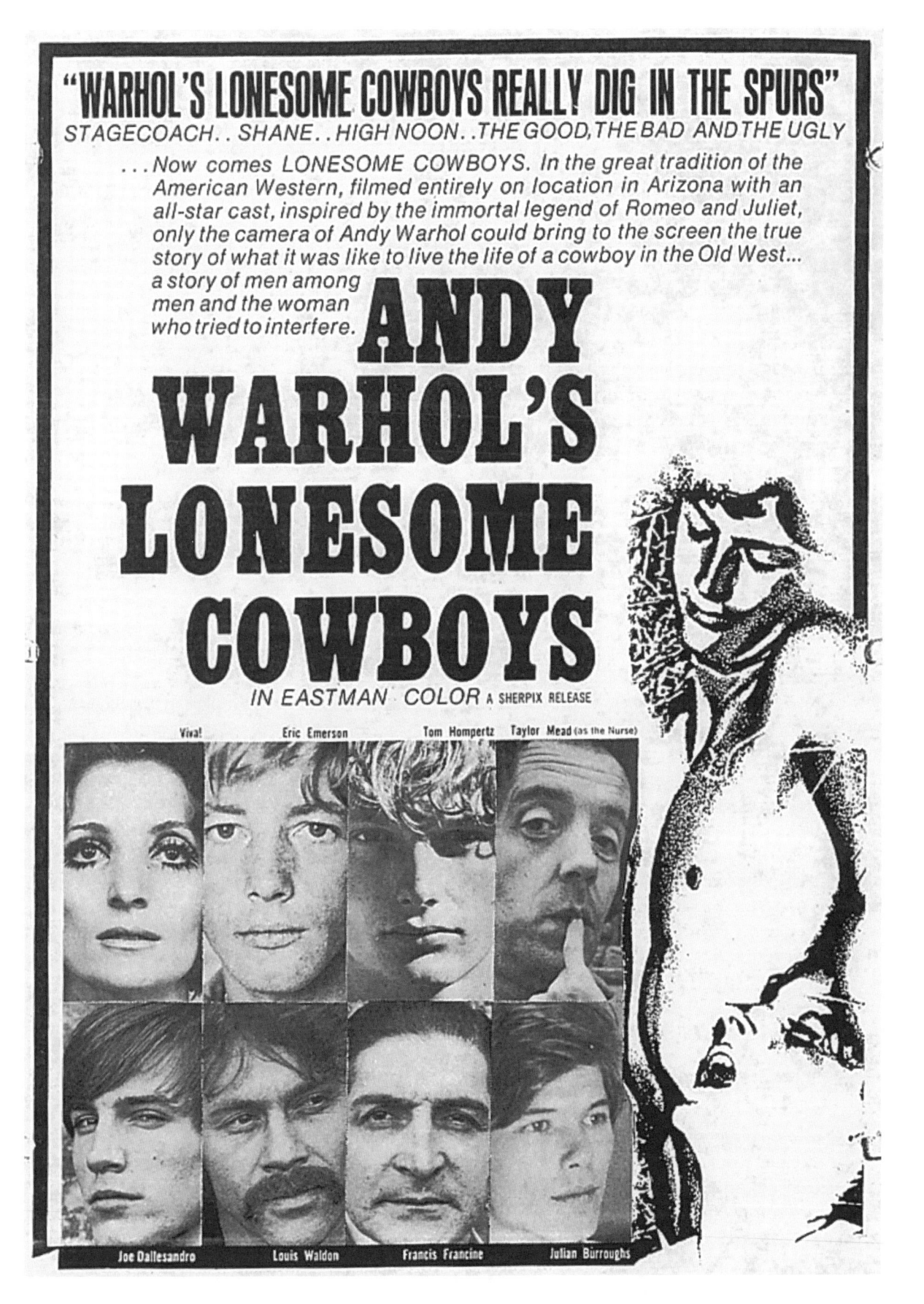

Courtesy Joe Dallesandro

an early review: "All the males in the cast displayed homosexual tendencies and conducted themselves toward one another in an effeminate manner. Many of the cast portrayed their parts as if in a stupor from marijuana, drugs, or alcohol. One of the cowboys practiced his ballet and a conversation ensued regarding the misuse of mascara by one of the other cowboys. There are other parts in the film in which men were revealed in total nudity. The sheriff in one scene was shown dressing in women's clothing and later being held on the lap of another cowboy. Another scene depicted a cowboy fondling the nipples of another cowboy. There were suggestive dances done by the male actors with each other. These dances were conducted while they were clothed and suggested love-making between two males. There was no plot to the film and no development of character throughout. Obscene words, phrases, and gestures were used throughout the film. It was rather a remotely-connected series of scenes which depicted situations of sexual relationships of homosexual and heterosexual nature."

Much has been made as to whether the "rape" was choreographed or spontaneous—a key determination for the Feds' case. A couple of months after the film was shot, Viva told the *Free Press* in Los Angeles that "they tore off all of my clothes and raped me. It's in the movie. I think it was planned." At which Andy interjects, "You know it wasn't planned," and Paul adds, "Stop saying it was planned."

The F.B.I. noted: "The female actress, Viva, said, 'Now look—you have embarrassed those children.' There were no children in the movie." They also, however, saw that the footage clearly caught vulgar horseplay and not forced sexual intercourse—the "rape" was not a rape, after all—and the rest of the flick was just a matter of similar bad taste, so they "declined prosecution because the movie was not obscene within the definition of that word as defined by the Supreme Court of the United States."

The *San Francisco Chronicle* opined: "Andy Warhol's **Lonesome Cowboys** may be a bit too much for many people, but that's their problem. (It's) a magnificent and very funny satire of the American Western that is liberally seasoned with our favorite 4, 8, 10 and 12-letter words and a cornucopia of nudity and sexual carryings-on that is—in combination—perhaps unprecedented!"

It was, of course, its particular kind of sexual carryings-on that made it so outrageously popular and controversial, though Vincent Canby writing in the *New York Times* felt it wasn't "so much homosexual as adolescent."

In August of 1969, while the film played its third week in Atlanta, it was seized by authorities who stated, according to a report in *Variety*, that it was "obscene, vulgar, and profane—just the type of thing that would ... make the ordinary person sick." The manager was arrested and, incredibly,

"when the lights went up, a man with a camera began snapping pictures of the audience. The theatre cleared in a hurry." Photos were taken of the seventy or so fleeing audience members so that they could be compared with photos of known homosexuals in the area and provide a record "of what kind of people go to these movies."

Looking at it today, it's almost too hard to imagine that this film could have had socio-political ramifications, because it's so free-spirited and silly and playfully queer. But maybe that's *why* it was seen by some as a threat. Its take on homos was too indifferent, and its target was an American institution—the frontier mythology of the American West. For gay audiences on the cusp of Stonewall, it must have been a real treat.

On the political front, Paul Overy, in his "Arts in Society" column in *New Society*, interpreted "Warhol's **Lonesome Cowboys** [as] art because it is honestly concerned with the instability of casual sexual encounters, specifically homosexual encounters—not because homosexual relations are by their nature casual or unstable, but because the pressures of a hypocritical society make them so. It points to the enormous current of suppressed homosexuality in those American myths of Hemingway-like hairy-chestedness and the archetypal Hollywood western hero, and it uses the unsatisfactory nature of most homosexual relationships in our society as symbolic of a deeper malaise."

The film was eventually cleared to be shown in Atlanta after six cuts were made, but it was only the first of several instances in which Warhol would battle censorship, as well as find himself victimized by the F.B.I. His **Blue Movie** (aka **Fuck**; 1968), which featured Viva and Louis Waldon getting it on, was also targeted for obscenity cases and seized by police in New York during the first week of August, 1969. As for **Cowboys**, the final mention of it in the released documents of his file indicate that the 3-page "review" of the film was sent to the Carter White House in 1977; perhaps because the President was about to have his portrait done by Andy for the cover of the *New York Times Magazine* and Jimmy was being briefed in advance about what the Feds had on the famed pop artist.

Lonesome Cowboys cost roughly $3,000 to make and didn't officially open in New York until May 5, 1969, despite a classic quote from Paul Morrissey at the time of the shoot. Asked by an Arizona journalist when the film would be released, Morrissey is reported to have said, "As soon as it comes back from the drugstore."

It took a little longer. Warhol had the reels, splicer, and projector sent to his home in August of 1968 and edited it while he was recovering from his gunshot wounds.

Morrissey then shopped the film to several exhibitors the following year, but none of the majors seemed interested. With the Garrick Theatre still available for rent, he booked it there and "executive producer" (that's how he's billed) Morrissey told one contemporary source that **Cowboys** grossed $35-40,000 the first week, with only $9,000 spent on advertising. A simultaneous booking at the 55th St. Playhouse ended up breaking the single-day housemark with a $3,837 take in the 250-seater at $3.00 a pop. The Garrick did $2,780 in business the very same day. The film also played the art houses for twenty weeks in Los Angeles and two-and-a-half months in San Francisco, now distributed by an outfit called Sherpix.

In an entertainingly headlined *Variety* piece on the film's success, "Homo On Range Of Comedy," the industry trade wondered whether Warhol's films could hold their own against first run "popular pornography." Would the competition drive him back underground?

Warhol didn't think so, especially since his films were never intended to be erotic. Establishing a line of thought that would run throughout his subsequent career as director, Paul Morrissey told the paper that "sex is the stuff of comedy," and that the secret to the films was the fact that they were improvised and "we shape our story to fit the people" in front of the camera.

"When they leave the theatre," Morrissey continued, "people don't say 'that was a great movie'; they say 'those were great people.'"

Not everybody agreed, however.

Time (May 23, 1969): "Interested moviegoers can watch Andy Warhol's merry band of junkies, faggots, transvestites and nymphomaniacs disporting themselves in...a series of dreary, druggy improvisational harangues by such luminaries as Tom Hompertz, Joe Dallesandro and Viva!, the superest Warhol superstar of them all. Now that Boris Karloff and Bela Lugosi have passed on, Viva! stands unrivaled as the screen's foremost purveyor of horror. By the simple expedient of removing her clothing, she can produce a sense of primordial terror several nightmares removed from any mad doctor's laboratory."

Playboy (November, 1969): "Populated by Warhol's 'superstar' Viva and such doe-eyed aides-de-camp as Tom Hompertz and Joe D'Allesandro, **Cowboys** is a mock western in which a gaggle of guys from the East Village try to make themselves at home on the range. They do so by acting as if they were still inside Warhol's foil-lined Factory, improvising dialogue ... Because Warhol's people are so downright unappetizing, and the homosexual motif so clearly in evidence even in the heterosexual encounters, the effect is far less erotic than pathetic."

"Joe looked fabulous in cowboy clothes in the movie," Andy Warhol told *Rolling Stone* for the cover story they were doing on Dallesandro. "He should be a cowboy. Cowboys look like hustlers. That's nice. Hustlers and cowboys are quiet. They don't know many words. When we made **Flesh** he was a hustler in that. And he was a cowboy in **Lonesome Cowboys**. He had his own horse. Joe isn't really a movie actor. I don't use actors. I use real people. People who can tell stories. Joe is able to tell a story and make it seem real."

Looking back on the **Lonesome Cowboys** experience today, Joe remembers an incident that perfectly illustrates the silliness of putting a kid from Queens in a western in Arizona: "The first day they put me on a horse, they put me on this unbroke stallion. So I got up on it, being the tough guy I am, and the fucking horse started running. I couldn't get the motherfucker to stop. The guy who breaks the horses came racing after me. My horse won't stop and I'm holding on for dear life. The only thing I know how to do is hold on. So the guy caught up to me and got the damn horse to stop, and then he starts screaming at me the whole way back: 'Why did you do that to the horse?' And I'm saying, 'what do you mean? The horse did it to me! Are you nuts?' He was just this Arizona wrangler more concerned about his animals than he was about the actors. You know? As far as he was concerned, 'Fuck you, I don't care if you fell off and the horse dragged you a mile, fuck you, you're hurting my horse!' And I'm thinking, hey, the horse took me! I didn't want to go anywhere. I wanted to stay exactly where I was. Look at me, I told him, I'm dripping sweat. Do I look like I was having a good time taking your horse for a fucking bolt?"

There's irony in a comment David Bourdon attributes to Joe in his book *Warhol*. While Tom Hompertz found himself utterly unable to do a monologue for Andy and Paul's camera, "From the sidelines, Dallesandro dryly observed, 'He's just a beauty, a pretty boy.'"

Joe was, of course, absolutely right. The irony is that Tom Hompertz was, for the moment, essentially prefiguring Dallesandro's roles to come. Little Joe would get his chance, however; hell, not only get his chance, but become a Superstar in the process and bring more to the part than Tom Hompertz ever could.

san diego surf (1968)

"From a cowboy movie with cowboys with New York accents to a surfing movie with New Yorkers who know nothing about surfing."

—*Joe Dallesandro*

(Also known as The Surfing Movie; Surfing) **With JOE DALLESANDRO AS JOE, Viva (Susan Hoffmann), Taylor Mead (Mr. Mead), Louis Waldon (Louis), Ingrid Superstar (Ingrid), Eric Emerson (Eric), Tom Hompertz (Tom). Directed by Andy Warhol / Paul Morrissey. 90 minutes**

Joe had been invited to play yet another supporting role in Andy's next location shoot, this time in La Jolla, California, where the artist took his cast of players in May of 1968, while doing a college lecture circuit. Joe tells me that they weren't sure what they were going to film when they got there, but it was mentioned that since they hadn't really played out the *Romeo and Juliet* thing in **Lonesome Cowboys**, they might have another crack at that. They had assembled pretty much the same cast, including surfer boy Tom Hompertz, whose sole spontaneous dialogue in **Lonesome Cowboys** comes at the film's end when Eric Emerson talks with him about surfing. That's something Hompertz knows about.

"Tom Hompertz was the dream man," remembers Joe. "Andy had met him on one of the tours or something. He was this little beach boy—really beautiful. I don't even know if he was bright, because I never spent much time with him. But he was an artist in his own way. He made these surfboards. And I think even Andy made one, as an art thing."

Joe recalls that there was also some discussion about shooting **Blue Movie** with Viva and Tom, but "they couldn't get Tom Hompertz to do what they could ask Louis and Viva to do. Besides, Tom Hompertz would never have been interested in doing that with Viva."

Blue Movie, aka **Fuck**, was made later that year, in October, and chronicled an afternoon of bedroom conversation and explicit lovemaking between Louis Waldon and Viva. It was to be her last film for Andy.

Rumor has it that it was decided to do an AIP-beach party movie spoof and Andy rented a mansion for the main house. Warhol's reputation had preceded him on the West Coast, however, and there was persistent hassling by the local police. Victor Bockris, in his book *The Death and*

Hanging out in San Diego/Courtesy Joe Dallesandro

Life of Andy Warhol, even details a search of Warhol and company's car on the side of the road. Louis Waldon is reported as saying, "I thought it was very undignified to see Andy spread-eagled."

Bockris also reports that Viva had grown increasingly irritated with Morrissey and told Waldon, "If you're a real man, you'll beat the shit out of (Paul) and save this film from his cheap commercial tricks."

The cast was housed in La Jolla for almost a full three weeks, but the longer they stayed, the less focus the footage seemed to develop.

"It was three weeks of hanging around doing nothing really," Morrissey told me. "It was hot and we were hoping there'd be some waves and the waves never came up. Then we'd go off and shoot people trying to surf. It was all a waste of time. In fact, it's really a film about the fact that nothing happens ... surfing is not very exciting, and people who think surfers are wild and far-out are disappointed. So it was one of those empty dramatic stories that I've done once or twice and turned around to regret. It's very hard to make something hold your interest if of its own nature it wants to be undramatic."

The film was aborted at some point in its scheduled shoot, at least as far as its location footage was concerned. Things weren't going exactly as planned and nobody seemed to know how to use that failure to advantage.

In Warhol's transcribed book, *Popism: The Warhol Sixties*, Andy indicates that the location simply failed to cause the usual filmable friction between cast members. He tried to provoke a few fights, he says, so he could capture them on film, but nobody seemed up to it. "I guess that's why the whole thing turned out to be more of a memento of a bunch of friends taking a vacation together than a movie."

Why Warhol would find that more objectionable than **Taylor Mead's Ass**—one of his minimalist film experiments—is a bit of a mystery and may provide even further proof of Morrissey's overriding influence.

"They got me out there to go surfing," Joe remembers of the haphazard shoot, "and I know something's wrong when I'm laying out there underneath the surfboard with my arms and legs wrapped around it upside down."

The 90 minutes that were hodgepodged together included footage from the West Coast and some additional stuff shot back in New York, where I assume at least one beachfront scene was filmed—because Joe is positively shivering to death from the cold. "Salt water is good for my nose," he says. Viva tells him it'll also help clear up his skin.

San Diego Surf remains the only film of Joe's eventual eight for the Warhol crowd that never had a theatrical run. It was only recently preserved by the Andy Warhol Foundation for the Visual Arts, which tentatively planned on screening it in selected exhibitions as the only unreleased Andy Warhol feature. [By now, that may have already happened.]

The movie opens promisingly enough with Viva, garbed in black, delivering a monologue to the camera about the stupidity of surfers, one of whom she says told her that "surfing is better than having an orgasm, so I think he's probably never had an orgasm." Her theory is that surfing "is all repressed homosexuality; in fact, they don't even raise girls in California, just boys." Sure, she enjoys "a wipe-out every once in a while, but you've got to be sick, sick, sick to make it a way of life." In very much the same way that the lifestyle of a cowboy was saddled with being queer in **Lonesome Cowboys**, surfing has now become the metaphor for gay boys at play.

The bare premise has Viva married to Taylor Mead and the unlikely couple renting out an extra beachhouse to a group of surfers sent by "Mr. Morrissey" of La Jolla Realty. The two have a grown daughter, Ingrid, who says she's pregnant and needs a husband. Mead tries to pawn her off to any half-interested surfer he can find. Meanwhile, Viva wants a divorce from her boy-crazy hubby and he becomes the attention of Luana, a black woman who sings *"The Muffin Man"* while Viva squeezes a cyst on Louis Waldon's back.

Waldon espouses the surfer's credo—"One for one and all for all"—and mock-fellates a piece of banana during his improv with Ingrid. Ingrid can't seem to hit it off with any of these guys, though. While talking to one scruffy-looking surfer boy, she asks him about space exploration and all he can say is that he thinks it's "groovy, maybe they can find some waves there, too."

A mustachioed Eric Emerson shows up for a single scene in which he tells Ingrid that "everyone should have all that is desired." He then admits he was married three times only because he was trying to prove that he was a man after an entire life spent being called a homosexual.

Joe Dallesandro is also given precious little screen time.

"Joe was in on **San Diego Surf**, but again, he sort of checked out and didn't have much to say," recalls Morrissey. "He didn't like to compete with people—certain types of people, people he knew or considered his friends. He didn't see acting as a competitive thing."

Joe shows up for four scenes and a quick silent shot at the film's very end where he and Tom Hompertz, both outfitted in white pants, stand together looking out on the deep blue water. Out of the hour-and-a-half running time, Joe's footage comes in at just 16 minutes and he barely makes an impression—save for one moment sure to startle viewers nodding off.

Taylor Mead is singing an improvised nursery song to a baby he holds in his arms. Behind him and over a fence top, we see a surfboard being hefted. Turns out that Joe is doing his morning exercises.

While Mead tries to flirt with the uninterested young man, Viva joins the group and complains about the damage done to the beachhouse. Mead says she's just harassing Joe because she's jealous. Look at those muscles.

"You know how he got those muscles?" she asks. "Ripping the fabric off the walls" of their house.

The couple launch into a marital squabble. Viva is holding the baby now and Mead says that he and Joe are going to have their own baby. Viva wonders where, "in his womb?"

With his back to the camera, Joe assures them both that all he's interested in is his surfboard—"Is there anything else?"—as Mead registers disappointment. Another child wanders into the scene and Viva stoops down to pick him up, causing the baby in her arms to flop forward head-first toward the cement driveway!

In a lightning reflex that demands the VIDEO REPLAY, Joe bolts forward and catches the baby before it hits the pavement, righting it and replacing it in mom's arms.

Viva looks into the camera with one of those smiles you give people after you've narrowly averted disaster in front of them, and Taylor Mead, with a great comic's timing and wearing a sardonic smirk, says: "You were nearly a complete failure as a mother."

Morrissey told me that "what we shot in San Diego was so tame and so innocuous and mild—it had a certain charm, you could say—but it was sort of a reaction to some things we thought were a little extreme in **Lonesome Cowboys**. Of course, when I say 'we,' I mean 'I,' because I don't remember Andy doing too much thinking. Or stating his thinking. He sort of agreed with everything I set forth. **San Diego Surf** didn't really seem like something we could release after **Flesh** and **Lonesome Cowboys**. Remember, **Cowboys** came out much later than **Flesh**, so the idea of putting something like **Surf** out after both of them didn't seem a good idea. It would have been a step back."

He was right on both counts. **San Diego Surf** is a rather shapeless and occasionally even boring film There's too much footage of dialogue that doesn't sparkle, of scenes that don't gel. It's as if the East Coasters were taking in too much sun and the heat was causing their brains to cook, their bodies to slow down. That Warhol and Morrissey reportedly shot 28,100' of film and could only come up with these 90 minutes is proof that, this time out, their famously improvised style of making movies didn't produce results that satisfied them either.

Morrissey also made mention of a scene that was considered beyond the pale even for Warhol. It comes during the final reel in a long, drawn-out encounter between Taylor Mead and the boy-beauty Tom Hompertz. Tom was glimpsed earlier in the film during Joe's first scene in which the novice Dallesandro asks Mead how to surf. Mead calls Tom over because he's graduated "from ripples to waves," and Hompertz quietly admits that he sometimes waits days for a good wave.

In the film's final reel, Hompertz is waxing his board when Mead, decked out in black swimming trunks that the head of his dick can be seen poking through, stops by to torment the innocent boy.

Hompertz begins to play the scene seriously by answering Mead's questions about surfing, telling him that "you have to love the sun and the water and all that." Mead says he only wants to learn how to surf so that he and his wife can obtain status in the local community. He pulls a giant harmonica out of his bathing trunks and sings a raunchy ditty, then insists that the silent Tom tell him something dirty.

With a shy smile, Hompertz offers quietly, embarrassedly even: "Squat on your scrotum." It's such an incredibly non-sensical, sweet response, and he smiles again as if he knows he's said something "dirty."

Mead is looking for something more graphic, though—he's just come to the wrong place—so he tells his own dumb story about a dolphin sucking a swimmer's penis until both parties were dead. The pair washed up on a movie star's beach where the surfer was recognized as a lover and the star had both man and animal embalmed and entombed for $8,000. Then:

"Tom, baby, will you piss on me?" asks Mead. He wants to be initiated into the surfer's world and thinks this a perversely funny way of doing it. "I'm not suggesting anything, but have a drink," he adds later, handing the naive and nervous Hompertz a beer. For the next several minutes, Mead goes off on his urinary tangent, making a pun of Barry "Goldwater" and spouting philosophical gibberish about golden showers to an obviously uncomfortable Hompertz.

"Piss on me," he says again. He talks Tom into lying down on his surfboard—the bottom of the surfer's feet are black as coal—then directs him to take off his shirt. Mead pretends to be masturbating himself and continues to drone on, working himself into a terribly tiresome frenzy.

"We middle class people suffer when we watch you surf," he says. "Can't you just piss on us?"

All right, all right already. Between takes, poor Tom has now been talked into pretending to comply with Mead's rants. He shucks his shorts—seen only from behind—and stands on his surfboard.

Cut to a close-up of Mead's grotesquely made-up face as a stream of liquid splashes onto his head and foams from

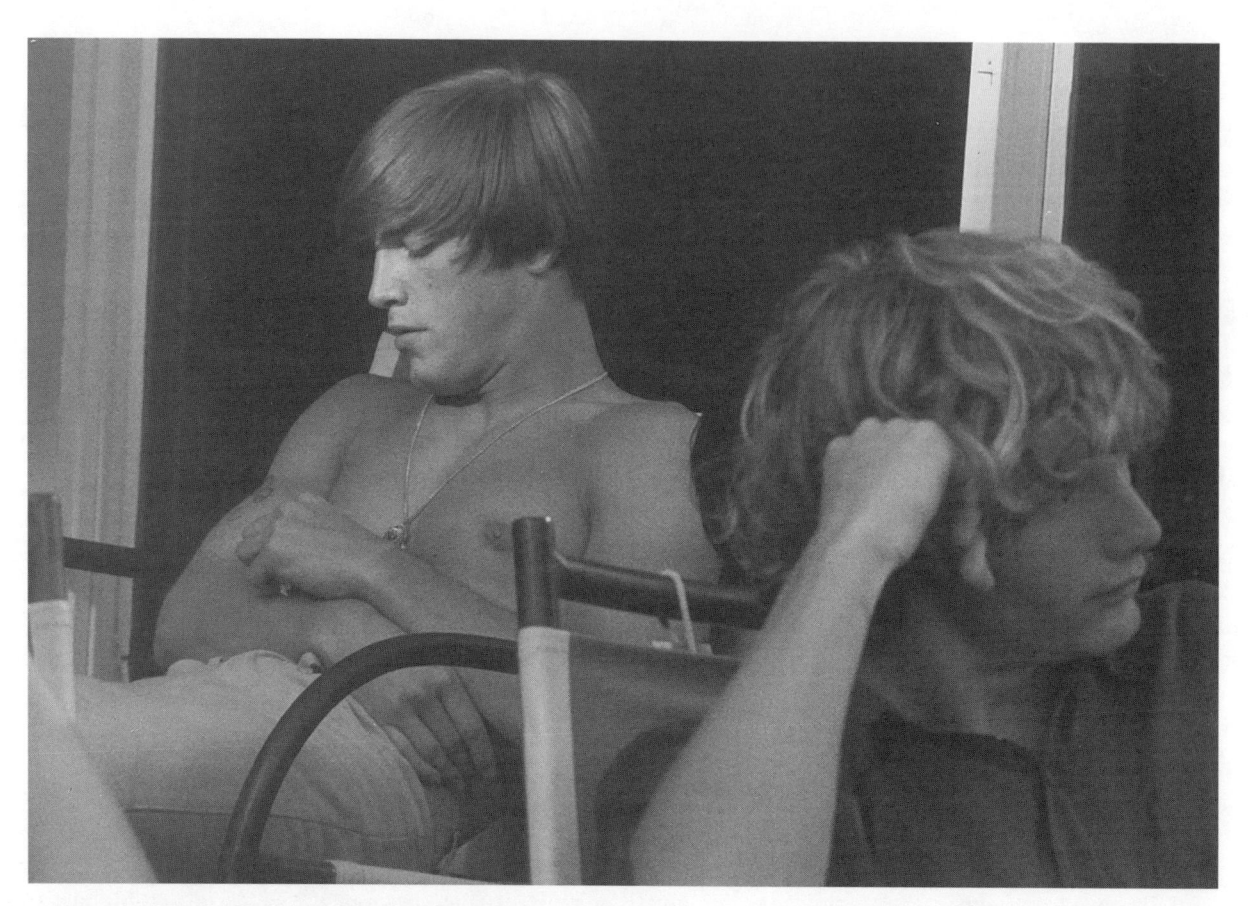

With Tom Hompertz—two silent beauties/Courtesy Joe Dallesandro

Whiling away time in a shot that does not appear in the film/Courtesy Joe Dallesandro

his mouth while he writhes in ecstasy.

"I'm a real surfer now."

No wonder Tom Hompertz didn't make any more films for Andy Warhol. Even Joe wouldn't have agreed to be a part of that nonsense. (Believe me, I'm not being a prude here; the 20-minute long scene just doesn't work—it sounds funnier in a grotesque and daring sort of way than it actually plays.)

Mead lamented the limbo of **San Diego Surf**, as well as a couple of other publicly unavailable Warhol films, when he told *Christopher Street* magazine in 1978: "They're sitting there like gold bars. There's a great sickness in Andy and Paul suppressing those films. Some idea that the later films won't be worth as much. Or some kind of weird awful uptown-gallery rationale where you would release a few paintings at a time and hold back the rest to drive up the price."

Callie Angell, adjunct curator of the Andy Warhol Film Project, writes: "As Warhol understood, the absence of his films, whether physically unwatchable or simply unavailable, has consistently worked to increase their value in the marketplace of cultural discourse, where a growing body of recollections, descriptions, and interpretations, projected on the often blank screens of Warhol's cinema, has come to replace direct experience of the films themselves."

Joe tells me that even though he's never seen the film, it may have gotten the customary screening at the Factory. Though he hastens to say, regarding any and all of the films, that "I didn't even want to go watch them," he adds, "the reason I got to see any of those things was because I was the projectionist at the Factory."

I share with him all of the reports I've ever heard about the fate of the Warhol surfing opus, particularly that it was never even "officially" finished, rumored to have been shut down by police in California over an incident involving a few marijuana seeds.

"Here again, we're doing an Andy Warhol movie," he tells me matter-of-factly. "An Andy Warhol movie doesn't have a beginning, middle, and end. An Andy Warhol movie is just a free-for-all for anybody who wants to participate. So to say it was never finished, what constitutes finishing an Andy Warhol movie? What constitutes *beginning* an Andy Warhol movie?"

For Joe, his own association with Warhol was anything but finished. He was hired on at the famed Factory where he performed any number of jobs, from answering phones to helping with paintings to screening out visitors to running guests up and down in the elevator where celebrities who had just seen him on the screen in one of Andy's movies often wouldn't recognize him as the little guy operating the lift.

"Sometimes Joe Dallesandro ... helps out with the phones and daily work of the Factory," observed writer-critic Stephen Koch. "It's astonishing to watch the half-visible way in which he sexualizes the dreariest details of life in a business office, eroticizing every moment of human contact and virtually every object he touches."

The secret to his enormous appeal: Joe seemed completely unaware of his charms. "I remember basically my job was to keep as many people out of the Factory as I could," he recalls. "It wasn't so much that I was the star of the movies as I was there to frighten other guys off. 'Cause I was a scary little kid. So they set me at the front door with a stuffed dog."

Joe and the stuffed dog—a Great Dane dubbed Cecil and allegedly once the property of C.B. DeMille—were the latest security measures after the June 3, 1968 shooting of Warhol by Valerie Solanas. Solanas had made a single appearance in one of Andy's films, **I, A Man** (1967), in which she confronts star Tom Baker on an apartment stairwell and gives him a little of her now-legendary feminist affront. Shrouded almost completely in shadows, Baker is having trouble getting this cheeky woman who supposedly goosed him in the elevator to come to his apartment. Getting nowhere because she keeps insulting him, he finally takes off his shirt and asks, "You dig men's tits? You don't know what you're missing." In classic sex-role reversal repartee, she tells him, "I wanna go home and beat my meat."

The reason she shot Andy Warhol depends on whose interpretation of her warped mind you subscribe. Solanas told the *New York Post*, "He had too much control over my life."

The attempt on Andy Warhol's life obviously left the famed artist and filmmaker with irreparable physical, emotional, and psychological scars. He would never be quite the same, many said, suggesting further that the shooting robbed much of his personal drive and creativity.

But there were still movies to be made. **The Loves of Ondine** would premiere within two months of the shooting, **Lonesome Cowboys** would be edited by Andy himself while convalescing at home, and Paul Morrissey would step autonomously into the director's chair with a little film of his own. **San Diego Surf** was summarily consigned to the vault. It's not even mentioned in most texts chronicling Warhol's or Morrissey's films. In a way, though, it's the ghostly buoy marking the change in tide at the filmmaking Factory.

For Joe Dallesandro, it meant going from supporting player to full-fledged Superstar.

flesh

(1968)

"Has Warhol brand and will appeal chiefly to voyeurs and cult followers."

—*Variety* (10/2/68)

With JOE DALLESANDRO AS JOE, Geraldine Smith (Geri, Joe's wife), Maurice Braddell (the artist), Louis Waldon (David), Geri Miller (Terry), Candy Darling (Candy), Jackie Curtis (Jackie), Patti D'Arbanville (Patti, wife's girlfriend), Barry Brown (new hustler on street), Bob Dallesandro (new hustler on street), John Christian (young john). Directed by Paul Morrissey. 89 minutes

Andy Warhol was in the hospital eagerly getting reports on all the behind-the-scenes gossip he could cull from Paul Morrissey about the day's shooting. Paul had made a short film with Ultra Violet (an exotic fringe Factory dweller who made much more of her association with Andy than there ever was) and the result was being projected as part of the multi-media background for the party scene. Taylor Mead, Candy Darling, Pat Ast, Jackie Curtis, and even Joe Dallesandro were hanging around waiting for their moment in front of the cameras.

John Schlesinger's cameras.

Midnight Cowboy (1969) was in production and for a groovy sequence in which country-boy-stud Joe Buck (Jon Voight) attends a psychedelic party that, in effect, "parodies" the Factory scene, director Schlesinger wanted Warhol to play a role as an underground film director and bring along his groupies.

"They asked if Andy would be in this movie," Morrissey recalls. "He's supposed to be giving an underground movie party. And I said, well, no, he wouldn't, because he's too frightened of everything. He's terrified of saying anything in front of a camera. He just trembles and can't get anything out of his mouth. Then I said, 'just for your own information, Andy has never given a party ... ever.' He certainly never gave a party and ran around with a camera filming people, which is a continuing idea that people have; even when Oliver Stone made his dopey movie **The Doors** (1991), he had Andy sort of giving a party. And he certainly never took a camera to a party like he was some sort of newsreel. He never knew how to do anything himself. Someone else had to set the camera up on the tripod and he just pushed the button on and off. So all these things are so inaccurate. And they said, we don't care, it's in the script."

ANDY
WARHOL
presents
FLESH
Starring Joe Dallesandro
IN COLOR RESTRICTED TO ADULTS

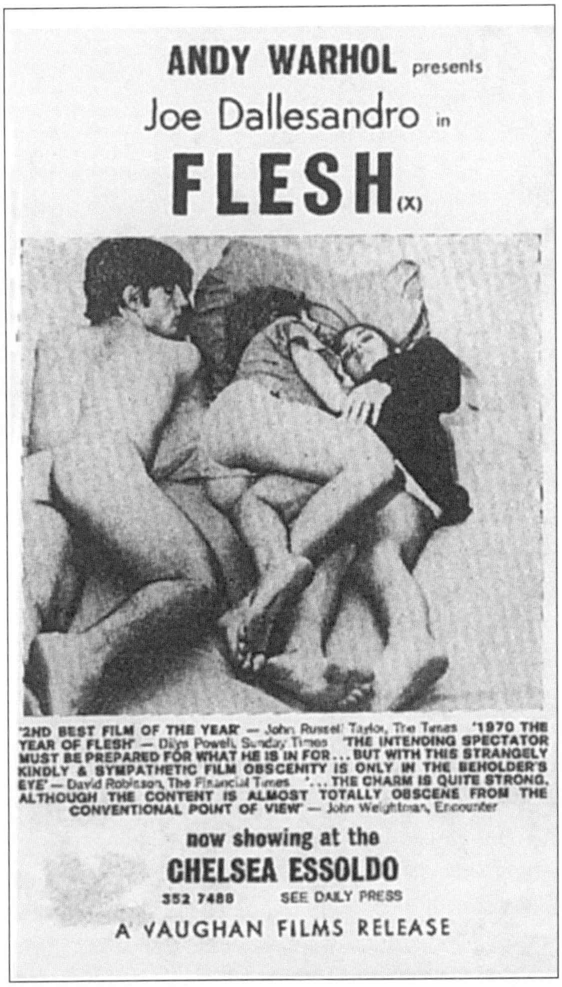
ANDY WARHOL presents
Joe Dallesandro in
FLESH (X)
'2ND BEST FILM OF THE YEAR' — John Russell Taylor, The Times '1970 THE YEAR OF FLESH' — Dilys Powell, Sunday Times 'THE INTENDING SPECTATOR MUST BE PREPARED FOR WHAT HE IS IN FOR . . . BUT WITH THIS STRANGELY KINDLY & SYMPATHETIC FILM OBSCENITY IS ONLY IN THE BEHOLDER'S EYE' — David Robinson, The Financial Times '. . . THE CHARM IS QUITE STRONG, ALTHOUGH THE CONTENT IS ALMOST TOTALLY OBSCENE FROM THE CONVENTIONAL POINT OF VIEW' — John Weightman, Encounter
now showing at the
CHELSEA ESSOLDO
352 7488 SEE DAILY PRESS
A VAUGHAN FILMS RELEASE

Joe
Dallesandro
in
LUITPOL
THEATER
Täglich: 15.30, 18.00
Andy Warh

In the case of **Midnight Cowboy**, Andy suggested Viva play his part.

"I was asked to recruit some underground film types," continues Morrissey. "To which I said, there are no underground film types."

Though certainly aware of the numbing conventions of Hollywood moviemaking, Morrissey was spending a lot of time just standing around on Schlesinger's set. It was a joke, particularly for the company of players he brought with him who were accustomed to instantaneous film stardom. All you ever had to do to be in one of Andy's movies, to paraphrase Joe, was just show up. You get in front of the camera and somebody turns on the switch and you just start doing it, whatever it might be, whatever you might feel it should be.

Warhol was disappointed in Paul's reports from the big-studio frontlines for several reasons, not the least of which was that he wasn't seeing any cash out of the deal, but also, because Hollywood was at long last finally tackling a subject in his cinematic domain. ("I kept feeling they were moving into our territory," he said.)

Male prostitution was considered a very daring and controversial choice of subject matter for Hollywood, but for Andy, it was old hat.

"Andy said, 'Oh, wow. Is that what it's about?'" recalls Morrissey. "'That sounds like something we did before. Didn't we do something like that once?' I said, well, yeah, sort of, we did one of these experiments called **My Hustler**. He said, 'yeah, we did that three years ago. Oh, that's terrible.'"

Warhol had shot **My Hustler** way back—relatively speaking—in 1965, an irony that wasn't lost on Paul Morrissey either. Perhaps it was time to do another take on that particular storyline and do everything Hollywood couldn't and wouldn't even dare.

Morrissey remembers that "Andy was out of the hospital maybe two or three weeks and I spoke with him on the phone at home. It was always difficult to make conversation, but he asked what happened with that big Hollywood movie. 'Did they use all our kids? Did they have good parts?' And I said, no, none of them got near the cameras as far as I know. We just sat around all the time. Then he said something very interesting: 'Why don't you go out and make a movie like that and we could have it out before theirs. And you could use all the kids that they didn't bother to use.' And that was what really gave me the idea. Furthermore, I thought, you know, that really is a good idea, because I finally won't have Andy operating the camera. He really had no good visual sense and didn't know how to use a camera in any way that was interesting. He just did the same thing over and over again. He didn't even frame well, and kept the camera running too long, and I had to keep stopping him. So this was a good chance to disengage from Andy having to be there to push the button."

With Warhol at home recovering from his bullet wounds, Paul Morrissey decided to take the invitation to do his own feature, and he knew precisely who was to be his emblematic star: Joe Dallesandro. "I was there every day (on **Midnight Cowboy**) and I had to sit with the extras and that's when I really got to know Joe a little bit. Joe came every day, too, and he was quiet, but he seemed like an interesting person, and I saw a different side of him then than he had made available before."

According to Joe, he and Paul originally toyed with the idea of doing a very different kind of film than the one they eventually shot.

"It was supposed to be a story about a boxer," recalls Joe. "You see, me and Paul would sit down and I would tell him stories about my life or the people I'd known on the street and he'd say, 'Oh, yeah, we've got to make a movie about that.'" Perhaps the boxer idea was just a ruse to secure Joe's participation since Morrissey seems to have known the kind of story he wanted to do all along. In any case, Joe made the thematic transition without argument.

"Since I ran Andy's office every day, I never had any time during the week to make movies, so I just did it on Saturdays and Sundays and maybe one week day," Morrissey said. "There were very few shooting days and only two or three hours a day. And, of course, when I say a day, it wasn't seven in the morning, it was like two in the afternoon and it was over two or three hours later at the most."

Thus, **Flesh** was shot mostly on weekends (for a total of about five days) in August/September of 1968 for approximately $1,500. Essentially, it details the picaresque tale of a lazy young man named Joe who supports his wife and baby daughter by hitting the streets and peddling his sculptured physique. The tale is told episodically in distinct sequences that effectively mark the day(s) on which they were shot.

It opens with a tight close-up of Joe's face on his pillow as he sleeps. The shot lingers for a full two and a half minutes (it seems even longer) while the entirety of a creaky old tune with the refrain, "Making Wicki-Wacki Down in Waikiki," plays on the soundtrack. In what may be Morrissey's visual epitaph to the aim, crank, and walk away stasis that was a trademark of Andy's film work, the long, long, unveering close-up also gives us time to contemplate the handsome profile of the sleeping youth in much the same way that Warhol's static eccentricity forced us to think about what we were looking at it in his movies.

When the camera does change perspective, it simply

widens out the frame and presents us with Joe in naked slumber, exposing his contoured beauty (the shapely white roll of his buttcheeks) for voyeuristic bottoms-up indulgence. It is precisely this motif of Joe as passive sexual object that would become the cornerstone of his underground fame.

If you listen closely, the first word you hear in the film by an actor is an off-screen Geraldine Smith asking Paul Morrissey, "Now?," before she walks into the scene and tries to rouse her dozing husband by whipping him with clothes and pummeling him with a pillow. Smith is having so much fun doing this that she can't keep herself from laughing.

Joe, who appears to be genuinely tired and perturbed, gives her a good return slam with the pillow, but also insists that there's no reason to get up, there's nothing to do, and that his giggling and abusive wife really is insane.

"You're the one that's a fucking nut," Smith counters.

She wants him to get up and go to work so she can give $200 to a girlfriend who needs an abortion. The actress was given no information other than the premise that she was supposed to be Joe's wife and wants him to get the abortion money, so it's fun watching how much she's enjoying playing out the role of flippant head of household. There's little doubt who wears the pants in this family. (Joe certainly doesn't have any on.)

When Joe asks her to "C'mere, and talk to me," he's doing his job to set-up a little one-on-one with his wife for the camera. He's also in full nude display the whole time they banter. Sub-consciously improvising the relationship to a tee, Joe asks her, "What are you gonna do today," then immediately, "What am I gonna do today?" and his tone suggests that he's asking for her to tell him.

"You have to do something with me," she giggles, suddenly deciding she'd like to get in a little nuzzling with this hot naked kid who's supposed to be her husband.

They kiss and kiss and the action gets pretty hot and heavy, with Joe finally climbing on top of her—he fully naked, she fully clothed—and gently humping.

Smith may have gotten a little surprised by what was developing, because you can hear her say, "What are you doing ... clothes on," and when Joe rolls off of her and sits up against the bedboard, we can see that he's hard. (Joe claims "semi-erect.") When Smith reported back to Warhol that Joe got a hard-on during their scene together, Andy was ecstatic.

In this opening sequence, Joe has been laid out nude before us only to be teased and abused by his wife, who also hits him with a pillow in the head, pulls his hair *hard* (as if she were going to wrench his noggin off), slaps his face, and paws his naked body all-the-while she remains fully dressed. The reverse sexism allows for an unusual dynamic and it's about to get even more interesting.

The couple exchange barbs about his mother (she calls his mother a "cunt" and says "I know all about your mother," to which Joe answers in classic retort, "Yeah? Well my mother knows all about you"), and the fighting is precisely the kind of silly bickering in which couples engage, but at one point Smith gets the weird idea that she'd like to tie a strip of white linen around Joe's genitalia.

She's so taken by the idea, giggling away and making comments like "good things come in small packages" and declaring it "scrumptious," that Joe can do little but put up with the ritual and smoke his cigarette. She's delirious with intent and playfully asks his approval, to which he smiles and says, "It's the only way for it to be."

Joe has only one retaliatory concern throughout his being used as a playtoy and it comes with such natural delivery and so unexpectedly that it never fails to bring down the house.

"Why do I always have to tell you when to do my laundry?" he asks Smith in a sympathetic whine while she's smothering him with kisses.

"Do my laundry, will you? Without me asking...just once?"

She's too wrapped up in herself and fondling him to reply.

"I make you happy, don't I?" he asks. "You want to make me happy?" Beat beat. "Do my laundry."

Not too shabby a request from a guy who's willing to sell his ass to put food on the kitchen table for you.

Not that he goes without a squeak of protest, though. He tells her that he's not in the mood to go to 42nd Street (she tells him to go somewhere else then) and explains that, "I can't hustle 25 hours a day." The improvised flub goes a long way toward telling us about his character and what he thinks of his work.

"It's very painful and I don't like that kind of work," he says softly, poignantly.

"Are you gonna do it?"

"Yeah."

Before he heads out, however, he takes time to play with his baby daughter on the floor, to feed her a cupcake and talk with her. The two minute segment plays in absolute silence, but it would become one of the most effective and remarked upon scenes in the entire film, bringing an unexpected tenderness to Joe's character, and revealing a warmth and natural charm in the young actor which were felt by critics and audiences alike.

"I told the story to Paul about how I taught my baby how to shower, how to hold on to the soapbar rack with one arm and then change hands," says Joe. "I taught him to take a shower at a very young age, because I thought the kid should grow up to be a man and take showers. You know, get away from that bath routine, because men don't need to be taking baths. Our bodies sweat in a different way and we're not meant to sit in our own funk. We want to wash it off, so we stand up to do it. Paul thought that was a great story and he wanted to shoot the scene that way, with me and my baby naked in the shower and my teaching him."

But his ex-wife wouldn't let him. "She wouldn't have anything to do with it."

So another child was substituted, this one a little girl, and a different scenario was decided. The only problem now was that there was some anxiety about having both Joe and the baby naked together. Though it would have seemed completely natural, and the baby *is* naked with Joe in the famous photos that were eventually used on posters, the decision was made to keep the baby girl clothed during the scene, which was shot at the Factory.

The tender exchange almost didn't make it into the finished print, however.

Paul Morrissey was editing the film—without the use of an editing table—on the very same day he had to walk the print over to the theatre for the first show at noon, according to Joe.

"The movie was going into the theatre," Joe recalls, "and I said, 'Paul, I want that scene in the movie. I have to have that scene in the movie. Why is the movie opening? It isn't ready.' So he went down and he got the footage—no sound on it yet—and he cut it into the film."

A remarkable bit of insight for a 19-year old. "Not that it's any great thing," he adds. "But I knew it had to be in there."

And he was right.

The rest of the film follows Joe through a typical workday. Morrissey's camera does a slow tilt up Joe's body as he stands on the street looking for lookers. Dressed in tight blue jeans, a light blue shirt with black T-shirt underneath, and a red kerchief tied around his head, Joe is a strapping young buck and the director has deliberately made us the leering john.

Business seems slow today, though he does manage to turn a $20 trick in what seems to be the young john's own house. At last, a spindly, elderly gentleman passes through the frame with cane in hand, then comes back to chat the boy up.

"Do you know anything about art?" he asks the young man, who admits he's done a little modeling.

Splendid, precisely what he had in mind, and for the hundred bucks Joe is asking, "you'll have to take all your clothes off for that."

The bespectacled Brit takes Joe back to his apartment, and after a moment's pause as the two actors stand in the doorway and wait for a cue to start, he begins a seemingly endless lecture on the aesthetics of the Greek statues, "simpatica," and the politics of "body worship." The artist's lengthy ramble, which is actually quite humorous in places, immediately establishes Joe as the clueless *objet d'sex*.

His silence has in fact inspired the old man to pontificate. Joe can only listen to the haze of self-aggrandizement with priceless facial reactions—communicating boredom, feigned tolerance, a tiny bit of polite interest, and finally exasperation.

"I never really thought of it like that … cause like … well, let's get started, it's getting late. It's good to know that really."

The old man rationalizes that his speech was intended to give Joe some pride in his profession, but its purpose is clearly to vent his intellect and stroke his ego now that other types of more tactile and sensual stroking are beyond him. In its own way, it is his attempt to seduce Joe, having not the youthful good looks to do it any other way and even justifying the queer relationship by suggesting that it's the responsibility of someone with a beautiful body to accept the worship of someone without a beautiful body, as if it were the noble thing to do.

The effete artist has Joe strip completely naked and stand on his bed, where he turns and twirls and poses the young man into noticeable fatigue. Each pose is related to its classical equivalent, as if the artist were sculpting with human flesh and then filling in the back- and foreground in his head. He wonders if Joe could hold that pose for 10 minutes, or maybe this one for 35.

Joe has less than subtle, but incredibly well-timed ways of letting his more practical interests be known.

"It's like, if I pick up a violin and I can't play the damn thing, what the hell use is it?" prattles the old man, with the camera in close-up on his face as he speaks to Joe, who is presumably on the bed off-screen right. "Might even be a Stradivarius. It wouldn't be any good. You've got to have the music …"

"What are we havin' for dinnah?" comes Joe's voice suddenly—unexpectedly—interrupting his teacher.

The artist's eyebrows pop up in warm surprise. His erudite lecture has been sabotaged by the simply stated desires of his audience.

"Yes. Food."

"What kind?"

The actor laughs at the startlingly honest reply.

Maurice Braddell plays the artist. He was an old-time British actor who had appeared, most notably, in William Cameron Menzies' seminal sci-fi flick of H.G. Well's **Things To Come** (1936). Morrissey was working as a social worker when some of his clients told him about the old English guy they knew who used to be in the movies. Braddell was then cast in Morrissey's very first feature length film, **Sleep Walk** (1964).

At the time the actor agreed to appear in **Flesh**, Joe tells me, he was restoring paintings for museums.

With his $100 made, Joe returns to the streets where he meets up with two young men who are new to the world of tricking and have some questions for him. For all those who've criticized Joe Dallesandro for not being a spontaneous talker in his movies, this is one scene in which he's very much in verbal command, probably due to the fact that he was able to improvise from the heart. It's hard to resist applying the rationale he espouses as hetero hustler on the streets to his own real life just prior to making the film.

"Are you straight?" he asks one of the boys (his real brother, Bob Dallesandro). "Hey, nobody's straight. What's straight? It's not a thing of being straight or being not straight. It's just … you just do whatever you have to do."

To Joe, worrying about what other people think of you means that "you're not in your bag." His wife, "she knows where I'm at, we've already had a kid…why should she get uptight, it's feeding her?"

So why should these guys worry if they know why it is they're out here, he reasons. When one of the boys insists that it's hard to get used to doing "that," Joe boils down his entire street philosophy: "He's only gonna suck your pee-tah, man," and then you're out of there, off to do your own thing.

Evoking Andy Warhol's famous **Blow Job** (1964), Morrissey teasingly cuts to an implicitly explicit sex act for which we, the audience, must provide the visuals. Joe's jeans-clad behind is shown with Geri Miller's fingers to either side of his hips, undulating and caressing him as she goes to work up front. While the servicing continues, two transvestites sit on a couch just a few feet away and read from an old Hollywood magazine.

"That's a very petty trick, you know," says Candy Darling in her whispery voice to Miller. "Trying to make the likes of me jealous."

Candy Darling, unequivocally the loveliest of all the Warhol transvestites, started out life as James Slattery, but his preteen obsession with Lana Turner advanced to an addiction to Kim Novak and a persona of platinum blonde fantasy became reality. Candy Darling was a Superstar. She was not only the most beautiful of the Factory transvestites, managing to be oh-so exotically glamorous and oh-so seductively witty, but she also would become one of the most tragic. (She was played by young Stephen Dorff, whose hairy torso required some waxing, but whose performance is touching, in Mary Harron's **I Shot Andy Warhol**.)

After lighting up the screen one more time for Paul Morrissey's commercially unsuccessful **Women In Revolt** (1971) and then landing a key role in a production of Tennessee Williams' **Small Craft Warnings**, she withered away from leukemia and died at age 25. For a while, she was taking hormone injections and was said to have intended to make the ultimate transition. (A series of famous photos exist of her from a session Richard Avedon shot while visiting the Factory on October 30, 1969. In several, including some in which she's standing opposite an equally unclad Joe, the bewigged Darling not only let down her hair, but pulled down her pants, too.)

Candy's co-star on the couch in **Flesh** is Jackie Curtis—sporting a decidedly more noticeable five o'clock shadow—who can be heard asking Geri out-of-the-blue whilst Geri is still in the process of going down on Joe: "Do you know any poems? I'm starving for culture."

John Holder, Jr. had too mannish a face to pull off the transvestite transition into femininity, but he also went in for a much louder and flamboyant look. His appearance in **Flesh** is probably the most conservative he ever adopted. Jackie came to Warhol having already had some of her own plays produced off-off Broadway, including **Glamour, Glory and Gold**, which marked one of Robert DeNiro's earliest stage appearances (or more correctly, several of his earliest stage appearances, as he played all ten male roles in the production). Jackie was also reportedly seriously considered by Ross Hunter for a role in **Airport** (1970). Didn't happen, unfortunately.

As witty and prissy and glamorously self-obsessed as the transvestites in **Flesh** are, the scene's only bonafide woman, a stripper named Geri Miller, turns out to be the funniest. With the "girls," the comments are calculatingly funny, but Geri just opens her mouth and what comes out is naturally funny.

She has no idea, but she's writing great dialogue and creating a quirky and interesting character from the moment she finishes with Joe and joins the others for a sit down and says, "I have a frog in my throat."

Dressed in black, with a 60's mountain of jet-black, synthetic-looking hair and inky false eyelashes, she says she dresses this way because she wants to be a vampire. She launches into a bizarre story to Joe about a time she was raped and then rejected him the same day when he wanted to make love with her. And then later she saw her attacker at the nightclub. "Do you know what it's like to dance topless in front of someone who raped you?" she asks Joe in all seriousness. She danced her best, though, she says, showing the guy that if he had only been nice, he could have had her real groovy, instead of how he did, "cause when he raped me, I was real stiff." (As with several players in the Warhol/Morrissey films, Miller's story comes with enough baroque detailing and free-flow of expression that you have to imagine that some or all elements of the freaky story being told are true, brought in from life off-screen. Miller professionally stripped at Al Goldstein's M & M club, as well as at the Metropole. She also once popped out of Mick Jagger's birthday cake.)

Geri's thinking about getting her breasts enlarged with silicone or maybe this new thing, "juice from a plant." Joe thinks it's a good idea after he examines them.

"Why don't you develop your brain instead of your bust?" asks Candy.

"My brain can't be developed any more than it is and I think I'm cute," she replies. "If I learn too much, I won't always be happy, cause the more you learn, I think, the more depressed you are."

Joe has been pretty much silent the whole time, clearly unaffected by Geri's stories. When Jackie sits down next to Joe, she tells him, "You know, you're sweet, you really are."

"I try hard."

Jackie has Joe read a "Dear Audrey" letter from a friend. Joe's reading, including natural stumbles trying to decipher the handwriting, is punctuated by wonderful reactions as he comes across lines that begin innocently enough but end otherwise, such as the one about having some photos enlarged that suddenly ends with "picked accidentally the one with my hands on my cock." (Joe's genuine surprise comes complete with a "hmmm!," raised eyebrows, and pursed lips.)

Whether aware of it or not—and he isn't—Joe is inextricably tied up in all these people's sexual lives. The johns on the street, the artist, the new hustlers, Geri, and now even Jackie are all vying for this gorgeous kid. They all want a piece of him.

Joe's visit to his gym-buddy's apartment continues the Joe-dependence motif as he rarely gets a chance to speak unless it's about how much the other guy means to him. Played by Warhol regular Louis Waldon, David, who's now got a gut and is approaching middle-age, wants Joe to move in with him.

He tries to convince Joe that he's made a mistake marrying ("She's so ugly, man, she can afford to be upset") and that, though "we're not queers," they've got something special together. As with the jabbering artist, David's need for Joe comes with a self-serving justification. The kid is learning things from the older man. Joe wants $30 on this visit so he plays along half-heartedly even when David takes out a porno book and reads aloud a graphic story of homosexual sex. We only hear jump-cut bits and pieces of the raunchy text because of Morrissey's stop-and-go camera, but David asks for an opinion, looking for approval, and Joe quietly declares it "beautiful."

Joe is just as much a purchased sexual stimulant as the porn is, however. David unknowingly underscores the theme when he asks Joe to strip down to his undies and reproduce a pose from the magazine: a pose that David says he could have done himself back before the war wound. (He shows Joe his unusual scar, inflicted across the underside of his upper arm and armpit by a flame-thrower in Korea. When Joe is at his most cuddlesome, because he's looking to get the cash, he plants a tender peck on it.) For David, Joe is his idealized link to a healthy, younger self; he even takes joy in squeezing a pimple on Joe's face, declaring it "a nice one." David's sexual prods, just beneath a veneer of maintained masculinity, are as much mental masturbation as anything else, a fact further evidenced by having him begin the scene by telling Joe that he can't get a hard-on anymore these days.

Even to his wife, Joe is clearly something to selfishly

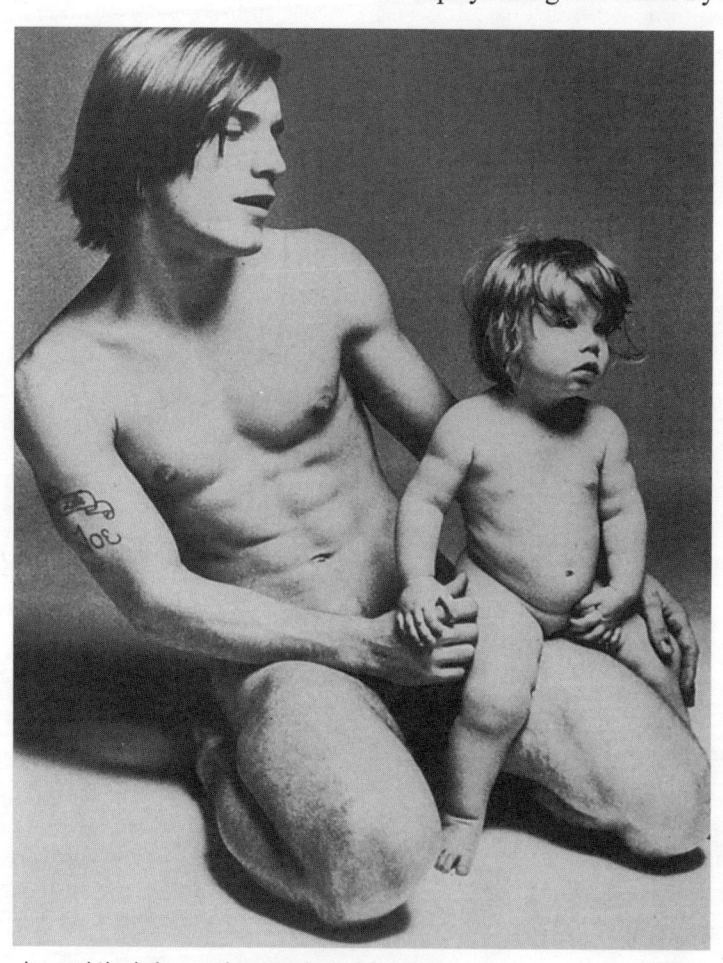

Joe and the baby—an image adopted for foreign posters and advertising/ © Francesco Scavullo, reprinted with permission

In this rare still from a shot that doesn't appear in the film, Joe prepares to head out for a day on the streets at his wife's request/Courtesy Joe Dallesandro

With Jackie Curtis, Candy Darling and Geri Miller's hands

flaunt and provoke. Her wrapping up his penis in the first scene not only accessorizes and commodifies him, but has her so excited that she wants him to stay that way so she can show her girlfriend.

When Joe finally meets the girlfriend (Patti D'Arbanville) in the film's last scene, he isn't even there two minutes before his wife has him stripped naked and is laughingly showing him off: "There it is…there it is!" But the women—both actresses appear to be either drunk or on drugs—want each other. Joe seems interested in their cuddling, but isn't invited. He has served his purpose. So off to sleep he goes, bringing the film full circle.

"Here was the way we shot films," Joe explains. "We would sit down and Paul would give us a paragraph of what the storyline was and then we'd talk about it a little—talk about going from here to here—and we'd improvise dialogue around that."

That's an amazingly risky way to make films, of course, because odds run against your getting enough good material; that Morrissey managed to consistently beat those odds is an enormous tribute to his extraordinary players. In Joe's favor, he now had a director who believed in his potential and knew just exactly how to put it to use.

"I did the Andy Warhol movies and I did the Paul Morrissey movies which Andy Warhol produced, and they're two different things totally," he is quick to point out. "**Flesh** was not made with anything of Andy's. **Flesh** was made with Paul's own stock. The only thing Andy Warhol did on that film was lend his name to it."

The film was, naturally, prominently advertised as an Andy Warhol film, carried the title "Andy Warhol presents … **Flesh**," and has also been known simply as **Andy Warhol's Flesh**. Director Morrissey, surprisingly comfortable at the time existing in the commercial shadow that Andy's name cast, said he didn't mind, famously equating Warhol's name on a film as being not unlike Walt Disney's. Andy ran the movie factory and his name ran above the title, but he didn't necessarily draw Mickey Mouse. (Okay, so he may have painted him, but you get the idea.)

Those who didn't get the idea included not only a handful of snobby critics who saw **Flesh** negatively, as a formal separation from the aesthetic Andy had established, but also members of the Factory entourage who felt unhappy with the change. With **Flesh**, Paul Morrissey had established himself the resident Film Director and his opinionated, talkative, and occasionally caustic personality apparently rubbed a lot of the old guard the wrong way. Jackie Curtis is said to have demanded that Andy be behind the camera on **Women In Revolt** (1972) because Paul made "only Joe look good" in his movies.

Defections are a natural part of any coup, political or creative, but the truth is that Paul Morrissey didn't steal the moviemaking from Andy, he simply took it up, and Andy didn't seem to mind very much. And who, besides a smattering of critical elitists, could have possibly cared that Morrissey meant the end of Warhol's peculiar brand of automaton filmmaking?

"I just realized that people who said things like that were stupid," says Morrissey. "They didn't know what they were talking about. They didn't understand what was going on, what the experiments were and what they were leading toward, and how they moved towards that constantly. It was my idea to move them constantly, yet they moved slowly over that period. This stupid notion of conceptual art shit, which is that you just put the camera on something and you watch it for eight hours, which they think is such wonderful conceptual art-crap, is just childish. It's hardly anything Andy sat through or wanted to see. It was just that he understood if you're going into moviemaking with no money, you do something that will wave into that crowd, into that sort of public relations image that comes out of the art world to get their attention. Then you move on from there. And that's all it was meant to be at the beginning. The stupid idea that you would continue to do that is beyond infantile. Andy was very happy that these films were traveling around the world, bringing in income, but more than anything else, all over the world and here in the United States, the films said, 'Andy Warhol presents …,' so Andy Warhol's name appeared in the papers thousands and thousands of times each year in different cities. It made his name as a silk-screen; you know, a huge industry, and he benefited, because there was more money in the silk-screening and the Polaroiding than there was in the box-office returns, comparatively. So it was of enormous benefit to him. He was hardly objecting."

Purists—i.e., those who enjoyed the thematic and aesthetic audacity of Andy Warhol's paintings and films and therefore enjoyed celebrating an intellectual appreciation of concepts the art world and the public failed to grasp—could never have admitted they appreciated the work of an acerbic conservative like Paul Morrissey.

Morrissey's desire to tell a story, to actually have some semblance of a plot, was nothing short of an artistic sell-out, they said. But a sell-out to whom? Did Morrissey forbid Andy to make movies after his recovery from the shooting? Did Morrissey stifle Andy's cinematic experiments? Only if you see an artist like Andy Warhol as living in a vacuum, which he very definitely was not. He had been asking friends, acquaintances, rivals, and critics for ideas from the very beginning. Andy was influenced, perhaps far more than the romantic notion of an artist expressing his inner self, by his outer selves. Andy painted and filmed surfaces.

He shamelessly went not only to the crass culture around him, but to his fellow consumers for ideas.

It bears repeating. Paul Morrissey told me point blank, "Andy said 'yes' to everything I said."

Morrissey's influence was not only inevitable, but sought out. He was a source of concentrated opinions and had very definite ideas about how to communicate them. The only way he couldn't have taken over the filmmaking when the circumstances allowed is if he'd taken a hike after **My Hustler**, frustrated by the deathly stillness of it all.

Then we'd probably be blaming Gerard Malanga— "one of the most important and influential creative forces behind Andy's paintings," according to Joe—for changing Warhol's movies, or, just as probably, for not changing them at all. In which case, we wouldn't be talking about the films much at all, because they may not have ever emerged from the underground closet.

"Andy had the idea of making films cheap, throwaways, you could say," commented Morrissey to the *New York Times* in 1973. "They're Andy Warhol films sui generis. Like there are Italian films, Hollywood films, musicals. They got the underground label because when they began, there was no other place to put them ... Andy discovered the technique of using the form of the film as the actual subject of the film, and avoiding the subject. But the subject is somehow inherent in the form."

Warhol reviewed his own career as filmmaker when he said, famously: "The camerawork is bad, the lighting is awful, the technical work is terrible—but the people are fantastic."

If one can presuppose a legacy in that statement, a torch to be passed, then Andy would have been hard-pressed to find a worthier successor than Paul Morrissey, who understood from the very beginning the importance of his stars. He chose with uncanny good instincts actors whose looks and whose personalities would imbue his screen with life, with story, with pathos and humor.

"He invented us all," Joe says of his mentor. "We gave him story ideas, but he gave us characters, and that's what a director does."

I, for one, see no reason to blame anyone.

The perception of real evil, it seems to me, came from the fact that Morrissey's films were commercially viable. They resembled films in the more traditional sense of the word and so the critics needed someone to finger for the change. It was a change that wasn't nearly so radical as they imagined, for not only did Warhol also love Hollywood and all its superficial glamour and glitz, but he had famously contributed to a revolution in the art world by turning to commercial iconography in his paintings and silk-screens. (Andy once prophesied, "The new art is business.") Paul Morrissey helped Andy Warhol reach a wider audience, an international audience, by bringing unconventional convention to his movies.

Flesh opened at the New Andy Warhol Garrick Theatre the last week of September, 1968, and played for seven solid months, averaging $2,000 a week—but pulling in $10-12,000 for the first six of those weeks—before moving to the 55th St. Playhouse in May of 1969. It was by far the most financially successful film under the Andy Warhol banner.

"For the first time, Andy started making money," says Joe. "Andy's movies never made money before Paul came along and started making our films. Andy would paint a painting and make a movie, because Andy made movies just to make movies. He didn't even make movies for people to go see. He didn't care if people saw them."

"It was the first film that we ever had that played in a theatre and went to other cities," recalls Morrissey. "It was the first film that really had a life of its own as a film."

Rex Reed raved that it "was the first Andy Warhol movie of any importance I've ever seen (probably because he had nothing to do with it except lend his name to its release), featuring the first naked Warhol superstar who can act (Joe Dallesandro) and dialogue so sharp even Joe Mankiewicz would be proud to have written it." Reed's quote was adopted for future ad blurbs where his compliment to Joe was curiously and quite erroneously truncated to: "Featuring the first naked Warhol Superstar."

Reed also made note that the film had been largely ignored by mainstream reviewers and the Garrick Theatre subsequently bannered an ad that used Reed's comments with: "The longest running film in New York is now starting its sixth month. Acclaimed by the public, it is finally being noticed by the critics."

The *New York Times* original review (of 9/27/68) wasn't so much a review as a description, but critical quotes were lifted out of context in an effort to make it look like a rave in the ads. "The saga of a pursued Adonis" and "reminiscent of the early Brando" were comments referring to Warhol's previous film **Bike Boy**, which shared similar themes. The *Times* reviewer actually thought **Flesh** proved "once again that even audacious, unadulterated sex can be a trashy bore ... It might rate marginal credit as a social document if it weren't so leeringly obvious."

"Public service warning," advised the *Village Voice*. "It's to Dallesandro that the flesh of the title belongs almost exclusively. A somewhat ambiguous figure, probably doing more real acting than you might assume at first, he seems to have more staying power than previous Warhol matinee idols, this being his second or third try already depending on how you figure it. Possibly his greatest asset is a sweet, shy, slowly dawning farmboy's smile, which he keeps wisely in reserve for very special occasions."

The reviews improved, for the most part, as the film moved west. While the *Chicago Daily News* hated it and called it "a flop on every level," a slightly hairier Gene Siskel gave it ★★★1/2 in the *Chicago Tribune*, emphasizing its worth by asking himself the question: "How can you tell if a film employs nudity simply to make money? Decide if you'd watch it even if everyone were clothed. For me, with respect to **Flesh**, the answer is 'yes,' an emphatic 'yes.'"

The Hollywood Reporter, after cogently comparing Warhol's Factory with 1930's Hollywood and then skillfully deciphering Paul Morrissey's influence on the Warhol films by using this one as a marker, remarked that "Morrissey also appears to have asked of his star, Joe Dallesandro, that acting rather than participation alone assume greater importance. To the degree that they are successful in fulfilling the conception, **Flesh** emerges as an almost documentary equivalent of **Midnight Cowboy** ... One sees what appears to be a basically decent and likable young man submitting to continued pawing simply because it is the only manner in which he inspires attention. It is the more poignant since he clearly appears to understand the limits of his communication and the immediate time limit of his appeal as a commodity."

Kevin Thomas, writing in the *Los Angeles Times*, found it a "surprisingly poignant film," whose "point, not surprisingly, is that everybody regards D'Allesandro, an Adonis-like street urchin with a Dead End Kid accent, as an object rather than a person. But D'Allesandro thinks he can sell his body and keep his soul. For how long, one wonders and even cares, for D'Allesandro is actually a kind, likable guy."

The *Herald-Examiner* noted that "comparisons with the new Schlesinger film, **Midnight Cowboy**, are nearly obligatory. But **Flesh** makes its points with more subtlety, force and validity than the over-stated, leering **Cowboy**. Dallesandro's performance has the kind of openness and authenticity that award committees—for shadowy reasons of their own—seem always to neglect."

In San Francisco, not too surprisingly, the film resonated deeply. Writing in the *San Francisco Chronicle*, John Wasserman said, "If one seeks meaning from **Flesh**, it is nothing more complicated than people should mind their own business, and a suggestion that words like normal and natural are entirely subjective and used as weapons far more than explanation. Sure, sure, we all know that. But if the Warhol syndrome does nothing else, it conclusively demonstrates that the prejudice against sexual and societal nonconformity is no more laudatory than prejudice against the color of a man's skin."

From *The Sun*, a British newspaper—February 5, 1970

The Advocate, the gay movement's national newsmagazine, gushed over **Flesh** and said, "at last, a perfect film has emerged from the Warhol Factory ... D'Allesandro is a man of shifting appearance and nuances, and expresses a world of emotion within the framework of his low-key characterization. Prediction: Within two years, Joe will be a top American film star. Hopefully, Morrissey will be directing him." In other words, Joe made gay men drool.

But because the Warhol gang lived and worked in New York, it was the New York criticisms they heard loudest and to this day Joe talks about the trashing they got from reviewers. When I tell him that there were plenty of good reviews of **Flesh** here in the States, he's completely amazed.

Some critics, clearly confused by the true authorship of the film, maintained it was Warhol's work because of a curious "signature" involving the film's editing. Actually, Warhol came rather late to using the device. Since **I, A Man** (1967; only the year before **Flesh**), Warhol (and Morrissey) had begun using a strobe effect in-camera editing technique. The Auricon camera they had was popularly used by documentary and newsreel filmmakers and it facilitated the editing process by "inserting" several white frames and an audible "blip" whenever the camera was switched off.

Andy got in the habit of leaving those interrupting white flashes and hiccuping noises in his final film because, he said, "it makes the movie more mysterious and glamorous." He also saw it as a good joke on all of those people who said he never turned the camera off once he got it rolling in his earlier ("boring") films.

Gene Youngblood, of the *Los Angeles Free Press*, wrote perceptively in early 1968: "It's sort of a Brechtian-Godardian ploy which distances the viewer by interrupting a scene to remind him that it is, after all, only a movie shot with a camera that can be turned on and off, giving birth to, or killing, cinematic life with the flick of a switch."

In that sense, the strobe effect is entirely consistent with Andy's earliest dictum that he always wanted us to know that we were watching a movie and that's why he deliberately focused poorly, zoomed haphazardly, and loaded up the print with as many scratches and dirt as he could.

Variety spent half of its negative review on the technical aspects, finally conceding that taking so much space to cover the "gross technical failures of a film is truly a pity since the mechanics should be second nature to any real filmmaker. Also, there are so many struggling young innovators in the business with that elusive ingredient called talent, who may never receive half the notoriety of Warhol, simply because their 'life-styles' are not that 'far out.'" (The berating concludes with the trade reviewer even criticizing the tail end of the film he saw projected jamming and melting, as if it were intentional!)

The start-and-stopping of the camera comes randomly, interrupting a sentence mid-stream, cutting us off from an interesting line or look, so that the initial experience can be somewhat frustrating for the uninitiated. Like all good films, though, **Flesh** gets better and better with repeated viewings, even moreso here in the sense that the flashes simply become part of the film's language—its urban rhythms—and they take on a fractured reality that comes off feeling like documentary. (For the film's eventual release in Germany, Joe tells me that the white flash-frames were actually removed by Morrissey and then edited back in by the Germans, who knew Warhol's films contained them and thought they had been edited out of their prints!)

The strobe cuts also work nicely to frame some of Morrissey's shots like still photographs or paintings. The scene with the baby is edited at one point by breaking down the images into quick flashes of beautiful composition: a close-up of the baby's pink little hand reaching out; a succession of isolated close-ups of parts of Joe's body, including an artful rendering of nipple and armpit—which sounds funny, but in fact serves to explore in striking terms the title concept, flesh. (Compare Gus Van Sant's sexual still-life tableaus in **My Own Private Idaho**.)

The fragmentary editing also provides an interesting temporal dichotomy. Though both Warhol and Morrissey would often say that the cuts were employed to chop out the boring bits, the effect also effectively compresses time while psychologically elongating it. The artist's lengthy speech about "body worship" is snipped to ribbons, but each time a cut occurs and the old guy's still talking, the effect works to make Joe's stay seem that much longer. No wonder he's sweating, bored, and wants to get down to posing. Later, when David reads Joe a portion of a dirty story, the frequent cuts not only heighten our interest in the nasty stuff he's reading (the neat trick is we get caught trying to fill in the words between the edits), but it also mirrors David's mounting desire to ... well, mount.

What is consistently surprising to fans of **Flesh**, as well as the other films Morrissey made under the Warhol banner, is that they appear on the surface to have been made as camp by free-thinking, free-loving, and freebasing counterculture freaks, but were in fact the deliberate product of an all-too serious and very conservative thinker.

To Paul Morrissey, who says his inspiration for this film came from the 1960 Mauro Bolognini film **La Giornata Balorda** (scripted by Pier Paolo Pasolini), this wasn't camp so much as it was lampoon. He was making fun of the lifestyles he almost appears to espouse. He was genuinely fascinated by the people, but genuinely turned off by their drug use and sexual excess. And all of his films resonate with those themes, as we shall see.

It's been reported he may have shot as much as eight hours of film on **Flesh**, even if the finished product looks as if, as Andy recalled, he used just about everything he shot. For the record, the running time on **Flesh** is 89 minutes, not the 105 minutes listed in nearly every film reference book, and even in several contemporary reviews, since it was released in 1968, though there has been some discussion about this. Morrissey has confirmed that there is no missing footage from his final cut of September, 1968, which seems corroborated by the odd off-screen infraction, including hearing the director verbally cue his actors with the word, "Now," during the last scene. A rough-cut used for the original workprint came in at approximately 106 minutes, so that may be why the running time error has persisted. Morrissey has said that he just guesstimated the earliest running times when he gave the info to the press. (Of course, further editing even after the films opened theatrically was not unheard of for Factory product: both **Bike Boy** and **The Loves of Ondine** were clipped after the fact.)

Regardless of running time, Joe remembers that there were a few extra snippets here and there that weren't used, one of which is represented by the rare still, from his collection, showing him reflected in the bathroom mirror readying to head out for the day.

For Joe Dallesandro, who appears in every scene in the film, this is a star-making performance, much more because of what it isn't than of what it is; which is to say, it is not a performance in the studied, classical sense of the word.

Morrissey wouldn't have stood for it.

"Whenever I read an actor has prepared for the part, I know they're phony, untalented frauds," said Morrissey to the *L.A. Weekly* in 1988, "because this preparation for the part is an excuse for not having any inner resources."

A kid from the streets himself, Joe imbues the screen with a beguiling natural charisma, an ingenuous smile, and a teeming sexuality embodied in a short, muscled frame still glowing with youth. He may have been the male as movie sex symbol fully exposed and glorified, but he is more than just a pin-up boy. There is a sweetness in his Brooklyn accent, a refreshing playfulness in his demeanor, and a marvelous transparency to his face that all great actors must have, that Joe possesses simply, completely unaware of it.

In fact, to "act," to engage in the art of recreation, was strictly forbidden on Morrissey's set. Make no mistake, then—this *is* a performance; a performance in the sense that a young man without a second of formal training in his life allowed himself to be photographed playing out what began as tales of the city he had shared with his director and became jumping-off points for improvisation.

If there was a problem at all with doing the role and handling all of the attention and fame—and eventual worship—to follow, it was in having the character he played in **Flesh** be so closely identified with himself. The identification was part and parcel of the remarkable following the films developed and the equally remarkable emotional response they engendered.

With "actors" appearing in "home-made" movies in which they made up all of their lines, the line between what was acting and what was real had been all but obliterated. Morrissey insisted that his films were about personalities and that he fit a story around those personalities, so audience members could hardly be blamed for thinking that the people they saw up there on screen were in fact the people they played. It provided a powerful vicarious dynamic to watching the films.

An audience member who saw Joe in **Flesh** had little thought that they weren't getting the real thing. It was a real guy they saw up there on screen, not some actor pulling a stunt. And what's more, he seemed like a nice kid at heart … he seemed accessible. Yeah, this was a Joe that could be had.

"Almost every young man in Warhol movies portrays a street arab, tough but tender and wounded—like the young Marlon Brando in **On the Waterfront** and **The Wild One**," said *Playboy*. "On film, all of these lads convey either bisexual ambivalence or overt homosexual appeal." (Actually, both. Simultaneously.)

"I consider myself bisexual," Joe tells me. "It wasn't that I was sexually attracted to men *per se*, but you know, if you do something for awhile you can acquire a taste for it. There will be certain parts of it that you like. Though you may not desire a relationship with a man, you may have other types of relationships with men. See, the whole part where you put a sexual inference between a man and another man—you see, I don't want to have sex for sex's sake. I always came from the mindset that there has got to be something more.

"For me, it's not a person telling me they love me that makes me feel loved, because I had that. The person that loved me beat me every fucking day. That's not love to me. Love to me is having loving actions towards another person. Now, loving actions could be that you pick up a person from work everyday or you show up and look for things to do with that person because you want to spend time with them. It's not me telling you everyday that I love you that makes me love you. It's me thinking about you throughout the day, thinking about what we'll do together, or how I'd like to prepare a meal for us, and then how you want to do that for me in return."

Asked whether he was aware of what he meant—as

image, as icon—to audiences at the time, if he was at all clued in to what his mentor was doing with him, he says, "I was quite aware of what I meant to an audience. Yeah, I knew that I was people's fantasy. But it didn't affect me, it didn't make me feel like I was beautiful. I just felt great because people liked me ... and I needed that love. I went through a childhood in which I was missing a lot of that love."

Provocative ads for **Flesh** asked, "Can a boy be too attractive?," and featured Joe's naked upper-half while hinting that his lower-half was similarly unattired. The sexual dimension to his appeal can hardly be underestimated; it's just so relentlessly pervasive.

By trade, his character in **Flesh** is willing to be had by either sex, and that willingness to allow himself to be admired is the primary reason the actor attained devotion from a gay audience, but there's more to it than even that. His affectless manner and his laid-back personality created a sexually ambiguous canvas of flesh and muscle on which every assorted fantasy from every assorted audience member could find expression and meaning. His was a beauty devoid of ego. His was a sexuality without regard for puritanical sexual mores.

Though male nudity was not a new thing for the underground film, or for Andy Warhol and Paul Morrissey, it was still quite daring and controversial as far as Hollywood/mainstream theatrical exhibition was concerned.

The Brits had offered teenaged Leonard Whiting's shapely white buns in **Franco Zeffirelli's Romeo and Juliet** (1968), and Alan Bates and Oliver Reed would wrestle naked in a grunting exhibition of their manhood in Ken Russell's **Women In Love** (1969), while **Midnight Cowboy** (1969), which was awarded an X rating presumably for sexual "content," managed only a flash of Jon Voight's doughy ass.

If there is anything revolutionary about Joe Dallesandro's full-frontal nudity in **Flesh**, and there is, it's how completely casually it's presented. Joe is so utterly un-self-conscious about being naked on screen that he even puts the viewer at ease. He challenges the presumed erotic charge of seeing a gorgeous guy naked by transforming his flesh into an aesthetic appreciation of the male body as a thing of beauty, as a thing worthy of art.

After Dark magazine asked a 19-year old Joe: "In **Flesh**, you probably spend more time wearing less than any actor in any other movie shown for public consumption. Did you have any trouble overcoming self-consciousness about this?"

"No." End of interview.

In comparison with **Midnight Cowboy** (1969), which managed to nab a Best Picture Oscar (the first and only X-rated film to do so), **Flesh** is far and away the better film.

It would eventually gross in excess of $2,000,000, with that figure considerably due to an unprecedented reaction to the film in West Germany.

Before Germany, though, there was Great Britain.

Flesh began its exclusive run in London at a theatre called The Open Space on January 15, 1970. Reviews of the film were mostly negative, with critics declaring it a bore.

"During the making of **Flesh**, Mr. Warhol was shot by a lady who was said to have taken extreme exception to his films. And though this is obviously going too far (happily Mr. Warhol survived the incident), it is easy to see what got on her nerves," reported a British paper in tabloid style, with characteristic distortion of the facts. "The artlessness with which this director surrounds himself carefully prevents us from caring. Beautiful people? Well, there is always Joe d'Allesandro's body, if you go for that kind of beauty."

Paul Morrissey could not have been pleased.

Apparently, neither were the Metropolitan Police, who raided the Open Space on February 3rd three minutes before the film ended, shut it down, seized the print, the projector, all the sound equipment, detained and questioned members of the audience, and confiscated the theatre's membership book and files of correspondence while invoking the "Obscene Publication Act."

The reaction from the public, mirrored in the juicy headlines of the press, caught law enforcement by surprise. Within a couple of days, the police admitted that they didn't have a warrant under the obscenity act, but were considering a Common Law charge of "debauching and corrupting public morals."

By week's end, in the bare face of allusions to the Nazi's burning Magnus Hirschfeld's Institute of Sexology in 1933, the "official" reason for the seizure was the question of whether the Open Space had proper licensure to exhibit motion pictures. It was technically a theatre, not a cinema. A week later, given the fact that the Director of Public Prosecutions had said he would not pursue an obscenity case, the issue became one of "fire code violations."

As the story gained more and more exposure in the press and the details of the film's content were disseminated, the case for blatant government censorship—no matter what the diluted charge—took hold. A Member of Parliament rose in the House of Commons and expressed his "greatest exception to being told what I may or may not see by some half-educated bigot at Scotland Yard who is answerable to no one for decisions of this kind."

Scotland Yard replied by saying, "We aren't zombies," and further stated that the call to action was made by a local precinct captain.

Parliament, meanwhile, was preparing to debate this latest assault on civil rights. The debate would become the loudest and most vociferous outcry over a common practice of club raids that numbered fifty or sixty annually.

Coming just weeks after a few erotic lithographs done by John Lennon were nabbed by coppers at the London Arts Gallery, the attack on **Flesh** effectively spawned a national debate on censorship hashed out in newspapers from city to college, on street corners and television, and over scones and tea.

Britons have never been renowned for their tolerance, particularly toward homosexuality, but **Flesh** turned out to be a "dirty" movie that wasn't even very dirty. "It's clear that those concerned in making the film had a real knowledge of the world of the male prostitute, whereas those concerned in making **Midnight Cowboy**, which has almost the same theme, did not," wrote Paul Overy in *New Society* a month and a half after the seizure.

In late February, 1970, Morrissey went to London to join Warhol's British distributor, Jimmy Vaughan, in defending the film. They met with John Trevelyan, director of the British Board of Film Censors, who quickly came out in support of the Open Space Theatre, as well as the film, and was almost apologetic about the embarrassing situation. Morrissey said people should be much more offended by all the violence in movies than all the silly sex.

Still, a cold wind was blowing through the United Kingdom and the University of Edinburgh announced it was canceling its proposed showing of **Flesh** because visiting police advised that even if the film wasn't prosecuted in London there was a very real possibility it would be prosecuted in Edinburgh, with said prosecution extending to the person or persons who knowingly allowed the film to be shown.

Twenty students responded by locking themselves inside the University's theatre to protest the cancellation. Earlier the same day, the film was being shown to a large audience at a main lecture hall when word got out that the cops were coming and the film was switched off. A local councilman announced to the press that he would seek the expulsion of every student who attended the screening. The "barricaded" students were finally persuaded out of the theatre after a two hour vigil.

Back in the States, ads for **Flesh** cried, "Banned in Swinging London," and at the 55th Street Playhouse in New York City where the film was about to make a triumphant return engagement due to all the overseas press, the theatre announced that "all persons with British Passports will be admitted free."

With Trevelyan in open support of the film (he called it "innocent and honest") and the public outcry at last silencing the police who had run out of reasons—moral or otherwise—to hold the print any longer, **Flesh** was finally returned to The Open Space on March 10, where it finished its successful and sporadic run.

Warhol had become a rallying figure for the college set—the film's most likely and intended audience—and **The Chelsea Girls** (which had previously run a full year at an art house) and **Lonesome Cowboys** opened up in London a few weeks after the **Flesh** debacle.

So why had the police allowed the film to play for three weeks before they raided the cinema? Just what prompted this particular raid at this particular time?

Joe says he knows the answer.

Behind the "complaint of a general nature" that the Chief Superintendent admitted set the whole affair into motion was something either far less or far more insidious: marketing.

"Jimmy Vaughan had some of his friends complain to the cops," says Joe with a big smile. "It was a set-up."

A set-up by the enterprising British distributor that even Paul and Joe didn't know about until after the whole thing played out and they were promoting the film in Germany.

"Paul was pissed when he found out. We had such good press going into England because we came in not as underground films, but as legitimate films, and Paul's first reaction to the censorship thing was that it negated what we were trying to do, which was find a wider audience."

Vaughan finally let the cat out of the bag, says Joe, "because it was just too sweet a thing not to tell anybody. Even I thought in the back of my mind that something was going on, though, because Jimmy Vaughan seemed too fucking happy. He was too much in control."

Despite the wishy-washy reviews, the film's rise to cause célèbre brought it publicity even Andy Warhol wouldn't have been willing to pay for, and the publicity paid off at the box office.

Officially, Morrissey explained to *The Times*, "A strong reaction is better than these reviews—'a not-too-well-made, but nice film.' I do think it should have produced a little more reaction. But it was made for a popular audience, and doesn't give critics much to talk about."

In the end, he could have cared less. Morrissey had finally come around and realized the beauty of what had been foisted on his movie, enough to play up the irony of his own politics when he told *The Sunday Times* that "I believe in censorship. That way you don't get so many assassinations."

Without intending to, **Flesh** figured in a cultural debate in Great Britain whose verdict was being heard: Kenneth Anger's **Scorpio Rising** and Jean Luc-Godard's **Week-End**, both ripe for "obscenity" charges, received certificates and played without incident.

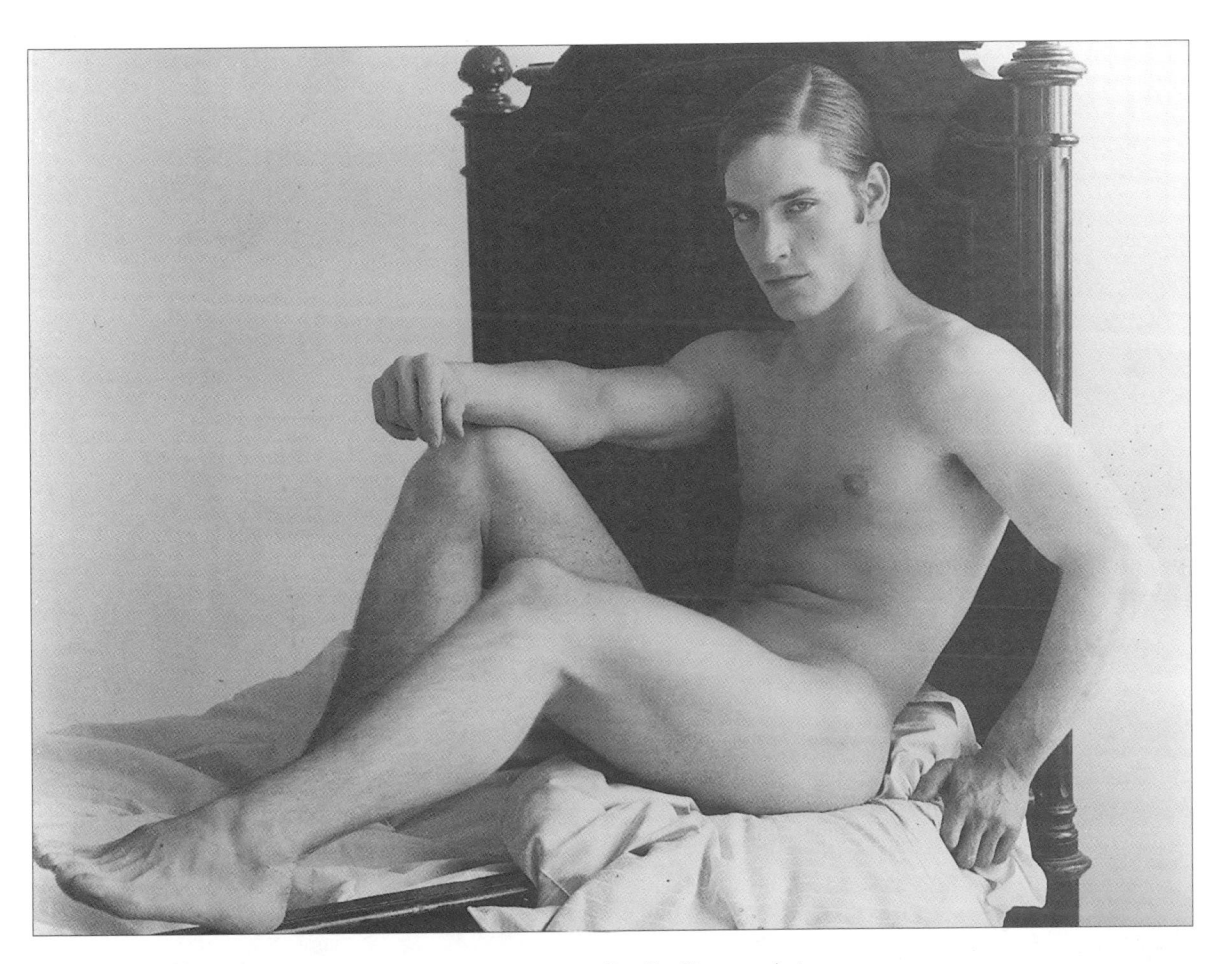

A sultry Joe Dallesandro selling **Flesh** in Europe, two years after the film was shot.

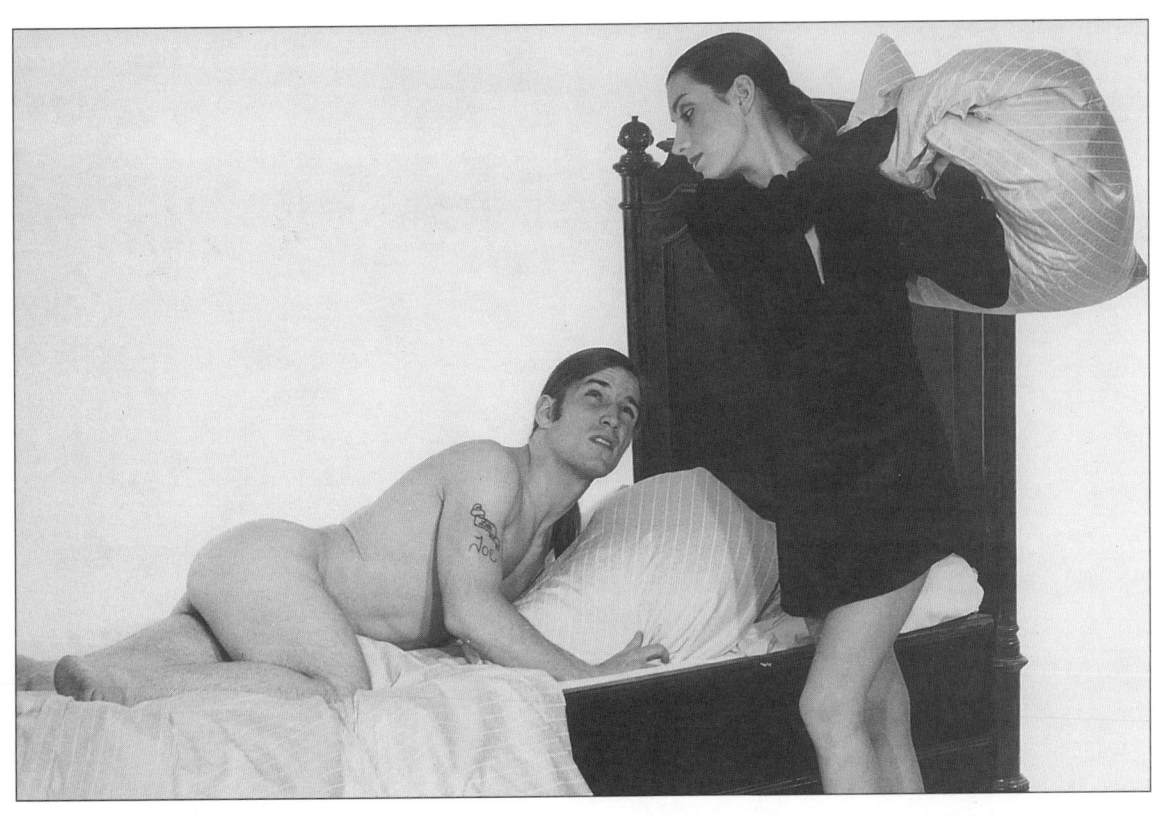

Geraldine Smith re-enacts her assault on her husband for German publicity cameras / Courtesy Joe Dallesandro

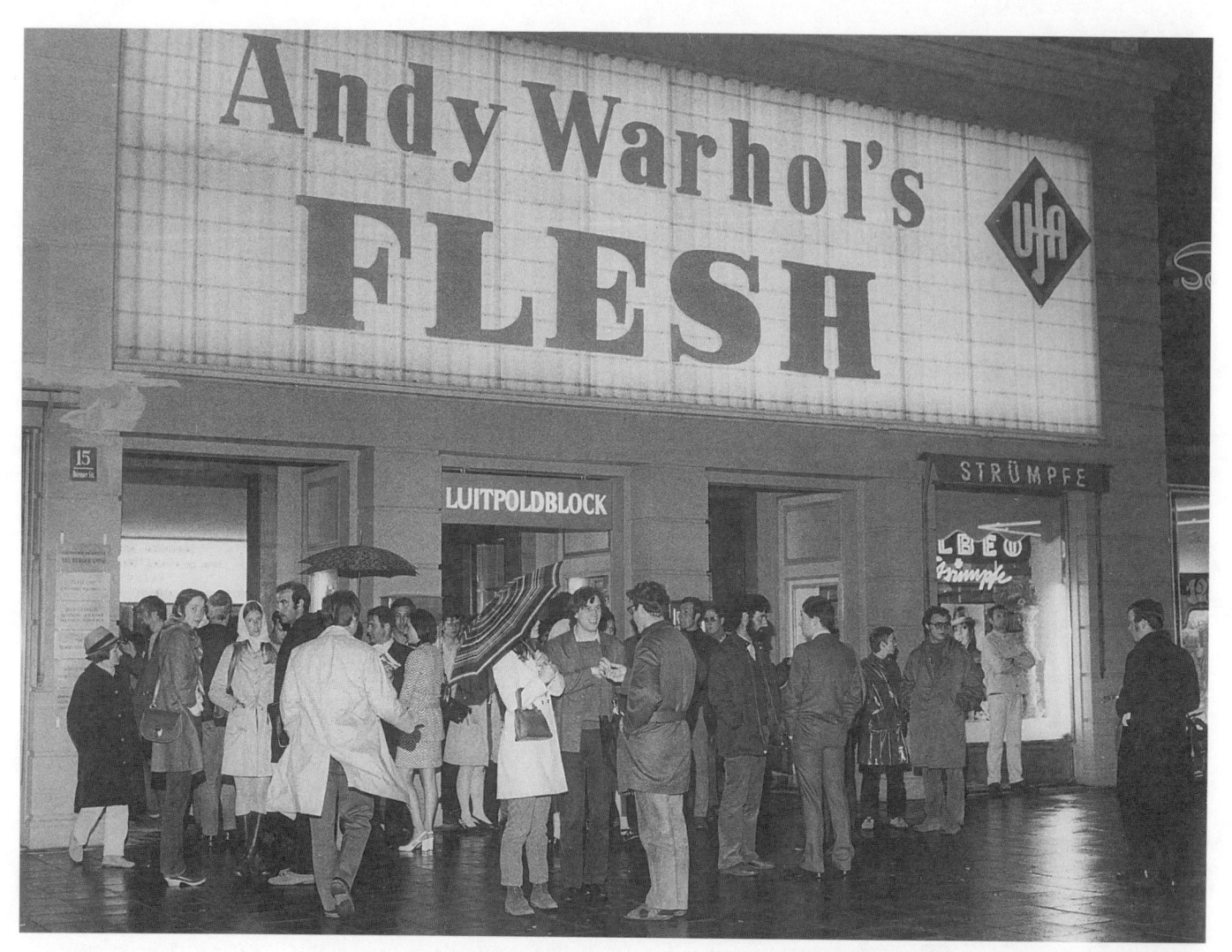

Courtesy Joe Dallesandro

German lobby display/Courtesy Joe Dallesandro

86

In June of 1970, the Brit-conquering Jimmy Vaughan sealed a deal with one of West Germany's biggest distributors, Constantin, to enjoy the distinction of booking the first American "underground" film into mainstream cinemas across the nation.

Flesh was greeted in Germany with a warmth and respect and critical reception simply unprecedented for a film so firmly identified as an art film. It played to sold out audiences at the Astor in Berlin for months (Joe has got a copy in his scrapbook of an ad heralding the 11th smash week) and continued to do extraordinarily well as word-of-mouth spread.

Vaughan had brought Morrissey, Geraldine Smith, Jane Forth (upcoming star of **Trash**), and Joe Dallesandro with him for a star-studded tour through Germany that Joe will never forget.

They were fêted at lavish hotels, assigned a personal photographer, granted tours of all the major cities and castles and sights, given columns of space in local newspapers, and granted royalty status at film festivals where **Flesh** repeatedly won accolades and Joe won Best Actor.

For once, they truly were Superstars.

"That was amazing," says Joe, shaking his head in disbelief. "I would have loved to have gotten even half that kind of reception back in the States, but it never happened. That was a real stroke for me. And what was nice about it was that the Germans were kind of like the old movie studios who protected their stable of stars. Everything was organized down to the minute. They never tired you, because they had everything so well planned. You'd get off the plane and you'd have a car waiting there and they'd take you to the hotel. Then you'd freshen up and go to the press conference—and we would do several cities sometimes in a single day, if they were close—and the fact that we didn't feel drained had nothing to do with the thrill of it all, but simply because they were so attentive. At the press conferences, they had just so much time allotted and only so many questions, and certain questions couldn't even be asked. They prepped everyone there. They took thousands of photographs of us on our little vacation tour through the castles. The fortune they must have spent on the photographer who went with us and took photographs all day!"

Flesh was nothing short of a phenomenon in Germany, where it was available in both English and dubbed versions. Joe told a British newspaperman that the only thing they added in "was some extra heavy breathing." Over 3,000,000 people went to see it at the nation's theatres—setting box-office records in several—and it ended up one of the top five moneymakers of 1970.

Constantin took options out on **I, A Man**, **Lonesome Cowboys**, and **Blue Movie**. Germany was hooked.

Neighboring Italy wasn't nearly so receptive. Joe recalls that they couldn't find a distributor there because the Italians claimed they didn't have an audience for that kind of film. When it finally did show up years later, it was edited for content. (Switzerland, too, banned the film after a single screening.)

On their triumphant return home, the stars stopped off in London. Joe and company met again with British Board of Film Censors' John Trevelyan for a chat ("He was a real fan," says Joe), a photo opportunity, and a marketing push for Britain to follow Germany and book the film as if it was Hollywood product.

"It was really an amazing thing that this film was such a huge success and yet could be made so quickly and so economically," says Morrissey. "Yet I wouldn't have been able to make it probably if I hadn't been paying attention to all the experiments that I'd been making for Andy over all those years. I mean, I was able to learn patterns of improvisation between certain types of actors, because I kept staging these things in these experiments and I could see what might work and what might not work. It was a great learning experience for me. I think Andy learned nothing, except that he realized there could be success and he didn't have to push the button anymore."

Looking back on **Flesh** today, Joe isn't entirely satisfied.

"Why go to the trouble of making the movie if nobody can hear the dialogue because the sound is so fucking awful? When I look at a film like **My Own Private Idaho**—a film I really admire—I think, we could have done that kind of film. But we didn't. We had that potential, but much of it was wasted. I loved the section of **Idaho** when the hustlers tell their real-life stories directly to the camera. That was brilliant. I think my portrayal in **Flesh** was more fantasy than real."

Yet when I ask Joe which of all of his films he's most proud of, the answer comes with just a little bit of hesitation and characteristic ambivalence.

"I've said it for years, and I've got to come to terms with it. It's kind of sad, because it's a film that I don't really want to like, but I've got to say **Flesh**. It was my first lead and it got so much attention and was talked about all over the world, but, in a way, it has caused me more dilemma and more pain and more happiness than any performance I've ever given. The happiness comes from the tremendous way people responded to it and from all the opportunities it gave me to see the world and launch my career. But it's also caused me pain because of the way people have perceived it as something that I wasn't. I was an actor playing a part—a kid who knew about the life but was so much more than that."

It was, of course, Joe's **Flesh** that audiences came to see. It really is his movie, and as ambivalent as he is about the film, he is also understandably a little possessive.

"First of all, this was supposed to be a movie about boxing and Paul took this little story about hustling that I'd told him and made it into a movie he wanted to do with the drag queens. I participated in anything he ever asked me to do. I'd show up and the drag queens are there and I'd say, 'I'm fine with it, let's do it.' 'Cause me and Paul had such great rapport. Anything he asked me to do I would do. We could fight about stuff, but that was him training me not to fight, teaching me to verbalize. Because when I sat down with him, he'd tell me that I really had a way of telling a story. I could convince him of just about anything I wanted to talk about, make it seem as if what I was saying was legitimate and that there was a damned good reason I was feeling a particular way. In the end, I was in charge. It was my idea. It was my story. It was my film. The only thing I allowed him to do was put drag queens in it."

In April of 1969, Andy announced his next film project would be the movie adaptation of *Los Angeles Times'* writer John Hallowell's unpublished book *The Truth Game*, which followed a young reporter on his beat among the stars.

"My book ranges from an interview with Barbara Streisand to studies of a male hustler and dirty movies," said the author. "It might be subtitled, 'The Stars and the Gutter.' Naturally, Andy will focus on the gutter."

Both the book and the film were to be released simultaneously in September. Warhol and Morrissey had prepared a treatment and altered the story to chronicle the exploits of an off-Broadway actress (Candy Darling) who has various encounters with a hustler (Joe), a major movie star (they hoped to find one to play herself), and Viva and the Factory Regulars.

In late May of '69, Warhol, Morrissey, Jed Johnson, Geraldine Smith and Joe flew out to Los Angeles to schmooze (while staying at the Beverly Wilshire) and try to get an initially interested Columbia Pictures to bankroll the film. The project never got off the ground, even after the proposed $100,000 undertaking was announced in the trades as being financed by Leslie Caron's new hubby, Michael Loughlin, and was to include cameos by Caron, Clint Eastwood, Natalie Wood and Troy Donahue. Joe told the German press that Rita Hayworth was set to star.

Andy was also mulling around the idea of filming couples, threesomes, and even sextets having sex for a film called **Orgy**. (The **Blue Movie** twosome was as close as he got.) And he told *Playboy* in late 1969 that he was also interested in doing a television series for NBC.

"In New York, apartments have a channel five which allows you to watch anybody who enters the front door. That will be my show: people walking past the camera. We'll call it **Nothing Special**."

(Who ever said Andy had run out of good ideas? He also toyed with doing a Civil War costume picture starring his players.)

No wonder Paul was making the movies.

When Andy came back from the hospital, a wall was built in front of the elevator at the Factory for security reasons, so that visitors couldn't see the layout of the room—where everybody was—when they stepped off, and then they could be ushered into designated areas after passing snuff with the guy at the first desk. Paul Morrissey was strategically moved to Andy's old desk; jokes Joe, "so that they would see Paul first and shoot him."

VIDEO REPLAY: With Joe on screen in every scene of the film, I'd really suggest you simply rewind the tape and watch the whole thing again. But if I'm going to choose a moment, I'd choose a close-up of Joe's profile during the scene in which the elderly artist is having him pose as a runner. There is a focused intensity on Joe's face—his skin is luminous—and when he hears the artist say, "And you're gonna take off!," he tenses and moves almost imperceptibly forward as if he really hears the runner's start and is about to launch his muscles into motion. In that tiny action, Joe Dallesandro demonstrates the greatest truth in the art of acting and reacting: he's living the moment.

trash

(1970)

"People thought I had a lot of power at the Factory, but I had none. Basically, I was the fucking doorman. I was the doorman that made them a lot of money."

—*Joe Dallesandro*

With JOE DALLESANDRO AS JOE SMITH, Holly Woodlawn (Holly Santiago), Jane Forth (Jane), Bruce Pecheur (Jane's Husband), Michael Sklar (Mr. Michaels, the Welfare Investigator), Geri Miller (Go-Go Dancer), Andrea Feldman (Rich Girl), Johnny Putnam (Boy from Yonkers), Diane Podlewski (Holly's Sister), Bob Dallesandro (Guy on Street). Directed by Paul Morrissey. 103 minutes

During Warhol, Morrissey, and Joe's trip to California in the summer of 1969 to see if they could hook Columbia Pictures into backing a project, the New Yorkers were invited to a Hollywood soirée thrown by Jane Fonda and friends. The group also went to a screening of **Easy Rider** (1969), which Paul Morrissey disliked.

He probably disliked it even more when he saw how well it was doing at the box-office. Warhol certainly did. He knew that the Factory could do the subject proper justice.

"We really hate all that hippy, flower-power, love-generation stuff," explained Morrissey to the British press. "Just look at that **Woodstock** picture. 'Three days of love and peace,' they said. Like hell. It was like the Nuremberg rally, with drugs."

If **Flesh** was Morrissey's humorous take on the peddling of skin, on the objectification of the human body in an era of proclaimed sexual revolution, then **Drug Trash** (the original title) was going to be his scathing tragicomedy on the human degradation of surrendering to the drug culture.

And Joe was towing the party line, telling *Coast FM & Fine Arts* in 1971: "Well, we just got very tired of looking at stuff like **Easy Rider** and **Woodstock**. Dope is sick. People who are on drugs don't say anything related to real life because they're not really living. We're weary of seeing drugs glamorized. Getting high is just not too cool. There's nothing at all positive about dope in **Trash**." (With pop-cultural irony, the film would open in New York the very next day after Janis Joplin's notorious heroin overdose death.)

Trash, as the title eventually became, was shot mostly on Saturday afternoons over three weekends in October, 1969, with a final scene picked up on a Saturday the following spring. Thanks to its director it came with a craftily conservative agenda.

Morrissey imagined telling the story of a couple living in utmost squalor who dream of one day getting on welfare; it's the life-goal to which they aspire. The young man would be a junkie and the woman would collect trash from the neighborhood and sell it to make ends meet. The director certainly had a lot of raw experience on the subject upon which to draw; consider his stint working in a social services office.

One of the things that bugged Morrissey about **Easy Rider**'s take on the drug culture was the age of the characters. "It really pissed him off, because he saw these older guys going through their problems with drugs, and basically, they should have been over all that at their age," says Joe. "They should have been done with their drug and hippie thing. It was too obviously a stupid thing to be messing around with. It was all right to see kids doing it, though. Which ties right in with Paul's desire to work with so many young actors. Instead of having some middle-aged actor 'acting' it, you take some young kid off the street who pretty much is going through that problem, at least dealing with it in some real way, and then you have them play the role. That's who it's about, after all."

For the junkie, Morrissey knew he was going to star Joe. Following the logic just given, not only was Joe still quite a young man, and not only was he the Factory's newest shining superstar, but he had also known the world he was about to evoke on screen.

For the girlfriend, Morrissey's casting choice was among the most unusual he'd ever made. Not because he was about to cast the lead female role in his film with a guy (he'd done comparable), but because he cast her without ever meeting her.

He read about her.

Holly Woodlawn was the name Harold Danhaki adopted somewhere along the way between being born in Puerto Rico, taking flight to Manhattan at age 15—where life on the streets eventually led to Candy Darling, Jackie Curtis, hormone shots, and hanging around Max's Kansas City (the Schwab's of Warhol's "Hollyweird" Factory)—and doing a bizarre little play that caught the attention of a local underground newspaper. With characteristic gusto, Holly Woodlawn told the paper that she was a Warhol Superstar.

Andy was nervous when he saw the piece (remember he'd already had a major run-in with a woman who claimed she was part of his clan), but Morrissey was positively struck by the brazen personality he sensed coming off the interview page.

Holly Woodlawn, whoever she was, was his Holly Santiago. It was the first and only time this director known for his acute casting eye and ability to size up personalities cast a major role without ever having met his star.

The shooting was done in the basement of the East Village brownstone where Morrissey lived, along with Joe and his girlfriend Terry. A few ratty trinkets half-resembling furniture were thrown in front of the lights. That first afternoon, Holly met her director, her quiet, unassuming and indecipherable co-star, and the simple method behind their madness: this is the set-up, now go and do it.

Holly was paid $25 a day for her few hours work and most scenes were shot in one or two takes. Only the final scene, all but ruined by the artifice of actor Michael Sklar as a shoe-fetishist Welfare Investigator, took five or six takes, because Sklar kept coming up with more ideas about what he wanted to say.

Famously, the film—like **Flesh**—opens with a naked

With Holly Woodlawn and Jane Forth. Photographed by Jack Mitchell / Courtesy Joe Dallesandro.

shot of Joe Dallesandro, this time a close-up on his blemished behind as stripper Geri Miller tries to jump-start him for action up front. Joe, with his hair now grown down to his shoulders, couldn't be less interested. It's dope that Joe needs to get off. His penis looms lifeless as a third character in the scene. Geri, who's already tried strip-dancing for him and keeps looking down at his limp dick, knows the dope is responsible and encouragingly suggests that sex gets her high.

Joe's half-closed eyes open up with interest. "Sex gets you high?" he inquires. "What kind of high is it?"

"A beautiful high," Geri tells him.

"Is it really? I never got high."

"When you came," she asks, "wasn't it so beautiful that you just...?"

"No," Joe answers without a beat, "it was over." His voice trails off as he realizes he can't use this particular bit of would-be inspiration. Geri doesn't have too many other tricks to try on him either. She tells him at last that she'll give him some money if he can make it with her, so she lies down, he lazily climbs on top, and after a few short moments: "Nothing's happening."

Cut to a shot of Joe picking at his buttcheek in boredom as Geri asks, "Does politics turn you on?"

Back home, Joe arrives to find his girlfriend Holly in not such a good mood. With buck teeth and scraggly hair and more blue eyeshadow than the entire decade can own up to as fashionable, she tells her dopey live-in, "You're startin' to look like a bum." Then she pauses to add another descriptive term that heart-winningly reveals a wickedly natural sense of humor: "… a big juicy bum."

Holly wants to rob the poor box at the local church, or at the very least go pick up some furniture she saw. "I found it out front of a church, so you know it's gotta be good. You know these nuns, they don't use nothin' cheap."

But junkie Joe is too tired and passes out on her bed, leading her into a tirade during which she shoves him off onto the floor. He's nothin' but a "fucking mooch!"

Basically, the film chronicles the story of a girl named Holly and a boy named Joe who live in a seedy Lower East Side apartment decorated with other people's refuse. "Just because people throw it out and don't have any use for it doesn't mean it's garbage," explains Holly. She might as well be talking about herself and Joe.

Holly has a mission: to get on welfare, something she feels she's owed and deserves. It would also make things easier for her and Joe, but first she's got to try and convince him to break his dope habit, which has left him completely impotent and caused her to seek sexual encounters right under his nose.

Holly searches for household furnishings in the streets to accommodate her pregnant sister's impending stay (a drawer is to serve as a bassinet) and then decides she'll fake her own pregnancy to obtain the welfare money. Joe tries to rob a whining young socialite who tells pornographic personal stories, wants him to partake in a rape fantasy, and hasn't the slightest interest as the camera forces us to watch him stick a needle in his vein and inject his dope.

Trash is really not so much Joe's film as it is Holly Woodlawn's. For a full account of the fascinating and funny and certifiably freaky story of Holly's life, you can do no better than to go to the source and read her autobiography *A Low Life in High Heels* (St. Martin's Press, 1991), which she put together with the help of Jeff Copeland. If books can talk, and occasionally they can, then this one has a voice all of its own.

She truly gives an Oscar-caliber performance, combining gutsy, no-holds barred explosions of rage with scenes that are tender, touching, and very funny. No less than Hollywood Golden Age director George Cukor personally lobbied for her nomination as Best Actress for the 1970 Academy Awards, though there was some understandable confusion about the category in which she properly belonged. (John Lithgow, Linda Hunt, and Jaye Davidson had yet to be consulted.) Morrissey rushed the film to the West Coast for its qualifying run in Los Angeles the week of Christmas, 1969.

Some folks thought he was joking, but he wasn't, and shouldn't have been either.

Of his detractors, the director told *The Hollywood Reporter*, "People like to think our films are so peculiar that they're not worth talking about in any context. They never compare our films to others. And our films are really the Hollywood type … we have our stars and we find vehicles for them. Our actors are so good and we like them so much, we subjugate ourselves for them. That's why we're in Hollywood—to attract a little attention for our actors."

A great deal of attention was paid to Holly's infamous masturbation-with-a-beer bottle scene. It's often unfairly played up in print to exploit the idea as merely degenerate movie madness, when, in fact, it comes as a poignant and tragicomic event.

Joe is beyond arousal, of course, so, "why dontcha just use the beer bottle," and Holly responds almost as if this bizarre suggestion had been made on other occasions: "You're right, if I have to, I have to." The notorious notion belonged to Morrissey, who came up with the idea between takes after Joe came back from one of his regular runs to the grocery store to pick up beer for Holly.

The scene that ensues may just be her equivalent of Divine-eats-dog-shit in the telling, but it's a whole different affair when you see it played out on screen. As she awkwardly tries to get off, Holly's voice is pleading, resigned, yet hopeful ("you're better than that beer bottle, Joe" and "oh, God, I want welfare!"), and she reaches out to touch Joe as he lies on the floor below her bed. Morrissey's camera pans in close-up to catch him gently holding her hand amidst all the huffing and puffing—Joe even asks her how she's comin'—and then a close-up on Joe's face reveals a watery, perhaps tearful eye, whether mustered for the scene or simply the result of the lighting hardly matters, because a peculiarly emotional moment has been captured.

Conversely, the scene where Holly brings home and tries to seduce a high school senior who's come along for drugs exhibits her extraordinary gifts as a comedienne. The kid with the mop-top hair, lamb-chop sideburns, and wire glasses is played by Johnny Putnam, Holly's 16-year old "boyfriend" of the time. He came down to the set to watch filming and Morrissey put him in the scene.

Holly is absolutely lascivious next to Johnny, making slurping sounds when she asks him if he likes blow-jobs, and it's even funnier when you know they're a real life couple. She's all over him, touching him, cuddling up against him and quizzing him about all sorts of things. Naturally, she's *very* interested in what he does for sex at his school, and when he says the girls are loose, she moves in tight and tells him with all of her radically seductive powers that, "I'm loose...I'm *very* loose...Are you loose?...Do you wanna get loose?"

He's really there just for the dope, though, and while she runs to another apartment to get it, a sleepy-faced Joe, who'd been sweeping up the place at the beginning of the scene only to watch his girlfriend drool all over this young squirt, sizes the kid up by describing him as "a drug-taking, hippie-groupie-type person."

"Yeah, well, we don't call ourselves that," says Johnny with a smirk.

"*We* call you that," throws back Joe.

When Holly returns, she's got a horse needle in her hand and a needle is precisely what the kid didn't want. Still, she manages to coax him into dropping his pants by reasoning with him in her lust-crazed logic: "No needle ... it's like a penicillin shot."

Morrissey's druggy camerawork, which consists of fluid and fuzzy shots that amble across the actors in claustrophobic pans, adds immeasurably to the delightfully weird characters, as Holly looks away and finally jabs the needle in Johnny's butt and he quickly collapses onto the floor with his pants down around his ankles.

Providing yet another of the brilliant little verbal gems that Morrissey's actors consistently seem to come up with while in the heat of the moment, Holly is heard (but not seen, because she's out-of-frame) asking Johnny to give her his glasses, and then we hear her ask of the drug-tripping naked boy she's ravishing in front of her boyfriend, "You're blind, you know that? Are you near-sighted or far-sighted?" You don't even have to see her doing it to find the unexpected image in your mind's eye of her taking the time to look through his glasses funny. It's so completely out of left-field that there's no way in hell a screenwriter would have thought to have included it.

Morrissey gives Holly all the credit for the performance she gave in his film. "At the end of the day," the director told me, "I'd simply say to her, 'Thanks, see you next week.'"

Writer Tom Wommack said, "Her performance would make any Tennessee Williams' heroine nervous."

What works particularly nicely in the film is the underlying sweetness between Holly and Joe that can be found just beneath all the surface cutting and screeching. In the very first scene when she throws him off her bed and screams names at him, she's still playing softly with his hair and feeling bad about the fact that he's unconscious.

As much as Holly dominates the screen, however, this is not to suggest that Joe has been completely overlooked. Once again playing the boy whom everyone wants to fuck, this time he is also the boy who simply cannot fuck and doesn't really give a fuck about not being able to fuck. His dazed, glassy-eyed Joe is played so naturally, so without mannerism or pretension, that the lack of artifice was easily mistaken for something else, such as real drug use. (More on that in a bit.)

Pauline Kael would write of him in **Trash**: "He isn't just impotent; he's barely alive." She's right. But Kael didn't mean it as a compliment, thinking the film too caught up in its own self-conscious lethargy. "What is sometimes called decadence may be just lack of energy." Director George Cukor, no less, disagreed, saying, "he really made me understand, more than any other film, what a drug addict was."

"Nobody gives him credit," says his co-star Holly Woodlawn today. "I love him. I adore him. I think he's a really good actor."

Joe's quiet, nearly buried responses to those around him are constant sources of deadpan humor: when caught trying to burgle the house of a young newlywed (Jane Forth), he tells her he was "just visiting ... just coming to see what there was here that I could use at my house," and his classic attempt to talk his way out of being caught by Holly with her pregnant sister ("I was just practicin', that's all, to see if I could do it") is inspired improvisation.

Sixteen year old Jane Forth, originally from Michigan

(Above) with Jane Forth and Bruce Pecheur (Below) with Geri Miller

and a friend of Warhol "business partner" Fred Hughes, looks like a painted porcelain doll, and even pursued a successful modeling career in New York. If her face, with its skin-tight black hair and Picasso-plucked eyebrows, wasn't enough to draw attention, then the voice that accompanied the Olive Oyl body would do it for sure. In the long tradition of affected vocalizers, Jane is second only to Andrea Feldman on the chalkboard scale.

Whiny, with a pinched-nose drawl of spurious nouveau riche, she was poised to be a Warhol superstar of the first magnitude. "Andy says not to bother learning to be an actress. Just be a star. It's easier that way," she'd tell the press in London.

Though Joe is an intruder in her lovely home in the movie, she berates him for picking a house that has no valuables (not even food, she says, because "we're on a diet"), then matter-of-factly asks him what he wants to do now, that he might as well stay, and inquires after details about his sexual crimes.

Joe is wholly uncomfortable with being put into yet another sexual situation, not to mention the class clash, as Jane coyly asks if he could rape someone on *that* couch— indicating the one in her living room. She actually implores him to engage in her rape fantasy, but Joe nervously backs off. He's not up to this.

When her husband (Bruce Pecheur) suddenly comes home, Jane decides she'll have Joe some other way. She has him strip down for her in the bathroom, making comments on his anatomy as he does ("My, you're rather large, hmmm"), then sits on top of the closed toilet watching him as he shaves and bathes. The whole time, though, she tells him a graphic story about the first time she ever saw a man's penis, then asks Joe if he gives good rim jobs, if he's ever slept with boys, and if he'd like to sleep with both her and her husband. She's even planning a facial and a haircut for him, despite the fact that after he's bathed and shaved off the scruffy little beard he was growing, Joe's skin transforms to lucent near-perfection and his face defines "handsome."

When her husband screams at her to watch Joe shoot up (as we must, in agonizing close-ups), Jane could care less. Though still naked, this isn't the Joe she was looking forward to having anymore. He's now her berating husband's life-lesson to her, so she just goes on gibbering about totally unrelated things while Joe collapses into a stupor.

What's amazing about Forth's performance is its absolute consistency, its complete single-mindedness (and she was only 16!). When she brings Joe his needle and considers the possibility of hepatitis if it isn't clean, she asks rhetorically, "You know what that would look like to the neighbors?" Later, during Joe's dropping out, her husband warns that "OD'ing goes to stop breathing."

"Then what happens?" she wonders. "Oh my, do you think we should draw the shades?"

Joe is in an absolute daze, his entire body limp as a rag doll and jarringly shot by Morrissey from an atypical overhead angle which has been read as invoking Christ-figure metaphors. Jane and Bruce argue and Bruce makes her pick up the nude junkie and throw him out the front door, something she objects to between funny drones about egg facials and her brother in Vietnam sending them a kangaroo with a beer bottle opener on top of it. (On the subject of brothers, during an early scene in the film on the streets at dusk, Joe talks briefly to his real-life brother Bob, whose face is never fully seen.)

Joe's bizarre dichotomy as sexless sextoy is further explored when he's approached in silhouette by an actress whose voice prophetically precedes her. She wants some "Lucy in the Sky with Diamonds," and she wants it now. She has "$20," she says, but when she gives it to Joe it's only a buck. He better keep it, she tells him, and by the way, has he seen her grandfather and would he like to see all the toys she's got with her?

"You're weird," Joe tells her.

"Yeah, well when you take LSD, you have to be weird," she expertly improvises.

She is Andrea (An-DRAY-ah) Feldman, aka Andrea Whips Feldman, aka Andrea Whips Warhol, and for the next few minutes, she'll turn **Trash** into her movie and her movie alone.

It is impossible not to wonder where the hell she hails from, because she is as eccentric a creation as one can imagine. Her vocal pattern has to be heard to be appreciated; it comes in a lilting, sing-song, completely affected and bizarre and thereby utterly fascinating style.

With frightening blond hair, deathly white skin, pug nose, and black smears of eyeshadow, she's a sight to behold—and a sound to hear. Joe's smart enough to just sit there and let her go, occasionally offering a comment or two about how really nice a person she is. He's preparing to shoot up in her apartment and she's supposed to be a "rich girl," but the wealth is apparently part of her dementia.

In typical Warhol/Morrissey fashion, her character may be tawdry as all hell, but she's also absolutely infatuated with wealth, social strata, and the idles of the upper class. During her free-association sing-song, she displays "cards from my mother saying, 'get better fast, because compared to you everyone else looks sick. Keep smiling. All my love, Mommy.'" She then relates a rambling story about her girlfriend who tells her "she's God," before at last settling down to watch Joe get off and suggesting, "Why don't you take off your unholy socks and take a shower."

Courtesy Joe Dallesandro

As in **Flesh**, Joe is immediately sized up as sexual prey.

"I hate to see what you have inside your pants," the rich girl says out of nowhere. "You've probably got crabs." When she matter-of-factly examines his pubes, she suddenly exclaims, "Oh, my God, I found a crab over there!" and gestures in disgust, all the while sounding as if she's delivering the punchline at a comedy club in the East Village.

Just as suddenly she gets up and says, "Wanna see me?," which must have brought groans of recognition to anyone who'd witnessed her act in the back room at Max's Kansas City, the neighborhood eatery near the Factory that served as the trendy hang-out for New York's coterie of musicians, actors, poets, and the Warhol gang. Andrea's sudden, piercing cries of "It's show time!" followed by her stripping off her top and dancing on the tables were often rewarded with her expulsion amidst a barrage of screamed profanities. (In *Popism*, Andy mentions a night she did this while Joe was there along with Jim Morrison and Jimi Hendrix.)

In the film, Andrea's bizarre behavior sends Joe into a fit of rage and he strips her of the rest of her clothes and attempts to rape her, something she protests in screams, but then seems terribly disappointed he can't pull off.

Sheepishly, Joe buckles up and tells her, "If you took dope you couldn't get a hard-on either."

"Sure I could," she says.

And you know, I believe her.

"I wish I wasn't a girl," she tells Joe at one point.

"What would you like to be?"

"I'd like to be a cock," she says. "One big cock."

Precisely what she'd like Joe to be. Precisely what everybody in the film wants Joe to be.

For Holly, at least, who bemoans her inability to "jerk him off" or anything, her love for Joe allows hope to spring eternal. The film's last line is actually the film's optimistic capper after all other dejection: "Joe, let me suck your cock."

"We're thinking of doing a movie in India," said Joe in an interview in 1970. "They've got jungles and palace ruins there. It'd be sort of a Tarzan movie, a jungle picture. We're also considering a remake of **The Blue Angel** where I play the Marlene Dietrich role. Then again we might not make it. We always talk about movies we don't make."

It's interesting that while **Trash** opens with titles spelled out in marquee lights that zip across the screen diagonally, music sampled from **Der Blaue Engel** (1930) plays on the soundtrack. The same music plays at the finale, too. There was lots of talk about the Factory doing a version of **The Blue Angel** with Joe playing the sexy nightclub performer and an actress—faded and famed or fresh from the Factory—playing the older woman ruined by her obsession with him.

It has been suggested that **Trash** is essentially that story, as Holly is stuck in her horrible situation in large part because of her dependency on Joe. But given that loose interpretation, **Heat** (1972) seems closer to the concept.

What I find most instructive here is the famed relationship of Dietrich with her director Josef von Sternberg, the man whose personal obsession with the actress resulted in him almost completely recreating her from slightly plump actress to extraordinary movie goddess. Not only did he see in her the makings of a star, but he pruned her, preened her, lit her, and taught her, and through this inspired cultivation came her own sharp understanding of what he was doing. She was a student of clay, but she became a practitioner of exotic glamour, shining like a perfectly cut gem. Through seven films they worked out their relationship and in every single one of them—no matter how successful or unsuccessful as drama—there remains a fascination that contributes to the exquisite tapestry of her seductive power over her mentor and certainly over us.

It is no mean stretch of the imagination that Joe Dallesandro might be considered Morrissey's Dietrich. The director caught a glimpse of natural beauty and charisma and charm and proceeded to cultivate it through seven films, each marking another point in their relationship. The sex object that was **Flesh** calls to mind the sex object that was **The Blue Angel** and the sour end that was **Dracula/Frankenstein** parallels the bitter irony that was **The Devil Is A Woman** (1935).

Like von Sternberg, Morrissey also appeared to control the behavior of the actor off the screen, too.

Even journalists noticed. When Joe was late for a particular interview in 1969, the reporter said the actor suddenly came running in and Morrissey, without so much as a "hello" to his delinquent protégé, turned to the writer and said, "This is Joe Dallesandro. He's sorry he's late."

One has to be careful about reading too much into events like these, because Morrissey loved to talk—Joe didn't—and was quite used to doing it for an equally reticent Andy Warhol.

No doubt, too, some of this is just good show business. A German newspaper noted that the director was ever-present with his star. "When Joe is asked how he feels and what he feels when he portrays the male prostitute (in **Flesh**), the superstar runs his thumb along the angle on the right side of his mouth, opens his mouth and the voice of Paul Morrissey is heard.

"'Joe feels nothing,' says Mr. Morrissey. 'Joe is a naive person, a simpleton. He only does what someone tells him to do. He has no relationship with what he does. He just does it.'

"Joe Dallesandro nods. No contradiction crosses his seamless face. The Valentino of the Underground is happy that he does not have to think about what he does."

Clearly, it's easier to be the guy who doesn't talk, only nods.

Warhol remembers hearing the director yell at Joe during the shooting of **Trash**, "Stop the Method moping—just talk! And whatever you do, don't smile unless you don't mean it!"

"A smile is a kind of surrender to fate," said Morrissey years later to professor Maurice Yacowar. "It eliminates any kind of tension. It implies acceptance and therefore a kind of commitment."

The control exercised by Morrissey included advice not to smile in public, either, as well as enforced admonitions not to smoke or drink in public. Joe says it was the latter edict that stifled his desire to go to any of the famed Warhol social outings.

"Because, shit, I was a kid. And I can't have a drink? Hell, then I don't want to go. My life wasn't over yet. I was still young."

Nevertheless, on many levels, he accepted the control because it seemed to bring discipline to his life, gave him a sense of direction. He wasn't going to easily forget all the good that had come into his life under Morrissey's tutelage.

"The reason it was all right with me," says Joe, "is that I was not a stupid person. When somebody gave me a piece of information, I'd go and find out if it was the truth or not before I'd buy into it. And 99% of anything Paul ever told me was the truth. He got the facts, he had an education, he was a bright man. I shared a lot of stories with him, it's true, and lots of that stuff went into the movies, but he shared a lot of stories with me, too, and he shared his films with me."

Joe was clearly Morrissey's Superstar now, even though the director would probably take exception to all this talk of "control" and "ownership." Whether it's a matter of reading into the relationship or not, the inescapable truth is that Paul made movies starring Joe and Joe starred in movies made by Paul.

Were other actors a little miffed because Dallesandro became so much the focus of the films?

"Not because I became the focus," says Joe, "but because people saw what Paul and I were trying to do with the films and they saw for the first time that people were going to see these movies in phenomenal numbers and they were getting a lot of good reviews. We were changing the attitude towards what our movies were."

"Today Hollywood is making movies about what it feels to be important issues," said Warhol to the press, "but we can do the same thing more quickly and more honestly...We care how a person is rather than *why* he is that way. We look for the same qualities that made a star in the 30's—superficial beauty, charm and personality."

Morrissey certainly would have agreed. But for him, outside of the Golden Age of Hollywood, the Italians were the world's master filmmakers and he has said that he saw **Trash** as the equivalent of an Italian comedy starring Anna Magnani.

Yeah, it was a comedy, but he had very definite and serious ideas about what he wanted the film to say and to that end Joe gives him a lot of credit.

"He portrayed us the way he wanted us to be, which is part of what a director does. We just carried the image."

Morrissey's style was to provide suggestions for a scene's story, never to dictate where it was to go. He felt that if a director's influence could be seen by the audience then he had failed.

"The director's only job is to say, 'say it louder' or 'say it softer,'" he told me.

Joe jokes that his mentor enjoyed being behind the

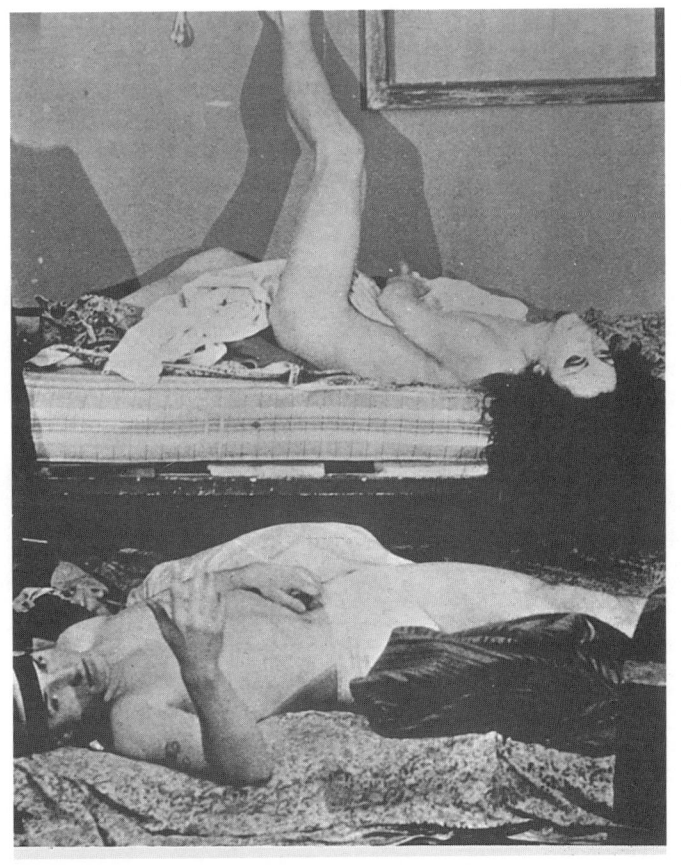

Holly's infamous beer bottle masturbation

camera, "but Paul would rather be me any day," adding, "with his brain, though, because he's so smart."

The film's entire anti-drug message is vocalized in a speech a frustrated Jane makes to an entirely unarousable Joe-in-the-tub: "God, junkies are never interested in anything! They don't want sex, they don't want wives, they don't want babies, they don't want to help people, they don't want plants that cost $300, they just don't want anything out of life except junk."

It's not entirely clear whether Morrissey's attack on liberal notions of free love and drug experimentation registered on audiences back then. It's even less likely they'd even be contemplated today since the demoralized environments he exposes have achieved a level of curious nostalgia as the sixties have become thoroughly mythologized.

Bob Colacello quotes Morrissey barking: "Why do you kids say you're experimenting with drugs? You're experimenting with ill health. Now that polio and all the other childhood diseases have been eradicated, you kids take drugs to find out what it's like to be sick!"

He told the Brits in 1970 that "we're ahead of our time. The entire drug business is dying out. The next generation is going to see a huge conservative backlash."

"I was living in the East Village when this was all going on," says Joe. "I was there for the whole hippie thing, so I knew how people had come from all parts of America to New York to get involved with the hippie culture. It was funny and pitiful, because by that time, for people on the Lower East Side, drugs were going out. Just when it was becoming most popular elsewhere, that's when it was going out for the people who were really involved in it. You see, by then it had beaten them up so badly that they knew they couldn't do it. But now it had finally caught on, it had become the thing to do, so people are coming from all across the nation to New York to be a part of something that was already over. Yet you can't just end something when you have such a great demand, even for something that should have been over with long ago. Paul tried to state that in a movie, about where it's at for drug users and how horrific it was, and why even drug users were seeing that it's over."

Whether recognized for their social messages or not, both **Flesh** and **Trash** still retain the power to entertain, shock, amuse, and inform us.

Trash marks the second of Joe's naked performances. Attracting devoted fans as much for his full-frontal exposures as anything else, he once famously commented to *After Dark* that, "If you watch closely, you'll see that my best performing comes when I have my clothes off. When I'm dressed, I really don't give very good performances ... Next time you see a film where I'm naked, watch my face and you'll see what I mean."

It's not true, and the look on his face when I bring up the famous quote suggests it was just a clever line to give interviewers back then and not the way he really felt. But it does point out the unusual dichotomy of Joe Dallesandro as an actor so completely embodied as a sexual object and so refreshingly unself-conscious about his nakedness that too many critics have seen the meat and not the message.

As Danny Peary points out, though, reviewing **Trash** in the first volume of his excellent series *Cult Movies*, "a film where the male lead has acne on his rear and the female lead is played by a female impersonator is not meant to satisfy a viewer's prurient interests."

"Joe Dallesandro is the center of **Flesh** and **Trash**," writes Stephen Koch. "His naked body, curving buttocks, dangling genitalia, classic torso, and good-boy face are *the* center of the camera's erotic attention. Everything else is farce. The camera's task is simply to pay attention to that body, and the relation between camera and object couldn't be simpler. Visually, the camera wants. Visually, Dallesandro gives."

Even by 1970, the male nudity quotient in a Warhol/Morrissey film was light years ahead of their Hollywood counterparts. Morrissey contended that if you put too much of anything on screen all the time, though, it can't help but become boring.

And that would be true, strictly speaking, if there was nothing else going on in the films, or, more importantly, if there was nothing else that Joe had to offer. But he has plenty more to give.

When John Lombardi sarcastically asked Paul Morrissey in *Rolling Stone* if he thought Joe was a good actor, Morrissey said, "Yeah. I think Joe is probably the best film actor around under 35, one of the best actors in the film business today." When the interviewer suggests the last three or four Warhol films have been too similar and could the director take, perhaps, a Buzz Aldrin, and make a film about going to the moon, Morrissey offers: "I don't know him, and I don't think we'd want him in any case. I think that it would be a better movie if we put Joe in an astronaut's space capsule and told him to be an astronaut."

Morrissey liked to bring up John Wayne's name, not only as one of the greatest actors in movie history, but in parallel to Joe. "We've developed a style of acting taken from the traditional American film acting, stars like John Wayne, who are always themselves, actors who maintain their own dignity," he told the Brits. (The *New York Times* reported that Morrissey saw **Flesh** as his "tribute to John Ford," and Joe told *Newsday* that Wayne "is the only one I can identify with, because he is always John Wayne and that is how I would have to be. I'd always be Joe Dalle-

With Paul Morrissey and Jane Forth/Courtesy Joe Dallesandro

Andy, Jane, Paul and Joe on tour in Germany/Courtesy Joe Dallesandro

sandro. Whatever I was supposed to play.")

When I spoke to Morrissey, he told me he saw Joe as being akin to Alan Ladd or Charles Bronson, the strong silent type unfettered by "acting school crap."

"I don't think good actors need acting classes," the director explained. "It makes them too self-conscious. Acting talent is what you see. They're a good actor or they're a bad actor. No acting class teaches you to be a hero. They just teach you to be an emotional basket case or a lower class creep."

"I never went to that school," says Joe. "I never went to the New York school of acting. I came from the New York school of the streets. Then I was told, 'okay, now you're an actor—learn camera movement, positioning, and just tell me what you know already.' And what I knew already was street talk."

His performance in **Trash** is nothing less than first-rate. Perpetually stoned or lethargic, exhibiting only occasional fits of life-energy, he so ably transcends the notion of performance that a few fans wrote the Factory imploring him to get off the dope. None of them had an inkling that he was actually married (a second time) and had a baby son of his own now (Joe, Jr.), living somewhat quietly outside of the Factory noise, though still working there daily doing any number of odd jobs.

This assumption of reality lent the films a powerful vicarious dynamic and it's no small tribute to the actors. (No doubt adding some confusion was the unusual fact that many of the players were known on-screen by their off-screen names.) Even writers who did profiles on Joe seemed forced to remark how surprisingly different he appeared to them in person.

"If it's possible to be a man with the combination of frank sensuality and vulnerability that Marilyn Monroe had and still come across masculine, it's Joe," said writer Tom Wommack after meeting the actor and noting "how un-funky" he was, with "clean hair, healthy skin, bright eyes; Shy. Courteous."

But, because the film seemed so down and dirty, and probably also because of Warhol's nasty reputation for housing and "exploiting" an entourage of drug addicts and "deviants" (an opinion not held by Joe), it was perhaps only natural that many viewers mistook the people they saw up there on the screen for the people they portrayed and assumed they were really living the lives captured on camera.

"Everything that they saw there, that had to be me, that had to be real, that was a documentary of my life," says Joe, shaking his head. "The only extent to which it was a documentary of my life is that we improvised dialogue." (Morrissey concisely told the *L.A. Free Press*: "We're making a documentary of good acting.")

As to the infamous, excruciating close-ups of Joe shooting up in **Trash**, he explains, "it was just water. You've got to realize that we're shooting a movie, a full feature, which is a lot of footage, and we're shooting it in three days. When the fuck do I have time to nod out? If I nod out, who's doing the next scene? There was no time to be drugged up."

Dallesandro isn't pulling his punches here. There was a period when he experimented heavily with drugs as a youth, but the entire time he was with the Warhol group, he tells me, he was completely straight. Paul Morrissey demanded it, even so far as to confiscate drugs from others who worked on the films. (Morrissey told me he certainly had no control over his actors before they got to the shoot and often couldn't tell if they were on something or not.)

The only thing more spine-tingling than the needle close-ups is the scene when Holly's sister (Diane Podlewski; whose last name appears as "Podel" in the opening credits) comes on to Joe, too. Pregnant to the point of imminent explosion, her figure's spindly white arms become shockingly disproportionate beside her huge pink belly. All Joe can do when she tells him not to worry about making it with her because "nowadays, anything goes," is mutter, "Oh, wow." (As succinct an indictment of the sixties youth movement as Morrissey could have dreamed.)

Trash opened in New York City on October 5, 1970 in Don Rugoff's Upper East Side art venue, Cinema II. Rugoff was a well-known distributor of offbeat fare who had respectably handled **Z**, **Putney Swope**, **Elvira Madigan** and **The Endless Summer**. His Cinema V distribution outfit would handle **Trash**'s bookings nationwide.

Holly Woodlawn couldn't attend the premiere, however, because she was in the slammer. She had been caught impersonating a French diplomat's wife while trying to withdraw a couple more thousand out of the socialite's bank account and was summarily hauled off to a woman's detention center until she was ordered to hike up her dress and drop her panties and she became an instant he.

Sitting in jail and unable to pay the $1,000 bail, she tried contacting Warhol, but he wouldn't take her calls. *Daily Variety* caught wind of the story and headlined "**Trash** Star Found in Trash Can," creating an instant celebrity and a surprising intervention. She was finally bailed out by artist Larry Rivers.

Vincent Canby, of the *New York Times*, while joking "that it's the best American film made in New York that I've seen all day," actually sort of liked the film. He returned to it less than a week after his initial review in an essay curiously reading it as a celebration of Spiro

Agnew's status quo America, remarking that it was conventional and reassuring in the same way that old Ruby Keeler and Dick Powell musicals were forty years beforc!

With the film doing well at the box-office, the *New York Times* saw fit to revisit it yet again two weeks later when Peter Schjeldahl wrote, "Nuttiness is, of course, the stock-in-trade of Warhol's people, if one may stretch the word to include simple cutting up, rampant exhibitionism and an occasional chilling whiff of real psychosis. To truly watch a Warhol movie (that is, not to just sit and condescend to it) is to get entangled in the emotional lives of real, gifted, suffering human beings."

Of course, not everyone liked it. Stanley Kauffman, who called any audience who mistakes the film's grubby naturalism for deeper meanings "suckers," ended his review by stating point blank that "**Trash** is disgusting, not for what is on the screen but for what is in the minds of the people who made it."

Turns out that negative reviews about the subject matter were far less a problem for Joe than reviews that pointed out all of his films' technical shortcomings.

"That was very difficult to hear and it's what pissed me off the most," he says. "All my critics pointed out that the films were impossible to watch because of the bad camera work, impossible to hear because of the bad audio, and there was some truth to that. We had the crappiest equipment you could ever have and in such a state of disrepair. And I would scream, 'let's get the fucking camera repaired!' I didn't even know it was broken until Paul pointed it out to me. I said, 'well, I think we're making enough money to get it fixed. I think we're making enough money to get a whole new camera. Aren't we? I mean, I wear dungarees and a jeans jacket no matter what season it is. There are no cashmere coats in my closet.'"

The Hollywood Reporter said **Trash** was "the closest thing to a sexual, sociological portrait of 1970 that the year is likely to see." *Rolling Stone* called it "a masterpiece, and the 'Best Movie of the Year.'" It even played at Cannes out of competition (as a critics' prestigious entry). A moralizing projectionist put his hand in front of the projector to censor Geri's opening blow. The audience was pissed. Morrissey laughed it off.

During the film's run for Oscar consideration in Los Angeles, Joe's performance was singled out by reviewers. "Morrissey is more interested in story-telling, and now in **Trash** he actually has somebody convincingly playing someone other than himself," wrote Kevin Thomas in the *LA Times*. "That somebody is his Adonis-like hero Joe Dallesandro, a natural actor who plays a junkie quite effectively although in reality he doesn't touch the stuff." Bridget Byrne, writing in the *LA Herald-Examiner,* referred to Joe as "that matinee idol of the streets ... Dallesandro has what in other contexts could be termed glamour and presence. We can follow the minutest emotions forming and fading in his mind."

Liz Smith, writing for *Cosmo*, told her readers that "this film proves that Warhol is one of the most moral prophets of our time" and that if he is putting us on, then "he still succeeds as a moralist by not succeeding ... Joe Dallesandro is wonderful, a Michelangelo nude pockmarked by needle tracks and addiction pimples ... **Trash** is hard to take, but hold your nose and swallow. It is important—as meaningful to our moment as hell was to the Middle Ages." A week later she published a letter from a reader who wanted her $2.50 back after seeing the film on the critic's recommendation.

The returns on **Trash** were quickly mounting up to give **Flesh** a run for its money and they were inevitably double-teamed in October of 1971, billed as "Wall to Wall Warhol." As with its predecessor, reaction abroad was even

Autographing memorabilia with Jane Forth/Courtesy Joe Dallesandro

more clamorous than here in the States.

West Germany, once again, proved the most fertile ground for Morrissey's film and this time even Andy went with Paul and Joe and company to experience the extraordinary reception, though curiously, Holly Woodlawn was absent.

"They didn't invite me because they were afraid of me," says Holly. "They were silly. It's okay. I don't mind. It's one of those things. I got over that. After **Trash** opened and I became a big star, I was invited here and I was invited there, but I was young and I couldn't deal with all that insanity and superstardom."

Trash was booked into Munich's 1,100 seat Luitpold theatre where it played to a capacity crowd and was followed by an extravagant reception held at the Arriflex studios. Photos of Joe and Jane Forth were gigantically projected on the outside walls.

And, once again, sightseeing tours through all the local attractions were provided during the week's tour of five cities. Joe was named Best Actor and Morrissey Best Director by the newspaper, *Abendzeitung*, which held a gala dinner, and the film went on to become the number two moneymaker of 1971, right behind—ironically enough—**Easy Rider**.

On the return trip, England proved a little dicey. The battle had been fought and won once before (with **Flesh**) and that at least made the issues familiar, but there was still plenty of stiff upper-lipped debate. The film had appeared at the 15th London Film Festival at the National Film Theatre, but the only authority to grant it a permit for exhibition was Berkshire. The British Censor was unhappy again—they had a new one, Mr. Stephen Murphy—and Warhol, Morrissey, Dallesandro and entourage were subsequently invited to the House of Commons by a Conservative Member of Parliament, Sir Norman St. John-Stevas, who was very much in their corner and wanted to see **Trash** released; he may have "found it repellent, but it was not pornographic."

Jimmy Vaughan, via the distributor Constantin, decided to wait out the latest debate and not even issue the film for club or film society screenings, ostensibly because he wanted a commercial market. The primary concerns, strangely (or aptly) enough, had to do with objections to the drug content. Apparently, the anti-drug message heard by critics in the States eluded the British Censor entirely. *Sight and Sound*, the International Film Quarterly, which found **Trash** "unmistakably a very good film" and "one of the most evidently moral" on the subject of drugs, took serious exception to the "totally incomprehensible" stance taken by the Censor, and thirteen film critics signed a letter of protest in *The Times* that criticized the Censor for not certifying **Trash** while granting certification to other films that featured disturbing violence, namely **Straw Dogs**, **The Devils**, and **A Clockwork Orange**.

"It's unlikely anyone will exit **Trash** anxious to shoot up for goodtime's sake," noted *Variety*, "and the vein-puncturing close-ups are more graphic and disturbing than any of the recent tv anti-drug spots."

It wasn't until February 8, 1973 that **Trash** finally got its release in Britain. It was booked into the first-run London Pavilion Theatre, a 1,000-seater owned by United Artists, making it the first Warhol film to receive a significant commercial venue there. Though the film had already established a track record of European box-office success (it was also very popular in Holland), when the Brits finally gave it the go-ahead, they not only awarded it the anticipated X rating, but they saw that three-and-a-half minutes of cuts were made. Bye-bye Holly and the beer bottle and all of Geri's hidden blow-job. (Even more shocking, when the film played in France, it was reportedly cut by an astounding 21 minutes!)

The West End release also came just as David Bailey's British television documentary on Warhol—shot over three weeks in New York and including vulgar language and nudie clips from some of his films—was served with a court injunction banning it from the British airwaves. This sparked yet another heated debate about morality and censorship in the modern age.

It was a good five years before the film saw release in Italy, but when it did bow it was in a dubbed version overseen by famed director Pier Paolo Pasolini, who liked the film so much that he considered doing an Italian "remake." With Pasolini's name attached to the project, **Trash** did exceptional business and was identified as the film that brought the underground "overground."

"When Pasolini did the dubbing on **Trash**," recalls Joe, "he picked out a real street kid to do my voice, and later, when I learned to speak Italian, I spoke with the same inflection and the same 'voice' as the guy Pasolini had chosen. It was amazing. Part of the reason there was a delay in Italy is because what we would do is we would sell **Trash** or **Flesh** and then part of the deal would be that we'd make them take two other films—Andy's product—which they never wanted. But they were told if you wanted this one, you have to take these other two. Which was real unfair to my product, because that's what they really wanted in the first place and that's what they were giving money for, and then they had to take Andy's pieces of shit, too, which nobody wanted because there was no audience for them."

Made for approximately $25,000, and that includes the costly blow-up to 35mm prints, **Trash** would reportedly gross over $3,000,000 worldwide.

Holly Woodlawn—who, importantly, is never *once* portrayed as anything but a complete woman in the film—followed up her success in **Trash** by co-starring in Morrissey's **Women In Revolt** (1971), but she was surprisingly intimidated on screen when working with fellow drag queen superstars Candy Darling and Jackie Curtis. She appeared in a few other low-budget films, including **Scarecrow In A Garden Of Cucumbers** (1972) and **Broken Goddess** (1973), before famously telling a lamely inquisitive Geraldo Rivera in 1976, who wanted to know "what" she was, that it didn't make any difference "as long as you look fabulous." She would also co-star with Divine in the campy stage hit **Women Behind Bars**. Today, she's still very much sought after for interviews, during which everybody eventually asks her about what it was like working with Joe.

"The first thing they ask is did you go to bed with him?" she tells me. "I wish I could have, but, honey, I was so in love (with Johnny Putnam) and I'm a one man woman. Joe and I were working. All he did was uncork a bottle of wine and light my cigarettes. I was so terrified of him. And I think he was terrified of me. But working with Joe, he made me so comfortable. I didn't even look at his cock and stuff. He was just a nice guy, a real gentleman. He really was. I hope that won't ruin his image by saying that he's a sweetheart."

They still keep in touch, and Holly says she'd work with him again in an instant. Back in 1979, she almost got her second chance.

With Joe thinking seriously about returning to the States after all hell broke loose in his personal life, there was a lot of talk about Warhol and Morrissey doing a sequel to **Trash** called **Trash-ier**, or simply **Trash II**. The script was being worked on, according to Andy's diaries, by Paul and Nelson Lyon, who reported to Warhol that Robert DeNiro might help get the money together to see the project realized. The plot involved Joe, who was still a junkie and now working at a pizza joint, and Holly, a nightclub entertainer, hoping to move out of their Lower East Side squalor to Lodi, New Jersey, "the town with the chemical spills." Joe and Holly have four dope-pushing kids and they decide to bankroll their new move by arranging for the oldest one to be hit by a taxi so that they can then sue the cab company. In May of 1980, Warhol reported that he wasn't certain if they were interested in a 25% deal being offered by an associate of Alan Ladd to do the film.

Sylvia Miles was then added to the cast as a school-teacher who seduces both Joe and then Holly's 17-year old son, while an incest theme was also being worked out involving Holly and her eldest boy. Pretty sick and potentially funny stuff.

Morrissey was certainly seriously considering doing the film, particularly since he wasn't having much success finding other film projects. He told me he always felt it was a miracle each and every time he got a film made and surely felt trapped by his identification with weird subject matter. "I'm cursed by that stupid word underground," he said in 1980.

So what about Joe? Did he ever seriously consider making another film with the people that made him famous and with whom he bitterly split?

Absolutely zero interest, he tells me.

"What the fuck kind of story is this? Like that was such a great story to begin with that you want to continue it? Never. Not with that storyline. Besides, I had no idea where my career was going to go when I came back. The main reason that I returned to the States was to get my health back, and one of the things I couldn't stand was the cold, so I had no intentions of staying in New York City. Plus, I drank all of my father's liquor and it was time to move on."

In 1973, shortly before his break with Morrissey and Warhol, Joe told the magazine *Viva* (in what he announced was to be his last interview ever) that acting—as a career—"became serious to me with the movie **Trash**. I saw that it was an important movie … it kind of caused me a hard time later because people were believing I really was a drug addict, so that it was almost impossible for me to work. Of course, I've really changed and I'm trying seriously to take this thing that started as a joke and turn it into a serious career."

VIDEO REPLAY: Joe's priceless reaction shot after Holly's sister tells him that Holly and she "used to make it together anyway," is followed by Holly's tirade when she catches them. Joe rises to his own defense in an impassioned speech that calms her down—telling her that he only got on the methadone program for her sake, because he was happy on drugs and he's been sick since he stopped—and the anger eventually resolves itself with the two of them willing to give their relationship another try. Even when arguing, Joe displays a sympathy and a tenderness that gives his character whole other dimensions. In the ugly face of it all, dammit, he cares for Holly and wants to see their relationship work.

heat

(1972)

"In my movies, everyone's in love with Joe Dallesandro." —*Andy Warhol*

With JOE DALLESANDRO AS JOEY DAVIS, Sylvia Miles (Sally Todd), Andrea Feldman (Jessica), Pat Ast (Lydia, the motel owner), Ray Vestal (Ray, the producer), Lester Persky (Sidney), Eric Emerson (Eric), Gary Koznocha (Gary), Harold Childe (Harold), Pat Parlemon (girl by pool), Bonnie Walder/Glick (Bonnie, Jessie's girlfriend), John Hallowell (John, the gossip columnist). Directed by Paul Morrissey. 100 minutes

The third installment in the Morrissey trilogy is probably the easiest of the trio with which to warm up the uninitiated; **Flesh** has its herky-jerky style, **Trash** has its gutter inspiration and close-ups of Joe shooting up, but **Heat** is the closest Morrissey came to making a "Hollywood" feature during this period. It's a very funny comedy with a sufficient number of weird and memorable characters to give one a taste for the earlier stuff.

Just prior to **Heat**, Morrissey and Warhol had lensed two of their "women's" pictures and there was no place for Joe. First was **Women in Revolt (P.I.G.S**; 1971), an hilarious send-up of women's lib starring Jackie Curtis, Candy Darling and Holly Woodlawn as Politically Involved Girls. Second was **L'Amour (Beauties**; 1972), a $100,000 feature shot in Paris, detailing the relationships of three American girls in the city of love in a story that ironically swirls a great deal around the subject of toilets and the deodorant cakes used in urinals.

The decision was made to shoot a film in Europe to capitalize on all of their international success there. Morrissey said at the time that Joe didn't join the cast in Paris because "he's a very quiet type of person and if there are a lot of people in the scene he won't compete; he'll just clam up. He only speaks when he has to. I think this is very good because I think this is, you know, the tradition in men's acting on the screen—like John Wayne; you only speak when necessary."

In **Heat**, as in all of his films thus far, Joe plays another Joe, though this time he's been given a decidedly "other" identity. Joey Davis, a former child star on a television series called **The Big Ranch**, is now in his early twenties and trying to get a music or movie career going again.

Short on words, long on hair (Joe's ponytail dangles to the middle of his back), he moves into a seedy little Hollywood motel where he meets the flipped-out lesbian daughter of an aging movie queen he once worked with on the TV show.

The daughter, Jessica, played with singular exception by the irrepressibly odd and wonderful Andrea Feldman, recognizes Joe as he suns himself poolside. She tells him by way of introduction, "You probably don't remember me. I saw you on that TV show **The Ranch**."

Within seconds she's telling him all about herself, rambling on about all the health foods she eats ("Did you ever try a nut? I'm into ecology"), rapping off a recipe for artichokes and avocados, and informing him that all she wants from her mother, the ex-star, Sally Todd, the ex-chorus girl whoring all over town, is money.

When her mother arrives, Jessica is grilled.

"Is this the kind of place to bring Mark up in?" Sally asks, referring to Jessie's baby.

"Yes. Definitely."

Feldman's responses are off-handed and unexpectedly to the point, yet they can come dressed up in weird free-associations, too. Her mother rants that she's already given the girl thousands of dollars, to which she responds, "Well, I need more." Shortly thereafter she takes a cue about time in a mental ward and goes off on an inexplicable riff involving somebody having her baby pictures in the asylum.

There's an hilarious exchange about Jessica's possibly confused sexuality during which the word "lesbian" comes up as a funny punchline a good half dozen times.

"Do you sleep in the same room with her?" Sally inquires about her daughter's roommate Bonnie.

"Sure. How else can I be a lesbian?"

Where does the baby sleep? In the same bed? "He'll be a lesbian."

The motel is run by Lydia, a grossly overweight, frizzy-haired harlot played to the absolute hilt by Pat Ast, who worked as an assistant to Halston and therefore had all her muumuu's designed by him.

She's already told us with a sarcastic wince that "some of these people around here are just downright disgusting," but certainly excludes herself from that company. What makes her so funny is how glamorously Ast plays her.

She's completely serious when she plops down next to a shirtless and sunning Joe and asks him if there's anything she can get him ("How about a hamburger?"), then offers her services as a masseuse.

The ensuing scene, in which Joe is outfitted in only a jockstrap and Lydia massages his back and coos in his ear, was earmarked by one British writer as one in which "either Warhol or Morrissey has an extraordinarily keen sense of the pathetic fragility of beauty and the aggressive beauty of ugliness."

When Lydia, who's wearing her hair in a tight bun, oooh's and ahhh's over the beautiful mane that Joe is sporting and asks him what he does to keep it like that, he says he just lets it grow. She says she's been letting her hair grow for six years "and it's nowhere near that length. I don't know, sometimes I think I have a deficiency."

Joe seems quite willing to handle any and all of her perceived deficiencies so long as he can get a break on the rent. He squeezes her breasts and she groans in ecstasy, telling him quite quotably that it's "just like a little bit of semi-heaven!"

Jessica, with deep black eyes and skin pale as a corpse, shows off her cigarette burns to Joe. She says her girlfriend burns her and beats her. Then it's off to mom's house with Joe in tow for more money.

Her mother takes one look at her and says, "You look like a black widow spider!"

"This is how they dress in Greece." A frantic call from girlfriend Bonnie, hysterically taken by a screeching and panicking Jessica, has her running out of the scene and leaving Joe and Sally Todd to get re-acquainted.

Spending time alone in her 36-room mansion (a cavernous old place once actually owned by Boris Karloff; full of Hollywood lore but now quite conspicuously empty, thus thematically appropriate), Sally and Joe have their lengthiest verbal exchange with one another; after Joe's silence prompts her to engage in a long speech about her many marriages, Joe finally does the most talking he'll do in the entire film, playing up his role of a sweet, pessimistic wounded boy who needs mothering. Sally falls for it hook, line and sinker. She wants to see what his hair looks like when he lets it down.

He does so, telling her it's his strength, but that "today, people aren't into hair anymore."

"Well, maybe not everybody's hair." Sally moves in for a smooch and tries unsuccessfully not to drown in the silken blanket of Joe's mane. It's a funny visual gag, probably because it seems just as likely that the actress is trying to move the hair so her face can be seen by the camera as because it's falling all around her.

Sylvia Miles, still riding high on her Oscar nomination as Best Supporting Actress for essentially a single scene in **Midnight Cowboy**, had seen **Trash** and knew immediately that she wanted to work with Joe. The actress' reputation for surrounding herself with gorgeous specimens of the opposite sex (exponentially younger than herself) surely had no bearing on her enthusiasm to do a film with a naked Joe Dallesandro—though the nudity quotient has dropped a bit this time out and Joe offers no full-frontals. (At one point, however, after he's bedded her and knows he's got her in the palm of his hand, he poses nude like a Greek statue in her home and when she comes out of the bedroom balling and whining for him, he turns on her and

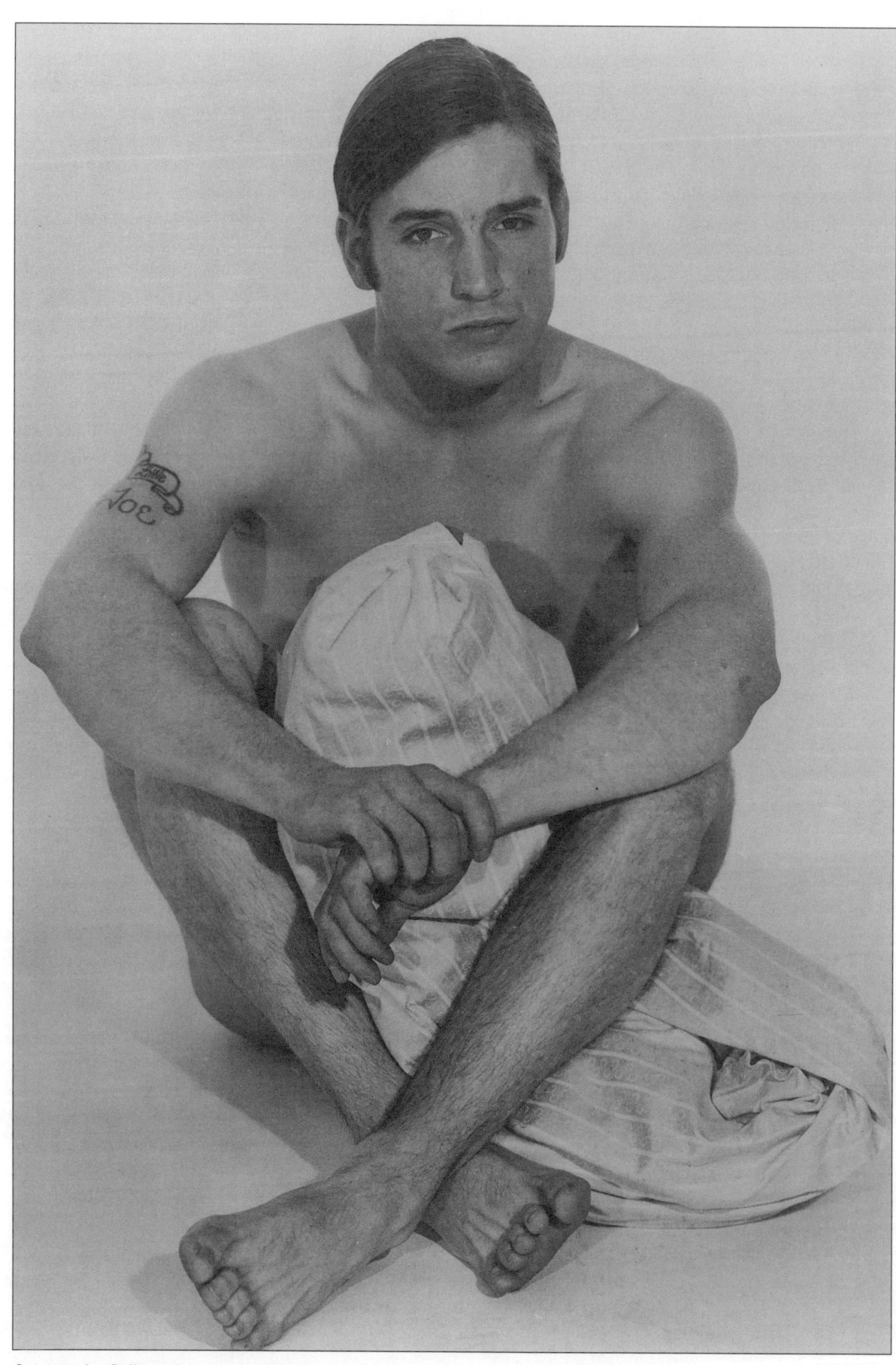

Courtesy Joe Dallesandro

tells her to "shut up.") It's interesting to watch the film and read into Miles' performance an off-screen lust for the guy, accurately or not.

When it came time for the sex scenes, which were shot in a rented house back in East Hampton, Ms. Miles was apprehensive about what she'd have to do in them. She supposedly made it known to Warhol that she was *not* going to go down on Joe, but wanted to do something to make the scenes special. When she decided to take Joe's hand and suck on his fingers after one of their love bouts, Andy was thrilled when he saw the printed scene.

Miles was reportedly nervous about working with Feldman—she even asked Andy one time if he thought she was dangerous or just plain crazy— and it's said that Warhol and Morrissey fueled off-screen rivalry between Miles and Pat Ast in order to heat up their exchanges. Again, it's fun to watch their few scenes together when you know they didn't really care for one another. Both give memorable performances.

Twenty-four years later at a sold-out screening of **Heat** at the Castro in San Francisco, Miles chimed to the gay boys in attendance: "Come on, did you come to see me, or did you come to see Joe?" She described the actor as having "the warmest skin in the world."

In the Morrissey films, Dallesandro became an increasingly somber, chiseled beauty. In **Heat**, he's lazy, self-centered and spoiled, though still desired by everyone— girl or boy. Everyone talks about him, wants him, has him, and he remains entirely unmoved, entirely self-absorbed and utterly indifferent, simply biding his time to see if all this attention is going to get him somewhere. Reinforcing his importance to all those around him, Morrissey's camera lingers over Joe's face and chest during dialogue between other characters in the scene, who are often dishing about him as if he weren't there or were perhaps on display behind plexiglass. At last, Joe had become the plastic inevitable Warhol loved to play; the notable difference being that Joe had the exquisite body and handsome face to boot.

In fact, Joe is probably the most radiantly healthy and handsome he's ever looked in a Warhol movie; somehow quite fitting considering the semi-autobiographical aspect of his character. Replace the child stardom of Joey Davis with the underground stardom of Joe Dallesandro and you have both real and fictional characters hoping to make the transition to Hollywood feature films.

The scene in which Sally arranges for Joe to meet her producer and a Hollywood columnist is particularly funny because it seems that all of the potential projects that the producer is looking to cast ("a young, fresh-faced kid from the streets of the Bronx" who becomes the leader of the Mafia) would be perfect for Joe, but the Hollywood idiot just can't see it.

Joe is virtually silent for the entire exchange, yet Morrissey's camera stays on him, because he is the meat that's being marketed. When Joe is asked to talk about his showbiz experience, he says he started in the chorus of a kids show called **Mousetime, U.S.A.**, then dryly adds that he was fired, leaving one to wonder what a little squirt had to do to get canned from a kiddie show and why you'd tell a prospective producer that. When the producer says that the show must have been a good learning experience, Joe says in another beautifully realized, off-the-cuff response that, yeah, it was, because he was "realizing that you had to do it everyday for five days a week," and that sounds like such a drag.

He's his own worst enemy and he can't even see that. When nothing happens in his career, when Sally has proved she can't make the connections he needs, he unceremoniously dumps her. Naturally, she blames her psychotic daughter ("She can't even make a good dyke") who has

A posed still, with Sylvia Miles and Pat Ast

moved in with the two of them with her baby.

The baby is "played" by Joe's real-life son, which caused dad to be a little apprehensive at times, particularly for a scene in which Andrea walks in with Joe Jr. in a shopping bag.

"Whaddya carry your baby in a bag for?" Joe asks her on-screen, revealing the joke we haven't noticed yet.

Dallesandro thought Morrissey was nuts for wanting to put his baby in a shopping bag, mostly because Joe felt uncomfortable being that far away from his son, particularly when Andrea was around.

"Remember, we already fucked him up when we took him out with the forceps," says Joe, referring to his son's difficult birth and the temporary condition of his elongated head. "The last thing I wanted was to have him dropped and smash up his pretty little head when it had just gotten back to being the right shape."

Did he know the baby was going to be in the bag?

"No, she just walked in and then I realized and I had to play it. Sometimes we got things in one take, sometimes it took two. Well, this was an instance where we had to do it three times. Most of the things we did with Andrea we did two or three times."

Rounding out Morrissey's cast of characters in this Tinsel Town long ago tarnished and bespeckled with pathetic egocentrics, gossipmongers, and meat-rack opportunists are Sally's ex-husband (played by **Hair** producer Lester Persky) and his effeminate live-in ex-child star "Aunt" Harold, who has an ocelot, wears an ascot, accidentally calls Andrea by her real name, and goes down on Joe. And then there are the poolboy brothers, Gary and Eric, who have a stage act together at a local club.

After Gary explains that their act consists of singing and dancing and then fooling around on stage, Jessica, not very quick on the uptake, says, "I heard you went to bed with your brother!"

"Yeah, but only on stage."

She figures he must like it or he wouldn't do it.

"Well, it's a living."

The brother, a conspicuous mute, is played to creepy effect by Warhol veteran Eric Emerson, who wanders about in a white dress and masturbates a lot.

"Eric Emerson was kind of a bulldozer type," recalls Paul Morrissey. "When I did **Heat**, Eric said, 'oh, I want to be in **Heat**. I want to go to California and meet one of my children that I've never seen. I have to go, please take me.' And I said, awwwww! I didn't want him in it because I know how he hogs the screen. So I said, all right, you can come. I'll give you a ticket. You can be in the movie, but you have to play a deaf mute. It was very clever of me, because he was actually quite wonderful. If he started talking, he would just go on with this sort of gibberish, because he loved talking."

Heat was shot in the last week of June and first week of July of 1971 in Los Angeles for approximately $50,000; the Factory's second most expensive film. Though it appears to have even more structure than the previous two films, it was still improvised, working from a treatment developed by Morrissey and John Hallowell, who's credited with the idea and also appears in the film as the gossip columnist. Hallowell was the journalist who had unsuccessfully pitched his *The Truth Game* to Columbia the year before when Warhol and the gang came out for meetings and who recounted another failed pitch session with the studios while trying to team Warhol's Factory Players with—presumably—Mick Jagger. (I could be wrong, as he's described only as "rock god" in the *Los Angeles Times* piece.)

Before Andy headed back to New York and let Paul alone to direct the film, the entire crew appeared on a local television show where a flustered Regis Philbin tried to get Andy to talk. Naturally, Morrissey did all the talking. Andy and Joe just sat there silently while Paul told off live callers to the show who were misinterpreting his films.

With Hollywood apparently rebuffing the New Yorkers, it's easy to read **Andy Warhol's Heat** as an acerbic attack on a long-faded Tinsel Town and its sleazy inhuman remains. The film was even known as **Hollywood** in some of the foreign markets.

Riding in on the financial and critical success of **Flesh** and **Trash**, **Heat** played at several film festivals (including Cannes and the Venice Film Festival) and it had a distinguished opening on October 5, 1972 as part of the New York Film Festival, two years to the very day that **Trash** made its bow.

The standing-ovation screening—with Joe, Paul and Sylvia captured in the spotlight—was followed by a panel discussion that included Morrissey, Miles, and—oddly enough—Otto Preminger, who stated that the film didn't represent any Hollywood with which he was familiar, but added he would consider acting in a future Morrissey project. Elia Kazan was also in attendance and said he liked the film, especially its quality of motivational ambiguity. Morrissey described his improvisational style and Preminger wisecracked by asking if the director had auditioned "the young man who masturbated."

A pair of small parties capped the evening, one at Pierre's, the other at Sam Green's and hosted by Candy Darling, with Joe and his wife mixing it up with the likes of Lauren Hutton, Alice Cooper, Warren Beatty, and Jack Nicholson.

The film was also screened for a "star-studded" premiere at the Director's Guild of America in Los Angeles that Andy, Sylvia and Paul attended, arriving in a 1929 Cadillac convertible and emerging with wolfhounds. The event was a little too light on big names for Andy's liking, but was eventually rescued by attendees Jack Nicholson (again), Ann Miller, Lorne Greene, Rona Barrett, George Cukor, Russ Tamblyn, Goldie Hawn, Jan Michael Vincent, Dean Stockwell, Lucie Arnaz, Jim Bailey, showbiz columnist Dorothy Manners, and (close-but-no-cigar) Mae West.

Warhol, Morrissey and Miles chatted up the local press, but the studios still seemed a bit indifferent to them. Columnist Joyce Haber's account of the visit was headlined: "Are they Superstars or superbores?"

Heat has most often been read as Morrissey's seedier version of **Sunset Boulevard**, and to a large degree that comparison works, right down to the final scene in which a jilted Sally Todd marches in and tries to unload her empty pistol into a wet Joey Davis as he climbs from the motel pool.

Morrissey definitely saw **Heat** as his 1950's film, but he thought more along the lines of **Written on the Wind**, with Sally as Dorothy Malone fifteen years down the road.

Another inspiration, albeit a little indirect, was all the attention **Last Tango In Paris** was getting in the press. Warhol remarked, "Now that's very dirty. It's a triple X movie. It's a funny thing. Here's Brando doing a Joe Dallesandro. And in **Heat** it's vice versa."

Sally's gun failing to go off, Morrissey would remind us, is a joke at the expense of **Last Tango**. The gender reversal of a May-December romance has Brando's emotionally tortured role assumed by Sylvia Miles in **Heat**, with Joe substituting as the young woman of his objectification. In **Tango**, the gun does go off. In **Heat**, Morrissey wouldn't think of giving in to such a cheap emotional release. His characters are terminally frustrated by their obsessions. Joe doesn't end up raped and murdered on the streets in **Flesh**. Holly doesn't end up on Welfare and Joe doesn't OD and die in **Trash**. And in **Heat**, Sally doesn't get to snuff out the object of her neurotic desires and Joe doesn't sign a deal and become a star in spite of her.

In the Morrissey trilogy, for better or worse—there's just no escaping it—everybody lives to see the next day.

Unfortunately, that was a different story off-screen. On August 8, 1972, just two months before the New York festival premiere, Andrea Feldman committed suicide. Reported with enough variations to make the details suspect, it has been said that her dramatic exit from this world was accomplished by leaping from the 14th story window of her apartment building clutching a rosary and a Bible (some versions substitute one or the other for a can of Coke). A note addressed to all of her friends, including Andy Warhol, included the phrase, "I'm going for the big time, I hit the jackpot!" Criticisms that Warhol was contributing to and then capitalizing on the drug-ravaged lives of his company (a charge also famously associated with ex-Warhol superstar Edie Sedgwick's early demise) came to a head when **Heat** premiered and some reviewers found Feldman's painfully disturbed appearance—they couldn't possibly see it as a performance—painful to watch and obviously an example of Warhol's irresponsibility and bad taste.

Peter Schjeldahl, writing in the *New York Times*, pulled no punches, citing that "Miss Feldman, with her twisted little face and frightening laugh, was clearly in a bad way, and the pitiless exposure of her suicidal mood makes **Heat** a repellent document."

Time magazine called it "a faggot rehash of **Sunset Boulevard** … (that) exploits the sorry selection of freaks who have been recruited for the cast. What is despicable about **Heat** is the way it both flaunts and mocks the grotesqueries of its cast, who seem generally neither to notice nor greatly care."

Joe disagrees.

"The only concept that Andy Warhol created that I liked was the one where everyone was a star. The trouble that Andy ran into with that concept was that the people who came to him were so insane. Very ill people. And when you allow them to be the star, you seem to be exploiting them. It looked that way because you look at the movies and say to yourself, 'obviously these people are ill.' But Andy wasn't exploiting them. You walk down any street and you'll find people who want to be in the movies, to be a star. Even if it's the furthest thing from their minds, if you give them the opportunity to do whatever they want to do and be the star of a movie, they'd love that."

Joe worked with Feldman on both **Trash** and **Heat**, so he knew how crazy she liked to get, how wild and uncontrolled she could be. He also knew that Andy and Paul were giving her precisely what she wanted. Demented or not, Andrea (who often used the surname "Warhol") wanted so much to be a Superstar, and Paul Morrissey gave her the chance to do it. Her tragic death would have happened with or without Andy Warhol and company. They merely provided a place for her to express her manic fantasies.

"Andrea was going to do what she was going to do," says Joe, not callously or coldly, as he genuinely liked her. But, "how can you protect someone from themselves?

"Andrea and Geraldine (Smith) would come to my apartment in the Village. Anything that I would say to them would go back and be written up the next day in *inter/VIEW*, because they'd make up a whole bunch of shit about me for Andy. It had nothing to do with anything that was remotely real, so I'd get upset with them.

"They would come to my house and I would have this

thing with them: You're not allowed to come to my house if you're going to act crazy. And they would be on their best behavior. They could hold it in for a half an hour and then they'd go right into their nutsy act. I'd tell them I couldn't take it, to get out of here, and they'd go into their squealy voices. 'You people aren't real,' I'd tell them. 'Get the fuck out of here.'

"But since I'd got them to be normal for about half an hour, I knew it was all an act. Because if you're able to do that, you wouldn't know what normal was unless it was an act. Paul could get Andrea to behave for six or seven hours. He would treat them like they were his little children. He would scold them like they were infants.

"What Andrea would say to me a lot—and she used the expression in the film—'you're nothing, you're nobody, you're nowhere!' And there was a part of me that knew she was right. All this Superstar bullshit. I'd ask her if she was fucking with me, because I could be her friend or I could be someone who doesn't talk to her. And they so much wanted friends. In fact, when she did her suicide routine, she was calling everybody. I wasn't in town, but I would've gotten the call. And I would have been the one who told her, you gotta do what you gotta do. Then I would have been the inconsiderate one, like Andy supposedly was, because you can't believe it when you deal with it on a regular basis. How do you know what's true anymore? When you've cried wolf so many thousands of times, how do you know what you're really going to do? I felt real sorry that Andrea had to lose it and die, because anybody who commits suicide, for whatever their pain, it's sad, because they wind up killing a person they never knew. If you have that much fear, you haven't been living yet."

Paul Morrissey also has some thoughts about how foolish it is to blur the personality with the opportunity. No one who wrote about the incident knew the first thing about her troubled family situation and difficult life off the screen, he told me. Idiots just assumed Warhol and Morrissey were to blame because it made good press—easy, irresponsible, ignorant, and incorrect good press.

"She had been given some scenes in the 25-hour movie, some stuff in **Imitation of Christ**, and that's where I realized how wonderful she was," says Morrissey. "Yeah, she was one of my favorites."

Peculiarly, though there was an attempt to downplay Andrea's death for stateside screenings so as not to cast a pall over the end results of everyone's hard work, when the film received its press screening in England, Jimmy Vaughan told the audience that the actors were "more or less acting themselves" and then announced Feldman's suicide. **Heat** was also snipped by four minutes for its Great Britain bookings.

New York Magazine thought Feldman's performance was the most striking of all in its very positive review, and also found that "Joe Dallesandro, who indicated in **Trash** that he was something more than a superstud, proves it with the cool, calculated sensuality with which he plays the field in his own conviction that he is the big star."

Vincent Canby, in the *New York Times*, liked the film, too, saying that "Joey wears his hair down to here and looks great and doesn't much care who does what to him as long as he doesn't have to do the work." His only complaint was that the film seemed a little mild and that he missed the Factory transvestites, comparing the picture to "an Our Gang two-reeler without Spanky, Alfalfa and Buckwheat—and sweet little Darla Hood."

In the previously mentioned Schjeldahl *New York Times* attack entitled "What's So Hot About **Heat**?," the writer felt that the change of locale for Morrissey might be partly to blame for the film's shortcomings. Strange, since Morrissey has always felt that **Heat** was essentially thoroughly a New Yorker's movie that just happened to be set in Hollywood.

With Sylvia Miles

"For the third time," Schjeldahl writes, "Morrissey has structured a movie around the person of taciturn muscle-boy Joe Dallesandro, who again functions as a kind of phallic statue beset by sex-hungry chatterboxes in whom he maintains at best a flickering interest. This is a serviceable formula, but one that can be only as good as its active elements—which emphatically do not include Dallesandro, who is present strictly to be gawked at, yakked at and pawed." Talk about not liking a film because it succeeds in doing precisely what it set out to do!

Rex Reed loved the film, especially Sylvia Miles (whom Rona Barrett told was a shoo-in for an Oscar nomination). Reed said it was "the most important film to ever emerge from the tropic underground movement, providing freshness and excitement." *Variety* caught it at the Director's Fortnight at Cannes as early as June, finding that "it is all ego, sex and the old film system ... Dallesandro is again the malleable sex object who can not resist fat, predatory femme motel owners, old stars, daughters for that matter, not to forget a gay actor kept by one of the star's former husbands. If he does much of it to keep going, he also seems to enjoy it, in a cool, laconic way ... There are some excellent acting bits, especially the girl, not available in credits here, who plays Miss Miles' daughter."

The film's musical score, comprised of bookend pieces heard at the opening and ending of the film, was composed by John Cale, member of the Velvet Underground. Cale would also serve as composer on several French films in the 90's, as well as on both **I Shot Andy Warhol** (1996) and **Basquiat** (1996).

Cale's title music comes over images of Joe posing on a deserted soundstage and then standing amidst the wreckage of the latest studio casualty. A title card tells us: "In 1971, another film studio, the Fox lot on Sunset Boulevard, was torn down." An era had ended and, ironically, the closest thing to Hollywood's studio system still in operation was Warhol's Factory where Joe Dallesandro reigned as their number one box-office attraction despite the fact that he wasn't raking in the big bucks nor did he have his own trailer, limo, and lavish estate in Bel Air.

Since **Flesh**, Joe was supposed to be paid 5% on all of the films he did at the Factory, but there was a dispute over the first film's interest because, Joe says, Paul didn't tell Andy that he was supposed to receive a percentage. On **Trash**, Morrissey mentioned it, but "they were still hemming and hawing," so on **Heat**—for the first time—the 5% deal was put into Joe's contract.

Warhol must surely have known how important Joe was to the success of their films. While in Italy, a country that took its sweet time in finally playing the trilogy, Andy relates (in *The Philosophy of Andy Warhol*) running into a high school student in the small town of Boissano who knew only five words in English and that four of them were **Flesh**, **Trash**, **Heat**, and Dallesandro.

Joe has a very practical sensibility about these things as they relate to the larger picture. When I talk to him about his screen presence and the qualities he brings to the Warhol/Morrissey films, he chuckles at the idea that they had anything to do with his longevity at the Factory.

I ask him, (I believe) rhetorically, that if he were to screen **My Hustler**, **I, A Man**, **Bike Boy** and **Lonesome Cowboys** or **Flesh**, which one of those young guys would he want to have stick around and make more movies, he answers:

"The one that doesn't want any money."

It's the perfect Dallesandro improvisation, skillfully and naturally delivered without even a moment's thought.

So you would have been canned, I ask incredulously, if ....

"If I pressed for money, I would have been gone." A big smile crosses his face. "But I did it the sneaky way, because I sent my brother to work there and he ended up getting more money than I got. He made a real salary."

It's hard to seriously believe that money, or the absence thereof, was the primary reason why Joe Dallesandro stuck around for eight films and became the most popular and well-known male superstar of the underground cinema. He seemed so right in so many ways for what Paul Morrissey had envisioned and what Andy Warhol himself seemed to invoke: a powerful attraction to an image.

On the occasion of a retrospective of his work at the Film Forum in December of 1995, Morrissey explained to the *New York Times* his successful formula: "In the center you have an abnormally good-looking person, better looking than anyone on the planet, and on top of that you build a story about young people and their problems. Is it realistic that Brando would have been on the waterfront? It's ridiculous. In real life he'd have been the top male model in the world ... Joe was not an improviser. He was a quiet person, the eye of the storm, and this lunacy going on around him therefore became very dramatic. I thought he turned out great."

Whether crafted carefully or by happenstance, the enigma of Joe is central to the maelstrom. When Holly Woodlawn was interviewed for a book on Andy's films and was asked to talk about Warhol, she hesitated, because she said, "usually I'm asked about Joe."

Why? Because the picture *is* worth a thousand words.

The drag queens and the other Superstars were interesting, quirky, witty, even fun, but they were also on some level threatening. Joe, on the other hand, inspired fantasy, dreams of an afternoon fuck. This was a Joe that could be

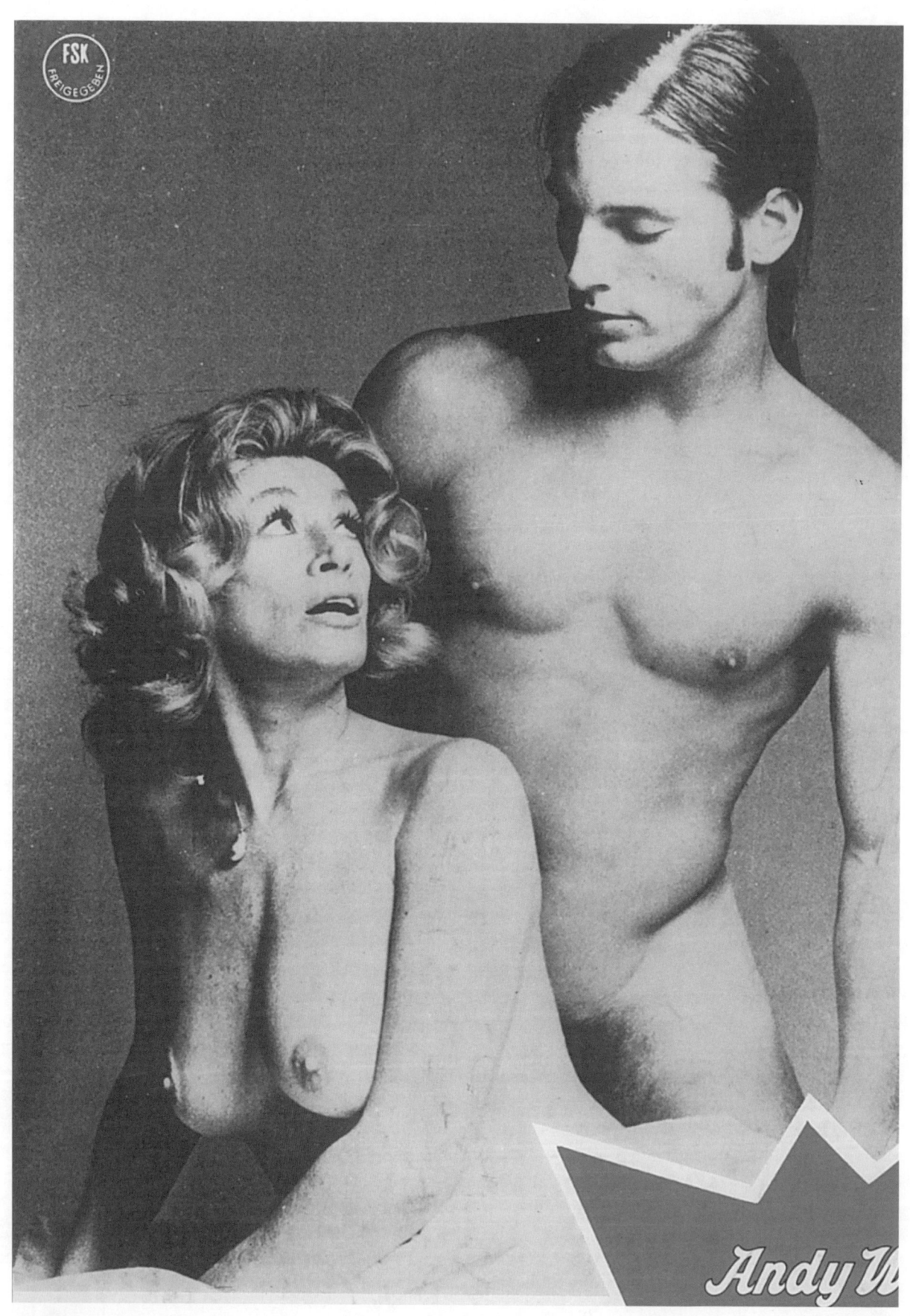

Aka **Hollywood** for the overseas market

had. Even at his most cold and calculating, as in certain scenes in **Heat**, one never thinks he couldn't be tamed, couldn't be taken care of or persuaded to stick around just so long as you were willing to treat him right. You'd *know*, after all, going into the relationship, what kind of guy he was, what he wanted. You'd be ready for him. You wouldn't be caught making Sally's mistake—wearing blinders. In other words, you'd play the hustle, if not exactly hustle the hustler.

Silent enigmas are fascinating; especially sexy ones, ones that inspire lust.

The genius behind Joe's blank looks and Morrissey's directive not to smile is that it enables the audience to project their thoughts and attitudes onto him. We can read whatever we want to when we look at him. The silence only deepens the power of the image, because it cannot invade or contradict the context we've provided as the looker.

The precedent is drawn from the earliest of moving image experimentation. Eisenstein discovered emotions could be "assigned" to the image of a woman's blank, staring face if it was placed before and after other images that in proximity made an emotional connection for the viewer. An image of a woman's unsmiling face followed by the image of a baby crying followed by the same image of a woman's face followed by an image of a baby giggling followed by the same image of a woman's face followed by a soldier dying on the battlefield all induce different emotional responses projected by the audience onto the woman's countenance. The actress hasn't "acted" at all, yet we have assigned appropriate and very different responses to her face by emotional transference. Our perception of her face has changed based on the feelings we're assigning.

The key, of course, is that the frames of the woman's face are all identical. Audiences project much the same way that actors and the very film itself does. We are the key interpreters of the language—bringing associative meaning and emotional nuance and resonance to still photographs fluttering before our eyes.

Look at nearly any nude study, classical or whack-off-able, and you notice how often the models in solo poses smolder in inexpression. The smileless smile allows the viewer to imagine a relationship with the subject that best suits his or own tastes. Is the naked pretty-boy being coy, cheeky, obstinate, teasing, apprehensive, seductive, inviting or is he playing hard to get?

All are correct responses.

This phenomenon is particularly evident in nude male photography where men are invited to objectify and eroticize the image in a very carnal way. Nude men can be and are photographed for the sheer beauty of form and aesthetics, but any male nude is also likely to inspire desire on a more primal level. The model who imparts too much personality runs the risk of turning off part of the viewership who do not find a particular attitude appealing. Models who can project personality and charm successfully *and* remain appealing to a wide audience are rare finds.

Joe Dallesandro was such a find. Morrissey's brilliant edict that Joe not smile was a masterful stroke from an artist familiar with classical sculpture, the psychology of the image, and the history of great movie stars.

"We had faces then." Indeed.

Joe is quick to downplay his contributions to the Warhol/Morrissey films as a talker, as an actor who couldn't rattle off juicy bits of improvised dialogue, but he also, I believe, doesn't fully appreciate his enormous potency as an image. He tells me he can't understand, in light of all that is available today, how or why anyone would sit through one of the Warhol/Morrissey movies. That probably has a lot to do with personal overkill and the contempt that comes from familiarity, but it also stems from an understandable lack of objectivity. To Joe, the films "were what they were." And now they're over and done with.

Can a boy look in the mirror and see the beauty others see? Yes. And so could Joe, though he'd be hard-pressed to admit it. More to the point, can a boy look in the mirror and see the desire or the fantasy he's inspired in others when they look at him? No. The best he can do is guess at the appeal or attempt to project similar feelings he may hold for someone else. (Yes, of course, pretty people know they're pretty, but it's an abstract.)

Joe Dallesandro doesn't have to say anything to his audience to speak to them. Importantly, though, Joe transcends the simple awe and drool allocated to any of a thousand gorgeous men glimpsed riding buses, getting ice creams at the mall, or staring back at you from the pages of a book or a magazine. Pretty boys inspire, but they can also be replaced. You have to do more than look good to attain the longevity of a Dallesandro.

And that's what Paul Morrissey gave Joe, who's fond of saying—even when he's being critical—that "they gave me a career." The context of the image is as important to making a good movie as lighting is to shooting a good photograph.

Neither Morrissey nor Warhol appear to have fussed much over lighting in their films, but the context in which they placed Joe—as the street beauty desired, accessible, and even down and dirty—embellished the plain fact that he was a good-looker and thereby gave him "light."

This is not to suggest in the least that Joe contributed nothing more than his body to the success of the trilogy. He often told interviewers in repeated variations on the theme that all he really had to do for these films was show up. In a profound sense, he's absolutely right. There's a purity to that statement that's undeniable, and charming as all hell, too, but he also had to give. Unstudied in the mechanics of acting, he reacted naturally to the situations that swirled around him and legitimately gave a performance.

"My performance always stayed the same," says Joe. "I told Paul, 'I don't have much depth, it's not going to get much different.' And he liked that. That's what other directors who I would go on to work with kind of liked, too. They say, 'you know, I can have you do a scene 20 times and I can count on you doing it 20 times exactly the same. Even if I'm asking you to do it differently, you'll still do it exactly the same.' I used to ask Paul if that was a good thing or a bad thing. He'd tell me, 'well, there are occasions when I think it's the greatest thing and there are occasions when I really just want to hit you one, because I know you hear me say do it a little differently and I know you've got to be purposely doing it exactly the same way.' No, I'd tell him, it's just because, basically, that's the only way I can do it. Show me another way, I'll do it your way."

Anybody out there ready to choke and sputter on an argument that Joe gave great performances in the trilogy—because his contributions have been seriously underrated (Leonard Maltin calls him a "zombie")—need only go back and look at the films. He fulfills all the requirements. He wasn't playing the Prince of Denmark to be sure, but he's not right for that role anyway (or is he?). Sometimes it's a matter of allowing an actor to create the perfect role, as Mike Leigh does with enormous success in his improvisatory films.

Sir Laurence Olivier once told Joe he admired his work when Joe visited his dressing room in London in the early 70's. "He's in the middle of finishing a performance," remembers Joe, "and he's obviously not looking for anything from me, he's not making a date, but he's obviously seen the work and appreciated them for what they were and was complimenting them. I had to take the comment graciously. I told myself not to let it go to my head when people like Laurence Olivier or Dustin Hoffman or Norman Mailer would say nice things about me. It was just that they appreciated my work in them and I knew that much of that was because of the person I worked with."

Due to all the graphic images—of naked men, of needles sticking in bulging veins, of polymorphous perverse sexuality—Morrissey's trilogy may appear to be decadent (and certainly it is quite easily enjoyed in that light), but it is actually very self-aware and socially conservative work.

The director used to tell interviewers that he wasn't interested in subtextual themes, lofty ideas or the sociopolitical interpretations that were fodder for pseudo-intellectual film students, critics, and a handful of fellow filmmakers who had succumbed to the heady pretensions of the "art" film. That may or may not be true, but certain messages are unavoidable, particularly when his films cavort in arenas of class and sexuality during an era when the very idea of the underground film was that it eschewed Hollywood fluff and narrative and was intrinsically "about" something, was supposed to reveal an intellectual agenda by the filmmaker, to make a statement, and thereby beg interpretation, discussion and debate.

Essentially, Morrissey made social comedies about young urbanites stuck in the mire of the culture's new drug and sexual freedoms and floundering in the stinking excess. For both Warhol and Morrissey, sex in their movies was always about not getting it, about wanting it but being completely unfulfilled.

Ultimately, the joys of **Flesh** aren't to be had in the hustling boy-beauty, but in what a guy is willing to do to support his family. The joys of **Trash** aren't meant to be

Courtesy Joe Dallesandro

had in the kitschy plight of a transvestite who collects garbage, but in the horrific consequences that drugs have exacted on the characters' lives. And **Heat** may be read as a call for normalcy in the nuclear family, with the cheap and tawdry world of misplaced values in Hollyweird sure to destroy any hope for an actress to raise her daughter clean, sober and straight.

Strained socio-political projections? Yeah, maybe so, but they speak to just how divergently accessible and entertaining this trilogy can be for the viewer.

It also strikes me how passive these films are, consciously or not. It's remarkable that in **Flesh**, for example, Morrissey doesn't retreat to a single scene of violence or physical threat while telling the story of a street prostitute. Instead of insisting on a hard-hitting, gritty tale of seamy encounters with dangerous johns or self-hating hustlers—the legacy of nearly every other film made on the subject, including the latest entries (**My Own Private Idaho, Where the Day Takes You, The Price of Love, Johns, Hustler White**)—**Flesh** forgoes the melodramatics to chronicle a single day of walking, talking, and standing around. By doing so, it also slyly, but perhaps unintentionally, assumes a morally non-judgmental take on its very empathetic lead character. No wonder Joe appeals so deeply to a gay audience. It's not the prostitution that's being condoned, of course, it's the sweetness of the boy who happens to make it his living. (A bisexual male prostitute in mainstream cinema—Hollywood or otherwise—would surely have been put to death in the scenario, with all the dark implications of being gay and thereby culpable intact.)

Of Joe's characters, he has gone from used to user, progressively withdrawing himself from the action around him. He slowly moved from the boyish charm and naiveté of **Flesh** to the deadened druggie trying to regain a little meaning and emotion in his life in **Trash** to the abject object—a deceptively agreeable, but callous Hollywood hustler—in **Heat**. Throughout the trilogy, he remains vitally important to the people around him. They exhibit an uncanny need to feed off him—or at least what they imagine he represents—just as much as he's expecting to get something out of them in return.

A sexually active, but naive lounger in **Flesh**, he was blissfully unaware of his powers. A limp and confused lounger in **Trash**, he was only aware that everybody wanted something from him that he couldn't give them. But in **Heat**, Joe is a lounger lusted after, hungered for, eaten up, gone down on, and very much aware of his powers over others. He simply lays back and allows himself to be had, complete with half-hearted "no's" or "stop that's" as he goes along. He has by now lost his heart and simply become a hard-on.

At the helm of this transformation was Paul Morrissey.

"I did the performances because I had a Paul Morrissey allowing me to do that," Joe says with sincere respect. "Paul knew my good things and he knew my bad things. For years, I didn't smile because he wanted to go for that Clint Eastwood look."

Paul Morrissey, eager, but not *too* eager to work in Hollywood, was offered an interesting tidbit during the run of **Heat**. Producer Robert Weiner announced to the press that he had tagged Morrissey to direct the screen adaptation of Gerald Walker's novel *Cruising*, a violent tale of a psychopathic killer of gay men in the S&M underworld to begin shooting in the spring of 1973.

Weiner was interested in casting either Jeff Bridges or Timothy Bottoms for the cop and Jan Michael Vincent for the killer. He said the film would be "sympathetic to and not exploit the homosexual community," and planned on having Jack Doroshow, who worked on **The Queen** (1968), serve as advisor "on matters relating to New York's gay world," with the film's bloody climax to take place at the Continental Baths.

Morrissey declined the offer—even before major studio funding couldn't be found—because, "I didn't care for the material. The premise just seemed too simple-minded to me. So I said, 'no.'"

Ironically, when the much-reviled film was eventually made in 1980 starring Al Pacino, it was directed by William Friedkin, who had directed the gay-positive **The Boys in the Band** (1970), and who said of Morrissey in the early seventies after screening **Flesh For Frankenstein**, "That young man will be one of the major film directors in the next 10 years."

As for Joe, he may not have had the stature of a Clint Eastwood, but he, too, was beginning to interest Hollywood studios. Just how these inquiries were dealt with by a Factory seemingly very possessive of their Superstar is a point of some contention.

VIDEO REPLAY: Joe comes downstairs dressed to the nines in a beautiful white suit and Jessica sits dejectedly to one side and says she wants to go out, too. No, this night is for Joe and her mom. She needs to stay home and take care of her baby.

"Listen, I gave my baby a sedative. It'll be asleep for about five hours."

the gardener

(1974)

"Joe Dallesandro needs no introduction. The man is a fucking god."

—*In-Touch magazine (#89), March, 1984*

(Also known as The Seeds Of Evil) **With JOE DALLESANDRO AS CARL—THE GARDENER, Katherine Houghton (Ellen Bennett), Rita Gam (Helena Boardman), James Congdon (John Bennett), Teodorino Bello, Anne Meacham. Directed by James H. Kay. 81 minutes, Puerto Rico.**

The irony—perhaps simple reality—that Joe Dallesandro's first film appearance outside of a Factory film was this cheap horror potboiler filmed in Puerto Rico is not lost on Joe. At a time when he said he felt constricted by his mentor and restricted by the notoriety of the Warhol films to the point that Hollywood suitors were scared off, he assures me that his inaugural step into someone else's project probably only got the approval because of what it wasn't.

"Paul's idea of the movie I should do was a movie called **The Gardener**," he says, getting wound up a little. "I should do this movie because, one, 'Joe, your first Hollywood movie should be a movie that preferably doesn't get released.' Two, 'you just want to do it so you can get a chance to work with a Hollywood group,' and then it'll get shelved after the experience. I couldn't understand that and I said, 'Paul, I'm not agreeing with you on this. I don't see why I can't do a good movie. I don't think I'd fail at it.' He says, trust me, trust me—and I did that. He gave me the go-ahead because he never thought it would be released, that it was such a piece of shit that nobody would see it."

How much **The Gardener** was like Hollywood, or exposed him to anything even remotely resembling a Hollywood production, is highly questionable. His co-stars, at least, had remnants of Hollywood about them. Katherine Houghton had played Tracy and Hepburn's annoying daughter in **Guess Who's Coming To Dinner**, and Rita Gam was a veteran of several films in the 1950's and was the ex-wife of Sidney Lumet.

The actresses play two snobby society women incessantly babbling on about inconsequential matters while sneaking comments about the new half-naked gardener.

"He really is something, isn't he? Not what you usually find in the tropics."

"Helena!" Houghton chides back with a whisper.

Courtesy Joe Dallesandro

Joe's movie image had been cultivated by Morrissey to the point where he became cold, callous, even silent. This career trek towards emotional ennui finds ultimate displacement here as he wanders around the grounds like some sort of zombified Tarzan tending his killer vines.

"I suppose you need a job?" asks Houghton after Joe's first female employer dies.

"I need a gah-din," he deadpans back.

Deeply tanned, with his hair now hanging down in a ponytail all the way to his butt, Joe appears to be toying with method-acting here. Given the role of a man at one with his vegetation, he is at his most hilariously flat and monotone as Carl, a performance so wooden that it can only be seen as foreshadowing his character's eventual transformation into a tree.

His face is so dead, his expression so comatose, that his performance reminds me of the style of acting Andy Warhol proclaimed to most admire when he dubbed the catatonically talky sci-fi cheapie **Creation of the Humanoids** (1962) his favorite movie.

What this cheesy little horror flick is supposed to be about is anybody's guess, though one gathers that the automaton gardener has supernatural powers and tends to give deadly plants to his employers, perhaps as some sort of revenge on mankind for deforestation.

Houghton's huffy hubby gets pricked by one of the plants while he's at the sink preparing for the evening's deadly dull soirée.

"If you want to turn this whole house into a jungle, well, okay," he gripes at his wife. "But not my bathroom!"

Later at the party, the husband gets a drink in him and offers the film's dirtiest—and thereby best—line: "Why don't you ask your friend, Carl? I'm sure he has just the right non-wilting blossom."

The only problem is that I don't think anybody thought it was dirty when they wrote, rehearsed, or delivered it. We're stuck doing all the work, fighting off the dorky music incessantly playing over dialogue as if this were some old studio picture, and forcing Freudian jokes both onto Joe's wanting to show Houghton "something special in the greenhouse" (turns out to be flowers that bloom at her touch) and the anatomically-correct close-ups of bright red pistils jutting from their crimson orifices.

One thing the film does nicely is show off its male star's very muscular and golden brown upper body. Joe's shirtless in every scene, wearing the same pair of tight tan pants riding provocatively low on his hips. He seems completely confused—or at the very least lost—during a couple of musical interludes showing him communing with his jungle of plants, but he certainly makes for a handsome specimen whilst strolling though the foliage.

Since this was the longest his ever-growing mane was captured on film and it had become something of a trademark, I asked him about his famous hair.

"It was fun having the long hair," he says. "But, you know, I always associated having long hair with being out of work. If you have long hair, you must not have a job. I remember when I went to Disneyland for the first time while I was visiting out here in Los Angeles and someone told me they had a policy about not letting men with long hair into the park. So to get in, I just dropped it down the back of my shirt. My hair was so smooth and tight when I had it pulled back that you couldn't even tell I had a ponytail if you saw me coming at you, so that's what I did. Then I let it out in the park and got paranoid that any minute I was going to get busted by Donald Duck."

The length of Joe's hair also helps us put **The Gardener** in its proper chronology. The film wasn't released until 1974 and quickly thereafter assumed **The Seeds of Evil** title (as it's known on video), though it was shot down in Puerto Rico in 1972, almost a year after he had done **Heat**, but, of course, before he went to Italy in early 1973 to film **Frankenstein** and **Dracula**, for which Paul had his Samson clipped.

Just in case you're not a hair fetishist, another way to enjoy the film is to turn it into a drinking game like those developed on college campuses to coincide with evangelist sermons (slam one for every "Jesus") or episodes of *The Frugal Gourmet* (slam another for every "gorgeous"). Only this time, you've got to down a shot every time a character calls the gardener by name. "Carl … Carl … Carl!" You'll be passed out in a pool of your neighbor's vomit in no time.

"On the releasing of it in the South," Joe recalls, "they sent a rose to people in the neighborhood as a flower from **The Gardener**. They didn't spend a lot of money on the thing, it was kind of low-budget, but much more than we ever spent on a movie."

Because he had worked briefly on both **Midnight Cowboy** and **The Magic Garden of Stanley Sweetheart**, when Joe did **The Gardener** he was told by the actor's union that he was a must-join who should have already paid his dues. He sent them back a letter that said, in essence, "Fuck you, I'm moving to Europe."

Ten years later, when he finally did join, they still had the letter on file.

VIDEO REPLAY: Towards the end of the film, shortly after Houghton takes a sickle to her girlfriend's arms because they've become entangled with living vines, the dazed and confused young woman fires a bullet into a beckoning Joe's chest. He takes off running into the night and his pants completely disappear from one shot to the next. The continuity girl was not fired.

flesh for frankenstein (1974)

"To know death, Otto, you have to fuck life in the gallbladder."

—*Baron Frankenstein*

(Also known as Andy Warhol's Frankenstein; Carne Per Frankenstein; Il Mostro E In Tavola … Barone Frankenstein; The Frankenstein Experiment; Warhol's Frankenstein; Up Frankenstein; The Devil And Dr. Frankenstein; Frankenstein) **With JOE DALLESANDRO AS NICHOLAS, Udo Kier (Baron Frankenstein), Monique Van Vooren (Katrin Frankenstein), Arno Juerging (Otto), Carla Mancini (daughter), Marco Liofredi (son), Dalila Di Lazzaro (female zombie), Srdjan Zelenovic (Sasha/male zombie), Nicoletta Elmi, Fiorella Masselli, Liu Bosisio (maid), Rosita Torosh, Cristina Gaioni, Imelde Marani. Directed by Paul Morrissey. 95 minutes, Italy.**

Not only is it one of the most unusual lines ever spoken in a film, horror or otherwise, but it is almost always misquoted as a prerequisite to writing about the flick in which it is delivered. One critic said it should go down in history as the single worst line ever uttered in a horror movie, but that guy was an idiot.

The inspiration came to Morrissey from all of the critical idolatry afforded Bertolucci's **Last Tango In Paris** (1972), not one of Morrissey's favorite films. He thought it was boring. Andy thought it was really dirty.

Post-stick of butter and pre-smelling the farts of a dying pig, Brando tells Maria Schneider that she will never find the One man she's looking for, the One love, "until you go right up into the ass of death; right up in his ass until you find a womb of fear, and then maybe, maybe then you'll be able to find him." This serves as prelude to his instructions to stick her fingers up his ass and the proctologic outpouring of some of the filthiest excrescence shat from a movie star's mouth while they were still in front of the camera and the film was rolling.

Critics were contorting themselves with praise (Pauline Kael said the date of its premiere—October 14, 1972—should be revered as a landmark in movie history) and audiences were lining up around the block to partake of its Europeany, arty nastiness rendered in golden goo and the first sexually "explicit" film of its type to get major studio backing.

Morrissey thought the "right up into the ass of death" line a ludicrous piece of dialogue, so during the shoot of his own film, he wrote something resembling what Baron Frankenstein says at the outset of this chapter. Udo Kier, who played the Baron, may have mixed up his "life" and "death" when it came time to deliver it, but it remains the signature line of dialogue from a very funny film; even more ludicrous than Brando's on the written page, yet equally as relevant to the finished scene.

Producer Carlo Ponti, the man who brought us **Two Women** (1960), **Doctor Zhivago** (1964), and **Blow-Up** (1966), among many others, and then-husband of Sophia Loren, was interested in financing a 3-D film project with Roman Polanski. Polanski was working on **What**? (a.k.a. **Che?**; 1972), a sordid tale of the sexual exploits of a young female hitchhiker while she stays in the mansion of an eccentric homo (Marcello Mastroianni). Some tests were made, and Polanski decided he didn't want to use the 3-D technique. He suggested that Ponti and co-producer Andrew Braunsberg (who went on to produce **Being There**) approach Paul Morrissey, whom he'd briefly met in Europe, about doing a horror film project using the process.

Morrissey felt it nothing short of miraculous that any of his films got made, so having outside money come to him with a deal must have been a very interesting proposition. He was already a devout fan of the Italian cinema, which he considers the best in the world since Hollywood's Golden Age, so the idea of actually working at the famed Cinecitta Studios must have also been an enticement.

He was asked by the producers how long it would take him to shoot the film and to estimate the cost, and when he pulled three weeks and $350,000 out of the air, the response following the raised eyebrows was unanimous: "Is that all? Then let's make two."

Flesh for Frankenstein and **Blood for Dracula** were shot in just that manner, back-to-back over a two month period beginning in early March, 1973, and thus they are so closely interrelated that it's difficult talking about one without mentioning or comparing it with the other. The casts were to share several key players, but according to Joe, it was his involvement that undoubtedly clinched the deal.

"The deal was that they would make these movies, that they'd back them for nearly a million dollars, but that they had to star Joe Dallesandro, they had to be directed by Paul Morrissey, and Andy had to lend his name, because that was the combination that they saw as a success with **Flesh**, **Trash**, and **Heat**," says Joe. Indeed, Joe gets top billing in both films even though he plays supporting roles in each.

He was damned reluctant to go to Italy, though, particularly since he said he was promised in the bargain even before he was asked. On top of that, he says, "they didn't put in a decent salary" for him, so he was upset from the start.

"All my life, I had this hustler mentality," he admits. "If I had a dime in my pocket back when a telephone call was a dime, then I would be okay. But I was getting too old to keep doing that."

Still, with no offers from Hollywood, and the opportunity to work with a professional film crew and a budget nearly ten times the size of his most expensive film, he ended up making the trip to Rome for what would become known as **Andy Warhol's Frankenstein** and **Andy Warhol's Dracula**, his last two outings for the men who made him famous.

Andy certainly never objected to the use of his name—he once told reporters who asked him what he did on the films that he just went to the parties—and he did drop by the set once or twice while he was both visiting Rome as a tourist and inexplicably showing up in Giuseppe Patroni Griffi's **The Driver's Seat** (1973), an abomination starring Elizabeth Taylor as a depressed woman seeking some unlucky fellow in Rome willing to bump her off.

Morrissey, of course, was used to working in an improvised fashion and originally intended to do his horror films the same way, but the international cast he had assembled, which included Germans, Italians, and a Serb, couldn't improvise their lines in English. Due to this, and perhaps also at the nervous behest of his producers, he had to work each night with script assistant Pat Hackett (the keeper of Andy's famed diaries) on lines for the following morning's shoot, which were given to the actors the same day they were to be filmed.

During the scene when the Baron is attaching his male zombie's head to the body and has to deliver a lengthy speech, the actor plays it as if he's just very preoccupied with the work he's doing, thus never lifting his head, but what he's actually doing is reading his lines off the table below him.

Frankenstein, originally titled **Meat For Frankenstein** until Andy uncharacteristically made a suggestion that they change it to **Flesh**, has been described by its director as "the search for the perfect nose."

Baron Frankenstein is looking to find the perfect "nasum" in order to realize the "Serbian ideals" of pure physical and intellectual properties said to descend directly from the Ancient Greeks.

For the Frankensteins, appearance is everything. They are elitists holding on to snobbish beliefs and rigorous class distinctions, but wallowing in depravity the whole while without seeing the least bit of contradiction.

The Baroness tells her silent children (the child actors didn't speak a word of English) that, "I've always looked for beauty … as a matter of fact, I insist on it," after which Morrissey cuts to a shot of the Baron lifting his nude female

The Baroness and the Shepherd Boy

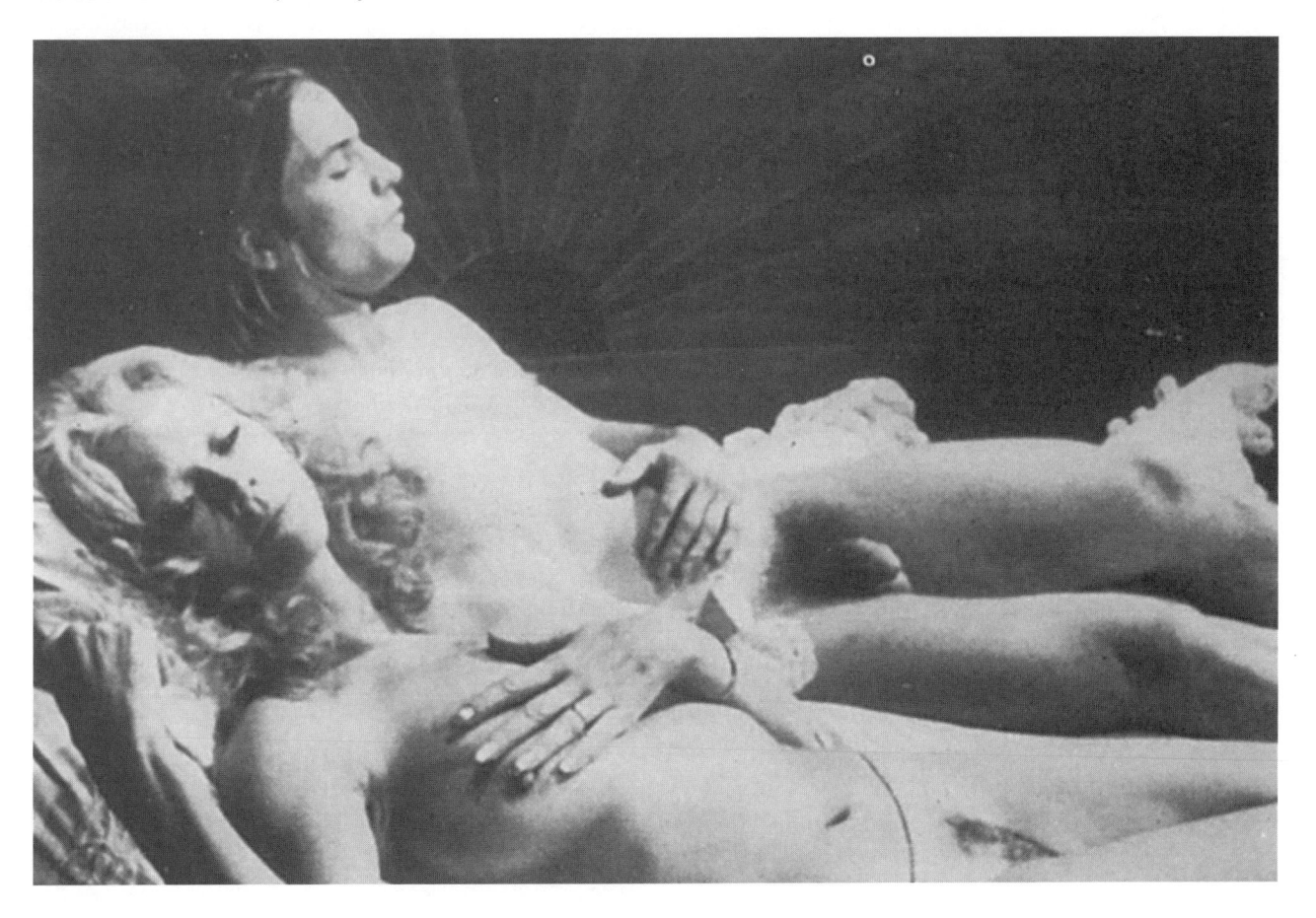

zombie out of the immense water tank in his lab, a sly visual play on the fish tank in the children's bedroom from the previous scene. (There are lots of little moments like that, such as having the two children sleep in the same bed together foretelling the revealed relationship of their parents and foreshadowing their own wicked futures following in Daddy's footsteps.)

Dalila Di Lazzaro, a gorgeous model whom the director saw in an Italian TV soap commercial, reportedly panicked while in the tank on her first day of shooting and the shot had to be postponed. The tank itself is certainly not the first one used in a Frankenstein picture, but the entire laboratory set for Morrissey's film, designed by Enrico Job, seems to have heavily influenced the cheaper version on view in **The Rocky Horror Picture Show** (1975).

The Baron is played to the proverbial hilt by German actor Udo Kier, who also played a Baron in the notoriously vicious **Mark of the Devil** (1970), a brutal sex and gore show grandstanding nudity and torture and wrapped up in a tale of 18th century witchcraft trials and tribulations.

Morrissey met the actor on an airplane. The director not only enjoys casting for faces, he also casts his actors for voices, committing himself to the rule of "stylized people for a stylized picture." Kier's voice is nothing if not stylized; his German accent sharply modulated and enunciated in what nearly resembles parody. The actor would follow his famous pair of Warhol films with key roles in the works of Rainier Werner Fassbinder and Lars Von Trier (for whom he is currently shooting just 10 minutes of film a year over a full decade for a project to be released in the new millennium).

American moviegoers re-discovered him humorously engaging River Phoenix and Keanu Reeves in tableau-style sexplay as Hans, the salesman of "pieces" for automobiles and the buyer of their motorcycle, in Gus Van Sant's classic **My Own Private Idaho** (1991). Since then, he's appeared in projects as varied as **Ace Ventura: Pet Detective** (1994), **Johnny Mnemonic** (1995), **Barb Wire** (1996), and **Breaking the Waves** (1996). (He even did a popular commercial for Milky Way candy bars in 1997.)

As Baron Frankenstein, Kier veritably quakes with emotion, spitting his ill-humored lines with hilarious precision, his whole body convulsing with spasms of disgust, particularly when it comes to the subject of sex.

Here we have a Frankenstein for whom flesh is both the physical stuff of his work and the antithesis of his repressed and perverted desires. He's really a fascinating guy, this venting mad doctor, so committed to his work—which involves the creation of life from death in order for sexual union to take place and foster a genetically superior race—that he's subverted his own sexuality.

When his assistant Otto wants to know where they'll get the perfect nasum, the Baron tells his devout little toadie that he knows of a place in the village where dirty and disgusting women with huge breasts do dirty and disgusting things. While still in school, the Baron says, his friends used to try to lure him away from his books to go there and indulge, but he would have none of it.

His sexual retardation proves his ultimate undoing. Not only does he naively talk of getting a male to "fall in love with my female zombie," but he's married to his sister (for the children's sake; whose or what are they?). He spies on the nympho Baroness while she makes love with that "peasant boy," and hasn't a clue as to why his male zombie isn't responding to his female zombie while trying to incite an erection.

It could be that the Baron's increasingly hysterical nine recitations of "Kiss him!" are simply a very funny way of showing how completely ignorant he is about varieties of sexual stimulation, or how prudish, but they also work as a knowing parody of Colin Clive's increasingly hysterical eight recitations of "It's alive" in the original **Frankenstein** (1931).

Beyond the joke of having his male zombie's brain belong to a monk-wanna-be, the utter failure of a genius who can reanimate dead flesh but hasn't the slightest idea of what animates limp flesh is very funny stuff. (Another joke involves the "preparation" of impossibly outsized seminal vesicles which are held in front of our noses in 3-D and then dropped in a beaker and stirred up indelicately; the Baron adds a bit of solution and it looks very much like a bad cooking show, or more exactly, like a couple of little boys playing mad scientist.)

Frankenstein's only personal sexual expression comes in one of the film's most notorious sequences. Bloodily snipping open the long (vaginal) stitching on his female zombie and massaging the leaking blood over her breasts, he announces, "I now go into her digestive parts," and proceeds to fondle her insides, breathily calling out, "spleen, kidneys, gall bladder, liver," pulling out some of the sweet and sour innards (sheep guts which were by then stinking up the set to high heaven) and kneading them in ecstasy.

The entire scene, which is far from over yet, is scored as a scene of romantic passion featuring Claudio Gizzi's quite beautiful love-theme melody on the soundtrack. The Baron is a man very much into his work, you might say, but the fact that Morrissey is treating the vivisection as a sex scene is brilliant thematic counterpoint considering the eternal commingling of sex and death, the literal jab at horror film conventions, and the poking fun at a bookworm scientist whose only socialization has been with the dead; the scene also precurses the severed head giving head in Stuart

Gordon's **Re-Animator** (1985).

When he actually gets on the operating table and "mounts" his zombie by lying on top of her and thrusting his hand inside her bloody gash and grinding his hips, the Baron meets Otto's voyeurism at the spectacle with a verbal scolding: "Vy are you looking at me you filty sing (thing) ... turn around!" Kier skillfully manages to invest the parental rebuke with shades of guilt and humiliation perfectly appropriate for the sexual pervert who abhors sex but has the bedroom door opened on him while he's screwing his blow-up doll.

Otto obeys and pretends to be busy cleaning instruments, splitting us up with his bulging eyes and a Mr. Spock raising of one eyebrow, while his master finishes his delirious auto-erotic organasm, finally calling Otto back over to let down the table. A delicious sound effect is heard as the Baron's crimson-colored lab coat separates with a suctiony unsticking from the gory object of his affections and then there is the delivery of the gallbladder line, to which Otto almost does a doubletake and then nods.

Otto is played by Arno Juerging, a young man whom Morrissey remembers meeting quite unexpectedly in New York when the actor's mother dragged the kid into the Factory offices and practically demanded they put her son in one of their movies. **Flesh** and **Trash** had, of course, been huge hits in Germany and Arno was apparently a big fan who yearned to work with the people who made them.

He got his chance. It's interesting to note that Kier said Juerging wanted more and more screen time, so a degree of earnest competition was taking place between them, which perfectly plays into their relationship on-screen. Otto, an obedient dog, worships his master but aspires to even greater things. He corrects himself when using "we" instead of "your" while pumping up the Baron's ego with praise for his accomplishments, and it's ultimately his own ego—spiteful-ly unleashed after a particularly nasty chiding from the Baron—that leads to his destruction.

Of course, in Morrissey's film, it's sex that really does him in. In both instances—the first with a maid whose red guts hang through a grating into our faces in 3-D, the second with the female creature, whom he accidentally destroys—he shows himself a sexually moronic copycat by attempting to "enter" the girls just like his master. The bit with the female zombie is made all the funnier by his lascivious tongue-wagging over her sutured scar. He lowers her genital bandage to show Joe her pubic hair, but apparently has no idea what to do with it, because he summarily re-tapes the bandage and continues to lick at her scar.

Juerging's Otto, with his great bulging eyes and his ridiculous devotion to Frankenstein, makes for a great pairing with Kier and they would repeat the teaming with equal success in **Dracula**.

The first thing a fan might notice coming across Joe is that his beautiful mane of hair has been cropped to the quick. After letting it grow for so many years and having it become something of a trademark for him, I wondered if he minded losing it.

"Paul had decided that the hair had to be cut," he says, without a hint of remorse. "I felt that anything Paul was asking me to do for a film, well, that's the way it's supposed to be. I always followed his direction. So snip, snip, snip and off it came."

Joe plays Nicholas, the horny shepherd whose asexual best friend Sasha gets his head sheared off in a case of mistaken identity when the Baron wrongly assumes that the head he's just gorily detached belongs to a man of great sexual prowess. He needs such a head to top off his male zombie so that it can mate with his female back in the lab.

He doesn't count on Joe subsequently appearing as an employee of the castle—a love-slave, no less, to the Baroness—and recognizing the stitched-on head of a new guest at

With Monique Van Vooren

the dinner table.

Joe's darkly handsome features and laconic sexual buzz are perfect for the role, though he continues his trend toward seriously underplaying his part and one is never quite sure if it's deliberate or merely a reflection of his unhappiness at the time.

He is, of course, entirely out of period synch with his surroundings, yet strangely, it is his comically anachronistic accent and apparent apathy towards being onscreen that fuels his appeal in this campy and very funny gore show. He comes off like the most vapid of stilted horror movie heroes—a David Manners from Queens—and achieves some level of brilliance when reciting dead dialogue about having to get into the Baron's lab while the Baron's nympho sister/wife loudly sucks and laps away at his armpit during an erotic tryst.

The armpit oral sex scene, reportedly actress Monique Van Vooren's answer to her director's request to do something original with Joe, is among the most absurdly funny sex scenes Morrissey has ever done and he calls it a personal favorite. Sex is silly, he tells us for the umpteenth time in his films, something to laugh at. Indeed, sexual obsessions and repressions are the very things that directly lead to the bloody destruction of all the film's characters.

The Criterion Collection laserdisc release of **Flesh for Frankenstein**, which includes a supplementary audio track commentary by Morrissey, Udo Kier, and Morrissey-academician Professor Maurice Yacowar, features the original "European" cut of the X-rated film in letter-box, but with only a single scene change from the stateside original X. Saying it was suggested to shoot a frontal of Joe for the German market, where Joe's casual full-frontal nudity helped fuel the phenomenal success of **Flesh** and **Trash**, Morrissey re-shot the famed armpit-slurping scene with Joe entering Monique Van Vooren's bedroom stark naked, though in medium long shot. He lies down on the bed—still nude, but with his genitalia obscured—as Monique goes to work on his pit.

Though it's usually interesting to see an outtake and sometimes it's fascinating to see footage shot for a foreign market, in this case, I prefer the clothed original. There are far less serendipitously effective slurping and smacking noises in the "nude" version and Joe's reactions aren't quite the same, so it's not nearly as funny. I wish Criterion and Morrissey had kept the original version in the film proper and then added the alternate nude take as a bonus track at the film's end. Though the print is somewhat variable, going from a bit murky to quite gorgeous, it is still the most unedited and only wide-screen version of the film available and it's a shame that such an important scene has been replaced by a far less effective take.

Van Vooren is a scream in **Frankenstein**, snapping off her lines with all the hauteur of a true imperialist. The actress has said she wanted to make the Baroness thoroughly unlikable, but her persistent bitchiness and impatience makes her every stinging comment that much funnier.

Her performance is, in fact, perfect in every tiny detail and what's so wonderful is that you can read every bit of her character's true self beneath the stern, eyebrowless facade. She chastises Nicholas the shepherd only so she can get him to come by her bedroom for a further "reprimand." When he gets there and relates the horrible experience of getting knocked unconscious and waking to find his best friend beheaded, the ice on her tongue melts ever-so-slightly with, "That's a very unusual story." Prepared to berate and threaten to fire him, now that he seems eager to leave, she abruptly changes course and essentially asks him why he's in such a hurry to go; whatever works, so long as she gets him to stay for a romp in the sack.

Her completely self-centered world, a world devoted to her pleasures, is beautifully illustrated when Nicholas comes crashing into her bedroom to tell her what he's found in the lab, to warn her in case she wants to split before it all hits the fan.

"How dare you wake me up in the middle of the day when you know I have insomnia!" she screams. After Joe gives her a really good wallop across the face and runs from the room, she cries out at him, "You farmer! How dare you walk out on me!" (Shades of Sally Todd in **Heat**.)

When her hysterical brother screams that he watched her—his wife—have sex with Joe ("I watched you!"), she counters hilariously: "Up to father's old tricks?" Of course, she too will be destroyed by her sexual preoccupations, literally hugged to death by the sexually-inexperienced male zombie.

Belgian-born Van Vooren comes to her most famous role from a fascinatingly odd career which includes playing Lyra the She-Devil, giving Lex Barker back some of the abuse he's said to have heaped on off-screen wives, in **Tarzan and the She-Devil** (1953), a small role in Dean Martin's first solo feature **Ten Thousand Bedrooms** (1957), a bit in **Gigi** (1958), a bit in Pasolini's **The Decameron** (1970), bedding Jon Voight in his bizarre film debut as **Fearless Frank** (1967), and a key role alongside Mary Woronov in the cult film **Sugar Cookies** (1973). She also did a cameo in **Wall Street** (1987). A real socialite and very popular with gay audiences via a nightclub act, she was friends with many of the Warhol people, as well as Rudolph Nureyev (one of only two men she's known with "translucent skin;" the other is Joe), and she claimed to have discovered handsome Hiram Keller, the only American in **Fellini Satyricon** (1969), and "a very beautiful boy," according to Joe.

Fools thinking they're oh-so-clever by actually taking the time to point out that Dallesandro's accent and acting seem to belong to another film may have even more trouble handling the truth: In 1973, an Andy Warhol movie just wouldn't be an Andy Warhol movie without Joe Dallesandro. Like Walt Disney, the Andy Warhol name really denoted a company, a logo, a type of product, and Joe Dallesandro was their Mickey Mouse. That he'd been injected into the European milieu was not only very deliberate, but contractually practical as well.

Peter Lorre shouldn't have played Mr. Moto, either, but he was great in the part. Tony Curtis doesn't belong in a costume picture or as a Roman slaveboy to Laurence Olivier, but if you've got a bankable star under contract, you use him.

What's so great about Joe in both of the monster films is that there is absolutely no attempt to hide his being an import. When you get Joe Dallesandro, you get the accent, the mannerisms, the whole kit and caboodle. Love him or hate him, understand the implicit humor of having him in the films or disregard the star system and lament his participation, Dallesandro was key to how and why **Frankenstein** and **Dracula** got made in the first place and both are all the more entertaining because he's there.

The male zombie in **Flesh for Frankenstein** is played by a Yugoslavian "experimental film" actor named Srdjan Zelenovic, whom Morrissey cast, naturally enough, for his height and his distinct nasum.

Joe remembers him as a nice enough fellow, but when Joe's wife Terry, who didn't want to stay in Italy, went with Zelenovic to Yugoslavia on a "vacation," he wasn't particularly happy about it. Terry subsequently called Joe and told him that she wanted to sponsor Srdjan so he could come to America and that's when Joe knew the couple were an item, or at least that Zelenovic wanted them to be.

"He didn't have a mean streak in him," says Joe. "It's just that he wanted to survive Yugoslavia. The reason he'd come to Italy in the first place was to get out of the military."

The movie's celebrated gore scenes play even funnier today than I suspect they played originally, if for no other reason than that we've become so sophisticated about our special effects that even the cheesier stuff—body parts that look like mannequin pieces and a gurgling decapitation with giant shears in a badly-disguised day-for-night shot (a necessity due to the light requirements for the 3-D)—are read as knowing parody on cheesy horror movies.

That's an effective diversion, because when special effects man Carlo Rambaldi, who seven years later designed E.T., is asked to pour it on, he does so with considerable aplomb. The female creature's sexual vivisection, the Baron's shocking hand job, and the penultimate spear through the Baron's torso hold up very well and still shock and amuse. A considerably fuzzier, though not particularly insightful Gene Siskel, who senselessly described Joe as "forever nasally-congested," told his readers in the *Chicago Tribune* that "Director Morrissey told me last week his intention was to show just how silly gore can be. I suspect you will fail to get the joke." (Who the hell was he addressing?)

The film's enormously effective music, which includes the tinkle of a child's music box over the Baron's discussion of one day having his new race of zombie children and then a dramatic trumpeting of brass as the Baron forceps the severed head and begins to attach it to his male zombie, was composed by Claudio Gizzi, his very first original film score after impressively arranging the Mahler pieces for Visconti's **Death in Venice** (1971). All Morrissey had to know was that the man worked with Visconti. Good enough for Luchino, good enough for anybody.

The film was shot in the 3-D process known as Spacevision, a one-camera system with a split prism that was supervised on this production by its French inventor, Colonel Robert Bernier. The resulting image provides crisp and clean dimensional planes, so that even though the actors had to be concerned about observing their marks and not moving around a lot within the layers of a shot, Morrissey was still able to include effective close-ups and gorgeous tracking shots, such as the one that opens the film in which the Baroness and her two children are seen riding in her carriage through the woods with pillars of white-barked trees gliding by in both fore and background. It really makes for an exquisite display of the 3-D effects.

Though often read as parodies of the sexy and bloody Hammer Films of the late 50s, 60s and early 70s, neither **Flesh for Frankenstein** nor **Blood for Dracula** was intended as such. Morrissey rarely mentioned the Hammer films in connection with his monster duet and it is highly unlikely that he saw the British products or cared much for any of them if he did. (Besides, Polanski had already done a knowing parody six years earlier with his **Dance of the Vampires,** aka **The Fearless Vampire Killers, or: Pardon Me But Your Teeth Are In My Neck**.)

Fortunately for both films, they aren't parodies subservient to anyone else's work, though the absurd amount of blood and the silliness of all the sex scenes humorously points out the comic liabilities already very much on view in the waning Hammer output. Morrissey was simply interested in doing his own versions of these oft-told tales of a scientist's passion to create his own super-race and a vampire's frustrating quest for a good suck.

Owing in-jokes to no one, they are very much Paul Morrissey films and are direct descendants of the themes and characters and ideas you find running through all of his other work.

With Arno Juerging

With Udo Kier

Given the formal beauty of **Frankenstein**, accomplished with more money than he'd ever had to work with, a crew of sixty (easily 20 times more help than he'd had before), a production designer—Enrico Job—who was a sculptor and both husband to Lina Wertmuller and set designer for her many films, a cinematographer—Luigi Kuveiller—who knew how to light faces, and all of their work captured on 35mm (this was the first time the "Factory" used the standard professional stock), there are those who contend that the horror films are not the work of "underground" experimental filmmaker Paul Morrissey at all, but rather Italian director Antonio Margheriti (aka Anthony M. Dawson). A false conclusion.

The confusion comes from the fact that when the films were released in Italy both bore Margheriti's name as director to oblige financial subsidy by the Italian government. Margheriti, who directed a score of schlock before and after his best film, **Castle of Blood** (1964), did work second unit on **Frankenstein** (perhaps a single day), but his influence on the final print is negligible, no matter how much he prefers to claim otherwise. The actors, including Joe, concur that the films are indeed Morrissey's, and any first year film student will come to the same conclusion.

Working under the constraints of a filmmaking process that required Morrissey not employ the type of camerawork he'd used in his cult experiments, and having the resources—both monetary and professional—to make a slicker production, we're allowed to see him play with painterly tableau (particularly for the dinner table scenes and the scenes of Monique and Joe posing elegantly in bed), but the thematic result is essentially **Flesh**, **Trash**, and **Heat** with a nicer camera.

For the star of that trilogy, the distinctions cut much deeper.

Tensions ran a little high at times, particularly between Joe and Paul, firstly over Joe's insistence that he, too, be provided with scripted dialogue.

"For the first time," Joe says, "Paul had Pat Hackett there trying to fumble the best they could through writing some lines. That's why the lines are so inept. That's not my dialogue. That's not my improvising, that's theirs."

Secondly, there was the not-so-little matter of money.

"What they decided was fair was about $23,000 on **Frankenstein** and $27,000 on **Dracula**," he reports. "Well, I got $25,000 for **Seeds of Evil**. Now how can I go to a company that never worked with me before and make them a movie for $25,000 two years earlier and come to make a movie with you for less than what I made with them? I had made these people so much money, there wouldn't even be a movie if I decided not to make it—the producers would probably pull out, because they had no success rate or track record with anybody else. What are they gonna say, 'Yeah, do it with Candy Darling? With Louis Waldon?' Sure, all of them are Warhol stars and interesting people in their own right, but audiences were not going to the films because of them."

He also says that a $5,000 a month expense allowance was allocated and was supposed to make up for the small paycheck, but "it was paying for the villa, for the food. We were renting Polanski's villa (the Villa Mandorli off Appia Antica), the one he usually rents out, and it was all coming out of my expense allowance."

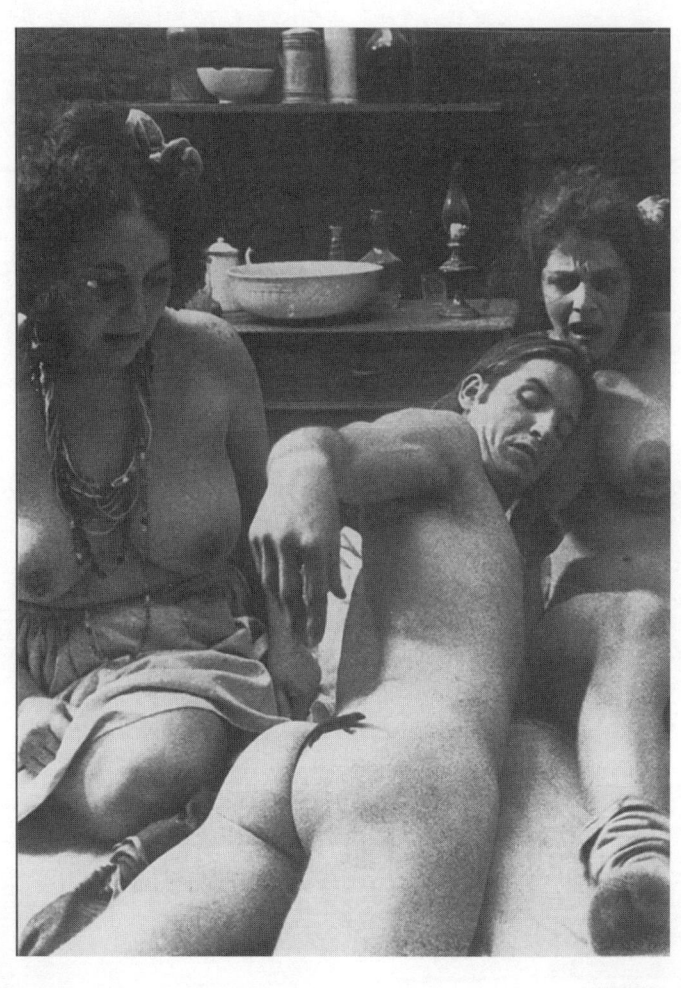

Debates about money on the set also became debates about money off the set. **Andy Warhol's Frankenstein**, in 3-D and even with an X-rating for the gore, still managed to gross over a million dollars in less than two months of its limited release. Originally, the trades indicated that MGM would be distributing both the "Warhol" monster pix, but the honors went instead to Bryanston Pictures, which then took the liberty of chopping out some of the gore on a portion of the prints in order to play them in more theaters with an R rating. For international markets, both Italy and Germany played the film intact, but Great Britain demanded 8 minutes in cuts.

By the end of the year, the film would gross over $5,000,000, a certified success that would compound internationally. It would go on to see a surprisingly healthy return engagement eight years later beginning in May of 1982 during the brief revival of 3-D that spawned **Jaws 3-D** and **Friday the 13th Part III in 3-D**, among many others.

The rough guess was that **Frankenstein** had grossed some $20,000,000+ worldwide, a figure that both interested and frustrated Andy Warhol and his legal counsel, who were wondering where their proper share of the returns was going and why there seemed to be so much difficulty in getting a true accounting of the proceeds. Andy even contemplated serving Ponti with a summons via his wife, Ms. Loren, who he was supposed to meet for lunch one day in 1977. Warhol's lawyers did file suit against Ponti, who later got into legal troubles with the Italian government to the tune of four months in jail and a $25,000,000 fine for smuggling currency and art out of the country, but he was by then a French citizen and could not be extradited. Warhol makes mention of the money Ponti owes him for **Frankenstein** and **Dracula** several times in his published diaries.

The rights have only very recently been returned to director Morrissey on the series of films he made under the Warhol banner beginning with **Flesh**. **Frankenstein**, as well as **Dracula**, led a very haphazard existence since its release in 1974, with rights changing from company to company and prints hacked up indiscriminately and repackaged for double bills (where **Frankenstein** was shown as a "flat" print—no 3-D).

Several versions of **Frankenstein** and **Dracula** were also released for the video market—including a letter-boxed 3-D version said to be quite effective—but most often in R-rated cuts where the quality of the prints left much to be desired. Thankfully, the Criterion laserdisc versions, particularly of **Dracula**, were struck from very good and uncut originals. The films can now be enjoyed in a manner befitting the work of all involved, not the least being cinematographer Kuveiller, whose gorgeous camerawork the *Hollywood Reporter* described as having "the allure of a William Blake drawing."

Said colleague William Friedkin of the director's work here: "Morrissey does things in that film that are incredible. Clever and inventive."

Flesh for Frankenstein was screened in Paris as early as February of 1974, where *Variety* caught it with **Dracula** and reported that "some cult usage may develop for this pair of elegant horror pix," in which Joe Dallesandro was "in fine stud form."

A pair of sold-out shows presented by Filmex after the Academy Awards in Los Angeles went over particularly well. Monique Van Vooren's friend Rudolph Nureyev was in attendance and told Morrissey that he was convinced that 3-D was the perfect process with which to capture dance on film.

The Hollywood Reporter found the movie "discreetly beautiful" and "the acting is more controlled than it has ever been in a Morrissey/Warhol film, especially the wry performance given by Joe Dallesandro who is, as ever, the sensible, reasonable street urchin trapped in impossible, absurdist situations."

For Udo Kier, the film is an unqualified tour de force, an actor's playground, and easily as funny in its own way as Gene Wilder's frizzy "Fronkinsteen" in **Young Frankenstein**, released the same year. (In Brooks' film, much is made of the pronunciation of the family name; in Morrissey's, the name is never once uttered.) It's no wonder that Kier admits to owning only two of his films on tape, **Frankenstein** and **Dracula**, because both are performances to relish. Nearly every line has a verbal hook—"populate" becomes "pa-poo-late," then it's "Why must you always pick on muzza (mother)?"—and his zeal knows no bounds, evidenced in a lengthy crescendo during which the man who stitches together human bodies tries to re-assemble himself by ludicrously sticking his severed hand onto the spouting stump from which it came. It won't work, of course, so in an inspired moment of childish frustration, he throws his hand at Joe, screaming, "It's all your fault!"

Even impaled, with a hunk of his shiny guts thrust 3-D into our faces, he manages a funny last speech, telling himself that, "I'm not going to die in vwain." There's even room for a little bit of sanctimony: "I am no one, I just had a laboratory and a dream."

Lots of horror film history books need a page ripped out and re-written when it comes to **Flesh for Frankenstein**, which has been ignorantly dismissed by genre critics as some sort of half-baked freak show from the Andy Warhol weirdos. It is, in fact, a very well made and extremely funny entry in the long saga of **Frankenstein** films and well worth scholarly reappraisal untainted by pedestrian write-offs about gobs of gore and misquoted profane dialogue that lump it in with exploitation.

It's not an exploitation film. It's a seriously demented comedy.

blood for dracula (1974)

"He makes no particular attempt to act in conventional terms, his monotone New York accent playing in funny contrast to the high style, Old World ambiance otherwise lushly evoked."

—*Hollywood Reporter, November 5, 1974*

(Also known as Andy Warhol's Dracula; Dracula Cerca Sangue Di Vergine E … Mori De Sete; Dracula Vuole Vivere: Cerca Sangue Di Vergina; Andy Warhol's Young Dracula) **With JOE DALLESANDRO AS MARIO BALATO, Udo Kier (Count Dracula), Arno Juerging (Anton), Maxime McKendry (Marquisa Di Fiori), Vittorio De Sica (Marquis Di Fiori), Milena Vukotic (Esmeralda), Dominique Darrel (Saphiria), Stefania Casini (Rubinia), Silvia Dionisio (Perla), Roman Polanski (Villager). Directed by Paul Morrissey. 106 minutes, Italy.**

As the story goes, on the very same day they finished shooting **Flesh for Frankenstein**, director Paul Morrissey ordered haircuts for Udo Kier, Arno Juerging and Joe Dallesandro and they began filming **Blood for Dracula**. (There may have been some overlap, as Kier's hair inexplicably switches between two styles in **Frankenstein**.) The filmmaker had hoped to photograph **Dracula** in 3-D, as well, but the confines of the villa in which they would be shooting interiors made the process too cumbersome, so the idea was scrapped.

Dracula is, in many respects, and as befits its cinematic heritage, a twin to **Frankenstein**. Produced in the reverse order, the original **Dracula** was released in 1931 and was such a hit that **Frankenstein** was immediately rushed into production at Universal and saw its own release later the same year.

Both "originals" are classics in their own right, with **Frankenstein,** in the hands of director James Whale, given the critical edge. Tod Browning seemed to have lost interest in **Dracula** as the production wore on, though the opening reel in Transylvania and Bela Lugosi's splendidly exotic and iconographic performance rescue it from being just a creaky old stage play.

Morrissey, a film devotee, felt no one had topped the original films and had no interest in

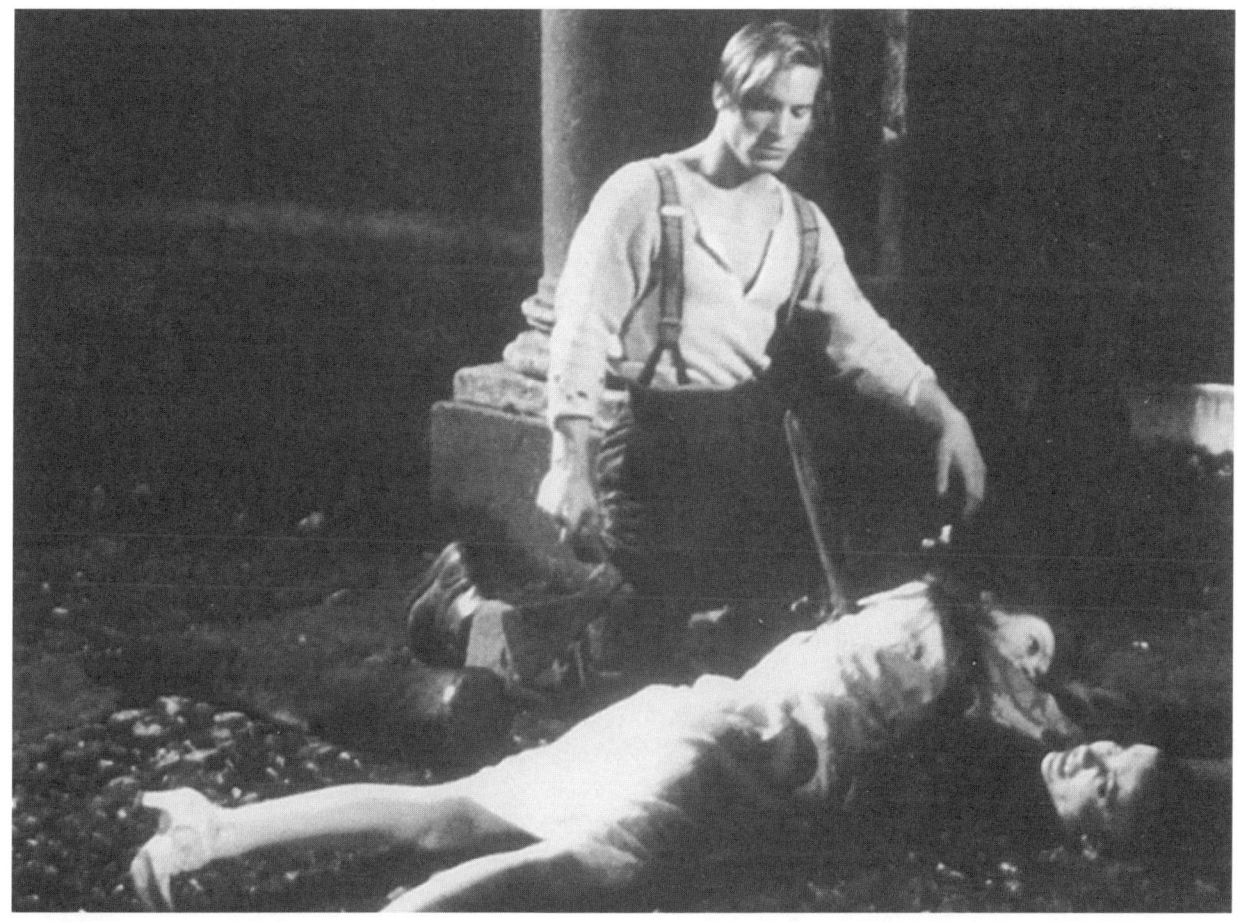

The Finale

ANDY WARHOL'S DRACULA
A FILM BY PAUL MORRISSEY

"Lavishly costumed and photographed in Italy."
—*Newsweek*

Joe Dallesandro, Udo Kier, Arno Juerging
Bryanston; Directed by Paul Morrissey
Color; Rated X, C; 106 minutes

Based on the famous Transylvanian legend, Andy Warhol's DRACULA follows the giant success of his FRANKENSTEIN. There's plenty of sex and camp humor and the faint-of-heart had better stay away—blood is not in short supply. Warhol regular Joe Dallesandro turns in his best performance yet as the gardener who beds the young ladies and finally does Dracula in. The old bloodsucker craves blood from only virgins in Warhol's version, and virgins are in short supply—even in 1930 Italy.

PUBLICITY AVAILABLE
Free Bulletin Board Posters
16mm Preview Reel

Rental $175.00
Rental Oct. 5 - Nov. 5 $250.00

re-making either of them. He did, however, borrow the time frame for his **Dracula** from the Lugosi stage triumph—the 1920's, when, as he says on the director's audiotrack of the Criterion laserdisc version, "the moral fabric of civilization started to tear … nobody ever questions what happens when people get what they want."

In an opening shot as classical in its own way as any afforded a Dracula film, we see a close-up of the Count (Udo Kier) applying dark make-up to his frosty eyebrows, then blood-red lipstick to his lips—which part to reveal fangs. There follows a wider shot as the Count paints black dye into his ghostly white hair before a make-up mirror in which, as the joke is realized, he casts no reflection.

Here is a Count Dracula who is pale and thin, sickly and weak, ready to die with his ailing sister in the vault of his castle if not for the insistence of his assistant Anton (Arno Juerging), who has arranged for the Count to travel by car to Italy in search of "were-gins."

Detailed with modern touches, such as the Count's concern about the heater working in the car and a shot of him in daylight as he locks the front door of his castle (Morrissey said he simply forgot about the effects of sunlight on a vampire, and when reminded, decided to have Dracula shield himself with his hat), the film isn't as earnestly funny as **Frankenstein**, but it's in many ways much more poetic.

Udo Kier bookends his manic Baron Frankenstein with a morose, pessimistic Count Dracula wasting away as surely as the aristocracy of which he was once a part. "That's the way it is with that rich trash," says handyman Mario with contempt. "They're all sick and rotten." The vampire is dying because of a new cultural decadence that makes finding women who are sexually pure an increasingly difficult enterprise. As one of the daughters he meets councils her younger sister, it's perfectly all right to have both a husband and a lover so long as you bathe and smell fresh in between. Ironically, it's the religiosity, the Catholicism, of Italy that brings Dracula there.

If the Count drinks tainted blood, we soon discover, he turns green-faced, his eyes cross, and he finds himself quaking and spasmodically up-chucking in the tub or toilet. Kier throws his entire lean physique into these paroxysms, making them so realistic that we can feel the weakness and the enormous drain on this pallid creature. And besides, when's the last time you got a good laugh out of watching someone convulsively urp a half quart of blood all over the bathroom?

Reportedly inspired by the great Peter Lorre, and deliberately avoiding an imitation of Lugosi, Kier invests his whole self into his Dracula. He manages to make him a seductive figure despite his depression and ill health.

He's also very funny, whether complaining about Italian cooking with "so much oil on everything," or quizzing Saphiria to find out if she's ever been with a man before.

"You don't know what boys do with little girls?" he asks in growing excitation, his eyes widening and his hand masturbating himself below frame (an action not made explicit in Morrissey's final cut of the film). He's so fucking hungry to sink his fangs into her sweet neck he can barely control himself.

"No," she lies.

"You're telling me the truth? I believe you!" he rattles off in the heat of the moment, springing from his wheelchair and clamping his teeth into her.

The puke scene that follows then becomes the first of several funny disengorgings and there's wonderful irony in the fact that almost all of the blood spewed in this particular Dracula movie comes from out of the Count himself. The only notable exception is Morrissey's pièce de resistance featuring the Count greedily lapping up the blood puddle resulting from Joe's de-virginizing the Di Fiori's 14 year old in order to "save her life."

On one of the shooting days, Kier was called away to fulfill a commitment on a German film and Morrissey shot the scene in the tavern in which Anton chats up the locals to find out about the Di Fiori family. The woman at the table (with her 14-year old daughter) who tells him, "We just stopped in for a quick one on our way home from the fields," is Juerging's own mother, the woman responsible for getting him the job in Morrissey's films.

At another table sit three peasant workers, only one of whom talks during the scene. The man in the middle is producer Andrew Braunsberg and the man on the right is screenwriter Gérard Brach. The most authentic looking of the trio and the man who invites Anton to join them is none other than Roman Polanski (whose next project would be **Chinatown**).

Polanski came up with the "You Can't Do What I Can Do" bit in which the seethingly proper Anton is shown up by the earthy peasant in a mirror game that he assumes is childishly simple. His humiliation is a slap in his classist face when he loses the game that is, indeed, childishly simple. (Polanski's invention adds a nice touch to the film. He would play a variation on it in his own **Bitter Moon** almost twenty years later.)

Juerging's Anton provides him with a larger and more important role than in **Frankenstein** and it's easy to see he's enjoying it. Morrissey thought the actor resembled Peter Lorre a little bit and certainly loved his voice and glaring-eyed stares. Here, he is as terse as the Baron in **Frankenstein**, but he's also a wonderfully comical little man whose intensity and wavering accent—he wants to know "if they are were-gins and awailable"—makes for some of the film's best moments. (Sadly, in real life, the actor eventually committed suicide.)

Adding to the potpourri mix of accents in the film is *Vogue* magazine food editor Maxime McKendry's nasally-British clipped diction. McKendry reaches the height of ridiculous aristocratic propriety when she comes across Joe deflowering her 14-year old daughter against the wall beneath a magnificent mural of a hunting party: "My God, you're just an employee! How dare you put my daughter in such an unfortunate position!"

The most impenetrable accent, however, belongs to another special guest star, Vittorio De Sica, the famed director of such classics as **The Bicycle Thief** (1948), **Umberto D** (1952), and **The Garden of the Finzi-Continis** (1971). Producer Carlo Ponti, who had produced several of De Sica's films, including **Two Women** (1960), **Yesterday Today and Tomorrow** (1963), and **Marriage Italian Style** (1964), asked his friend to put in the appearance even though De Sica was worried about the possibility of having to improvise in English during his three day stint.

His contribution to the film, as challenging to decipher as some of it is, proves to be a source of Old World charm. His Marquis has gambled away the family's fortunes, but through it all he remains the family poet, his voice twinkling with delight as he elocutes to wife and daughters who haven't the time or patience for his linguistic predilections.

To decide whether he likes the idea of this Count Dracula, he swirls the name around in his mouth like a wine-taster (he is, in fact, a self-professed "name-taster"), then lets it fall trippingly across his tongue in a vibrato repetition, dissecting the syllables and the etymological fragrance and timbre.

A bizarre farewell in which he assures his wife that all will be well because there's no indication that names ending in "ula" show any negative signs, followed by the peculiar admission that "I am getting the analysis of Count Dracula's urine made by Dr. Benson" in London, was of De Sica's own invention.

With **Dracula**, Joe gets an even juicier opportunity to wrap his thick Brooklyn-accent around dialogue delivered in Central Europe than he had in **Frankenstein**. Here he's the Marxist handyman, Mario Balato, who gets to scowl interminably and deliver enjoyably vitriolic speeches against the class system and about social revolution while bedding two daughters of an aristocratic family teetering on ruin.

The girls, who seem to be at least as much interested in each other as Mario, tease their lower class lover by telling him about the Count who has come to their house looking for a suitable bride. If one or the other should be chosen, he's not to worry, he can either be their butler or maybe a slaveboy.

"So, he's an aristocrat?" Mario grumps with contempt. "Is he broke, too?"

Now, now, mother allowed him to come and she...

"Your mother has some high-falutin' ideas for a woman who's got a crackpot for a husband and a house that's falling down. All you got is a title to put in front of your names and someday that's not gonna count either. You're gonna be on the bottom. It's gonna be just like Russia."

"Russia?" asks one of the sisters.

"Don't you know what happened in Russia, you dope? They had a revolution there, that's all. They killed all the rich people. Took everything they had and killed them. You won't even have this crummy house when it happens here."

His bedroom has a red hammer and sickle painted on the wall and he uses and abuses the girls like a sexual fascist. "I'm tired of you two tramps," he says sourly. "What about your sister? What does she do all night? I'd really like to rape the hell out of her."

"She's only 14. A real goody-goody."

"I'd treat her real sweet. She'd like that I bet."

When he finds out that the Count has come looking specifically for virgins, Mario famously asks, "So what's he doin' with you two hooers?," an exaggerated New Yawk delivery for a character who's supposed to be a second generation worker at the estate; yet it's comically echoed by the Count after one of his more excruciating vomiting sessions when he laments, "My body can't take this treatment anymore. The blood of these hooers is killing me. I just want my coffin back to sleep in."

Joe also gets to utter the film's last line, a succinct declaration of the plain simple truth as embodied by an entire history of horror movie peasant mobs: "He lives off other people, he's no good to anybody, and he never was." And in goes the stake. [But not before a chase scene that has Joe chopping off Dracula's limbs one spurting stump at a time—pre-figuring and possibly inspiring the famed Black Knight encounter in **Monty Python and the Holy Grail** (1974).]

When I tell Joe how impressed I am with the make-up job done to hide his tattoo, he seems to remember they "reversed the film. You're seeing the opposite arm." But both arms are on display in several of his butt-nekkid hump scenes, as well as during a sweaty display of wood-chopping, and the tattoo is virtually invisible. If his memory about the film is a little faded, it's easy to understand. The Italian monster movies are not ones he either visits

With Dominique Darrel and Stefania Casini

With Stefania Casini

often or holds in very high esteem.

He was plainly unhappy on the project.

"At one point, during the finale of **Dracula**," he recalls, "Paul tortured the shit out of me. Word got back to me that I supposedly couldn't do dialogue, so I made them write my dialogue every day like they were doing for everybody else. Then Paul would make me do ten rehearsals of a three word line. And I'd say, 'Paul, what is this? Are you trying to fuck with me?' And Paul would say, that's how it's done. 'I know how it's done, Paul, because you see how I'm doing it. I don't change because you make me do it over and over again. I'm still going to give it to you exactly the same way. If you put the two voice tracks over each other, they'd match up perfectly.'

"He was torturing me. He wanted to see if he could upset me into not being able to do what he suggested I wouldn't be able to do. Not only did I prove I could, but I proved it while I was working with people who couldn't learn their cue lines. I was giving them their cue with my foot. We had an Italian, a German, a Yugoslavian (on **Frankenstein**), and none of them were learning the cue lines. I'm thinking, how hard is it to learn—even if it's not your language—a couple of fucking lines? It's not like they had these long speeches, because Pat couldn't write that much. I think we did about three pages a day every day, maybe five, which was a lot of work. The whole screenplay was about seventy to eighty pages. Just pathetic dialogue."

The story goes that when Paulette Goddard—a "friend" of Warhol's—saw Joe in **Dracula**, she proclaimed him a "born star," adding only that he should study ballet and mime so that he might move more gracefully.

The camerawork and cinematography are gorgeous realizations of a visual aesthetic not previously associated with Morrissey until his monster films. **Dracula**, though, much more even than **Frankenstein**, has a design and composition suitable for framing. The shot of Dracula's black car loaded with coffin and with wheelchair on top driving over an arched bridge in the distance is as painterly as Visconti. One might be lulled into believing that it's just the locales, but you actually don't have to look very deeply to see how orchestrated the shots are. One of Morrissey's most effective techniques is to begin a shot in relative close-up and then zoom or dolly in reverse to allow all the elements to come into gorgeous tableau.

Blood for Dracula was reviewed as early as February of 1974 in Paris, but opened in the States in November. It was widely distributed and eventually double-featured with **Frankenstein** in early 1975. It was clipped of four minutes of footage to play in Great Britain. For reasons probably attributable to lack of the 3-D gimmick, it did far less business than its predecessor and was even retitled for a time as **Young Dracula** to play off the success of Mel Brooks' **Young Frankenstein**. (A David Niven vampire stinker of the same time was titled **Old Dracula**.)

Those who have seen the film in all of the myriad chopped-up and inferior dubs really need to see it in the 1996 Criterion Laserdisc edition where, I'll promise you, it will seem like you're watching it again for the very first time. It is often an astonishingly beautiful film to behold and the colors have never been richer.

As with **Frankenstein**, **Dracula** looks and plays better and better all the time. As late as 1992, Ben Sonnenberg reviewed it in *The Nation* and noted that "Morrissey's **Dracula** doesn't have a portentous subtext like most other vampire films. It's like a jolly season in Hell with someone who knows the turf. It follows the Bram Stoker novel in focusing on property, breeding and social class; in wedding an Anglo-Irish ghost story to Transylvanian folk tales; and in changing the vampire's gender to male."

Dismissal of the film as a mistaken product of Andy Warhol's derisable moviemaking talents in books by lazy and ignorant horror film "scholars," who really ought to know better, is a matter deserving of immediate redress. Indeed, Morrissey's film is a more than worthy contribution to Dracula's cinematic heritage and warrants an equal shot at genre study and analysis.

Announced during the early production of **Frankenstein** and **Dracula** was a third Euro-financed film for Morrissey entitled **West**, to be produced by Alberto Grimaldi and begin shooting in the summer of 1973. The idea had been considered as early as 1971, and the director told *Variety* that the spoof would be based on historical precedent.

"In the early settlements, there was maybe one woman for every 100 pioneers," he told the trade paper, "and under such circumstances, the men created their own sex frolics. The one woman in **West** is an amoral saloonkeeper. The others are all drag." Dallesandro was announced as heading the cast, with MGM distributing (!).

Joe remembers the project as "essentially a remake of **Lonesome Cowboys**, except with more drag queens. Paul's idea was that there weren't many women around back then. [to an imaginary Paul] I don't know what West you're talking about Paul, but I can tell you this, I don't think you should go walking around Texas telling people that because they might hang you from a fucking cactus."

For a short time after Joe's defection, the film was associated with Mick and Bianca Jagger, but never did get off the ground.

Meanwhile, back in the States, young Jed Johnson, whose twin brother Jay was also a regular figure at the Factory, was stepping behind the camera to do **Andy Warhol's Bad** (1976). The project was developed specifically for Paul Morrissey to do, but he wasn't interested and remained in Europe. Johnson had cut his filmmaking teeth on **Trash** (editor and soundman), **Women in Revolt** (sound and cameraman), **Heat** (co-editor), **L'Amour** (cameraman and co-editor) and had worked as co-editor on both **Frankenstein** and **Dracula**.

"The movie **Bad** was written for me and they called me up in Italy and asked, 'Joe, will you come back and do it?' And I said absolutely not."

It's easy to see him as the vagabond smalltime criminal played by Perry King in what turned out to be the Factory's final movie, a twisted tale of grotesque crimes and infanticide parlayed out of Carroll Baker's electrolysis clinic. Baker and Susan Tyrell give terrific performances, and Joe's flame from Italy, Stefania Casini, shows up as one of the nasty girls who enjoys tormenting Tyrell and inexplicably sticks a severed human finger inside a ketchup bottle.

"Perry King is a good actor, but I think Joe would have been much better," offers Morrissey. "Because Joe is a sympathetic actor and that's a very important quality. No matter what his characters do in my films, the audience still empathizes with him."

The budget on **Andy Warhol's Bad** came close to 1.5 million dollars, easily the result of the enormous success the Factory had seen with each successive film, but particularly so with **Frankenstein**, for which they put up no cash, but in which they had an interest that was constantly in dispute. The lurid subject matter and extreme characters were certainly akin to the stuff popularly associated with Andy Warhol, but it's interesting that just when Joe's dream of making better films with better equipment was coming to fruition, he'd had his fill.

In more ways than one.

"I was brought up a very strict Catholic. I believe the films I made with Andy Warhol are a sin—**Trash** and **Heat** and **Flesh**," Joe told the adult men's magazine *Oui* (July, 1974) in an issue that includes steamy nude couplings of he and Stefania. "But in New York I would go to confession and the priest would say it was all right, I should go right ahead. It was what I needed to survive and support my family."

He was also getting tired of all the nudie attention. "I want to do some films of importance without having to do nude things constantly," he told another adult magazine, *Viva* (June, 1974), in an interview which he said would be his last. "Males get undressed now. I mean, everybody does it. I think it's becoming boring. And now that the big stars have done it there's no reason for anybody else to do it, is there?"

When I ask him about the "sin" quote, I expect him to brush it off as something he said once when he was angry and the balcony outside his bedroom window looked out across the Tiber and took in the dome of St. Peter's at the Vatican, but, "That's what I honestly believed at the time," he says. Not only during the time they were making the films, "but for a long time after that."

Suddenly, an entirely unexpected dimension revealed itself; one in which the casual screen image of an open-minded young man comfortable with his body and seemingly comfortable with his sexuality and its multi-faceted effect on others has to be reconciled with an actor whose religious upbringing he's not entirely able or desirous to shake, particularly so twenty or thirty years ago.

"I understood that the perception of my personal openness was a great part of my characters' appeal to audiences back then, and I also understood that the audience didn't know that on some levels the stuff I was doing did disturb me."

Did it trouble you greatly?

"At times, it did trouble me greatly. And later on, it just bothered me."

He was also bothered by the idea that he wasn't being afforded the room to grow in his career, to seek out other opportunities.

He told *Newsday* as early as 1970: "I think there is a nicer way to use me in movies. I'd just like to attempt it some day and see if I can and if I fail at that then I will just give up the movie business."

"When I left the Warhol clan," he tells me, "it was because I had done so much work for them for so long and they weren't allowing me to go off and do other things. They were telling other people that they didn't think I could do it."

"There's no need for Joe to work in other movies," Paul Morrissey rationalized for a reporter in 1969. "Our films are more exciting. And our audiences are getting bigger."

It would perhaps be too easy to see Joe's split from the people who gave him this extraordinary career as being filled with anger and bitterness. Years after the actual event, he sees a much more practical rationale than evidenced in some of his subsequent interviews. Warhol comments on one in his published diaries when he mentions seeing an interview with Joe in which the actor claims he never hung around with or was even friends "with those Factory people."

"I was never bitter," he corrects me. "I was angry with them about something that I had a legitimate reason to be angry about. We had made money off these movies—a very decent amount of money—and Andy was able to buy (the beach house at) Montauk and Paul was able to buy his brownstone, and even that wasn't my anger. My idea when

I made these movies and we started making money was that we start making better movies, because when I got involved with it more and more, I saw that we were doing something that was fairly good and we had already captured an audience. We were making all this money and yet we weren't taking a dime to fucking repair the camera we were using."

What's even more frustrating for him is the sense that even while he had seen the popularity of his own films for Morrissey/Warhol grow, he didn't see that success filter down to anybody who acted in the films. On at least one point, Paul Morrissey seems to agree with Joe—that the Factory as a film factory with a company of players was in many ways just a myth.

"When Andy finally started making money," says Joe, "he could have had his troupe of people. They certainly acted like they were a troupe, with Eric Emerson, Louis Waldon, Viva. He had a whole bunch of people who kept coming back, hanging around and doing their films, but he didn't do right by them. I mean, Andy had enough to go around that everybody could have been comfortable. They didn't have to be greedy."

When asked about his interest in graduating to Hollywood films, Joe told the *Village Voice* in 1972: "I'm interested in making a very big salary. Not that I don't make enough money now, but I'd like to make more money." For the record, Joe drew a reported wage ranging from $124 - $150 a week as Factory employee in the early seventies, or, as one British paper put it, "roughly a New York streetsweeper's pay."

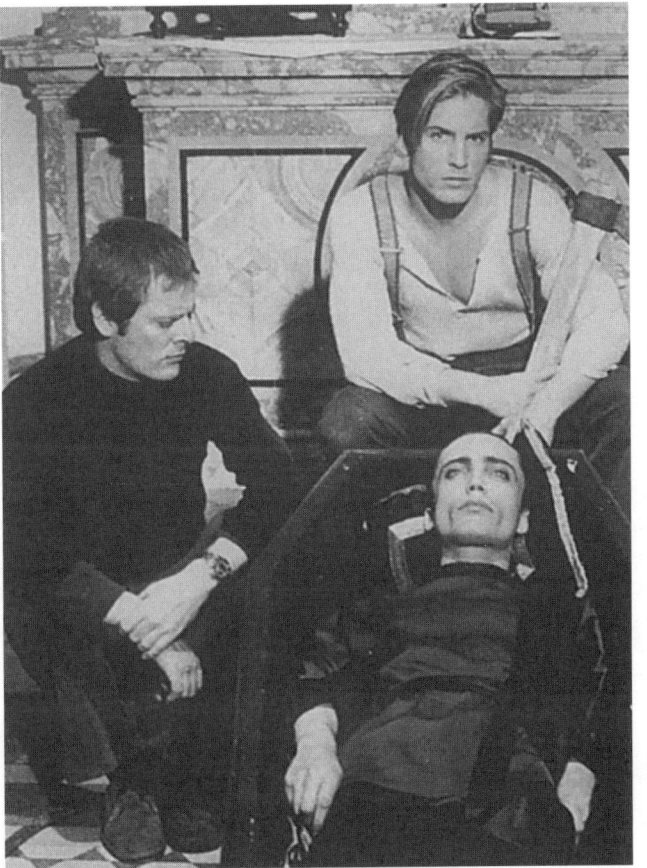

In November of 1967, Paul America, star of the Warhol/Morrissey film **My Hustler** (1965), threatened to sue Warhol for money he felt was owed him. No doubt begrudgingly, Andy gave him $1,000 with the possibility of $1,500 more if the film made money. Few have seen even that much return for their work.

Joe says, "The problem was that the nitwits would come in thinking that the movies made millions of dollars,

On the set with Paul Morrissey and Udo Kier

which they didn't. The only movies that ever made millions of dollars were **Flesh**, **Trash**, **Heat**, **Frankenstein** and **Dracula**," adding somewhat gleefully: "Andy and Paul both got fucked on **Frankenstein** and **Dracula**, so good for them. They finally got fucked like they did to other people. But they still got theirs, just like I got mine. I got a career. They got to make a million dollar movie, which they never would have been able to do on their own.

"Instead of seeing other studios doing our storylines and making them look better and doing them in better ways, I thought we could do the same. Then I'll look better, the product will be better, and there won't be a problem with saying that what we're doing is legitimate."

Fighting for legitimacy was at the crux of Joe's decision to stay in Italy and pursue film projects there.

"My agent said I had to do one art film a year and I told him I wanted to stay away from those. I'd had enough of art. So I tried to stick with shoot 'em ups. No westerns, because I was too short for horses, but anything else I wanted to do. I had three films signed to do before I finished **Frankenstein** and **Dracula**."

Of note, it was Paul Morrissey, who also stayed in Italy for a time following his horror comedies, who tried to steer his disgruntled discovery into a suitable direction. He introduced Joe to the work of director Marco Ferreri, the only director whom Morrissey thought might be able to utilize Joe's talents properly in Europe.

"I didn't know the man or his work, so I was introduced to it by Paul," says Joe of Ferreri, the award-winning writer-director of a series of acerbic social comedies, including most famously **The Wheelchair** (1960), **Dillinger Is Dead** (1969), and the suicidally gluttonous masterwork **La Grande Bouffe** (1973).

The two never did work together, but another relationship was fostered in Italy for Joe when he fell for one of his **Dracula** co-stars, the beautiful Stefania Casini, on whom he had to lie naked and simulate sex for the big screen. Casini said that she and the other actresses took note of this handsome American stud right away, but their mutual admiration was communicated in body language, since Casini didn't speak a word of English and learned all of her lines for the film phonetically.

Over the next year or so, the two grew to become quite an item, working together on at least two more film projects, and putting up with each other's idiosyncrasies and game-playing.

"I like everything about him," she told *Oui*. "But I hate people who hurt me. If Joe is away, I go out with another man if I want to. I do it to punish him. Sometimes I say to myself, 'Stefania, try to understand him. This is a terribly neurotic person who tries to put his neuroses onto others'... But I'm not so sweet myself. Sometimes he makes my nerves break. Living with Joe is like living with a superstar."

The relationship may be all that Joe Dallesandro can salvage from his memories of making the Morrissey horror films, which is a real shame, but an unavoidable truth.

"At the time, I did the best that I could, but there was still so much more that I could have done. That we could have been doing. It was a sell-out to do **Frankenstein** and **Dracula** for Ponti; it was a total fucking sell-out, because they couldn't get Hollywood to do it for them, and I couldn't get Hollywood to do it for me because of their bad lip and the types of things I was doing for them. C'mon, I was doing their films and on top of that they're gonna bad lip me? I mean, I still respect them and I realize that they gave me a career, but that still doesn't mean that I haven't taken offense to the fact that they shortchanged themselves and they shortchanged me."

VIDEO REPLAY: Saphiria comes to visit mean old Mario in his workshed and tries to communicate her dread of Count Dracula. "He's so ugly," she tells him. "Of course, he's ugly," spits back Mario. "You'll have to have babies from him and they'll be ugly, too. For the rest of your life you'll be with ugly people. You might as well get used to it."

donna e bello

(1974)

"You have to remember, it's a very small city. All roads lead to Rome. It is a place of great decadence. You sit down and eat lunch for three hours and then you siesta. The only thing you really have to worry about in that country is hemorrhoids."

—*Joe Dallesandro*

(Also known as Woman And Lover; One Woman's Lover) **With JOE DALLESANDRO AS WALTER, Andrea Ferreol (Ottavia), Marino Masé (Mario), Daniela Metternich, Massimo Sarchielli, Henning Schluter. Directed by Sergio Bazzini. 95 minutes, Italy-France-West Germany.**

Joe's first film away from under the clutches of Andy Warhol was this funny, rude, and entertaining sex farce set in rural Italy. Director Marcello Andrei intended to be the first to feature the actor, post-Factory, by casting him to play a cold-hearted street thug in **Il Tempo Degli Assassini (Season For Assassins** in the States), but first-time director Sergio Bazzini beat Andrei to it. Here, Bazzini gave Joe a most unorthodox debut into a movie world without Warhol.

A woman is cleaning out a stall in which a cow moos in annoyance, and then lets loose a prodigious sluice of piss. This apparently triggers the woman's own need to squat, as she does dutifully over the hay mound in the neighboring stall. Not long after she lets loose her stream, a muffled sound and rustling can be heard from the hay beneath her. She's peeing on someone's face! Thoroughly drenched, the unfortunate pushes aside the hay in half-hearted protest while managing a disgusting gurgled swallow.

"I'm sick," he moans.

The woman screams and runs out of the barn, followed shortly by a staggering Joe, who collapses to the ground.

The stables and servant's quarters in which he's stumbling belong to a woman in the employ of a fat old Count who owns the attached villa. The woman's husband, a surreptitious

Communist, has left for a term to meet fellow Reds, though he tells his fat boss—seen sipping tea and raising his legs with great effort to pass billows of gas—that he's off to the North Pole.

The Count, as it turns out, must be away on business, too, leaving the woman and her obese and retarded son to play host to a recuperating Joe. Joe plays Walter, not only a sexy addition to the middle-aged woman's meager household, but a forced destitute since the retarded boy found Walter's money and scissored out the faces to put on his pictures of half-naked women.

I really wish Walter would have been a good guy, a sweetie who brought life and liberation to the farm, but just when we start to get to like him and he's teaching the retarded son how to chug-a-lug (the son ends up pouring the booze over the top of his beret), and he's even seen slow dancing with the kid, we hear him grumble: "If the bitch kicks me out, I'm fucked."

Joe's a user again. Fortunately, there's plenty of bawdy humor to be played out given his situation.

During their first sex scene together, the woman, Ottavia, protests that Walter's hurting her inside. "Resist it," he advises, continuing to plow away while a picture of Lenin hangs on the bedroom wall. As her moans begin to crescendo, he interrupts with a lackadaisical, "How's it goin'?" She's apparently in ecstasy. Walter looks at his wristwatch.

The film's off-putting use of dark humor plays particularly well today. In one sequence, a girl is seen reading from a fashion magazine at the local boutique while Ottavia is getting all dolled up. The magazine's text is typically inane and preachy, mandating what every girl should know and letting us in on the fact that "legs are of great importance this year." The camera pulls back to reveal the reader as a wheelchaired double-amputee.

Dallesandro makes the most of his role here, using his matter-of-fact delivery to detail to Ottavia the odd story of a former flame of his, a girl who looked just like the one on the cover of this month's *Playmate* magazine. "She used heavy make-up to look younger," he explains, lying shirtless on the bed. "She took sleeping pills and laid down on the train tracks."

Beat beat.

"They never did find her head."

But that's not the kicker.

"Later on, the truth came out ... she was really 57 years old."

And boy, could she kiss. Not exactly kiss, though, says Walter to an interested and playful Ottavia, who'd like him to describe the woman's kisses, how she did them.

"She didn't kiss on the mouth. I called her the all-day sucker," he says. Ottavia still seems confused, so Walter squeezes and licks her belly-button. "You understand?"

Yeah, now she knows what he's talking about. She doesn't want to do it, though. Walter may represent the sexual liberation she craves (she's only had one man—her husband, had sex only once, and has a retarded child as a result of the union), but she has her own horror story to tell.

A freaky couple on a motorcycle show up at the villa. They're counterculture anti-guerrilla operators who subsist on astronaut food. He likes boys, black bikini underwear, and turning somersaults while the soundtrack cuckoos.

"This tube is life, this tube is death," explains the stranger to Walter while displaying little vials of astro pills, one containing sustenance, the other poison. "Which do you prefer?"

"I prefer chicken," says Walter.

Any audience member savvy enough to guess that these vials come into play later on in the film has nothing to be proud of.

Walter's dastardly political affiliations are revealed only after he's caught snooping around the Count's villa and taking a sniff out of a Nazi princess' shoe.

With a little cutting and some of the raw sex footage back in, this weird little flick could be a real hoot and it's unfortunate that it doesn't take its absurdities further than it does. Still, there are plenty of laughs to be had, there's Joe's naked butt, and there's an ensemble of actors apparently having a good time with the offbeat material. And Joe is looking good in the picture, too; marvelously handsome in several shots, particularly in profile, including the erotic little bed play in which we follow Ottavia's fingers in close-up as they march up his chest, past his nipples, up and over his chin and then the "member" between her "fingerman's" legs goes right into his mouth for thumb-sucking euphemism.

"There was no way I could not accept **Donna E Bello**," says Joe, reminded of how several directors were vying to launch his career after he'd left Morrissey and Andy Warhol. "I loved the actress so much. (Andrea Ferreol was the schoolteacher in Ferreri's **La Grande Bouffe**.) If you see the movie, you'd say to yourself, no wonder he wanted to work with her."

Variety said, "Bazzini has dipped into a dust-covered issue of *Playboy* to give the orgasm its rightful place on the human pedestal as a potential source of femme revolt," while further describing the film as "containing the most candid display of simulated erotica in Italian cinema, a complacent vein of cruelty and lots of faddism—political and otherwise. Entry is a marketable dish."

il tempo degli assassini (1975)

"And another thing. You realize that since I've been in here you've accused me of killing a friend, ripping off a jewelry store, and throwing a girl out a window all in one night? Don't you think you're pushin' things a little far?"

—*Pierro (Joe Dallesandro)*

(Also known as Season For Assassins; The Time Of The Assassin) **With JOE DALLESANDRO AS PIERRO GIARANALDI**, Martin Balsam **(Commissioner Katroni)**, Rossano Brazzi **(Father Eugenio), Magali Noel. Directed by Marcello Andrei. 102 minutes, Italy.**

Director Marcello Andrei was kind of upset that he didn't manage to swing Joe into his inaugural post-Andy Warhol role in this nasty little movie about a gang of delinquents tearing up Rome and the hard-as-nails police commissioner who's so tired of it all that he'd just as soon kill them as arrest them. The filmmaker's disappointment was all his, though. Dallesandro deserved better.

Joe gets to play a real vicious son-of-a-bitch, without a single redeeming feature, so it's tough to get any real joy out of watching his work here, though his tight-lipped sneers of pleasure while watching his buddies beat or rape people bring to mind the mischievous grin of a Jack Nicholson. Or a **Mr. Sardonicus**.

Joe plays Pierro, the bell-bottomed leader of a gang of young men who love to mix it up with just about anybody. They're a bunch of hard-boiled nihilists and—at times—the intractably downbeat movie seems to want to say this is what we've come to, this is the youth of today. That may or may not explain the strange title.

Though he's married and has a kid, Pierro spends most of his time on the streets with his friends. He meets an impossibly naive young woman with a high-pitched voice and a bowl haircut who admits she's a "little stupid." The pair have their peculiar moment in the sun, running along the beach (Joe in very tight shorts), frolicking in the water, and kissing in sunny backlit shots while a soft rock American beach tune plays on the soundtrack. The whole oceanfront sequence, including a shot of a woman noticing that the two young guys staring at her from behind a screen are also pissing in the sand, is out of place and perfunctory, but I really wished we'd seen *that* movie instead of the one we are watching. (I'd have loved to see Joe in a teenybopper sexploitation movie losing his virginity, losing his car keys, or even losing his lunch all over the front seat of his old man's convertible.)

We've already been introduced to these thoroughly unlikable characters—seeing them on the beach as playful youngsters does nothing to change our feelings for them. During the course of the film, we'll witness them (Joe included) smash cars, threaten a kid's head with a buzzsaw, strip and rape a woman who was making out in a car with her boyfriend, repeatedly kick a fellow in the nuts whom they've harassed on the bumper cars, and attack Pierro's girlfriend and rape her after Pierro finds out she's pregnant by him and doesn't want to have the abortion he demands. When his cronies show up at her apartment and she asks who they are, Pierro says: "They're friends. They want to get laid. I can't say no to friends."

Sure, on paper this movie sounds like a blast to anybody with even the slightest bit of interest in exploitation movies and I sure as hell would have gone to the drive-in to catch it, but the film is really pretty dead; it's too morosely self-serious to be much fun, at least in the blood and guts department. It just doesn't have the pacing, despite a couple of well-shot car chase sequences.

There is, thank goodness, some priceless dialogue. Playing a priest, faded Italian screen star Rossano Brazzi's first scene in the film has him looking at beaver shot collages Pierro has made and hung on his walls at home. When the irate youth walks in and sees the padre there, he accuses him of breaking his balls. To which Brazzi answers in all sincerity: "Now wait a minute, Pierro. Maybe I've broken a plate or two, but never anything else."

The well-meaning father is destined to become one of the film's innocent victims and is, in fact, beaten senseless by the gang of hooligans. A skinny teenager who's sort of the innocent kid associated with the gang is hauled in by an ornery Commissioner Katroni, who warns: "Don't give me any story about a priest falling down the stairs. The medical report indicates a blow to the neck with a blunt instrument and a staircase is not a blunt instrument." Then Katroni practically kills the kid in his office.

Pierro's drippy girlfriend, in a full nude shot on the bed after rolling around with him, asks him whether or not he's happy. Why, he wonders, uninterested. Because, she explains, when they make love he makes a face that looks to her like he's disgusted and "you make funny sounds, like you're mad."

"It's normal. All men do that," Pierro grunts.

Later, when she tells him she's pregnant, he scorns her with: "Listen sweetheart, I only came around for a couple of good fucks. But you know somethin'? I'd rather stay at home and jerk off then listen to your moanin'!" When she ends up getting gang-banged by his friends, surprisingly, Pierro gets sick and pukes in the sink while he flashes back on images of their beachfront romp. It's the only bit of humanity he shows; sort of like Timothy Van Patten playing the piano in the equally nihilistic **Class of 1984**. Her flashback, meanwhile, as she prepares for a suicidal leap from her apartment building, is the memory of her drawing a heart in the sand and Pierro coming up and stomping his foot on it.

So why did she die, asks Commissioner Katroni.

"How do I know?" answers Pierro. "Women are crazy."

If the movie had only lightened up a little, or seen itself as a sick parody of violence in our society, it could have made a nice companion piece to **Andy Warhol's Bad** (1976), the dark and relentlessly twisted violence of which is played out by a cast of characters so reprehensible you feel creepy satisfaction watching them in action.

That's not what **Il Tempo Degli Assassini** has in mind at all, however. It's dead serious. And occasionally, though

142

not as often as we'd like, that's kind of funny, too.

Martin Balsam's commissioner is such a fucking grouch that he coughs up his best and most biting lines to the priest—a pious symbol of peace. "Father, you keep vomiting up love," he tells the monk. John Waters couldn't have written it more eloquently.

"But you represent the law!" the priest argues.

"I represent bullshit, Father!" After all, he argues, the priest has Heaven to look forward to after his life on this planet. The Commish has only got his lousy pension...and that's if he sticks with it.

The phone rings. Balsam gets the news that the kid at the hospital died five minutes ago. He puts the phone down and looks at the priest.

"Be my guest, Father. Resurrect him."

The silly freeze frame at the film's finale has Balsam frozen in action as he smashes his gun to the ground. The only possible conclusion I can come to is that he's pissed he didn't get to put a bullet in Pierro's brain.

The only pleasure Joe Dallesandro got out of the deal, other than the paycheck, was getting the opportunity to work with the legendary Rossano Brazzi, once a major matinee idol in Italy of the 1940's and later a Hollywood success story in such films as **Three Coins in A Fountain** (1954), **The Barefoot Contessa** (1954), **South Pacific** (1958), and **Light in the Piazza** (1962). Within a decade, as Brazzi's looks gave way and he aged beyond what Mastrianni incorporated, his career hit the low-budget skids. He had just finished **Frankenstein's Castle of Freaks** (1973) when he came to this project.

Martin Balsam's participation can only be explained by a need to pay some bills while in Italy, and maybe the fact that Ernie Borgnine wasn't available. He looks thoroughly unhappy in the film (though that may just be his character) and had by this point in his career already accrued a resumé of notable film roles. He won the Oscar as Best Supporting Actor for **A Thousand Clowns** (1965), but had made even more commercially striking impressions in **On The Waterfront** (1954; his debut) and as the nosy Dr. Arbogast who goes on a vertigo plunge down the staircase while Mrs. Bates hacks away at his face in **Psycho** (1960).

Joe remembers Balsam as being particularly off-putting on **Assassini**, remarking that he stands out as one of a handful of the most difficult actors with whom he's had to work. Within a year, Balsam would be back in business in the States with a role in **All The President's Men**, followed a couple years after that with three seasons on **Archie Bunker's Place** as Archie's Jewish business partner.

Unfortunately, though a couple of different cuts of the film exist on video here in the States, none have the advantage of Joe Dallesandro's tough-guy delivery. Adding to the low-budget aura, everyone has been dubbed except for Balsam, who may have had it in his contract to do his own voice work. Joe was busy with his next project and his contract didn't stipulate that they had to use his voice for the final looping, a frequent post-production necessity even for English-speaking actors delivering their lines in their own language, because much of the sound recorded while shooting is used strictly as a wild track. Converting all the other Italian-speaking actors to English is most easily accomplished by re-recording all of the dialogue in a studio at the same time. Joe simply wasn't there to do it.

Il Tempo Degli Assassini was edited by Giulio Berruti, who three years later directed Joe to equal indistinction on **Suor Omicidio** (**The Killer Nun**).

l'ambizioso

(1975)

"I wore the heels basically for height, not as a fashion statement."

—*Joe Dallesandro on his boots in L'Ambizioso*

(Also known as The Climber; Ambitious) **With JOE DALLESANDRO AS ALDO (THE CLIMBER),** Stefania Casini (Luciana), Benito Artesi, Mario de Luca, Ferdinando Murolo, Raymond Pellegrin. Directed by Pasquale Squitieri. 103 minutes, Italy.

"I came to Italy to make commercial action movies and this is what **L'Ambizioso** is all about," explained Joe to the *Daily American* while living in Italy. "Joe Dallesandro breaks out of the underground" headlined the interview. Joe was doing exactly what he set out to do by breaking with the Warhol group. He was starring in films for other people who were willing to place him in leading roles and give him the opportunity to show his stuff in other genres.

L'Ambizioso proved a decent project for the young actor and was one of his better roles during the first half of his European stay.

The film tells the story of Aldo, a small time operator from New York, who nearly gets busted while delivering smuggled cases of cigarettes by boat as the film opens. He's a tough guy, a collector who cuts a rough-trade image dragging on his cigarette, squeezing money out of his clients, and cruising around Naples on his '68 motorbike. But he's also restless, looking for bigger action, and very interested in going into business for himself.

Such extracurricular notions get him into trouble and he's slapped around by some of the local Mafiosi's boys, who also have his beloved motorcycle tossed in the drink. Beaten and then unceremoniously dumped on a highway at night, Aldo stumbles to the nearest gas station where he meets a young woman, Luciana (Stefania Casini). She rather improbably agrees to give him a lift to Rome. Even less probably, this beauty lets him stay at her place where she proceeds to fall instantaneously in "love" with him, and he, figuring she's lonely, takes her to bed.

Aldo hits the streets to try and drum up some business and finds an old buddy of his, Carlo, who's now working at a local auto junkyard. Carlo introduces Aldo to Corrado, a fat homosexual shopkeeper who takes a fancy to the young hood and feels up his leg while describing a job he's got for him. Corrado wants Aldo to make a pick-up—diamonds from Holland.

The deal, not too surprisingly, is a set-up. Aldo recruits Carlo and they do make the pick-up, but it's heroin, not diamonds, so Aldo absconds with the treasure.

Skillfully imagining his future, Aldo switches the drugs with talcum powder. When he's caught by the Mafioso, he shrewdly cuts a deal to deliver the real drugs in exchange for his life, as well as having first dibs on killing his double-crosser.

Aldo makes good on that last promise in a nicely conceived and brutal scene, stabbing Corrado to death while muttering vulgar hustler metaphors. "You're gonna get every inch coming to you," Aldo tells the cowering creep before plunging in his blade.

This is just the beginning of the ambitious Aldo's offensive. In a unique reversal of his own image as nude beefcake, by the way, Joe is shown dressed to the tee in suit and tie while recruiting a boxer friend who showers full-frontal during their dialogue.

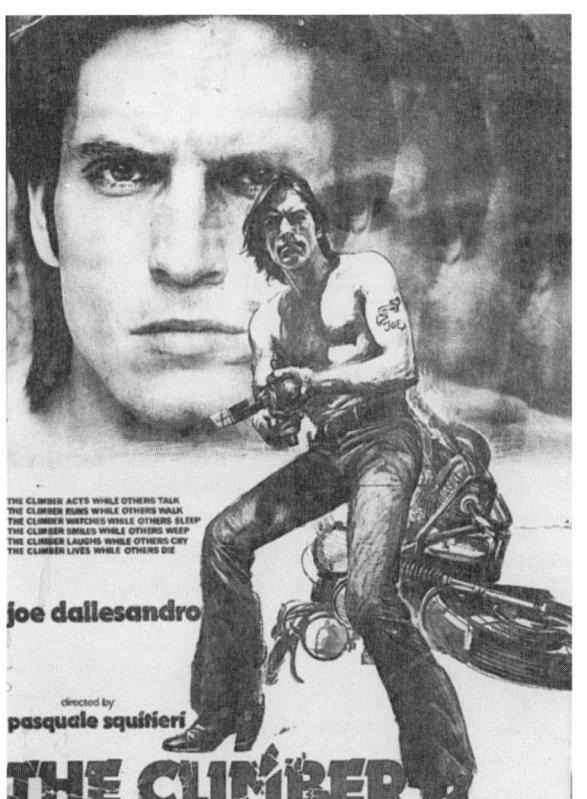

Aldo's first plan of action is to go after Corrado's queer customers; businessmen who've hired hustlers.

Eventually, Aldo has assembled a team of ten men— including a cool and silent marksman and a street gaming shark—all of whom return with him to Napoli to work the clubs and restaurants and stomp on his former bosses' territory. Luciana is in tow, but she wants to bail after an ambush on motorcycles leaves some of Aldo's men dead. Aldo, now ensconced in a posh new home, won't hear of it. He tells her he owns her.

The young gangster has exercised too much power to be ignored, however, and his enemy, Enrico, abducts Luciana and threatens to kill her. Aldo tells him to go ahead and do so. He could care less. Enrico plays a tape of Aldo's callous words to her and then after letting her go, she commits suicide. Aldo, as it turns out, was only saying those things so that she'd be released and not used as a pawn. Naturally, his revenge will know no bounds and he viciously guns down Enrico.

Courtesy Joe Dallesandro

Now the real war starts. The big boys step in as Aldo flexes his muscle and threatens to become too big for his britches. A hit man from Yugoslavia is called in, dragging a trailer behind his car, driving with a picture of Aldo clipped to his visor.

It's only a matter of time. Aldo is seen driving alone in a black Rolls Royce through the narrow city streets. Children follow his car in a metaphorical funeral procession. Then Aldo is blown away in slo-mo; his killer, a phantom in the night behind him. The Climber has fallen.

Joe has a real fondness for **L'Ambizioso** and it's easy to see why. Not only was it his first lead in an action film, but it was also a good role. He may not be quite as blankly cold and seductive as any number of Alain Delon gangsters, but he still manages to play bad smoothly, and he's an undeniably good-looking fucker outfitted in his form-fitting white T-shirt while buzzing down the street on his motorcycle or walking around shirtless in a black leather jacket.

What **L'Ambizioso** really needs is more of what it's got. The cast is good, the plot is interesting (in a **Scarface** sort of way), and the situation is ripe for development. With a bigger budget and an eye and ear towards an international market, the film could have realized some of the interesting ideas it starts and stops with here.

The shoot also provided the opportunity for Joe to work with his girlfriend Stefania again. They had met while Joe was filming the Warhol horror films in Italy and Stefania was cast in **Blood for Dracula**. She would also appear in **Andy Warhol's Bad** (1976) as a hired killer who short-cuts her latest murder assignment by severing a man's legs with an auto-garage hydraulic lift, then snips off his thumb and shoves it inside the family ketchup bottle. It's just that kind of kink that would have made her a much more dynamic character here.

"I'm a little tired of movies that make you think a lot," admitted Joe on the film's release in Italy. "I liked Bergman's **Cries and Whispers** very much. I thought that was excellent, but mostly I like movies with a lot of action. Like **L'Ambizioso**."

That's the kind of honest-to-goodness young actor charm you can't manufacture.

black moon

(1975)

"My son, who's six, saw it and he enjoyed it totally. He understood things that Louis explained to me before we shot it—things I didn't understand myself. Kids see things differently."

—*Joe Dallesandro, In-Touch magazine (#89), March, 1984*

With JOE DALLESANDRO AS THE BROTHER, Cathryn Harrison (Lily, The Girl), Therese Giehse (The Old Woman), Alexandra Stewart (The Sister). Directed by Louis Malle. 100 minutes (also 92 minute version), France-West Germany.

When it came time for director Louis Malle to cast the twin of statuesquely beautiful Alexandra Stewart, to whom he'd assigned the role of the Sister in his latest film, he had trouble. Months of trouble. Originally, he wanted Terence Stamp, but Stamp, who appeared suitably ambisexual in Pasolini's **Teorema** some seven years prior, shied away from the project.

Fortunately, Malle had previously seen Joe in Morrissey's **Heat** (1972) and when he heard that the ex-Warhol actor had settled in Italy to make films, he sought Joe out.

"When Louis Malle wanted to do this movie, **Black Moon**," Joe recalls, "he came to Italy to visit and I didn't know who Louis Malle was at the time. Remember, if the movie didn't play on Times Square, I didn't see it. When I met with him he had no script, but it was all in his head. That's why he was coming down there, to tell me the movie. He started to tell it to me and his English was not all that great—it was good, but not great—and everything to him was so deep, and I'm not all that deep of a person, so all I could do when he finished talking after about forty minutes was ask him: 'Do you see me doing the role?' And he did."

Malle told interviewer Philip French, "At the last minute, I chose Joe Dallesandro, which is one of the most surprising casting decisions I've made in my life."

But a fortuitous decision, as well. Being tossed into an improvised, highly unusual set of circumstances wasn't exactly new to Joe. If this was "art," he knew what it was like to be a piece of it. Malle would admit: "I don't think Joe Dallesandro ever really understood what it was all about. But he didn't mind. He was perfectly prepared for something that was eccentric, and I suppose for him it was no more difficult than a lot of things he'd done with Warhol and Paul Morrissey."

Shot almost entirely in and around Malle's own manor just outside Limogne-en-Quercy on the Causse de Limogne in the Dordogne Valley, the film is a bizarre hodgepodge of fairy tale, Indian myth, and war of the sexes inspired (sort of) by *Alice in Wonderland*. Actor Rex Harrison's 16-year old granddaughter Cathryn, as The Girl, runs down a barely discernible badger making its way across a pitch black country road only to drive right into the middle of a battle zone where male military thugs mow down captive women in a line-up. She narrowly escapes their clutches by driving off into a meadow where she abandons her car and strolls through the foliage. She suddenly becomes aware that the plants she is stepping on are crying out in pain and then is startled by a beautiful woman riding a black horse, a gaggle of naked children chasing a monstrous sow, and a sad, fat little horse with a horn glued to its forehead.

Continuing to wander, she ends up inside a large house, first encountering a pig in a baby's highchair cheerily snorting away when she attempts to reach a near-overflowing glass of milk on the table, and then a strange old woman who talks and talks and talks, initially to a big rat named Humphrey, and then into her screeching short wave radio microphone. Alarm clocks go off and the Girl tosses them out the window, sending the old lady into some sort of seizure. Thinking she's killed the woman, the Girl runs outside and encounters Brother (Joe Dallesandro) warbling an obviously dubbed bit of Wagner while trimming a tree. However, although this striking young man can sing, he cannot talk; he communicates with her by placing his hands on her shoulders and using his fingers. She understands him to say that his name is Lily, too, just like hers.

The woman on the black horse she'd seen earlier is his twin Sister and the three of them go back to the old lady's room. Brother manages somehow to prompt the ancient woman's breathing by holding a mirror to her mouth, and then the lovely Sister reveals her breast and suckles the old broad back to life.

Trapped by these queer people, Lily tries to make some sort of sense of it all, managing to glean that there is a civil war raging outside between men and women. When she tries to seek out the talking unicorn in the meadow, she comes across a dead female soldier who has a chicken pecking away at her tit. Brother shows up to bury the felled soldier in a big pit, tossing in her submachine gun. Catching a glimpse of the unicorn cutting across the garden, the Girl chases it and flips over the back of the giant sow instead. The gaggle of naked children then torment her. She eyes Brother and his Sister getting it on in the barn, then later returns to the house where the Sister is carving roast beef for the naked children (presumably her's and Brother's). That evening, while visiting the old woman, who smacks her lips in disgusting hunger, the Girl prepares one of her breasts with oil and lets the old lady have a suck. Downstairs, Brother and Sister and the gang of kids have applied make-up and are prepared to perform *Tristan and Isolde*, complete with a lengthy operatic recitation by one of the children while the Girl accompanies on piano.

Come the new dawn, everyone has disappeared from the house. The Girl is intrigued by a beautiful painting depicting a mythological showdown between a warrior and an eagle when a real eagle suddenly flies into the room and Brother, outfitted appropriately, slashes at it with a sword. Having successfully hacked off its wings, he remains statuesque while his Sister paints his face with the eagle's blood. The twins then remove themselves to the garden where they proceed to beat the bloody shit out of each other.

The Girl goes upstairs and climbs into the old woman's empty bed, strangely acquiescent when a snake slithers under the sheets and up between her legs. The poor-man's unicorn appears in one corner of the bedroom, failing to make good on an earlier threat to disappear for 154 years, and it begins making lip-smacking sounds identical to those of the old woman. The Girl readies her breast with oil.

Roll credits.

Catholic-school educated, Louis Malle, who had been making films since co-directing Jacques Cousteau's documentary **The Underwater World** (1956), was not a stranger to controversy. **Les Amants** (**The Lovers**; 1958) was lambasted for its overt sexuality, **A Very Private Affair** (1962) was a barely disguised film bio of star Brigitte Bardot, and **Murmur of the Heart** (1971), an adolescent coming-of-age story with incestuous undercurrents, has a boy questioned about masturbation by a suspiciously curious priest. It was, however, Louis Malle's next film after **Black Moon**—and his first in America—that was to launch his notoriety here in the United States: **Pretty Baby** (1978) contained all sorts of pretty explicit sexuality, but none was more potent than casting Brooke Shields as a 12-year old prostitute.

Black Moon was so odd a film, so obviously a director's indulgence, that few people outside of critics saw it here in the States and it is rarely revived. Even as an experiment, it leaves a lot to be desired, but there are moments that brilliantly transcend the otherwise ordinary way in which it's shot and effectively call to mind a fairy tale dreamland. The naked children skipping after the enormous sow, the mocking pig in the highchair, a kitten playing the piano, and a gibberish-squeaking rat all make for storybook illustrations and even a smile. The annoying old woman croaking incessantly in her bed is a bit harder to translate, because veteran actress Therese Giehse, who had created the title role in Bertold Brecht's *Mother Courage*, was asked to do the role in an imaginary language that was then redubbed afterward into something resembling English, but uninteresting and rambling nonetheless. Actually, it was Giehse who prompted **Black Moon** when she told Malle, after completing his **Lacombe, Lucien,** that "words hold you back. You should make a film in which dialogue has no importance." Ms. Giehse died six weeks after finishing this film and **Black Moon** is dedicated to her.

In fact, Malle didn't even have a sound unit on his "set" during the filming, opting to play with the sound and fill it all in after the fact, deliberately seeking to lay tracks out-of-synch. Of the two sound versions they recorded, French and English-language, he preferred the English. It was all part of his personal quest to spew forth a dream, a psychosexual initiation into questions of gender, sexual politics, and "the emotions and fears of puberty." The sexual conflicts work rather too obviously, complete with a genuinely funny scene in which Lily's panties keep falling down around her ankles on their own, but perhaps Malle wanted what was thematically obvious to be just that—as obvious as the moral to a fable.

The problem with **Black Moon** isn't that it's a failure to put a dream on film, but that it's someone else's dream and seems somehow very unsatisfying because of how often it fails to evoke recognizably dreamlike imagery. The choppy dream logic and associated magical happenstances are too weighed down by the film's mostly earthbound, uninspired style, though famed cinematographer Sven Nykvist's work is exceptionally good and Joe enjoyed hanging around with the master for some behind-the-scenes technical training.

Roger Ebert wrote of the experience: "To 'interpret' this material would be folly; we can't sort out meaning or sig-

*Looking like Lestat, with Cathryn Harrison at the make-up mirror on the set of **Black Moon**/Courtesy Joe Dallesandro*

nificance, and I don't think Malle intends us to. **Black Moon** is a sensual experience. We go to it and it happens to us, and whatever happened is what the movie was about…In the late 1960's, a movie like this would have been considered a trip; people would have seen it stoned or high. Now we just don't go. It's not the season for dreams."

Vincent Canby, writing in the *New York Times*, thought it "a poetic vision made to look so absolutely literal one doesn't question the validity of the images … The movie evokes the dream state without once resorting to the use of fuzzy filters, slow-motion photography or even lap dissolves. We see everything with the clarity with which Alice/Goldilocks observes it, though, unlike Lily, our tendency is to interpret what we see rather than simply to accept it. If one can accept the images in this way, the movie has a liberating effect."

Not surprisingly, the critical strata for such a strange film was wide-ranging, from critics such as Judith Crist deploring it for being "strangely pretentious" to Kevin Thomas of the *LA Times* declaring it "Malle's most challenging and surreal work, and maybe his best film—So intensely personal, beautiful and dynamic that it avoids pretentiousness."

Joe does a nice job with what he's been handed, looking particularly striking wearing a beautifully crafted necklace with an eagle spreading its wings across his throat. Pauline Kael, who wisely suggests that "Malle is a sane man trying to make a crazy man's film," offers that "as brother and sister, Joe Dallesandro and Alexandra Stewart have a handsome, blank twinship." Dallesandro offers more than that for fans, actually, though perhaps he's not expected to do so. Joe may be the flip side of an androgynous double-headed coin, but it's fun to see him so patently played as the silent masculine beauty, taking him to the obligatory next step of his iconography as established under Morrissey: a mythological male sex symbol needless of speech, communicating entirely through his body language and image.

"There wasn't much to do in that film," Joe admits. "But I gave everything I could give."

VIDEO REPLAY: The twins go at it. Joe explains: "They gave her (Stewart) a prop, which was like a sponge rock, and she went and made up her own with dirt and real rock in it, because she didn't think the one they gave her looked real enough. She threw it and hit me square in the head. It looks real, like I'm dazed, because I am. Knocked out almost. Then she got to swinging the sword. I had taken fencing lessons, but she wouldn't take advantage of the classes Louis was giving us. Next thing I know, she's swinging this thing at me—out of control—missing me only because I was athletic enough and had the good sense to move away from her. She was practically cutting me to shit while the cameras rolled. She was totally nuts. And afterwards, Louis said, 'I'm sorry, Joe. I didn't think she'd get that wound up.'"

With Cathryn Harrison

calore in provincia (1975)

"The cult of Joe Dallesandro might be called the cult of a non-actor, which isn't the same as being the cult of a Keanu Reeves, as temptingly appropriate as that may seem. The difference is that Reeves actually set out to be an actor and takes himself quite seriously in that regard. Joe Dallesandro, on the other hand, never set out to be in front of the camera and didn't take himself at all seriously some 30 years ago just because he was the guy who happened to have it pointed at him."

—*Cult Movies, Issue #17, 1996*

With JOE DALLESANDRO. Directed by Roberto Montero. Italy.

Translated roughly as **Heat in the Suburbs**, this exploitation film, according to Joe, "is about three friends who go out, kill a cab driver, steal the cab, and then go around picking up passengers and fucking them over and torturing the shit out of them. It was a trio of youths—me and my two buddies—who go nuts. We lose it. The irony is that we're kind of intelligent kids who go out and do these horrible things. Not just murder, it's torturous murder, like jumping on a forklift and chasing people down. Then I end up working for a computer company."

Sounds like one of those "gifted kids can be just as rotten as scum-of-the-earth kids" scenarios. Was it meant to be taken as serious social commentary?

"I don't remember. It was such a horrific piece of shit that I couldn't have cared to go see it. But they all thought they were doing their fucking Oscar winner. The thing is, I took the worst scripts that people would bring me and I'd say, yeah, it's a bad script, but I'll do it the best that I can. I'm not a scriptwriter and I'm not a director—I don't do those things—but what I will do is take everything you give me and make it look as real as I can."

Director Montero had a long history of making exploitation films before he came to do **Calore**, his 56th film since 1949.

fango

bollente

(1975)

"Warhol hero, hanging loose, mumbling, passive, yet with a distinct shining presence and no inhibitions about being natural, especially *au naturel*."

—Keith Howes on Joe Dallesandro, Broadcasting It

With JOE DALLESANDRO. Directed by Vittorio Solerno. Italy.

Boiling Mud, as it translates, left no impression on Joe whatsoever, and remains one of the few films from his European stay of which he has virtually no recollection. What does come to mind is the general difficulty of making films outside your native language, something he glancingly encountered while making the **Frankenstein** and **Dracula** movies.

"When you're working in a film in which everyone is speaking a different language, you have to at least know enough of the other language to know when to come in with your line," he says. "It was my job to understand the cues, so that even though we're speaking two different languages, I know my marks so that I can continue the flow of the performance. Some actors just don't take the trouble to do their jobs, though. One guy I worked with kept looking past me for off-screen cues. Sometimes it's nice if a character seems to be confused or distracted in a scene, but in this case, it wasn't confusion. It looked like the actor was stretching for dialogue, like he was aware of a prompter off-screen and was trying to reach behind the equipment for a line. There were people that I would work with that I'd end up having to give my cue by tapping on the floor with my foot."

Even off the movie set while Joe was living in Italy, he quickly became starved for doses of his American heritage. The young man who used to tell interviewers that the only book he ever read in its entirety was *Andrew Carnegie and the Age of Steel*, and that only to pass an English class, became a voracious reader. Frank Herbert's *Dune* series provided a particular source of enjoyment. His own cultural isolation in Italy turned out to be very fortuitous in its own way, allowing him the opportunity to read the novels he'd missed out on during his entire youth, and all because they provided a chance to read something in English.

je t'aime moi non plus (1975)

"Reminiscent of early Yank rustic dramas except for the homo aspects. In Yank pix, the male friends were macho and not gay, or did not admit to it."
—*Variety, March 17, 1976*

(Also known as I Love You No More; I Love You, I Don't; I Love You No Longer) **With JOE DALLESANDRO AS KRASSKY, Jane Birkin (Johnny), Hughes Quester (Padovan), Rene Kolldehoff (Boris), Gerard Depardieu (Rene la Canne), Jimmy Davis (Moise), Michel Blanc. Directed by Serge Gainsbourg. 88 minutes, France.**

Je T'Aime Moi Non Plus is a cult classic waiting to be discovered. Joe plays Krassky, a dump truck driver embarking on an erotic fable of sexual self-discovery. That we're to think of the tale we're watching unfold as a fable to be deciphered is made clear by writer-director Serge Gainsbourg from the outset when he has a black crow splatter bright red across the windshield of Joe's yellow garbage truck. Joe doesn't even use the wipers to clear away the blood. It's important. He'd no sooner wipe it away than a painter's subject would reach across the canvas and smear his creator's last brush stroke.

Gainsbourg raises his camera to show that Joe has someone else traveling with him in his cab. Another man can be seen resting his head in Joe's lap as the truck tools down the road. When they arrive at the dump, it's this other man, Padovan (Hughes Quester), who removes the dead crow from the windshield, folds it up in his hand, and then launches it into the air as if to give it flight. For a second you might even hope that it soars, but the moment you think about how neat that would be, the thing falls to the ground amidst the mock machine-gunning from Padovan.

Padovan has been established as the immature member of this male coupling. So what is Joe's role? Who is this Krassky now taking a pee atop a mountain of trash? He's the guy who picks up a dog's skull from the garbage and recites, "Alas, poor Yorrick." Padovan hasn't a clue. He's so earthbound that Gainsbourg has him machine-gun down the poetry.

Back on the road, they come upon a group of stranded fellows who blew a tire while out for a reckless joyride. All but one of the guys jumps into the back of the truck, the leftover sitting up front with Padovan and Krassky. Padovan looks longingly at the new man. Krassky notices and shakes his head. The truck passes Gerard Depardieu clip-clopping down the road on his white stallion. The passenger says he knows that guy and that he's a fag.

Padovan tells Krassky to stop the truck, then kicks the rider out on his ass. Krassky raises the dump truck and unceremoniously dumps the other fellows out on the highway.

The pair stop off at a roadside cafe along the barren landscape. Padovan immediately heads over to play the pinball machine while Krassky saunters study toward the kid behind the counter; the boy with the short red hair with his back to him.

This is Johnny (Jane Birkin), the waitress, much to Krassky's surprise. So why do they call you Johnny, he asks. "Because I've got no tits and a big ass," is the reply. Johnny is clearly interested in Krassky, who she eyes through the mirror when her back is turned again.

Krassky seems captivated by the girl even if she is a girl, or maybe because she's not quite believable as a girl. His motives here, and throughout the film, are never explicitly explained. Less is more and thus we begin the love triangle proper. Padovan is instantly jealous of the attentions Krassky gives to Johnny. When the obviously bored young woman is invited to join them for a ride in the dump truck, we see her run off the roadside to squat and pee, her jaunt framed in the triangular space between Padovan's arm and body as he rests his hand on the truck.

They pick up some horse meat at an outside market where Johnny tells Krassky that her old fart of a boss (Rene Kolldehoff, heard passing gas much of the time) sells the stuff as beef. When she comes running back to the truck wearing plastic glasses and a Cyrano nose, Padovan has had enough and flags down a bus to take off on his own.

At a local dance held inside an old airplane hangar, Johnny tells Krassky that her boss has told her that the two guys are queer. She doesn't believe it. Krassky calls her boss an old fart. Johnny says, "That's not an answer."

An amateur strip show is announced and arrives as advertised. The overweight women peel down to the stares of bored townspeople. Only Gerard Depardieu, the town queer, grabs at his crotch while these women bare just about all in a humiliating display. Strip show over and done with, Johnny asks Krassky to dance and they do while Gainsbourg introduces his lyrical love theme on the soundtrack and the two tentative lovers exchange kisses. Padovan arrives only to be confronted by the gang of fag-bashers he'd thrown from the truck earlier. They beat him and kick him to the sound of Gainsbourg's continuing love theme.

On the ground, Padovan screams out in anguish. Krassky arrives and disarms a switchblade-wielding gang member by twisting his ear. Padovan's calculated self-abuse tactics have worked. In what amounts to gay self-hate, he has allowed himself to be beaten in order to win back his man, further martyring himself by telling Krassky that it's "all your fault."

Gainsbourg cuts from a shot of the bickering male lovers in bed together to a shot of a topless Johnny in her own bed, hugging to her chest a little piggy doll that Krassky gave her and reaching under the covers to masturbate.

Krassky takes Johnny to a roller derby where the participants smash and collide into each other. She's enthralled and turns to him, naively asking him, "Are they girls?" To which he replies, "Yes, as much as you are a man."

Watching her wolf down phallic vegetable stalks dripping with cream at dinner that evening, Krassky is on edge. Johnny seems to know it, too. The sexual tension deepens precisely because when you look into Birkin's face, you think you can read knowing intent there. She still doesn't know or believe or accept that Krassky is homosexual—or does she? And does or doesn't she know just exactly what she's doing here?

Once in bed, she lies completely naked below him. He's still in his jeans and after slowly unbuckling his belt and unzipping himself, he stalls and lies down next to her. "I can't ... I just can't," is all he'll admit and she reaches into his pants as if to check.

"So Boris was right."

Krassky kicks her out of bed and plants his bare foot over her mouth while she calls him a queer. A moment of silence follows as she makes a decision and then slouches down further onto the floor, turns her back to him, and says, "I'm a boy."

With the love theme revisited, presented with her backside, Krassky becomes aroused and begins his amorous lovemaking. Johnny's screams of pain, accompanied by the pulling down of the plastic shower curtain on top of them, arouses a neighbor woman in the motel and the couple are kicked out mid-fuck. As Krassky passes the snitching neighbor lady, he tells her, "Whores always screw in silence."

They try several more times to get it on, but each time Krassky rear-ends her, her pulsating screeches of agony get them kicked out of wherever they are. Johnny's willing endurance of this pain—her screams are not protestations—provide an interesting sexual subtext. It's almost as if she's willing to do whatever needs to be done to accommodate the man she has come to love. He wants simply to get past the sexual barrier—do it and finish it so they both know it can be done—in order to continue their relationship.

The sexual politics are played against a backdrop as sparse as the American Southwest, where it has been suggested this film is supposed to be set. Cinematographer Willy Kurant (who photographed the Godard classic **Masculin-Feminin**) has done a nice job of making the space, both interiors and exteriors, seem barely occupied, thereby calling attention to the more theatrical choices Gainsbourg has made with his framing and his primary color schemes: yellow truck, black crow, red blood, Krassky's red kerchief, his white T-shirt and blue jeans, a bright red fuel pump, Johnny's orange-red hair, her friendly white pit bull, and her pink dress (worn after she reminds Krassky that she's a "woman").

Produced by Claude Berri, who would direct **Jean de Florette** and **Manon of the Spring**, **Je T'Aime** was inspired by Gainsbourg's breathy international hit song of the same title from his infamous *Comic Strip* album. The album is replete with weird combinations of jazz and folk influences mixed in a blender, but the four minute *Je T'Aime*, co-recorded with Birkin, is a sensational repartee of pre- to post-orgasmic moans, grunts, sighs and pants that give intimacy a whole new aural dimension. Both Joe and Jane appear on the cover of the motion picture soundtrack.

The cast is excellent. Jane Birkin, who was married at the time to writer-director Gainsbourg (their daughter is actress Charlotte Gainsbourg), brings physical beauty and ambiguity to her role of Johnny, a part one can't help not thinking about in probably inappropriate ways when you consider her husband wrote it for her. A veteran of over fifty films, Birkin would appear in Paul Morrissey's **Beethoven's Nephew** (1985) before dabbling in writing and directing films herself.

Hughes Quester, later of Kieslowski's **Blue** (1993), has also been carefully directed to bring shades of a "larger" character to bear on a rather simply told story. His Padovan's jealousies, temperamental displays, even eventual rage, are key to the tale, but we never learn very much about him. Most curious is an ever-present plastic bag he carries with him, coming off something like Linus' security blanket and open to several possible interpretations, from figural (the smotherer) to literal (he is, after all, a garbage man).

Gerard Depardieu, in a curious role early on in his career, makes his snuff-snorting part seem much more interesting and mysterious than written, perhaps partly because we recognize the actor playing it. His character, who rides a white stallion (Joe tells me that "Gerard's character likes his horses to have big cocks"), is the fairy in the fairy tale who decides not to grant a wish. When Padovan is mad at Krassky, he meets Depardieu's character in a field and doesn't have to say anything. Depardieu knows why Padovan is there. "You want me to stick it up your bottom," he says. Alas, he declines, boasting that he's sent more than one to the hospital with his prodigious member.

For Joe Dallesandro, Krassky was not only one of the best roles of his entire European career, but an example of superb casting on Gainsbourg's part. That Joe could handle the raw sexual appeal and physicality certainly came as no surprise, but what a joy for the actor to play something beyond that. This may be the only film in which you can hear Joe quote Shakespeare, compare a sea of garbage to the mythological River Styx, comment on a bitter world by tasting his own ear wax, then wax poetic by solemnly stating that "love is blind and has a long pink cane" or describe lovemaking as "a synchronous bout of epilepsy;" and those are all good things.

In a strange way, the film also explores Krassky's acceptance of his own homosexuality. Padovan may not be right for him. Too jealous, too immature. (Then again, even the job Krassky's stuck doing isn't right for a man whose intellect and humor flashes through from time to time.) But, Johnny isn't right for him either. At least not this Johnny. Krassky's decision—forced by an eventual act of violence—seems to me less about having to decide between these two people than having to decide who he really is.

"The whole story of the movie is that I'm after this girl who looks like a boy because I want to give her a good butt-fucking," summarizes Joe. "Um, not as unclassy as that, though."

Raymond Murray, in his excellent encyclopedia of gay and lesbian film and video, *Images in the Dark*, declares **Je T'Aime** "years—even decades—ahead of its time," concluding his remarks by saying: "Why this film is not considered a classic of 70's filmmaking is beyond me."

Joe may have the practical answer for him.

"It was a fun thing to do," says Joe of the movie, a portion of which we watched together (it was easy to see the affection he has for it). "It was a real time-right piece to do, too, in the era of a **Last Tango in Paris**. It was done right and if it only would have had some kind of release—but, you see, the problem with America is you have to shoot the whole damn thing in English. You cannot have anybody—*anybody*—out of synch."

In fact, they were shooting two versions of the film—one in French and the other in English. Gainsbourg told Joe, who could passably speak the former, that "when you speak French, your whole face contorts and you don't look like who you are. I can understand what you're saying, that's not the problem. It's just that your face becomes different." Thus Joe did not do a foreign language version, but others in the cast had to be dubbed and distribution in the States was minimal.

"At the time, I thought it was just a fancy way for the

With Jane Birkin

With Jane Birkin

guy to tell me he didn't like my French."

The set was a weird one to work on primarily because of the strained relationship between Birkin and her writer-director-composer husband, who was very much in the throes of alcoholism at the time, causing Joe to reflect on his own drinking, as well as his father's.

"He was a boozer," says Joe of his dad. "A real drinker. For me, that was a pretty hard thing to deal with. It was not unlike what Jane had to go through with Serge, watching a man drink himself to death. You just couldn't see it with my father because he looked so young for so many years, where Serge looked like he was dying right from the get-go."

Whatever off-screen tensions and personal imbalances were going on, they surely found their way into the fabric of the film, helping it in an odd way by lending it a subtextual buzz. **Je T'Aime Moi Non Plus** is an erotic art film, no question about it. Gainsbourg and the cast took this project very seriously.

Which is not to suggest that there weren't lighter moments while filming it. Joe remembers all the fun he had learning how to drive the Mack dump truck, which he almost drove through the front window of the cafe during his first outing behind the wheel.

During one scene in which Krassky and Johnny are naked and sunning themselves by floating in a reservoir on a huge innertube, it occurred to Joe that the director was getting awful close to their exposed heinies with the camera and shooting a hell of a lot of footage.

"We're just floating on the innertube going around and around and around," says Joe. "I'm saying, 'Jane, not that you don't have a beautiful butt, but I don't think we should be going round and round on this thing for hours with our butts hangin' out. Do you? I mean, especially if they use all of it. It's going to look pretty silly.' She said, 'no, he'll use the right amount.'" (Gainsbourg used over a full minute of the rotating rear-ends in the final cut.)

VIDEO REPLAY: While Krassky loads toilets into the back of the truck, he says to a brooding Padovan, "Imagine all the vaginas that have sat on these." Padovan, with a foreshadowing plastic bag over his head, says Krassky better shut up or he's going to be sick. Krassky smiles and makes a "vagina" with his two lips by flattening them with his fingers and squishing them back and forth.

With Jane Birkin

la marge

(1976)

"His physique is so magnificently shaped that men as well as women become disconnected at the sight of him."

—*Vincent Canby on Joe Dallesandro, New York Times*

(Also known as The Margin; The Streetwalker) **With JOE DALLESANDRO AS SIGIMOND PONS, Sylvia Kristel (Diana), Andre Falcon (Antonin Pons), Mireille Audibert (Sergine Pons), Louise Chevalier (Feline), Denis Manuel, Dominique Markas, Norma Piccadilly, Camille Lariviere, Luz Laurent, Karin Albin. Directed by Walerian Borowczyk. 95 minutes, France.**

La Marge provided Joe with the opportunity to work with yet another of Europe's great film directors (Malle and Rivette, among them). Walerian Borowczyk, a Polish animator and filmmaker, can be (and has been) argued to be the Franz Kafka of the movies. He began making visually complex and increasingly graphic and dark animated short films in 1957, experimenting with a variety of animation techniques, including painting, stop-motion, pin screen, and combining live action. His subject matter was challenging, bizarre, heavily psychosexual, and sometimes disturbingly violent.

Whatever the subject matter, though, Borowcyzk's films ask us to respond to them as works of art, as if we were standing before a painting in a gallery consumed not only by the beauty and the color and the form, but by how the imagery speaks to our psyche.

In 1963's **Renaissance**, he had us contemplate a room whose contents were blown asunder. As we watch, the fragments in the room begin to re-assemble themselves and connect in ways that are surprising, somehow reassuring, and yet very much a reminder of the forms and meanings objects have when they are connected to shapes and contexts we recognize.

He followed this with one of his most nightmarish animated shorts, **Les Jeux des Anges** (1964), featuring an audial and visual barrage of executions. Three years later he released his first feature-length animated film, **Le Theatre de Monsieur et Madame Kabal** (1967), in which he introduced a theme of sexual voyeurism that would soon stream through all of his subsequent films. It simultaneously won him fans and alienated critics who saw him as one of the greatest animators in film history gone sophomoric.

By the time he shot **La Marge**, Borowczyk had made four live-action feature films and those same critics had charted his move from artful, live-action extensions of his animator's dark genius to more lurid and sexually explicit subjects.

La Marge lies somewhere in the middle of the transition. Presented as a fable, though not as rapacious as his modern take on *Beauty and the Beast* in 1975's **La Béte**, the film also never reaches the carnality or carnage of later works, such as **Docteur Jekyll et Les Femmes** (1981).

Joe plays family man Sigimond Pons, still gloriously and romantically in love with his beautiful wife. When the film opens and we have yet to discover their relationship, they are playfully frolicking on the grounds of an estate, running through the rain and through the trees as if in Eden before The Fall. They might just as well be young lovers on a honeymoon. Further frolicking in bed has Sigimond anointing his naked wife's body and face with flowers.

"I promise never to betray you," he tells her, rolling over onto a branch of thorns and gashing his arm. The wound is severe enough to require bandaging, which conveniently covers his "Little Joe" tattoo for the duration of the film.

They are, we come to learn, husband and wife, with a cute little boy. Sigimond has been asked to go on the road for his firm and this means travel into the city and a lengthy stay away from his family. He is somewhat reluctant to go, but does so, driving out of this picturesque Eden and into … Paris.

Once in the city, he is immediately beset by streetwalkers, all of whom he ignores, save one. Sylvia Kristel is Diana. (Need I remind you that Sylvia Kristel is also **Emmanuelle**?) She has a more hands-on approach to Mr. Pons than her gaudy peers. She walks up and gives his crotch a nice healthy grope.

A dour Joe in Italy, circa 1969/Courtesy Joe Dallesandro

Sold! For 200 francs!

Their first love scene comes complete with plenty of nudity, including a tight close-up as Sigimond squeezes her nipple into full erection and an overhead shot of his tensing and releasing ass while on top of her, all played out under the familiar 70's pop tune, "I'm Not in Love." Later, during one of the few light moments in their relationship, we'll hear Elton John's "Saturday Night's Alright" underscoring the film's most remarked upon scene. Sigimond has brought two hard-boiled eggs with him and Diana practices rolling one from between her breasts down onto her midsection, where she strategically maneuvers it into the divit of her bellybutton, and then with a pop (!) of her stomach muscles, she launches it right into her pubic hair. Again and again she displays this remarkably entertaining party trick, after which she eats the egg and makes love to Sigimond.

Through some inexplicable cosmic predestiny, great ideas are often shared by two people at the same time. Also in 1976, director Nagisa Oshima brought to the screen his legendary tale of a couple's frightening immersion into complete sexual obsession, **In The Realm Of The Senses**, making even more startling and controversial use of a hard-boiled egg. Oshima has his male lead insert it whole inside his partner's vagina, then order her to squat and lay it like a chicken, after which she angrily forces him to eat it.

La Marge is a very simple movie. It chronicles the empty sexual escapades of a family man giving in to sexual desire without ever really exhibiting a need beyond the random connection he has with one particularly sexy hooker.

The country life of tranquillity and natural beauty and family that he drives away from becomes the city life of cheap sexuality that abounds everywhere. He partakes, the hooker thinks she may actually be falling in love (perhaps because he has at least some of the tenderness he brought from the country in him), and disaster strikes.

The city is filled with sex, sex, sex, and Sigimond succumbs to the desire, but without the heat and passion or even cheap thrills in the having of it. Sex for sex's sake is a rather vacuous experience and Sigimond participates in the emptiness of it, rarely smiling, never really connecting. It would be proper to suggest that Joe hasn't been glamorized to the point he could have been, because he seems far less sexually charismatic here than he did even in **Heat**, but I think that's precisely what Borowczyk was looking for. He took a sexy leading man and de-sexualized him; made him seem altogether ordinary. Sigimond loses the life-glow, the warmth he had when we saw him with his wife in the beginning of the film. That warmth returns momentarily to his character only in flashback.

Like Paul Morrissey, in whose morality plays open displays of male and female nudity abound in stories about the silliness and vacuity of sex, Borowczyk is also a strident voyeur insistently showing us lingering close-ups of the pubic hair of his actresses. His camera dallies so often at waist-level, enjoying the sight of Sergine picking the yellow flower buds out of her bush or displaying the silhouetted hairs of a panty-less maid as she presents her backside while stooping to pick up a vacuum cleaner in Sigimond's room, one wonders if the director might have seriously contemplated shooting the entire film framed from belly-button to knees.

The abundant nudity includes Joe Dallesandro's most extensive displays since **Trash** (1970), but it's also a stylized nudity, if you will. The pulling down of panties or stockings (for the women) and the shucking of his sheer black undies (for Joe) are filmed in a manner that belie their importance to both the story and the audience, but the subsequent lovemaking never really goes further than the initial charge of seeing someone's crotch revealed in medium close-up.

There's no rhythm to the sex, no developing passion or mounting sexual energy. During their first tryst, Diana breaks the action by telling him, "I will not mess up my hairdo!" (a Sylvia Miles flashback), after which he pays her more money and she concedes, holding the extra cash crunched in her hand while Sigimond gets it on with her. Borowczyk has quite deliberately made sex, even between two attractive people, quite mundane and rather unerotic. It is one of the primary themes of the film, though one review used in conjunction with the film's publicity in the trades warns us that "Borowczyk is too much of an artist to preach any doctrine."

Taken purely as a fable, Borowczyk's film punishes Sigimond for his selfish actions, or at the very least, uses him as an example to teach us what can happen if you forsake the family and "family values."

He received a letter from home while in Paris, but for some reason hadn't read it. Perhaps he was escaping the guilt. The last time he has sex with Diana, she goes down on him and ravishes and pulls and squeezes at his chest until it is red, finally running to the bathroom (presumably to spit) before running out of his life altogether. Significantly, when he goes to follow her, during his trek through the streets and to the subway station and then back to his room, we see no one else. He is alone. All alone.

And it is at this point that he reads the letter and discovers that while he has been away, tragedy has struck at home.

"I've never killed anybody, or hurt a soul. I'm not a liar or a cheat. I've never done any harm," he tearfully tells himself and probably his Creator while driving home. Though only three lines, it seems to be Joe's biggest speech in the entire film. The film could easily, in fact, have been made as a silent movie. There are long passages without dialogue and the story's primary communications are, after all, physical. Though not a very commercial idea, I think it would have been wonderful had the director decided to play it as a pantomime with music.

The film was produced by brothers Robert and Raymond Hakim, both producers of Luis Buñuel's hooker masterpiece **Belle de Jour** (1967), as well as some of Alain Delon's best icily gorgeous work, including **Plein Soleil (Purple Noon**; 1960) and **L'Eclisse (The Eclipse**; 1962)— part two of the Antonioni trilogy. Editor Louisette Hautecoeur also served as editor for Buñuel's **Belle de Jour** (1967) and **The Milky Way** (1969).

Among the cast of ladies, Isabelle Mercanton would also do **Spermula** (1976), and Dominique Erlanger would appear two years later with Joe in Jacques Rivette's **Merry-Go-Round** (1978).

La Marge is based on a novel by Borowczyk's friend André Pieyre de Mandiargues, whose short story "La Maree" was itself the basis for one of the episodes in the director's extremely popular **Immoral Tales** (1974). The book is set in Barcelona, making much of that setting, and so the move to Paris was criticized by some of the film's geographically-challenged detractors. It's said that Borowczyk originally intended to film in Spain, but the government wouldn't allow a reputed "pornographer" the permit. (The film was also cut by six minutes for the Italian market.)

To the charge of pornography, Borowczyk has said, while admitting that his deepest and most profound inspirations come from his dreams, "Anything that's beautiful is not pornography. The very word belongs to legislation, not to art."

l'ultima volta (1976)

> "I come from New York and the pace over in Rome was just so different. If, say, you have an appointment on Monday and you show up the following Monday, you're on time. Or if someone makes an appointment to see you on Tuesday and they're not there, but show up the following Tuesday, they're on time. It's you who fucked up."
>
> —*Joe Dallesandro*

(Also known as Gli Scippatori; Born Winner) **With JOE DALLESANDRO AS PERICLES,** Massimo Ranieri, Eleonora Giorgi, Pino Colizzi, Giancarlo Bandessi, Luigi Casellato, Dominique Demarest, Gianfranco DeGrassi, Severino Sattareli, Giovanni Ventura, with special participation of Marisa Mell. Directed by Aldo Lado. 87 minutes, Italy.

Another Joe movie in which you wish you could just make a whole other film with the same cast. What starts out as a possible teen-sex comedy about a good looking kid (pop star Ranieri) who works in the bakery, sneezes on fresh pastry, and then lands a job catering a posh birthday celebration only to be seduced by the hot young birthday girl, turns into a pretty dull buddy picture about a jacketful of stolen money and a lame motorcycle race.

Before it gets there, though, there's one last chance for the plot to get interesting, if you're willing to forgive the serious lack of credibility. As Pericles, Joe crashes the birthday party with a gun and robs all of the ritzy revelers. He orders everybody to dance and tells our young hero to "bring me a sandwich"—a very Joe thing to do, mixing the practical with the heat of the moment. Pericles manages to pull off the heist, but through subsequent circumstances and after stealing the kid's bakery van, he discovers the unlucky teen's name and shows up at his apartment for co-habitation.

The kid hardly even bats an eye of protest. Pericles is cooking.

During dinner, we find out that this handsome crook used to be a championship motorcyclist whose career was brought to a premature finish after a nasty accident. He is still haunted by the wipe-out and during his first night at the kid's apartment, the boy wakes up to see a butt-naked Joe wandering zombie-like towards an open window.

So, okay, it's going to be a buddy flick, we think, with bad-guy Pericles and bumbling young hero bonding and both becoming better people in the end. Pericles can teach the kid how to make it with babes and the kid can restore the older fella's shattered confidence by giving him something to care about again and turning his life away from crime. Or some such nonsense.

Nope.

Instead, the jobless kid begins to wonder how much purse snatchers make and the two become helmeted motorbike criminals. One successful snatch leads to the best paragraph of dialogue delivered in the whole film, a real treasure amidst the rest of the tripe. The kid has found a diary in the purse of a very good looking young woman (Eleonora Giorgi) and reads with increasing interest as we hear her voice-over of the following priceless entry:

"Is it possible to be in love and not want to make love? Or to make love when you're not in love? The fact is, I love screwing … a lot. And I also like an occasional girlfriend and I don't see anything wrong with that. I also adore Al Pacino and that sweet old Jack Nicholson. I think I'll go to the movies more often. I don't want to see anymore of Gaitano. He's one of those male chauvinists who say, 'It's my cock and I'll stick it where I like.' I must ask someone what other movies Robert Altman has made."

(Are we sure this wasn't improvised by Jackie Curtis?)

This babe is evidently too sassy to resist, and so our boy decides he'll call her and say he's found her purse. That way, he can get himself a girlfriend. Pericles thinks he's crazy, that it's too risky, but doesn't stop him. The kid actually makes paces, too; if only he hadn't let Gaitano's name slip in the midst of going down on her.

Pericles, meanwhile, with his tattoo smudged so we're not able to read what it is that's "Little," makes his own chick in typically rough and unromantic fashion. The girl he's boffing, however, turns out to be the fling of a senator who's planning to smuggle out a sizable chunk of stolen cash.

Pericles and the kid decide to pose as would-be money-holders in need of smuggling services only to find out that the operation plans to use Vatican credentials to take out this particular shipment for the senator. Our helmeted hooligans intercept the loot and make off while the idiot smugglers' vehicle inexplicably fails to give chase. No, it's not a plot set-up. It's a "I hope nobody in the audience will notice."

With the money sewn into the lining of his leather racing jacket, Pericles hangs out on a steamy resort beach with the kid and the chick, sweltering because he refuses to ever take off his coat. The Trofeo Maximoto motorcycle race just so happens to be going on and Pericles demands to stick around to compete. Naturally, he'll be wearing the jacket. The race itself is excitingly filmed, but certainly far less than suspenseful.

Pericles' victory is bittersweet, however, for a couple of reasons. First, because he's about to get killed. But more importantly, because his death comes in the single sequence in the entire film in which director Aldo Lado—who eighteen years later produced the Oscar-nominated **Farinelli**—cared about what he was doing: filming Joe in slo-mo as he raises both hands from his motorbike handlebars, cutting to a little kid eyeing the action through the viewfinder of his camera, then instantly intercutting with crosshairs seen through the scope of a sniper's rifle as Pericles is blown off and the bike continues to buzz down the track in front of him.

L'Ultima Volta, which was shot in September of 1976, isn't much of a movie, but I still can't shake the idea of wanting to play it out on any of several admittedly obvious tangents that the film could have or would have taken had it been made in the States: a sex comedy road picture with Pericles and the boy stumbling through conquests and defeats as mentor and pupil; an offbeat flick about sordid characters on the motorcycle racing circuit; or a buddy picture with bad-guy luring good-boy and sexy-girl into a life of petty crime that eventually catches up to them all.

Though he looks great all dolled up in black, with a spiffy designer tie and jacket, and later outfitted in his smart racing garb and posing with a cigarette dangling from his lips, Joe just can't save the picture on his own. Besides, even with those groovy sideburns, his hair needs to be cut to keep it from falling in his face all the time.

VIDEO REPLAY: Joe and the kid have their backs turned to the camera for a pantomime pee. Both of them do the requisite shake, adjust, and zip, and then as they turn to face the camera, Joe's hand glancingly "notices" that his fly is still open—and it really is, flashing his white undies—causing him to make the quick zip for real.

un cuore semplice (1977)

"I never went to school to study acting. There's nothing I ever did that said I qualify to get all this fame or even that I deserve it. I just kept showing up."
—*Joe Dallesandro*

(Also known as A Simple Heart) **With JOE DALLESANDRO, Adrianna Asti, and Alida Valli. Directed by Giorgio Ferrara. Italy.**

How's that for quotable filler? Truth is, I've been able to uncover next to nothing on this Italian entry in Joe's career and he remembers nothing about it either. It's possible that the film was never released, though it does show up in some filmographies; as it should, given the fact that it co-stars Alida Valli, who made films in her native country before going into hiding during the Second World War and re-emerging in America at the beckoning of David Selznick. (For a tidbit more on her career, which included films for Hitchcock and Carol Reed, see **Suor Omicidio** in this book—which marked the second time she worked peripherally with Joe.)

Director Ferrara's other known credit doesn't surface until 1991 (**Osada Venetsii**), so it may just be that this particular film never saw the inside of a movie theatre aside from an occasional screening to encourage backing. The distributor showed up with it at the 1978 Cannes Film Festival, but none of the trades reviewed it, and *Variety* noted that the company was in precarious financial straits, as indicated by their coming to the festival with product one to three years old.

The search continues. For now, it'll have to suffice that it is merely part of the record.

merry-go-round
(1978/1983)

"All the big sex symbols have last names ending in 'o'—Garbo, Harlow, Monroe, Brando, Dallesandro."

—*Paul Morrissey, as reported by Bob Colacello*

With JOE DALLESANDRO AS BEN, Maria Schneider (Leo), Francoise Prevost (Renee Novick), Maurice Garrel (Julius Danvers), Dominique Erlanger, Michel Berto, Jean-Francois Stevenin. Directed by Jacques Rivette. 160 minutes, France.

Arguably one of the great French filmmakers of all time, and a central figure of the French New Wave, Jacques Rivette is one of the most hotly contested geniuses of cinema since the 1960's, with most of his work simply unavailable to American audiences. As with most geniuses, the designation is foisted upon him or torn from him by the critics; in this case, an elitist corps of cine-intelligentsia that lord over the decision to bestow importance on this filmmaker as opposed to that filmmaker by virtue of "getting it" when others simply don't.

Spawned by reading Cocteau's account of the making of **La Belle et La Bete** (1946), Rivette's interest in film coalesced with his innate critical faculties and he began to contribute to the legendary *Cahiers du Cinema*. His essays on Hitchcock, Renoir, Hawks, and Mann are still insightful today.

His apprenticeship under Renoir was followed by work as cameraman on films for peers Francois Truffaut and Jean-Luc Godard, forming a philosophical alliance that came to be known as the nouvelle vague (New Wave). This was a theoretical rethinking of the formalist architecture of film that resulted in a wave of loosely-structured, elliptical, and very internal works that were read as personal statements from the film's *auteur* (its author): the director.

La Religieuse (1967), the tragic story of a woman forced into a nunnery and later sexually pursued by the Mother Superior (based on a play adapted from Diderot's novel of 1760), became Rivette's earliest success. Its temporary banishment in France made it notorious as a cause célèbre.

To satisfy our purposes here, let me say that amidst the tremendous amount of work Rivette has done over his long career there are two superficially notable characteristics that are of importance to us. First, he rarely indulged in working from finished scripts, preferring to allow his films to take shape through actor improvisations. It was often his practice to allow actors to create roles separate from one another and then he would conceive the outline for their commingling. Second, his films defied the standard running times of commercial cinema. He saw his films as works of art unto themselves, not to be limited by arbitrary constraints, such as when buttocks might start aching or at what point bladder and/or bowels might begin protesting.

L'Amour Fou (1968) runs 252 minutes (4h 12m). His next project, originally slated as a television eight-parter (but not sold), was **Out 1: Noli Me Tangere** (1971), which chronicled the labyrinthine rehearsals of 40 actors preparing two plays, and it came in at 12-and-a-half hours. It was shown in its entirety only once. A shortened version, called **Out 1: Spectre**, is still a healthy 260 minutes.

His masterwork may be **Celine et Julie Vont en Bateau** (1974, and a mere 193 minutes), an existential film exploring the relationship of two women, each of whom is integral to the other's immersion into a fictional reality in a haunted house.

As Joe points out, **Merry-Go-Round** was heading for the same running time stratosphere. And this on top of the tensions that were running high on the set because no one knew in what direction the haphazard project was going.

There were also off-camera personal crises complicating the lives of stars Dallesandro (drugs), Maria Schneider, and the director himself (on the verge of a nervous breakdown). It was only when Joe fell off a motorcycle and injured his coccyx that fate happily intervened on the frustrating shoot.

"I didn't want to, but it was the doctor's advice that I stop," Joe recalls. "I'm the kind of actor that if there's a limb hanging off me, I'm still going to work. The only way any of us could have left the film and got a breather from it, though, was for me to be accidentally injured like that, where the insurance then came in and paid everybody. That's what happened. Everyone got paid while I was healing. Rivette was going nutty, and Maria was attempting suicide, and so my crack-up gave us a week to calm down and get it together. Rivette was trying to make this movie last forever—we shot a ton of footage—and it was turning out to be one of those 24 hour movies."

The film originally came about as the answer to a contractual question left open when the director received an advance for an ambitious quartet of films, **Scenes de la Vie Parallele**, of which he had only made two (**Duelle**, **Noroit**). When investors forced his hand, he told them he would make the last two films as one and **Merry-Go-Round** was the product.

However, it turns out that **Merry-Go-Round** had nothing to do with either of its predecessors. Instead, it was a strange little detective tale about a man coming from New York to meet a woman whom he doesn't know coming from Rome after each are mysteriously summoned to Paris. Their only common link, it's discovered, is his girlfriend, who happens also to be her elder sister, but who has now vanished—perhaps kidnapped—along with a sizable inheritance. The pair set out to find the woman and are transported, according to *Sight and Sound*, into "a sort of parallel universe, and the suburban surroundings of the thriller, 'the dangerous, sad city of the imagination,' gives way to a natural world (sand dunes, a forest) into which they are assailed by hounds a la Zaroff, snakes, a medieval knight, and suchlike terrors of the mind." Quite a few segments are shot with a subjective camera.

With its totally "unrelated" and improvised musical track of bass and clarinet, the film comes complete with weird dream sequences—one reportedly involving characters trapped on the titular amusement park ride—which may relate to the film's original idea of having the leads psychically re-awakening their childhoods, and Andy Warhol reports in a diary entry that while in Paris, in 1977, he ran into a drunken and filthy Joe (his teeth "like licorice") cavorting loudly in a restaurant and saying that he was making a movie with Maria Schneider in which they played zombies! ("No, we weren't zombies," says Joe with exasperation. "I don't know where half this crap comes from. The *Warhol Diaries* are complete bullshit. You can't believe a thing in them.")

Merry-Go-Round finally came in at two hours and forty minutes, but Gaumont judged it unsuitable for release. It sat on the shelf for five years and finally opened in France the first week of April, 1983, where it received lukewarm reviews. One critic noted, however, that "a failed Rivette will always be more engaging than a successful Sautet or Woody Allen, because it speaks of the cinema, and the cinema's morality."

Joe was unaware of the delay and has always wondered—since he says his contract states that he owns the film for Italian distribution—why he never received prints or any of the related promotional materials.

suor omicidio

(1978)

"When I worked in Italy, they'd take all these old actresses who were overweight and they would put them in films with me and they'd ignite again, they'd have something going for them, because I wouldn't make them look like an old person. I play to everybody as if they were the most important thing in the world."
—*Joe Dallesandro*

(Also known as The Killer Nun) **With JOE DALLESANDRO AS DR. PATRICK ROWLANDS, Anita Ekberg (Sister Gertrude), Paola Morra (Sister Miture), Alida Valli (Mother Superior), Massimo Serato (Dr. Porei), Alice Gherardi, Ileana Fraja, Lee de Barriault, Daniele Dublino, Lou Castel. Directed by Giulio Berruti. 82 minutes, Italy.**

This is one of those horror movies that opens with a title card telling you that the story you are about to see is true. Now that may have worked for **The Texas Chainsaw Massacre** (1974)—which actually wasn't true, though it was superficially based on Wisconsin's Ed Gein case—and the makers of **The Amityville Horror** (1979) may have advertised their best-selling pulp fiction as "based on a true story," but it really doesn't make a bit of difference here. The film says the true events took place in an unnamed Central European country, though elsewhere I've seen it cited as coming from Belgium.

In any case, the basic story certainly could have actually taken place. There are no supernatural elements at work here. Anita Ekberg, the busty Swedish beauty queen in the fountain in **La Dolce Vita** (1960), stars as Sister Gertrude, a post-operative, brain-tumored nun working in a Catholic psychiatric ward who "could freak out at any second."

And she does, playing disconnect the IV, stomp on an old lady's dentures, go to the city, dress up like a real woman, and seduce a stranger for a stand-up screw. She pleads with the senior physician she has long assisted, as well as with the Mother Superior, to be allowed to go to the hospital for treatment. Her doctor callously says there's nothing wrong with her, that the tumor he removed wasn't even malignant. "How do you know? You're not a specialist!" she spits back at him. And Mother Superior? She simply reminds Sister Gertrude that "it is a nun's vocation to suffer."

165

Who can blame her then for walking around the hospital with the shakes, especially around scalpels? During dinner, she reads the tortures of the saints to her patients, detailing boiling oil poured onto gums, a red hot poker applied to the tongue, lips and cheeks pierced with searing needles, and a breast lopped off. As she reads, she becomes increasingly annoyed by the sight of little old Josephine's dentures sitting in her drinking glass on the table. She can finally take no more. She stops her litany of torture, grabs the teeth, flings them to the floor and repeatedly stomps on them while yelling, "Disgusting, disgusting!"

Later, she's sorry. She doesn't know why she did that. Her topless roommate, the dark-haired Sister Miture, comes to console her, and in the proces confesses that she's always loved her. On top of all this, Sister Gertie's got a drug problem.

Admittedly, it's almost always fun watching nuns shoot up on screen, and we get to here, but Ekberg is so darned serious about this tortured role that it's hard to laugh, even though usually it's the actors playing it straight that make bad movies funny. This is a flick probably best enjoyed, if at all, with a roomful of drunken Catholics, ex- or otherwise.

While Sister Gertrude goes into a drug-induced daze, we see visions of her brain surgery (with what appears to be a flap off an orange rubber ball filled with Karo Syrup doubling for her noggin). We also see her standing beside an unidentified man who lies completely and impressively nude on a slab in front of her. Meanwhile, in the non-dazed world, a patient who was trying to help the flipped out nun back to her bed is bludgeoned with a lamp, then thrown head first off the building into a lower courtyard to make his wounds look like a suicide.

Gertie manages to get the stuffy doctor she's been working for these last fifteen years booted from the staff. His replacement is Dr. Patrick Rowlands (Joe) and he's the cutest thing the film has to offer, so there's little surprise when Gertrude tells Sister Miture, "I've seen how you behave with the new doctor. Perhaps you're not as much a lesbian as you pretend."

You see, Gertrude has decided she'll go ahead and use her adoring roommate when it suits her, such as for going out to bring her dope. (This sounds more interesting than what we get to see, unfortunately.) In one scene, just begging to redeem the whole film, Gertrude tosses her bush-baring young nun a pair of stockings and demands that she put them on. "Put them on or I'll beat you," she says with spicy authority. Gertie prefers men, of course, but she's always ready to make love and "if I'm going to do it with a woman, she has to be wearing silk stockings." I like a nun who knows what she likes, but the movie-makers apparently had little idea what audiences like, because no love scene follows.

The director of the institute warns Dr. Rowlands that there's a great deal of suspicion among the patients that Sister Gertrude is behind the murders (there are now a few, including an old guy in a wheelchair offed after getting it on with a staff member). Says the young and painfully serious doc, "The way she acts, I'd put money on it." Too bad the film has been re-dubbed into English. It would have been nice to hear Joe's delivery on that line.

There's a bit more graphic torture, including a scene with a patient getting stuck in the face with little darts and a scalpel, but figuring out the real culprit and the motive isn't particularly tricky (was it the brain-tumored nun, the lesbian nun, or nun of the above?). The film ends on an abruptly unsatisfying note that betrays its fictional treatment of a possibly true story.

In addition to Anita Ekberg, whose career accomplishments include roles in Jerry Lewis' **Way...Way Out** (1966) and **Fangs of the Living Dead** (1973), the **Suor Omicidio** cast is honored to present Alida Valli for three scenes as Mother Superior. Valli, a screen veteran and cold beauty who had been making films since the 1930's, had also appeared in Hitchcock's **The Paradine Case** (1948) and Carol Reed's **The Third Man** (1949), then saw her career temporarily derailed by a well-publicized Italian sex-murder-and-drug scandal. She would later appear in the 1959 French horror classic **Les Yeux Sans Visage (Eyes Without A Face**; aka **The Horror Chamber of Dr. Faustus)** and Dario Argento's Italian horror classic **Suspiria** (1977), which co-starred Joe's girlfriend, actress Stefania Casini, and Udo Kier.

It's fun watching Joe in this very secondary role as a sober young doctor, garbed in white lab coat and tie and with a stethoscope in his pocket, and it would have been great to see him give an examination, but no luck. It's really quite a nothing part. Could have been played by anybody, so it might just as well be Joe. Then again, if I had Joe Dallesandro in my cast, I'd want to give him something to play with. His best scene comes about only in context, not because of anything quirky he gets to do.

Sister Miture, worried that Dr. Rowlands will have to report her drug-running activities to the police, is desperate to protect herself and Sister Gertrude. She cries out to him, pleading, then lowers herself in front of his crotch and plants a little kiss. "I'll do anything if you help me." The nub of her tongue runs gently up the front of his pants until she's standing again and they kiss. Apparently, our heroic Doc has decided to turn a blind eye so long as he's got himself a habit.

Joe doesn't even remember making "this piece of shit."

queen lear
(1978)

"(Joe) possessed a physically robust and voluptuous beauty and was comfortable with the knowledge that his physique aroused sensual appetites in both women and men."

—*art critic/author David Bourdon*

With JOE DALLESANDRO and Laura Garcia Lorca. Directed by Mokhtar Chorfi. France-Spain.

In one of his more unusual roles—which is saying a lot when you look over his career—Joe plays a husband who also sleeps with men (so far, it's just like **Flesh**). When confronted by his wife with his bisexual infidelity, he runs out of the house and gets mowed down by a semi, only to return time and time again during the course of the film in elaborate dream sequences after his widow drinks a vial of his sperm given to her by his male lover and immaculately conceives a child who wants to know all about his Daddy!

Joe recalls that most of the film was shot in Barcelona and that the script was some sort of play on Shakespeare's *King Lear*.

One particular set-piece has the family automobile rebuilt inside the living room of the house, with Joe's miracle son making a clubhouse out of it.

Co-star Laura Garcia Lorca, in her first (and maybe only) film role, is the niece of Federico Garcia Lorca, the famed Spanish poet (*Lament*) and playwright (*Blood Wedding*, *The House of Bernarda Alba*) who was shot to death in 1936 by Fascists during the Spanish Civil War.

Director Chorfi described his film to a French trade-paper as a "meditation on the power of love and on its mythology. Joe Dallesandro plays the role of a horseman of the apocalypse who laughs at love and has contempt for its most secret forms and expressions. Displaying his madness from one end of the movie to the other, he gives this story full of silence and fury its tragic dimension." He said further that it would "reveal a Dallesandro who is not only a perfect lover, but also a high class comedian, a dizzying presence on the screen...a fitting successor to Marlon Brando."

The highly unusual project remains one of the most sought after of Joe's European films that have yet to surface in the States.

About to get mowed down by a semi in **Queen Lear**/Courtesy Joe Dallesandro

6000 km di paura (1978)

"I was lured into that film as an opportunity for a vacation jaunt in Africa with my new girlfriend while I was playing a small role in the project. I didn't get the script until I got on the plane and it was only then that I came to understand I'm the star of the fucking movie. I said, 'Oh, my God,' because they had gotten me for very little money. I only did it for the chance to vacation, and now, not only does the script suck, but I get there and they want to sit around the table every day and have me involved in re-writing the thing."

—*Joe Dallesandro*

(Also known as Safari Rally) **With JOE DALLESANDRO AS JOE MASSI, Olga Bisera (Sandra Stark), Marcel Bozzuffi (Paul Stark), Enzo Fiermonte, Eleonora Giorgi (Lucile Davis). Directed by Bitto Albertini (Albert Thomas). 92 minutes, Italy.**

A Rome-Nairobi-USA co-production, **6000 km di Paura** took Joe to Africa to play the squarest leading man of his career. He's so square and so gorgeously primped with lustrously shampooed hair that, frankly, it's a shock to see him cast this way. There is so little of the Joe Dallesandro we know from the Andy Warhol days that you'd be hard-pressed to convince anyone he could play the roles that made him famous. This is all to his credit, of course, and there's more than a little joy in seeing him given the opportunity to so thoroughly shake himself loose of the sordid characters he was usually offered.

The film opens in Monte Carlo where a clash between arrogant teacher—car racer Paul Stark—and estranged pupil—Joe Massi (Dallesandro)—is underway. With some exciting shots of cars veering dangerously close to cheering onlookers in the night, it isn't long before Joe is involved in a terrific crash, "accidentally" caused by Stark, that sends Joe's car plummeting off a snowy mountainside. Miraculously, a passenger immediately jumps out unharmed and gives an unconscious Joe a few slaps on the face to try and revive him.

A handsomely half-blackened Joe crutches around his hospital room shirtless, bandaged, and showing off his tattoo during his recovery. A sultry visitor, played by Olga Bisera (of **The Spy Who Loved Me** Bond flick), turns out to be Sandra Stark, a former flame who's now wife to and navigator for his despicable ex-mentor. She still hasn't given up on the two of them, but Joe is clearly not interested. Like all great sportsmen, he has his sights firmly set on the next big competition—in this case, the Safari Rally.

"Not bad for an ex-corpse," Joe tells his navigator friend, Al, as they emerge from the car. Joe's sick and tired of always being the "#2 boy," with his cranky and jealous old instructor always #1. The two buddies walk along fully dressed (how else?) and then there's a jump-cut to a poolside stroll wearing only their tight little bathing trunks. They make friends with two bikini-clad women, a foxy journalist and her photographer partner. The journalist, Lucile (played by Eleonora Giorgi, Joe's co-star in **L'Ultima Volta**), wants to cover the entire race from a decidedly "different angle" and within minutes she and Joe are walking along the beach and he's playfully trying to go in for a peck.

Stark hasn't won the Safari Rally. In fact, it's the only trophy he doesn't have and he's none too happy that Joe is here as upstart challenger. "If you plan on beating me," he tells Joe, "you better get a plane."

Joe and Stark are both members of Team Kosmos, but everybody still races against each other. Mechanic Gianni makes a half-hearted plea to stop Joe from taking off in his car for an impromptu drag-race with Stark, screaming, "Those brakes are going to blow!" as Joe heedlessly speeds away. Stark gives Joe a good run for his money and then, in a wildly surprising and well-shot scene, Joe's car suddenly gets plowed by a speeding locomotive! His partner is hospitalized and Joe pleads with his racing management: "It was the brakes...not me...it was the brakes that didn't work."

Depressed, he heads off to seclusion with Lucile. He's seen lounging poolside at a resort, shirtless, and drinking his troubles away. Lucile consoles and lectures him: "At your age, you've succeeded where thousands of men have failed. But one little boo-boo and you come apart at the seams like a rag doll."

With Joe's blues nearly busted and his Ken-doll face smiling again, we're informed that Team Archer's driver is sick with malaria and so Joe has got himself another sponsor in the nick of time. A helicopter flight over the treacherous rally's track comes complete with such highly esoteric technical information as: "There are a lot of trees."

"I better be careful," says Joe.

Shot during the actual 25th Anniversary of the Safari Rally, the film mixes in footage of Joe racing along in Car #65 with documentary footage of attendance by Kenya's Vice-President at the opening ceremony, and for a good chunk of the ensuing film we get a pretty lifeless record of the muddy five day race.

Every once in a while, director Albertini, responsible for **Goldface, Il Fantastico Superman** (1969), **Black Emanuelle** (1975) and **Yellow Emanuelle** (1976)—and who Joe says was drunk so much of the time that the assistant director is really responsible—spices things up with some neat subjective footage from inside the cars as they buzz their way through panicking herds of giraffe, zebra, ostriches and a pack of cheetahs. These shots are particularly energizing because they add sound, exotic sights, colors and vibrations to the unspectacular and tension-less racing footage; perhaps even moreso because it appears obvious—from the lack of well-defined roads—that Albertini is deliberately charging these animals with his cars and not just encountering them along the "racetrack."

"Oh, no, a herd of elephants," laments Sandra matter-of-factly. "Just what we needed. Try to go around them to the right."

Though Joe suffers from a periodic bout of lightning knee pain, requiring his navigator to stick him with a hypo or risk having him faint at the wheel, his showdown with nasty Paul Stark is hardly nail-biting. A peculiar happenstance has Stark avoiding a little boy who has come out too far in the road to watch the race and thus veering off and coming to a fiery end with his wife by his side on the rocks below.

Meanwhile, the race is won by a suped-up Ford Escort! (Actually, I think that's sort of cool; a race movie in which neither the good guy or the bad guy wins—what a way to snuff out your audience's most basic expectations, making them feel completely unsatisfied and empty for having stuck with your worthless plot.)

Joe's performance is so different from anything he'd previously done that it's a kick just watching him play the handsome hero—the nice guy who doesn't swear, smiles a lot, and takes a shot at being the romantic charmer. Of course, he looks completely out of his element in his white racing uniform, especially when that squeaky-clean image is placed alongside a career's worth of offbeat movie characters. The fact that he's also dubbed with such an obviously "handsome leading man's voice" only adds to the sense of displacement. Robbed of his New York accent, his face nearly becomes someone else's.

In many ways, however, he's perfectly cast—as bland as can be, but that's only if you hadn't an inkling of what he'd done before. Strictly from the actor's point-of-view, it must have been a refreshing change of pace, as well as an extraordinary opportunity for the former bookbinder from Long Island to visit the Dark Continent as a movie star.

Two from the archives/Courtesy Joe Dallesandro

vacanze per un massacro (1979)

"Too bad the screenwriter was so completely oblivious to what he was doing here. A bad girl who gets bopped in the head, is forced to work with a pickax, and then seduces and gets fucked by the man responsible before ever asking who he is or what it is he wants is prime cult classic material deserving of a Paul Morrissey or even a John Waters."

—Paul Carruthers, Vine Street Reviews

(Also known as Vacation For A Massacre) **With JOE DALLESANDRO AS JOE BREZY, Lorraine de Selle (Paula), Patricia Bhen (Lillian), Gianni Macchia (Sergio). Directed by Fernando Di Leo. 91 minutes, Italy.**

If nothing else, this Italian drive-in exploitation flick ought to bring back buzzy remembrances of nights spent swatting mosquitoes and blaring your horn at the local passion pit while marginally shapely women with hard voices and lots of mascara cavorted their furry beavers across the night sky and kept at least half of the drunken audience hooting and horny.

Vacanze Per Un Massacro opens with Joe running through the countryside until he comes across a villa and decides to bounce a rock off a hapless fellow's head. Another fellow engages him in a little ballet with a pitchfork, but he gets the same rock bounced off his face. Then Joe pitches him with the fork for good measure, effectively killing off his witnesses so he can steal the car, light up a cigarette, and cruise down the road during the opening credits.

He breaks into a boarded up shack and walks suspiciously around the place looking for something, finally thumping on the base of the old fireplace. He isn't there long before a car is heard and he bails to a nearby rocky hiding place where he spies two women and a man unloading the vehicle. Turns out this shack is actually a vacation house of sorts, though it has to be something about the location rather than the place itself. (The filmmakers must have rented it in a pinch and were told to leave everything as it was, because the joint is sparingly decorated: a steel basket of fruit and a conspicuous wall-poster of a grinning John Travolta add to the charm.)

Turns out the threesome are two sisters and the older sister's husband. Young Paula is a bitchy little thing, allowing her brother-in-law to cop a feel when Big Sis isn't looking and demanding to know when the two of them will get it on. "We'll fuck, we'll fuck," Sergio tells her.

Joe watches all of this with a glinting eye from his hideaway and actually sits the whole night out in his rocky crag. Next morning, Joe is at the window spying as Sergio does a little implicit muff-diving with Paula. That transgression out of the way, the adulterous creep heads out to bag some game and can be seen aimlessly shooting off his shotgun in the air for cutaways meant to show he's having no luck. On at least one of these cutaways, actor Gianni Macchia decides to shake his hunting bag to "act out" that he's having no luck.

Back at the house, Lillian has left for shopping and Joe has at long last decided to move the plot forward by coming by and punching Paula in the head through the back of her sunning recliner. She's knocked cold and he carries her into the house, drops her, and starts slamming away at the fireplace base with a pick-ax. On Lillian's car radio, we hear the warning that Joe Brezy, a Corrections Prison escapee who was to go to the gas chamber on murder charges and who stole $300,000 five years ago that was never recovered (how, when, or why he hid it is inconsequential), has escaped and killed a local man. The license plate of the car is also given in the morning's newspaper, but it's completely unnecessary. None of the trio will spot the car and pretty soon they'll all know who he is, despite the irony that the radio describes the man as being "6', with blond straight hair and clear blue eyes." (Joe is 5'7", has brown hair and hazel eyes.)

Paula eventually wakes up to Joe's pounding and he tells her, "Behave or I'll split your head ... okay?" A little vixen who likes to walk around nude beneath her one-ply purple sundress, she tries to turn on the charm and visually seduce Joe with her long legs and near-spreads. Just when you think he might succumb, he gets her off her ass, hands her the pick-ax, and tells her to get to work.

"Harder!" Joe orders. She takes a few half-spirited whacks, then complains she's all sweaty and tired and runs her hands over her skimpy wrap. Joe just sits there. Interesting to see a film in which just about everybody gets naked *except* for Joe Dallesandro.

Big Sis comes home to find Paula tied and gagged and Joe threatens her with a knife. Sergio walks in the house and promptly gets hit in the back of the head (a favorite and effective target). Joe orders him to "dig."

Finally, the bag of dough is found. Then, in one of the more unusual moments in the film, Joe orders Sergio and Paula to get in bed and strip. While loving Big Sis looks on (the actresses don't look even remotely related and aren't even of the same ethnicity), Joe commands, "Now fuck." The pair look incredulous, so Joe points his shotgun at Sergio's crotch and orders, "Get hard!" Amazingly, the pair enact their little scene, while a cold-faced Joe calls from the sidelines: "With feeling ... c'mon, do it ... and you, do what men enjoy." The act consummated, Joe unloads his shotgun into the bedroom wall and walks out to reload.

Sweet Lillian, tormented by the knowledge of her husband's infidelities with her snotty little sister and having been forced to actually watch them go at it (in an unknowing stroke of Joe's psychosexual genius), is starting to give in to Joe's thugish charms. While a sappy English love ballad plays, she incredulously seems to respond to his kisses; kisses and pecks that go on for an eternity before Paula and Sergio decide to make their move and attack Joe with what looks to be a pointy black dildo pulled from out of the bedroom dresser. In requisite slow-motion, Joe blasts both Sergio and the wily Paula away. Then he asks Lillian to "come away with me." He reloads, but stupidly leaves the weapon in the house, walking to the car with the bag of money only to be shotgunned from behind, his face wincing and his arms upraised in freeze frame.

Vacanze Per Un Massacro has most all of the trappings of a really sleazy little action-sexploitation movie. What it doesn't have is the awareness to be just that. Made on a shoestring by writer-director Fernando Di Leo, whose earlier films include **The Cold-Blooded Beast** (1971), **The Italian Connection** (1972, which also had Gianni Macchia in it), **Stick 'em Up, Darlings** (1974), and **Mister Scarface** (1977), it's a movie without perspective on how joyfully dreadful you can make something like this, especially for cult audiences of today.

Simpler even than the nightmarish **Last House on the Left** (1974) in America, its plot is recycled horror/crime fodder with plenty of opportunities for nudity and sexual escapades. Nobody was in on the joke when they spent the few bucks to put it up on screen, so the result is an awfully ordinary exploitation flick that's begging for a sense of humor and a willingness to soak in the silly excess.

In **Vacanze**, Joe has the unenviable task of playing the whole thing straight, with lots of lingering close-ups as he drags on his cigarette and stares at his captives. He'd make an even better killer if the screenwriter would have only written him a part. Instead, though he's seen murdering two guys at the outset, he spends an awful lot of time lounging around puffing and there's absolutely no tension built or even the tiniest of threats managed by having him sit on the periphery for so long. Though it's nice to have him playing a "Joe" again and able to sport his tattoo, it seems all in a lazy day's work for Dallesandro.

© Francesco Scavullo. Reprinted with permission.

tapage

nocturne

(1979)

"The sexuality of Dallesandro is on the brink of what Ihab Hassan identifies as the shift from genital-centered, phallocentric modernist representations of sexuality to the more polymorphous and androgynous sexuality characteristic of post-modernism." —*Stephen Tropiano, Spectator*
USC Journal of Film and Television Criticism, Fall, 1989

(Also known as Nocturnal Uproar) **With JOE DALLESANDRO AS JIM, Dominique Laffin (Solange), Marie-Helene Breillat (Emmanuelle), Bertrand Bonvoisin (Bruno). Directed by Catherine Breillat. 95 minutes, France.**

At age 28, this was director Breillat's second film, and her second vocation. She made headlines at age 17 when her novel *L'Homme Facile* was deemed controversial for a teenaged author because of the amount of sex it included. Later, she would pen the novel *36 Fillette*, as well as write and direct the film version released in 1988, which follows the coming-of-age of a busty 14-year old and her seduction of a man her father's age.

With this film, Breillat has written another sexually-charged tale and brought it to the screen. It's the chronicle of a sexually adventurous young film director (Laffin)—perhaps autobiographical?—who becomes involved with a dispassionate young man who drags her through a soul-sucking relationship, thereby broadening her horizons on the politics of sex and male/female power-plays.

The film was critiqued for the sort of sexual relationship scrutiny that **Last Tango in Paris** engendered, which is apropos, since Breillat appeared in the Bertolucci film as Mouchette, but the reviews for **Tapage Nocturne** were not altogether kind.

The score was composed by Serge Gainsbourg, writer-director of **Je T'Aime Moi Non Plus**, which also starred Joe.

Variety noted, "Joe Dallesandro, a familiar sex object in Andy Warhol's iconography, makes a brief appearance as a familiar sex object," speaking fractured French.

the cotton club (1984)

"When I went to Europe it was with the notion that I'd come back Clint Eastwood … it didn't quite work out that way."

—*Joe Dallesandro*

With JOE DALLESANDRO AS CHARLES "LUCKY" LUCIANO, Richard Gere (Dixie Dwyer), Gregory Hines (Sandman Williams), Diane Lane (Vera Cicero), Lonette McKee (Lea Rose Oliver), Bob Hoskins (Owney Madden), James Remar (Dutch Schultz), Nicolas Cage (Vincent Dwyer), Fred Gwynne (Frenchy Demange), Gwen Verdon (Tish Dwyer). Directed by Francis Coppola. 127 minutes

Clean and sober, back in the country essentially to get his head together and figure out what he was going to do for a living, it didn't seem immediately apparent to Joe that acting in films again was going to be his ticket. For one thing, he had other priorities when he first arrived, and for another, when he did show a little interest, he was told that in order to get representation he should really have his latest work on tape for promotional purposes.

The Warhol films were known, of course, but they were the kinds of things he was hoping to avoid getting involved with if at all possible. Still, the Vista Theatre in Los Angeles celebrated his homecoming with a special screening of **Trash** on June 8, 1984, which Joe attended, even doing a spotlight Q & A after the show. But on the record, he was determined to distance himself, telling Robert Osborne in the *Hollywood Reporter* that "it was a great school for me" and "Paul was always telling me don't act. Just be yourself. I never felt awkward. Except that I was always asked to take my clothes off in front of the camera. And once or twice, okay, but come on. I didn't want to go through my whole life being photographed bare-assed," adding disingenuously, "Most of those films I didn't think would ever be shown in public. I was just a kid."

He'd made films for seven years in Europe, some for major directors, but much of that product wasn't making it across the Atlantic. Everywhere he went agents told him he had to have those work samples, if for no other reason than to prove to potential casting directors that he was still alive.

"When I first got back," remembers Joe, "people expressed how they thought I'd been dead. Because, of course, there were so many other people in the Warhol clan who were."

In 1983, after nearly a decade out of the American limelight, Joe Dallesandro got his break.

Francis Ford Coppola, the same director once said to be interested in him for **The Godfather**, cast him in the supporting role of mobster Charles "Lucky" Luciano in his latest epic film. Coppola was coming off the box-office disaster **One From The Heart** (1982) and had just completed his two "boy" movies, **The Outsiders** (1983) and **Rumble Fish** (1983), much to the dissatisfaction of berating critics who enjoyed gnashing at the larger-than-life director's egocentric dream of running his own movie studio, Zoetrope.

The Outsiders, presented as a wide-screen, drive-in, teenage-delinquent movie shot as if it were **Gone With The Wind**, is primarily remembered for its stellar cast of young discoveries (Swayze, Cruise, Estevez, Lowe, Howell, Macchio), but **Rumble Fish**, a stunning black-and-white teen art film with beautiful performances by Matt Dillon and Mickey Rourke, suffered a rather swift demise at the American box office. That the director of **The Godfather** films was adapting teen paperbacks at the behest of a librarian and her students from a Southern California junior high school was considered a professional joke.

The Cotton Club, suggested by James Haskins' pictorial history, was producer Robert Evans' baby and it was in trouble almost from the start. A man of some wild repute in the business, to say the least, Evans was coming off the phenomenal success of **Urban Cowboy** (1980) and apparently had some cash to spend on this fantasy project. Reportedly, he also got mixed up with modern day gangsters in the process.

Honestly, when he drafted Coppola onboard at the 11th hour, Evans couldn't have imagined it would help keep costs down (anybody remember **Apocalypse Now**?). The film went through as many as forty screenplay drafts, including work by Mario Puzo, and **Cotton** was spun into *gold* at an estimated final cost of $48,000,000.

Since it's somebody else's money, I've never much succumbed to the oooh's and ahhh's associated with movie budgets, particularly these days, but a feeding frenzy developed in the popular press—not unexpectedly—as the bills kept piling up and the pay-off was weighed against the expectation of Middle America's interest in a 127-minute film about a club in Harlem in the 20s and 30s that catered to gangsters and made black entertainers stars while refusing to let their fellow African-Americans in the front door.

The film's production schedule was sure to be a long one, and Joe was clued in to that possibility from the get-go.

When he went into co-producer Fred Roos' office during the casting phase, Joe was aware that he was being considered for the role of Luciano, but was worried because his hair was uncharacteristically buzzed into a crewcut for his limo driving job. He was concerned that he might have to wear a wig or something because he didn't look right for the part. Roos told him not to worry.

"You'll have plenty of time to grow your hair."

And he did. The film was so casually over-budget, with Coppola notoriously helming from his "Silverfish," a state-of-the-art trailer outfitted with all the video and audio techno-gadgetry known to man, that Joe sat around on the set for the entire first week without a single thing to do.

In fact, he even got a little restless because this job was cutting into his other job. One day, at the urging of a comrade, he went up to the director and informed him of his dilemma. "Oh, yeah, what's your other job?" Coppola inquired.

"I drive a limo."

A big grin crossed the director's face and Joe's most important scene, during which Luciano discusses a hit on upstart gangster Dutch Schultz with Owney Madden (Bob Hoskins) and Frenchy (Fred Gwynne), was shot at a booth in the club where a curtain could be drawn.

That way, you see, Joe could film all his dialogue in a closed environment. He wouldn't have to hang around for the endless days of filming in which his character would only have to be seen sitting at a table in the background of the shot.

The role of Luciano is a small one, coming only during the last fifteen minutes of the film, but Joe's slicked and stylishly wavy hair, classy Italian looks, and brooding demeanor in his very first Hollywood "A" picture seems far more legitimate than Richard Gere's dress-up act. (As an interesting aside, Andy Warhol reported in his diary that Gere told him in 1979 that ten years prior he had come by bus to New York, saw **Bike Boy** at a theatre in the Village, and decided he was going to be an actor.)

Setting a precedent for the kinds of roles he would now play, it's really a perfect part for Joe, giving him the chance to make a significant impression in a very short amount of time. ("Francis was good to me," he says. "He used just about every second of film he shot on me.") He's given several reaction shots, beautifully lit and from an imposingly low angle, as he silently watches over all the moll scrapping and mayhem that plays out before him; he's eyeing his new territory. This is a guy who's calm, cool, and very cunning. He's a killer waiting for the opportunity to do his stuff, and when it comes, it's as simple as moving into the backroom—where his silhouette plays against the wall—and making a phone call, muttering his instructions in Italian.

Even Vincent Canby in the *New York Times* took notice, remarking on the supporting work by "Joe Dallesandro, the one-time Andy Warhol star, who has aged gracefully enough to stand out in his brief appearance as Charles 'Lucky' Luciano."

In her own comparison to Gere, Pauline Kael wrote in the *New Yorker* that in "his brief appearance as Luciano, Joe Dallesandro, who's reminiscent of De Niro in **The Godfather, Part II**, has a much more romantic presence." (In fact, he looks as if he could be De Niro's brother.)

Too much of **The Cotton Club** feels like it's wrapped in plastic, though. It doesn't breathe, it doesn't come to life. The screenplay was pieced together from disparate plot line tangents, many ending up on the cutting room floor or abandoned altogether, and egos clashed and the studio demanded cuts and it was rushed into completion, miraculously coming in on schedule, but at the great expense of both dollars and its own hired-hand director's vision. Even most of its musical numbers lack pizzazz and there's an inexcusable fracturing of the shots during a potentially classic tap display by veterans of the Hoofer's Club. Why a director of Coppola's stature would even dream of cutting away from his dancers' feet is beyond me.

Symptomatic of this bubble-effect in which several excellent actors and occasional lame ones (a listless Gere and Coppola fave Diane Lane—who doesn't know how to give meaning to her lines) aren't able to make the period come alive is the fact that the best scene in an entire film about gangsters and the jazz age is a simple one-on-one between white guys.

Fred Gwynne and Bob Hoskins and a pocketwatch are the elemental ingredients to a certified all-time classic movie scene, which I won't spoil by detailing here.

Joe shares his scenes with both those actors during the film's "Cab Calloway Sequence" which shows the Cotton Club at its trendy peak, with notable celebrities in the audience, including Charlie Chaplin and Fanny Brice.

But Joe particularly remembers the fellow hired to play James Cagney, a young man named Vincent Jerosa, to whom he gave some curious advice.

"You should never speak to anybody," Joe told Jerosa. "You should just shut up and let them soak you in." Joe was positively enthralled.

"It was as if Jimmy Cagney had been reincarnated before he even died. I loved hanging around this kid, because I was such a big fan of Cagney's films, and that's all that I needed. I know that sounds weird, but the image was so complete. It wasn't as if the guy was acting like James Cagney, he *was* James Cagney. He gave me so much by looking the way he looked. He didn't have to do anything to win someone's friendship, because Cagney gave us such a gift, and his resemblance to him gave us such a gift in return, that he didn't have to do anything else. It gave you a sense of being with this legend when he was a young man. How else could we ever be in the presence of a young Jimmy Cagney?"

Funny, that's the first and only time I've ever heard Joe Dallesandro talk about someone with the kind of star-struck reverence associated with the cult of celebrity, the very thing he can't imagine ever inspiring himself. Laurence Olivier, David Bowie, Tennessee Williams, Dustin Hoffman—it doesn't matter what famous person he may talk about having encountered, because it always comes across as simply an event in his life and not a name-dropping ego trip—and yet here his voice assumed the silly, joyous excitation of an adolescent. How incredibly appropriate for a man who can't imagine his own photo arousing fantasies that the object of his adulation was nothing more or less than an image.

The underground star returns to America/Courtesy Joe Dallesandro

178

critical condition (1987)

"He's renowned for making the actor who is working with him laugh all the time. He won't let you keep a straight face even if the scene calls for it. They're beating me up, he's hitting me with this pipe and everything, and eventually I'm knocked out while Tex Cobb is holding me up in his arms. If you look, there's a little smirk on my face, because Pryor is making me laugh."
—*Joe Dallesandro on working with Richard Pryor*

With JOE DALLESANDRO AS JOE STUCKY, Richard Pryor (Eddie), Rachel Ticotin (Rachel), Ruben Blades (Louis), Joe Mantegna (Chambers), Bob Dishy (Dr. Foster), Sylvia Miles (Maggie), Randall "Tex" Cobb (Box), Bob Saget (Dr. Joffe), Garret Morris (Helicopter Junkie). Directed by Michael Apted. 100 minutes

The pleasures to be had sitting through this haphazardly conceived vehicle for Richard Pryor are too few to mention, though I imagine someone might get a perverse kick out of hearing Bob Saget say the "F" word on-camera as opposed to under his breath between takes on his television show. Pryor hides out from the mob in a hospital by pretending he's nuts and then escapes only to be mistaken for a doc during a hurricane. Joe shows up fully bearded and hobbling as a murderer and drug dealer who subsequently makes his own escape during a power outage. Relegated to a barely realized subplot that provides the film with a fight scene for a climax, Joe is given virtually nothing to do except stand around and look mean.

For Joe, it was another paycheck...and the chance to get kicked in the nuts by Richard Pryor.

Variety noted that the film reunited Sylvia Miles "with her old Andy Warhol partner Joe Dallesandro, but it's anyone's guess what he's up to here."

Sylvia and Joe have only one face-to-face scene together, but exchange no dialogue (Joe doesn't even look at her), so even the slightest joy of seeing Sally Todd and Joey Davis share the screen together again is completely lost.

sunset

(1988)

"I don't believe in studying acting. You can hone a craft, but there's certain things you just don't learn. I never even knew I had the talent until someone pointed it out to me."

—*Joe Dallesandro in LA Style, April, 1986*

With JOE DALLESANDRO AS DUTCH KIEFFER, Bruce Willis (Tom Mix), James Garner (Wyatt Earp), Malcolm McDowell (Alfie Alperin), Mariel Hemingway (Cheryl King), Kathleen Quinlan (Nancy Shoemaker), Jennifer Edwards (Victoria Alperin), Patricia Hodge (Christina Alperin), Richard Bradford (Captain Blackworth), Dermot Mulroney (Michael Alperin). Directed by Blake Edwards. 107 minutes

Five years after putting his stamp on Charles "Lucky" Luciano in **The Cotton Club**, Joe slicks back his hair again—this time as straight back as Bela Lugosi's—and adds a little tough-guy pizzazz to one of writer-director Edwards' less enjoyable outings, sandwiched right between **Blind Date** (1987) and **Skin Deep** (1989).

The **Blind Date** connection doesn't come near to explaining why Bruce Willis was chosen to play legendary Hollywood cowboy star Tom Mix, because it's doubtful even Willis' best friend would peg him for the role. Though he's not completely devoid of charm, he's pretty much left to fetishists who'll enjoy seeing him dandied up in all-white cowboy duds or sporting a black shirt with three gargantuan roses embroidered on the chest.

James Garner, on the other hand, is in his element, his voice now registering low enough and slow enough to evoke John Wayne's, and playing a role to which he first gave screen life in John Sturges' **Hour of the Gun** (1967)—none other than Wyatt Earp, this time fictionally called in to Hollywood to coach Mix on playing him in a movie, despite the fact that in real life Earp would have been one year and six feet under.

The unlikely duo eventually pal up when the owner of The Candy Store, a tinsel town bordello, is murdered while Earp is on assignment to locate the nasty studio boss' wayward son. While at the club, Earp spots the studio head's daughter (played by the director's daughter,

Jennifer) walking arm-in-arm with Chicago mobster Kieffer.

Garbed in brown suits that match his hair and set off his eyes, Joe cuts an imposing figure and makes short work of the gangster dialogue. On a visit to crooked studio boss Malcolm McDowell, he tells the crafty Brit with the flower in his hand, "I know who you are and what you are. I knew a guy just like you when I was just startin' in the rackets. Cocky little guy. Wore spats and a derby all the time. Used to brag about how smart he was. Until someone shot him in the mouth."

Even *Variety* took note, panning the film, but admiring Garner and one other actor in particular: "The other thesp to make a strong impression is former Andy Warhol leading man Joe Dallesandro, who is excellent as a supremely self-confident gangster."

It's fun to see Joe dressed up in black tie and in the audience for the film's pre-climactic evening at the very first Academy Awards, but you can't help wishing Edwards had just made a silly comedy instead of a half-serious murder mystery with 1929 Hollywood trimmings. Because outside of a few charming little moments—a mop handle becomes a convincing 12-gauge shotgun in the hands of actor Tom Mix, for one—the film doesn't ever seem to come to life or know what it's supposed to do. Frankly, we could care less about the murder because it happens to a character we never even meet.

Cross-dressing fans are left to ponder director Edwards having Mariel Hemingway wear a butch do and a man's evening clothes as the host/ess at the bordello with whom Garner briefly dallies. Of course, Garner had previously dallied boy/man/woman **Victor/Victoria** (1982), played by Edwards' wife Julie Andrews in the famed film Edwards both wrote and directed.

VIDEO REPLAY: Corrupt police captain Blackworth is in the midst of telling an intimidating Kieffer that he's not afraid of him when they both hear a large crash off-screen.

Blackworth: "You have a cat?"

Joe takes the proper beat: "Not that big."

An actor's headshot/Courtesy Joe Dallesandro

double revenge (1989)

"A lot of times it seems like I've got an attitude problem in interviews. But it's not like that. (He flashes a grin.) I'm really just a mean guy."

—*Press interview during the making of Double Revenge*

With JOE DALLESANDRO AS JOE HALSEY, Leigh McCloskey (Mick Taylor), Nancy Everhard (Susie), Theresa Saldana (Angie Corello), Chris Nash (Ray Halsey), Bobby DiCicco (Burt), Paul Ganus (Lewis), Robert Sampson (Ted McCray), Richard Rust (Sheriff Blanchfield). Directed by Armand Mastroianni. 96 minutes

Shot in Woodland Hills, California, in early 1988, **Double Revenge** was the first of a two-picture starring-role deal Joe had with producer Luigi Cingolani and his foreign investors. (**Private War** was to follow, and taken as a pair, they represent an interesting export of ideas about a crazy and violent America.)

In the small town of Morfield, California, dawn is breaking and one cozy couple get up to face the bright day with his good news that his landscaping business is on the verge of major growth and her secret news—just received in the mail today—that she is pregnant. On the flip side, we have dawn breaking on ex-con Joe Halsey (it's such a weird pleasure having Joe play a "Joe" again), who sits in his chair, shirtless—his "Little Joe" tattoo on display, smoking his cigarette and shining up his sawed-off shotgun. Little brother Ray is in the bedroom with his girlfriend, who's doing her best to talk the cute kid out of going with Joe on the morning bank job they've got planned.

Joe couldn't look meaner. He has, in fact, been very well cast (had to provide his own wardrobe, too), and there's a nice moment when he purposely shoves his brother's girlfriend out of the way only to open her dresser drawer, grab a pair of her black pantyhose, and slit it in half with a knife so that they'll both have masks for the job.

In case you couldn't have guessed, our sweet couple and our not-so-sweet couple are going to meet in one of those karmic moments of cultural incivility that make real life horrors the dramatic coincidence of movie plots. The bank job goes bad, Joe's brother is blasted away by cops when the nice guy grabs at the kid's pant leg, and Joe blows a hole in the do-gooder's arm and then wastes his beautiful wife by shooting her in the back for good measure.

At the trial, no one can positively identify Joe as the gunman and because of a series of law enforcement mistakes the bastard is released on a technicality. All hell breaks loose when the widowed nice guy (Leigh McCloskey, of **Dallas**, bad teen movies, and later **General Hospital** fame) is terrorized by Halsey and has to take the law into his own hands.

It's a very simple set-up, working along the lines of a vigilante movie, but with solid performances by the leads, and an eagerness by director Armand Mastroianni to milk the all-American tragedy angle, even to the point of overkill: he litters the film with American flags; the white-shirt and blue-jeaned good guy drives a red-and-white pick-up while chasing Joe in a blue one; Joe checks out his new weapon "hodware" in front of an American flag while our hero loads his pistol in front of a television signing off with the "National Anthem"; McCloskey is framed beneath purple mountains majesty as Harry Manfredini's tinny score swells during target practice in the countryside; a shoot-out in a bar is underscored when Joe avoids a shotgun blast and bumps into a jukebox, causing it to play "My Country Tis of Thee"; and all this patriotic irony reaches its nifty finale with an impressive slo-mo fall as Joe hangs from the rope of a flagpole mounted high on the facade of the American Furniture building.

The supporting cast doesn't hold up very well, some are so green they may be relatives, and there's some residual creepiness about seeing Theresa Saldana—the actress whose horrifying real-life stalking and near-fatal attack by an obsessive fan was also made into a 1984 TV movie—getting slapped around and then brutally strangled by Joe.

VIDEO REPLAY: Immediately after his release from court, a sardonic Joe walks down the street of the little town too careless to nail him for murder, stops at an ice cream stand, says, "Give me a cone," and then hands it to a little girl sitting on the front steps of a church.

private war

(1990)

"Mess with the best, die like the rest!"

(Also known as Operation Paratrooper) **With JOE DALLESANDRO AS VINCE RAYKER, Martin Hewitt (Phil Cooper), Kimberly Beck (Kim), Reggie Johnson (Cal Liston), George Shannon (Major Donnerman), Sam Hennings (Joseph Bates), B.J. Turner (Roland Caldwell), Robert J. Bennett (Angelo Rossi). Directed by Frank DePalma. 95 minutes**

This was the second of a pair of low-budget exploitation films distributed by Smart Egg Pictures that provided Joe with star billing. (The first was **Double Revenge**.) At the very least, it gave him the opportunity to show a side of him we haven't really seen before. He might appear improbably cast as a tough-as-nails Army sergeant, but, as I said, this is a revolutionary Joe and he's come prepared for the part: beefed up, with a military buzz-cut (bordering on flat-top), he delivers his lines in a gravelly voice and gives his grunts hell ... literally.

Joe's Vince Rayker is also psychotic, you see, so besides spouting inane strings of profanity (try "look who's got his finger up the cunt of genius" or "looks like you're feeding snowballs to a hot pussy" on for size), he's also using live ammunition during training exercises and taking his flashback wrath out on new recruit Phil Cooper, whose father served with the crazed sergeant in Nam.

The kid thinks Rayker is simply gung-ho, even after he takes a bullet in the arm from the guy, because his dad had written home saying that Rayker was simply the best. As far as the kid knows, his Dad is M.I.A., but we've already seen in flashback that Pops was purposely left to Charlie by a cowardly Rayker during a prison camp break.

That decision to leave his wounded friend to certain death has haunted the nasty sarge ever since, so when he's successfully booted and awaiting certain court martial for using a live grenade during an exercise (Cooper turns him in), he burns his military duds, prepares his weapons and follows the youngster up to a remote location where Major Donneman has planned a quiet hunting trip and asked the kid along.

Toss in a subplot about the Major cutting an arms deal with some local gun runners and a

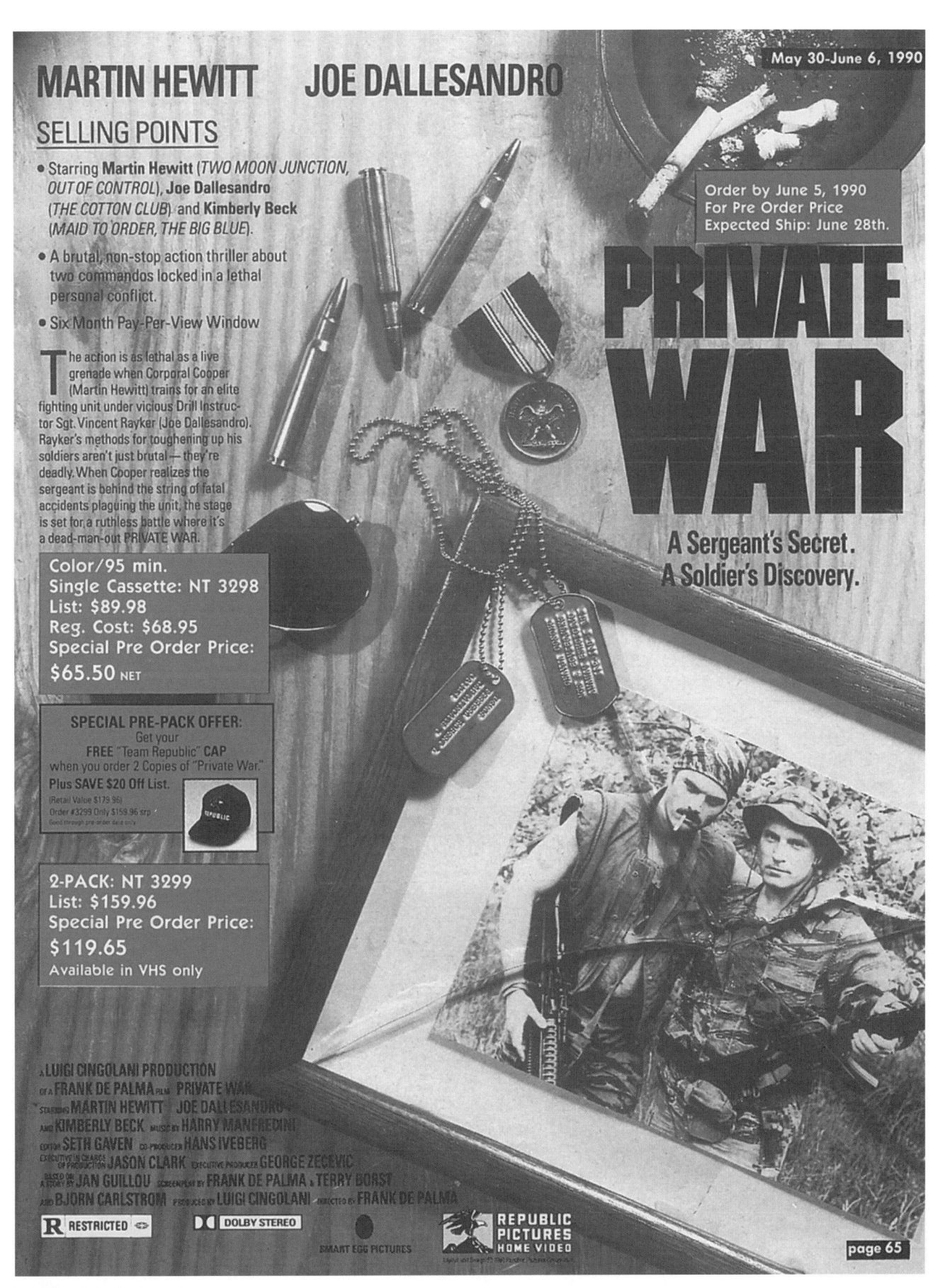

Courtesy of Joe Dallesandro

female journalist spying on the whole affair, and all you've really done is upped the body count for what quickly turns into a slightly gory slasher flick, with Joe as a camouflaged Boogie Man in green greasepaint, complete with his phony death and expected resurrection.

Rayker had a reputation in Nam for cutting off the fingers of his kills and you can better believe we're witness to some of that action. One-by-one the sergeant stalks the guys in the forest, either contriving to have them accidentally kill each other or putting to use tactics from the war and booby-trapping the forest with skull-gouging racks of catapulting spikes.

Martin Hewitt, who found himself a less than stellar career in low-budget films after baring his butt as Brooke Shields' teenage obsessor in **Endless Love**—the guy who listened to a bare-chested Tom Cruise's advice and burned down his beloved's house—does what he can in the hero role.

Kimberly Beck's résumé is appropriately dotted with appearances in **Massacre At Central High** (1976) and **Friday The 13th: The Final Chapter** (1984), and after giving Hewitt a thankful smooch, gets to say, "At least we still have all our fingers." Robert J. Bennett, who plays Angelo the Italian arms buyer, also played the "Headless Tarman" in **Return Of The Living Dead** (1985), and the film's score was composed by none other than Harry Manfredini, who scored all the "ch-ch-ch, ha-ha-ha's" for the original **Friday The 13th**! Even director Frank DePalma can't resist getting in on his own action. He plays Soldier #1.

The film is set in Italy, but was shot in Portoroz, Yugoslavia and completed in late 1988, thereafter languishing on the shelf for a year-and-a-half before getting a direct-to-video release.

Variety noted: "Dallesandro is surprisingly convincing in an acting stretch...(giving) an effective character performance."

Joe did all of his own stunts for the film, and while on the domestic front he and his girlfriend Kim had decided to live together for the first year, when it came time to marry, "I had just come off of **Private War**, and I had to do this flip, and I ended up breaking one of my fingers—my wedding ring finger! Man, I know whole fucking war movies that people work on that nobody gets hurt. But if you have an explosion in a movie that I'm in, I'm the one who gets blown up. It's just the nature of the beast. You know, the bullet is supposed to go into the tree and you're supposed to see some bark fly off; well, the bark's going to fly off and splinter my whole face."

VIDEO REPLAY: Dialogue during the first exercise as Joe gives his girls the once over before their aerial jump:

Rayker: You ever seen an ass-kicking wind like this before, soldier?

Soldier: No, sir.

Rayker: I'll say you haven't, 'cause the last time there was a wind like this you were suckin' up to your daddy's jism in your momma's pussy. Am I right? And I ought to know, because I was on the other side of her buttfucking her brains out. Am I right shit-face?

Soldier: Yes, sir.

Rayker: Don't ever call me sir. I work for a living.

cry-baby

(1990)

"Imagine our shame: our only child and he carries illegal weapons, drives fast cars, and wears clothes obviously designed by homosexuals!"

—*Joe Dallesandro in* ***Cry-Baby***

With JOE DALLESANDRO AS MILTON'S FATHER, Johnny Depp (Wade "Cry-Baby" Walker), Amy Locane (Allison), Susan Tyrell (Ramona), Polly Bergen (Mrs. Vernon-Williams), Iggy Pop (Belvedere), Ricki Lake (Pepper), Traci Lords (Wanda), Kim McGuire (Hatchet-Face), Darren E. Burrows (Milton), Stephen Mailer (Baldwin), Troy Donahue (Hatchet's Father), Mink Stole (Hatchet's Mother), Joey Heatherton (Milton's Mother), David Nelson (Wanda's Father), Patty Hearst (Wanda's Mother), Willem Dafoe (Hateful Guard). Directed by John Waters. 85 minutes

Perhaps John Waters' most underrated film, largely due to its relative failure to repeat **Hairspray**'s success at the box office, **Cry-Baby** not only deserves a midnight cult, it damn well better get one. In fact, I'll go so far as to predict it will have just such a following as the personal cult of Johnny Depp continues to grow and the new millennia looks back on one of the most profoundly original and eclectic careers of the fin-de-siècle. (Depp's, I mean.)

At first glance, Waters seems to have sold out from doing the raunchily subversive films of his own cultish youth (**Pink Flamingos**, **Mondo Trasho**, **Desperate Living**, **Female Trouble**, etc.), but that's all too superficial a blow. **Cry-Baby** is not only happily subversive, but it remains entirely consistent with the themes Waters has been jacking off all along. That he didn't want Johnny to eat dog shit isn't the point—he'd only be repeating himself, as he himself repeated to inquiry after inquiry about whatever happened to the Prince of Puke when this film came out—because it's something even more diabolical that he laces through his homage to the juvenile delinquent films of the 50's and 60's: he likes them. The cast list alone has "subversive" written all over it. From confessed alcoholic (Polly Bergen) to grown-up porn actress (Traci Lords) as daughter of world-famous terrorist (Patti Hearst) married to one of Ozzie and Harriet's kids (David Nelson), to 60's rocker (Iggy Pop), 60's ex-Pop figure (Joey Heatherton), desiccated 50's teen star (Troy Donahue), cantankerous author's son (Stephen Mailer) and underground film star

With Joey Heatherton, Mink Stole, Troy Donahue, Patty Hearst and David Nelson

(our man Joe), this is a virtual who's who of off-beat. And I haven't even mentioned a super-pregged Ricki Lake and a certifiable Susan Tyrell, one of the most frightening females in all of film history.

You don't have to be pop-culturally hip to enjoy what Waters has in store for you here, but it probably helps, and that's why I think this film is destined to eventually find a midnight showing audience. Too many people shied away when it hit the theatres in the spring of 1990 because it was marketed as a "teen flick" with a twist. Mediocre reviews didn't help and the few teens who went and saw it were simply the wrong audience at the wrong time. But in the cultural meltdown of the Information Age, when kids sharpen their heads on masses of accumulated microsplatter and pop culture becomes their favorite category on gameboard Q+A's, the time-trauma associated with generation gaps will be zip-drived and Hearst, Pop, Lords, Nelson and even Dallesandro will be trivial pursuits known, traded, and discussed.

No, **Cry-Baby** isn't wicked in the same ways that Waters' early greats are and it's not likely ever to replace **Pink Flamingos** or **Desperate Living** at teen video gross-out parties, but for legions of pop culture heads and their slightly older ma's and pa's, it's precisely the right response to the juvenile delinquent fluff Waters grew up with in the 50's and that's still available ad nauseam on AMC and TNT. **Cry-Baby** is the movie that the kids in **Hairspray** would have seen at their local drive-in on a Saturday night.

Johnny Depp, desperate to escape the prison of teeny-bopper TV star and about to go insane as he wound down the fourth season as Detective Tom Hanson on Fox's **21 Jump Street**, jumped at the chance to do **Cry-Baby**—what better way to turn an image on its ear than by playing it to the hilt?

Depp is Wade "Cry-Baby" Walker, the greasy-haired, leather-jacketed leader of the Drapes, a gang of bizarre juvenile delinquents proud of who they are, full of free-spirited fun and attitude, whom the goody two-shoe Squares revile with a spitting passion. Among Cry-Baby's entourage is a gal known as Hatchet-Face (Kim McGuire), a blond gargoyle, mean on the sax, sore on the eyes, but full of "character." When she's not beaming affectionately at a cow and sending it running in fear, she's crashing through the screen at a matinee of the 3-D film **Creature From The Black Lagoon** and sending the audience of hardened criminals screeching and flailing in terror.

In all of Waters' work, he's irrepressibly on the side of the social outcasts, the often larger-than-life freaks of nature who are as self-assured about who they are and what they are as the Munsters are sure that Marilyn is a sorrowfully ugly young woman. In **Cry-Baby**, it's the juvenile delinquents who have all the fun.

"I'm so tired of being good," laments pretty young Allison Vernon-Williams, the Square with the round corners who catches Cry-Baby Walker's dew-dropping eye.

Sure, Cry-Baby can talk tough and he can light a match with his teeth and extinguish it in his mouth, but he also wears his sissified nickname with family pride, the result of his predilection to shed big, gooey tears when he gets emotional. If you're not giggling yet, you ought to be. A teenage hood who cries in public, sings rock 'n' roll, and has an electric chair tattooed on his chest in memory of his serial bomber dad is just the kind of bad apple you'd call "Cry-Baby" and make a movie about. Okay, but you do if you're John Waters.

In his very first self-proclaimed "boy movie," Waters has lots of fun with his teen-idol star. Tapping into the dirty, adolescent fantasies—and more precisely, the dirty, grown-up fantasies directed at adolescents, the director indulges in the reworking of the spanking clean 1950's dreamboys by allowing his dreamboy to be anatomically correcting. When Cry-Baby Walker pulls his rod up outside the Vernon-Williams home and all of the prissy boys and girls and parental guidance inside run to the windows in a panic to look at the invader, we see this leather jacketed sexgod dismount and take a moment to dig at and re-arrange his goods—the epitomal gesture of uncouth and dangerously sexual youth made deliberately comical, self-aware, and somehow very sexy in all its male practicality.

Later, during an attempted escape from lock-up, Cry-Baby's prison pants get snagged and he's left to crawl through the tunnels in his slightly grungy jockey shorts, once again answering the call for teencake idolatry that had Pat Boone falling naked from a tree and covering himself with a sheep when discovered by nuns in **Journey To The Center Of The Earth** (1959). Waters knows how to handle a teen idol besieged weekly by fan letters stuffed with sub-human Polaroids and requests to trade tufts of pubic hair. If it's sexy boy you want, then it's sexy boy you'll get. (The underwear scene is played brilliantly, too, because it's so straightforward—not in the least a matter of the plot's attention or the star's embarrassment. A butt-shot would have been plainly gratuitous; though Depp's personal revilement for 1985's **Private Resort** has no bearing on the heinie shot he graciously provides there.)

John Waters said he felt like a "pedophile" when he walked up to the drugstore counter with an armful of teen magazines while he was researching (yeah, right) an actor to play the lead in this film. Johnny Depp's face was on the cover of every one of them, he said.

Sex has always been good to teenage coming-of-age films, even when it's presented as evil—maybe especially so. Teenagers who are aware of their bodies—the Cry-Baby Girls are all proud of their tits and even use them literally as weapons during rumbles—are just asking for trouble say the traditional movies of the drive-in 50's.

Not in a John Waters' teen movie. Not only does bulging Ricki Lake tell her approving grandmother how happy she is to "be all knocked up" again (she already has two little devils), but she and her "sisters" think Cry-Baby has "blue balls" for the Square, and sex in the Age of Innocence (pre-AIDS) is about to get a memorable endorsement in a PG-13 musical comedy by the Pope of Trash.

The French Kiss.

Tony Scott stuck it in his blue-light special silhouetted sex scenes in **Top Gun** (1986) and a few critics seemed to get the joke, while teenaged boys and girls giggled and moms and dads cringed watching Tom Cruise stick out his tongue and trade French kisses with Kelly McGillis.

The national news, meanwhile, was filled with mysterious references to safe-sex in the Age of the Sex-Plague and there were veiled references to avoiding the exchange of bodily fluids, even though kissing was considered "low risk" for transmission.

"Kiss me," says Cry-Baby to Allison, his face poised for maximum effect. "Kiss me hard." Leave it to John Waters to give us an entire sequence of lollygag Frenching, swirling, and sucking tongues between characters. Even the little kids join in, humorously trading their lollipops. In some ways, the French kiss seems as much a product of the 50's teen mythology as do ducktails. After decades of sweet and occasionally passionate kisses between hermetically-sealed idols in the movies, Waters was letting us have it.

And he doesn't stop there. The "gross out" is a trademark in Waters' films, even as he moved to more commercial fare. (**Hairspray** had a close-up of a zit being popped. Amazing how low the general public's tolerance is for such ordinary things!) In **Cry-Baby**, the gross out comes during a scene in which Allison, in a curious fit of ritual mourning, guzzles a jar of her own tears that she's been collecting since Cry-Baby was found "guilty of rampant juvenile delinquency" and jailed. Audiences gagged.

The irony of his being jailed is that, of course, he hasn't done a single thing wrong. Cry-Baby Walker is the rebel without a cause by virtue of his looks, his tastes in music and clothing, and his social choices. The Drapes have a code and it includes a respect for family, a commitment to a single girl or guy, and an edict to be true to yourself. The Squares, on the other hand, are smarmy little egotists, provoking fights, spewing racial epithets, vandalizing property, and quick at throwing the first punch. With short hair cuts and bleach-white clothes, they're the intolerant bureaucrats of the Eisenhower era.

"It's okay about my face," says Cry-Baby forgivingly to Mrs. Vernon-Williams after Baldwin throws a drink in it and fists him in the stomach. "It don't hurt much."

The clothes, the quirky characters, the attention to trashy time and place would have been enough, but the darn thing's a musical, too! Depp flawlessly lip-synchs to James Intveld's Elvis-y crooning on songs like "King Cry Baby" ("I had my first cigarette before I could walk and I was strummin' this guitar before I could talk"), "High School Hellcats," the **Jailhouse Rock** production number, "Doin' Time For Bein' Young"—a showstopper with inmates in blue jeans, blue shirts and James Brown doo's—and the falsetto jailbird lament, "Teardrops Are Falling," sung moments after creepy prison guard Willem Dafoe soundly slaps Johnny's butt and bids all the men to ask God to bless Ray Cohn and Richard Nixon.

Allison's numbers, including "A Teenage Prayer" and the saucy, "Please, Mr. Jailer," are vocalized by Rachel Sweet and less successfully dubbed.

The original music not only effectively evokes the period, but also the style of music that a teenaged John Waters lusted after while growing up in Baltimore in the 50's. It was the "colored" music forbade by adults because of its unnatural influence on the teenage sex drive, and precisely the kind of music that made losers feel empowered and winners feel superior. Because it was bad, every teenager in America wanted to hear it, and because it was bad, it was liberating.

The film was financed by Imagine Entertainment, where executive producer Brian Grazer (Ron Howard's partner) gave the green light on the $8,000,000 project because the only John Waters film he'd ever seen was **Hairspray** and he loved it. Incredibly, so the story goes, he was unfamiliar with any of the director's more notorious work.

Universal Pictures distributed and Waters must have enjoyed using the old black-and-white Universal logo with the plane buzzing around the globe as his opening image. He certainly enjoyed the opportunity to see one of his films shown at the Cannes Film Festival, where a midnight screening of **Cry-Baby** to a sold-out crowd resulted in a standing ovation.

Producer Rachel Talalay was also associated with the **Nightmare on Elm Street** series in which Johnny Depp made his film debut, and that explains why Depp was willing to do the cameo in the otherwise derisable **Final Nightmare** (1991), which Talalay directed, and in which his "brain on drugs" TV spot is the funniest thing in the entire flick.

The Joe Dallesandro-John Waters collaboration seems a natural and it's really kind of surprising that it didn't happen earlier in their careers. After all, Waters was making his films during precisely the same period as Morrissey was making his. What's more, Andy Warhol often had Waters screen his films at the Factory. So where was Joe?

"They kept us as far apart as possible," he says. "I was well protected."

The re-casting of an Italian Catholic underground film star as a barking evangelist works well and Joe makes the most of his limited screen time as one of the Drapes' disapproving parents.

The cable television airing of the film includes additional scenes cut from the theatrical version. Unfortunately, you get less when you get more. Cut from the cable version are several key pieces of dialogue (including Lake's "knocked up" line), the Frenching, and, inexplicably, all of Joe's scenes except for his first bit of dialogue in the courtroom, where he and his wife have been called because of the fracas out at Turkey Point.

The danger in spoofing a subgenre as silly as the drive-in teen movie is that the originals have dated so badly that they're already spoofs of themselves. You want to make fun of an old Tab Hunter or Troy Donahue or Fabian flick? Just watch one of them.

Cry-Baby is about shaking the timeworn stereotypes, about embracing "vulgar jazz words," about being true to yourself even if all the other kids bounce chalkboard erasers off your head. The most subversive thing about it is that it is essentially as moral and instructive in its own way as the "educational" films it means to razz.

VIDEO REPLAY: Preacher pop Joe and withering mom rise in the courtroom to let the judge know how they feel about their son's involvement in the debacle out at Turkey Point. Clutching his Bible and an oversized cross, Joe tells the judge they've been praying so hard for their son that they've got headaches. When his wife starts quivering and muttering in a fit of divine inspiration, Joe's eyes go wide: "You see that, your Honor? She's speakin' in tongues. God's in her gullet!"

almost an angel (1990)

"Tall, androgynous leading man..."

—Midget fact-checker's entry for Joe in
The Encyclopedia of Film, 1991

With SPECIAL APPEARANCE BY JOE DALLESANDRO AS HOOD LEADER, Paul Hogan (Terry Dean), Elias Koteas (Steve), Linda Kozlowski (Rose), Charlton Heston (The Deity), Doreen Lang (Mrs. Garner), David Alan Grier. Directed by John Cornell. 96 minutes

With Chuck Heston stroking ego as God, Paul Hogan as writer, executive producer, and star impersonating Willie Nelson and Rod Stewart, and even less palatable pseudo-religious goodwill than the **Oh, God** movies of the 70's, there is only one reason to sit through this lifeless, sappy little film: Joe Dallesandro. Even Joe wouldn't be enough reason except that you can see his entire performance in the film's first three minutes. After that, you're done. He's gone. He's never coming back. Except for the special billing at the very end of the end credits.

In the very first scene, set at a bank, Joe is the lead bank robber wearing a ski mask and wielding a .44 magnum while shouting orders. It might as well not even be him. And he agrees, joking that he sees a whole career of such roles ahead, playing the hooded bad guy whose face nobody ever gets to see but who gets special billing in the credits. Actually, it was a simple two day gig in mid-March of 1990 and the special billing was at the producer's discretion and agreed to in his contract. Well, it was a little work anyway.

The second time we get to see him it's outside the bank and inside the getaway car where he informs the incredulous accomplice in the backseat who just fired three rounds into Hogan's "Rod Stewart" that he "knew you'd flip out if anything went wrong, so I loaded your gun with blanks."

guncrazy

(1992)

"Skanks on Film: Harry Dean Stanton, John Holmes, John Belushi, John Cassavettes, Joe Dallesandro, River Phoenix, Keanu Reeves, Gus Van Sant, Alex Winter. They may look like mechanics, but they have the soul of poets."

—Galaxy Craze, "Skank Rules," Details magazine, November, 1991

With JOE DALLESANDRO AS ROONEY, Drew Barrymore (Anita Minteer), James LeGros (Howard Hickok), Billy Drago (Hank Fulton), Michael Ironside (Mr. Kincaid), Ione Skye (Joy), Rodney Harvey (Tom), Jeremy Davies (Bill). Directed by Tamra Davis. 97 minutes

A beautifully photographed redundancy (check out Arthur Penn's **Bonnie and Clyde**) that had a lot of promise. It starts off with enough quirky and interesting white trash characters to make it look like it might warp into punky social skewering, but nothing comes of it. An abandoned teenaged girl (Drew Barrymore) living out of a trailer in a California desert town is the butt of sexual jokes and the lay of the land because she knows no other way to respond to all the nasty men in her life.

One of the randy dopes calls her "sperm bank" during geography class and before the day is over she's on her back in an old drainage pipe showing him and his buddies that she guesses she likes them, too.

Back at her trailer, her runaway mother's drunken skag of a boyfriend, Rooney (Joe), sits in front of the little TV drinking beer and smoking cigarettes.

The first time we see him, as described above, Joe is so greasy and scuzzy looking that he might as well be the poster boy for all such sleazy movie slimeballs. It's amazing then how nicely he cleans up, coming home in his red pick-up to find his teenage ward blasting away at cans with his .38. There's a clever shot of Joe's face reflected in the dark brown curvature of a beer bottle target, serving him up in double metaphor.

Drew wants the slug to teach her how to shoot, which he does, telling her how to pull

With Drew Barrymore

the trigger by suggesting, "Squeeze it like a zit...slow and easy." Before long she becomes quite adept at blowing away things in the backyard and Rooney is duly impressed.

"Quick, there are some Cuban looney-tunes with hard-ons!" he yells inexplicably, prompting her to fire off her pistol with aplomb.

"You know, all this shootin's got me feelin' kind of good...if you get my drift," he tells her. She gets it all right. But that night, after he thinks he got his by breaking down the door and forcing her to have sex, he finds out what getting it is all about. While he's sitting in front of the TV watching cars blow-up, the pale blonde teen queen with a gun walks up behind the skunk and blows him away.

End of Joe. Beginning of a new Drew. A penpal project initiated in school was supposed to lead to an education about the world in which we live, but Anita Minteer wrote to a guy named Howard Hickok who was spending three years in Chino for manslaughter and an additional two for pistol-whipping his pa.

"I always dreamed of a girl who loved guns," writes back Howard, who has now turned to painting and whose gentle voice has the charm of a southern fried preacher. Anita says Howard should write a letter saying he's found Jesus so that she can get him a job with the local gas station preacher who sermonizes by having his congregation fondle poisonous snakes.

Howard gets paroled and comes to town, lands that job with the weird preacher (who privately admits his rattlesnake's head got run over by a truck and hasn't been able to bite ever since), and love blossoms between the two young lovers.

Sort of, anyway, because as in just about all movies about guys and their guns, the gun has other thematic properties. Howard, like Warren Beatty's Clyde, ain't so much into sex, really. That's okay, says Anita, who may have brought about the impotence earlier the same night of their first encounter when she handily proved she was a better shot: "You can still cum in my mouth."

Ten years after her own jaw dropped wide open in **E.T.**, she succeeds in dropping ours.

With a quietly effective performance by independent film character actor turned leading man, James LeGros, who was so good in **Drugstore Cowboy** (1989) and would be hilarious in an alleged spoof of Brad Pitt in **Living in**

Oblivion (1995), this film has all the raw ingredients of a great little road movie with enough quirks and violent jabs to come off as a **Natural Born Killers** primer via **Badlands**. LeGros is the nicest killer you ever did meet, and though 15 years ago they would have cast Gary Busey in the part, LeGros has the advantage of not being nearly so scary looking to begin with; it crosses your mind that he might just even be one of those nice guy killers who had their reasons.

But the script by Matthew Bright, who co-scripted the cult favorite **Forbidden Zone** (1980), loses its edge as the film moves out onto the road and follows Howard and Anita's occasionally bloody run from the law. The dialogue still manages to sparkle here and there in its particular context, such as when Howard asks Anita if she wants to say a few words over Rooney's incinerating body—because it's the Christian thing to do—and she offers, "Here lies a pig. May he roast in hell for all eternity." Or when the preacher warns Howard that Anita's "come of age. She's all pink and juicy. Remember, I used to be a farmer." But the situations become too conventional to keep the interesting characters interesting. [Check out Gregg Araki's incredible **The Doom Generation** (1995) to see how the teen-angst road movie can be gloriously born again!]

The film's title invokes the 1949 Joseph H. Lewis looney B-budget classic **Gun Crazy**, which has deservedly developed a cult following and brought about critical orgasms since its rediscovery in the late 1960's. The 1992 film is not a remake, so the title is just a tip of the hat, but the two films do share heroines who become sharp-shooting criminals and otherwise gregarious leading men who've had run-ins with the law and hope to find honest employment as test-shooters for a major gun company.

This was music video director Tamra Davis' first feature film and was originally intended as a made-for-cable Showtime entry. When a handful of unexpectedly good reviews came out, the film managed a brief release in theaters at almost the same time it was available on home video.

VIDEO REPLAY: "There's some Yoo Hoo left in the fridge," says Rooney to Anita, adding, "Your mom called."

"What'd she say?" asks the interested teenager whose mother up and left her months ago in the care of a degenerate boyfriend.

"She said 'Hi.'"

bad love

(1992)

"As a general rule, beware of movies in which your lead characters chain-smoke. A billowing cigarette is an actor's invite to chew scenery. Besides, every other word is 'fuck,' 'fucking,' 'cunt,' 'bitch,' or 'bullshit' during the emotional outbursts and the actors are left wailing and whining and beating their heads against a wall of infantile improvisation."

—*Richard Vollin, The Woodstock Sentinel*

(Also known as Love Is Like That; Wild Angel) **With JOE DALLESANDRO AS BOSS, Pamela Gidley (Eloise), Tom Sizemore (Lenny), Seymour Cassel (Uncle Bud), Jennifer O'Neill (Ms. Alman), Margaux Hemingway (Jackie). Directed by Jill Goldman. 94 minutes**

"I don't know how I got myself into this mess," our lead character tells us via voice-over while we see her body hauled in slow motion anguish into a waiting cop car. Peculiar thing if you think about it, though, because she's talking to us after everything has already happened. This is one of those movies that begins where it will end. Unfortunately, for the next hour and a half we're going to see just exactly how she got into this mess.

Pamela Gidley, seven years after essaying the titular role in **Cherry 2000** (starring Melanie Griffith), plays Eloise, a cute, chain-smoking office girl who's sick and tired of being hit on by her boss. Playing a cleaned up sleazeball this time, Joe plays the boss. He tells her that "my wife made plans, we'll have to skip dinner," then takes her to the local motel where they strip and he bangs her. She's not into this scene. It's simply a means to her end.

Then Eloise gets wise and tells her boss off. He doesn't even get a nice, nasty rebuttal, just a quizzical reaction shot. In just under nine minutes and with only three scenes to his credit, Joe is gone. A fan stays tuned, of course, just in case that sexist pig comes back to stir up trouble later. That's what fans do. That's what fans live for. But I'm here to save you the trouble.

wild orchid II: two shades of blue (1992)

> "It's just as much work for an attractive person not to have sex as for an unattractive person to have sex."
> —*Andy Warhol*

With JOE DALLESANDRO AS JULES, Nina Siemaszko (Blue), Wendy Hughes (Elle), Robert Davi (Sully), Brent Fraser (Josh), Christopher McDonald (Senator Dixon), Liane Alexandra Curtis (Mona), Bridgit Ryan (Ruth), Lydie Denier (Dominique), Tom Skerritt (Ham). Directed by Zalman King. 111 (107) minutes

The original title was just **Blue Movie Blue**, but softcore king Zalman King had reasonable success with his original **Wild Orchid** (1990), particularly due to word-of-mouth on a jaw-dropping overhead view of sexual intercourse between Mickey Rourke and Carré Otis that begged the tantalizing question: Are these two actors really getting it on? Never the darling of critics (his **Two Moon Junction** features a lez-be-frenz tease from a spunky Kristy McNichol), King received this peculiar review for **Wild Orchid** in *Leonard Maltin's Movie & Video Guide*: "Notorious simulated sex scene caused a stir, but it's all for naught; this picture is enough to make any two bananas roll over in Carmen Miranda's grave."

So the new movie became **Wild Orchid 2: Blue Movie Blue** and, alternately, **Wild Orchid II...The Seduction**, with the idea that the film's pre-title would designate it as belonging to a series of erotic films that each had different stories. (King would do just this with his **Red Shoe Diaries** films for cable television.) So **Wild Orchid II: Two Shades of Blue** is the **Halloween III: Season of the Witch** of its kind.

You don't have to see the first film to follow the second or third and vice versa. All you need to know is that it's Zalman King, the once-upon-a-time actor who turned to writing sexy movies, such as Rourke and Basinger's steamy, critically trashed **9 1/2 Weeks** (1986).

His style is lay-it-on-thick, and, as film critic Dave Kehr wrote in the *Chicago Tribune*, it's the type "that one associates with TV perfume commercials and his eroticism is roughly comparable." The images are slick and sleek and soaked in color, making the stories he's written to accompany the images pale in comparison.

Tom Skerritt was having a banner year, all things considered, for being cast in pseudo-erotica, first as an alcoholic family man seduced by a harlot teenager (Drew Barrymore, no less) in **Poison Ivy** (1992), and then here as a horn-playing jazz musician with a heroin habit who's traveling "somewhere in California in 1958" with his 17-year old daughter, Blue (Nina Siemaszko).

On his first night's gig in a place called Jules' Joint, he mournfully blows his horn and then goes back to his room with the shakes and sweats because he's also blown all his cash and he needs more junk, a habit we're supposed to believe he's successfully hidden from his daughter.

Blue's no dummy (then again...), so when Jules (Joe) stops by, the teenager comes face to face with a bad idea.

"You ever been with a man?" asks Jules.

"No."

He takes her up to his luxurious digs, complete with moose head on the wall, and starts to undress. Blue switches off the lights, but Jules turns them back on, telling her, "You might not like looking at me, but I love looking at you."

Okay, so Joe plays another sleazeball. At least he's just trying to help out this time. He's an old friend of the family (he shows her a picture from off his mantle of himself with her dad, her long-gone mother, and baby Blue herself) and seems willing to supply the old man so long as he can take it out in trade.

When the de-virginized daughter returns with a gift for dad wrapped in tin foil, it doesn't take him long to figure out what transacted and he smashes the room to pieces with his cane.

Jules runs in to stop him, shouting in defense, "I'm not the problem here and you know it!"

Apparently, he does. Because the horn-tootin' junkie dad with a cane kills himself that very night, effectively setting his daughter on a course of prostitution and effectively getting actor Skerritt, living up to his character's namesake of Ham, the hell out of the movie after the first fifteen minutes, despite (or in direct spite of) lead billing in the credits. As consolation, he immediately went on to star as Brad Pitt's preachy pop in **A River Runs Through It** (1992).

Blue begins her training after she has a fit at Jules' Joint and smashes plates and throws things through windows. "Fucking whore!" Jules screams at her. He stands to make 10% off her tricking so he can't afford to get too bent out of shape.

"There's girls you fuck and there's girls you marry," tutors a fellow employee, "and never the twain shall meet."

After a late night sneaky-peek into the various rooms and accompanying activities in the palatial house of sin, Blue finds herself chosen by a good-looking high school kid who's been brought in by his dad. The boy (Brent Fraser) jokes that he's only doing this because his dad thinks he's queer.

"I'm not queer ... I'm just a virgin."

This is the very same slightly hunky kid Blue was entranced by in the film's opening when she and dad came across him strolling down the road. He was a charming young goof—a romantic ideal—and she even took his photograph. Luckily for him, he doesn't recognize her on his visit to the whorehouse because she's such a good "actress" and is sporting one of her many wig helmets.

Uncontrollable, feisty, and spiteful, she's not an ideal hooker and Madame Elle knows it. A particularly nasty scene involving a senator who has her hooded, gagged, and stripped for his home movie cameras is interrupted by Madame's delivery boy and driver, the pockmarked Sully (Robert Davi).

Sully turns out to be a good guy who helps her run away from her corrupt life. She finds herself back in high school, where she belongs, and has a chance to fall in love with the sweet boy who still doesn't recognize her from the night she busted his cherry.

There are numerous opportunities for writer-director King to turn up the heat, to up the stakes, but not a single one of them is taken. Where are the steamy sex scenes, the splash of kink, or the roving voyeur's eye of the camera?

Nowhere to be found. Instead we get scene after scene in which actors appear to wade across floors steeped in molasses. Everybody seems to be in a trance, a contagious lethargy inexplicable beyond the desire to make a feature-length movie out of a *Red Shoe Diaries* episode or a *Playboy After Dark* cable special.

There's an extra four minutes of supposedly "hotter" stuff in the "Unrated" version of the film, primarily comprising of a lengthier version of the senator's black-and-white stag film that's used against Blue for plot melodramatics and in which two of the lady participants reveal nether lips.

"There's nothing that sexy about my scenes in the film," admitted brunette teen-dream Fraser to a magazine at the time of the film's release. "I had a clause in my contract that they could show only my bare ass, and they didn't even do that."

Case closed.

It would have been nice to see Joe play the role of Sully, the tough-as-nails chauffeur with a tender heart, but instead, he adds another sleazy character to his repertoire.

Oh well, at least he gets to live.

sugar hill

(1994)

"It's hard to know why a picture like this got made, but apparently some Fox executives decided we hadn't been getting enough movies linking blacks to drugs and violence."

—*Jonathan Rosenbaum, Chicago Reader*

(Also known as Harlem) **With JOE DALLESANDRO AS TONY ADAMO, Wesley Snipes (Roemello Skuggs), Michael Wright (Raynathan Skuggs), Clarence Williams III (A.R. Skuggs), Theresa Randle (Melissa), Ernie Hudson (Lolly Jonas), Abe Vigoda (Gus Molino), Leslie Uggams (Doris Holly). Directed by Leon Ichaso. 123 minutes**

Almost no one saw this somber drama of the streets when it showed up in theatres in the summer of 1994, even with a very popular Wesley Snipes in the lead. The problem was basically twofold: it was very emphatically a drama—released in an off-key box-office season for a serious film— and it was also very emphatically not a **New Jack City**. It was "black," but it also wasn't **Menace To Society** or even **Boyz 'N' The Hood**. What all of those films had, good and bad, was juiced violence and action sequences that helped drive home their messages about crime and drugs and death in the urban neighborhood. **Sugar Hill**, on the other hand, isn't hyped up much at all. Its highs are, in fact, its lows, so that the few times we are witness to violence, it packs a real punch.

Timing is everything in the movie business. If the last mediocre Vietnam film you saw was the first Vietnam movie ever made, you'd still hear people talking about it.

The critics should have known better and they really ought to take another look. If none feel compelled, then at least the one who wrote the ** entry in Leonard Maltin's popular guide should revisit, because here we have a sourcebook that's clearly missing the opportunity to point people in the direction of a literate, well-acted, and important film in the midst of drug culture overkill.

The dialogue is so good in this film that it's necessary to point out it was written by Barry Michael Cooper, a journalist who was born and raised in Harlem and also penned **New Jack**

City. He has written a black "Greek" tragedy, a moving tale of guilt and redemption and the destruction of family played against the backdrop of Harlem's Sugar Hill, the very place our two central leads, brothers who witnessed the drug death of their mother while children, now control as drug pushers.

"The boy you loved has become the man you feared," Roemello (Wesley Snipes) intones as chorus to his long-dead mother. As a man, Roemello has become victim of his own circumstances. Intelligent, well-schooled, and on the brink of a scholarship (he also once played piano) as a teenager, Roemello gave his promise away by seeking out and murdering the man responsible for beating and repeatedly shooting his father on a rooftop while Roemello, as a boy, watched helplessly pinned beneath a cop.

As in Aristotelean tragedy, it isn't necessary that Roemello be punished by society, only that his punishment be moral, guilt-ridden, and self-inflicted. The conflict is in how he might find redemption. For Roemello that means getting out of the foul business in which he's enmeshed. He still visits his drug-addicted father, **Mod Squad**'s Clarence Williams III in a strong performance, and tries to develop a legitimate and romantic relationship with a beautiful young actress (Theresa Randle).

Roemello knows what he's doing for a living is only an end to itself, but getting out is complicated by the bond to his high-strung older brother Raynathan (Michael Wright), who as a child was their mother's only choice to help tie off her arm for heroin injections. Raynathan is a mess, an embittered, emotionally unstable and immature man. Wright's melodramatic performance is on a different pitch than the performances of his fellow actors, making his character's pain hard to assess or truly appreciate, but the idea of casting an actor who looks younger when playing a supposedly older brother is an interesting choice. It adds to the notion that Raynathan never truly got past that day when he was 11 and his mother died in front of him. He's volatile, angry, despises his junkie father, and has learned to love no one but his brother.

The boys work for the local Italian restaurateur Gus Molino (Abe Vigoda), whose gang beat the hell out of their father. Gus' cousin Sal did the most damage and he's the one who got offed by a young Roemello, but Gus insists he doesn't know exactly who killed Sal. The relationship is amicably uneasy and business-like, but things get stirred up when Tony Adamo (Joe Dallesandro) shows up and tells Gus that a decision has been made to bring someone else into Harlem to secure the territory now ruled over by the brothers—a former boxer named Lolly.

Roemello's dream to liberate himself from the violence and the drugs which he knowingly participated in for so many years is precisely the kind of redemption we want to see him achieve. Having given us glimpses into the past that haunts him (and, perhaps, many urban kids), his struggle to forge a new future takes on epic metaphorical significance. This is a movie about the virulent scourge of drugs on black urban youth and the great tragedy that often robs the promise each victim of that world holds.

Much more than the entertaining and successful **Superfly** (1972), a film to which this one has been compared because of its tale of a Harlem cocaine pusher who wants out after a final superdeal, **Sugar Hill** tells its story without moral ambiguities; it is a vehement anti-drug film. However, the redemption and salvation of Roemello Skuggs can be achieved.

Joe's role in the film is limited to appearances in four scenes, with only the first having any dialogue. He makes such a threatening impression in that first scene, during which he tells Abe Vigoda, "Hey, if I even thought someone killed my cousin, I'd take care of him," that he seems primed to appear as a key player in the showdown with the brothers. After all, he's the one who brings in Lolly and unbalances all of the key relationships. He is, therefore, an integral player in the tragedy, but, alas, not given much more screen time, even though the final confrontation with Raynathan in Gus' restaurant just screams for his character to show.

His third scene in the film, a roundtable discussion at a café of what's to happen next in the battle for turf, finds him curiously silent.

Joe explains.

"They were looking for everybody to improvise and I wasn't ready to do that. They had some interesting New Yorkers who were willing, though, and that's why they seemed to give more of a performance than me. They just pulled anything out of a hat. And it worked, thank God. Originally, I thought they were just seeing if it would work and nobody said whether it was or wasn't, so I didn't do anything. If you ask me to do something, all I can do is tell you whether I can or not. And if you give me something to do, I'll do it the best that I can, but I can't read your mind. I might offer something that maybe you'll be offended by, especially if you're the one who has written or directed the script."

Joe said he enjoyed working on the project very much, however, and getting that bit of insight as to what was going on in that café scene makes it interesting to go back and look at. You can see that Ernie Hudson is talking to both men at the table and is looking for answers from either one of them. Joe's reluctance to say anything can almost be read on his face, though undoubtedly that has a lot to do with projecting his behind-the-scenes apprehension onto the image. With a turn of his head towards the "other" guy, allowing *him* to talk, Joe resorts to just the kind of re-acting in which he specialized in the Warhol films.

199

theodore rex

(1996)

"I think movies should appeal to prurient interests. I mean, the way things are going now—people are alienated from one another. Movies should—uh—arouse you. Hollywood films are just planned out commercials."

—*Andy Warhol*

(Also known as T-Rex) **With JOE DALLESANDRO AS ROGAN, Whoopi Goldberg (Kate Coltrane), Bud Cort (Spinner), Juliet Landau (Dr. Shade), Pons Maar (Theodore Rex), Richard Roundtree (Commissioner Lynch), George Newbern (voice of T-Rex), Armin Mueller-Stahl (Elizar Kane), Stephen McHattie (Edge). Directed by Jonathan R. Betuel. 90 minutes**

Joe marks up another career curio by appearing in the most expensive film ever to go directly to video. The $35,000,000 **Theodore Rex**, known for a time simply as **T-Rex**, is a disaster of the first order. A horrifically tedious mixture of semi-serious cop picture and little kid's dinosaur movie, it is impossible to tell just exactly who the intended audience is.

Writer-director Betuel had previously written **The Last Starfighter** (1984) and had written and directed **My Science Project** (1985)—which had its own encounter with a T-Rex in a high school gym—but not an iota of what was marginally good in those teen flicks manifests itself here. This is what makes the common man resent Hollywood: millions of dollars spent on dressing up garbage that someone ought to have known from the get-go was garbage. (In this case, the filmmakers who signed the dotted line had no choice but to finish the goddamned thing and managed to foist it on Germany for the 1995 Christmas season.)

The sets and dinosaur special effects, the latter involving large costumes and character robotics like we've seen on television's *Dinosaurs*, are expensive, as must have been securing the cooperation of Goldberg, but the screenplay is hopelessly uninteresting, unfocused, and unworthy of all the time and effort. Goldberg tried to bail on the picture and her unhappiness with the project was no secret in the trades, but she stuck it out anyway.

She was particularly nice to Joe, he recalls, making sure that he spent as much time on the set as possible. His role is thankfully small, though practically speaking it would have been nice for him to have made a little more cash, as well as get a little more screen time. As it is, we assume he's Whoopi's "grid police" partner when we see the two of them staking out a job from the colorful neon city rooftops.

"Seriously, Coltrane," Joe asks Whoopi the android cop, "you sure your CPUs are ready for action?"

Joe and Whoopi then hitch lines for a dead weight and less-than-graceful descent onto a speeding truck. Whoopi crashes through the roof into the back and Joe lands on the hood and battles it out with the driver through the broken windshield. The truck belongs to the nasty, ugly, and whiny bad-guy Spinner, a cousin to actor Bud Cort's equally disgusting character from the end of the Robby Benson horror film **Die Laughing** of fifteen years prior.

The plot involves a billionaire's attempt to destroy the Earth as we know it so that he can build his own "new Eden." A dinocide investigation launches the participation of our title character and he's teamed with Whoopi without so much as an off-screen death or re-assignment for Joe.

After his opening action sequence on the truck, in which he gets to trade sub-par banter with Whoopi ("I thought you said you had the front?" "I thought you said you had the back?" "You had the front?" "Oh, like you had the back."), Joe welcomes Whoopi's character on her return to the grid and we never see him again.

Theodore, with his love for cookies maintained by an at-home Cookie Shooter machine, lumbers through the rest of the movie with Goldberg and there won't be a conscious man, woman, or child in your house by the end. Turner's cable station had the guts to show this turkey as a world television premiere on Thanksgiving Day, 1996. What a sadistic way to prey upon kids gathered for the holidays!

VIDEO REPLAY: See how much fun Joe and Whoopi are having on the picture by replaying their awkward, three-ton descent from the rooftop on wires.

With Whoopi Goldberg

pacino is missing (1998)

"We had to provide our own wardrobe and I was wearing a pair of pretty raggedy shoes. They wanted to do a shot where they start on my shoes and work their way up to my face and I said, 'Hey, man, I'm supposed to be a godfather type character and I wouldn't be wearing a pair of shoes that are falling apart. The last thing I want to see on the big fucking screen is this giant pair of rotten old shoes from out of my own closet.' So they skipped the shot."

—*Joe Dallesandro*

With JOE DALLESANDRO AS SAL COLLETTI, Anthony Alessandro (Keno DeVito Franceschi), Joe Estevez (Joe Cicero), Tawnya Richardson (Raleigh), Orna Banarie (Marisa), John Harrington, Barry Tracten, Laura Selway, Todd Bridges, Burt Ward, Dana Plato, Kenny Rogers, Jr. Directed by Eric Galler.

Originally titled **Cheap Thrills**, this Twilight Productions comedy does a little **Get Shorty** tango in its story of a young Family man (Anthony Alessandro) who's sent to Los Angeles so that his relationship with the girlfriend of Sal, the Godfather (Joe), won't come to light. Once there, the kid decides to check in on one of the Family's west coast investments, Fantasy Machine International Pictures, and before you know it, he's re-organized the company, made himself president, and committed to cranking out five low-budget flicks in just six weeks.

Things get complicated by a sideline drug operation with the Cubans, the ever-watchful eyes of the Feds, and the unexpected appearance of the Godfather who's come looking for his moll.

joe-pourri

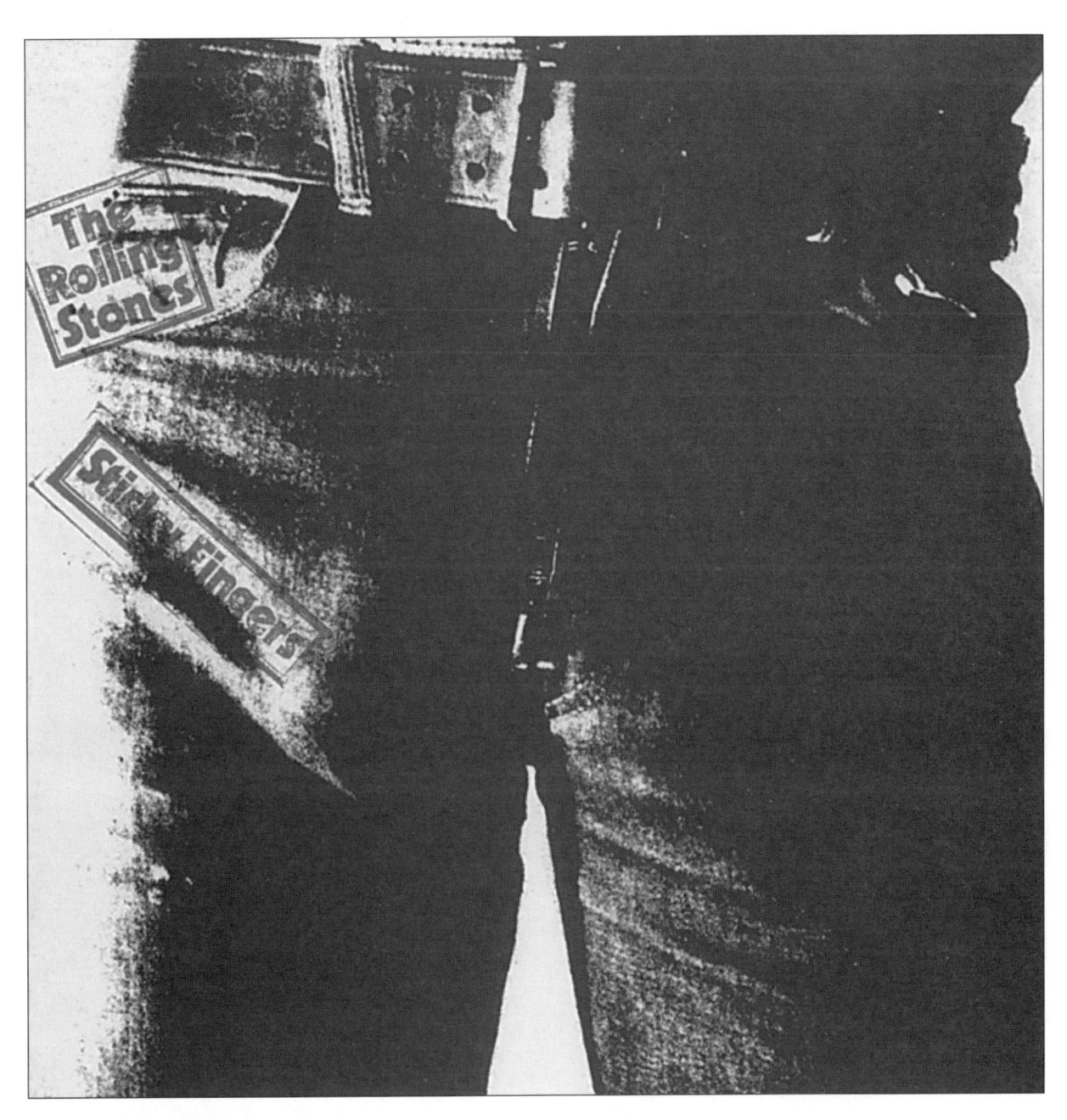

"Little" Joe?/Virgin Records

With Paul Morrissey, Jane Forth, and Andy Warhol on a stroll through Germany/Courtesy Joe Dallesandro

documentaries

Andy Warhol And His Clan
Germany (1970)
With JOE D'ALLESANDRO.
Directed by Bert Koetter. 46 minutes

Andy Warhol
(1973)
With JOE DALLESANDRO IN FILM CLIPS ONLY.
Directed by Lana Jokel. 53 minutes

Andy Warhol: Portrait Of An Artist
British Television (1987)
With JOE DALLESANDRO IN FILM CLIPS ONLY.
Directed by Kim Evans. 79 minutes

Scenes From The Life Of Andy Warhol
(1990)
With JOE DALLESANDRO.
Directed by Jonas Mekas. 38 minutes

Superstar: The Life And Times Of Andy Warhol
(1990)
With JOE DALLESANDRO IN FILM CLIPS AND STILLS ONLY.
Directed by Chuck Workman. 87 minutes

Homo Promo
(1991)
With JOE DALLESANDRO in the original trailer for Heat (1972).

Walk On The Wild Side
Great Britain (1993)
With JOE DALLESANDRO
Directed by James Marsh. 40 minutes

short films

music videos

Fred Brauner Prefers Beer
France (1979)
With JOE DALLESANDRO AS LEO.
Directed by Pierre Wallon. 30 minutes

"Never Let Me Down"
(1987)
David Bowie

Playboy's Inside/Out—"The Diaries"
(1992)
With JOE DALLESANDRO AS RICHARD.
Directed by Lizzie Borden. 13 minutes

"Molly (Sixteen Candles)"
(1995)
Sponge

Transformer
(1995)
Directed by Doug Aitken. 7 minutes

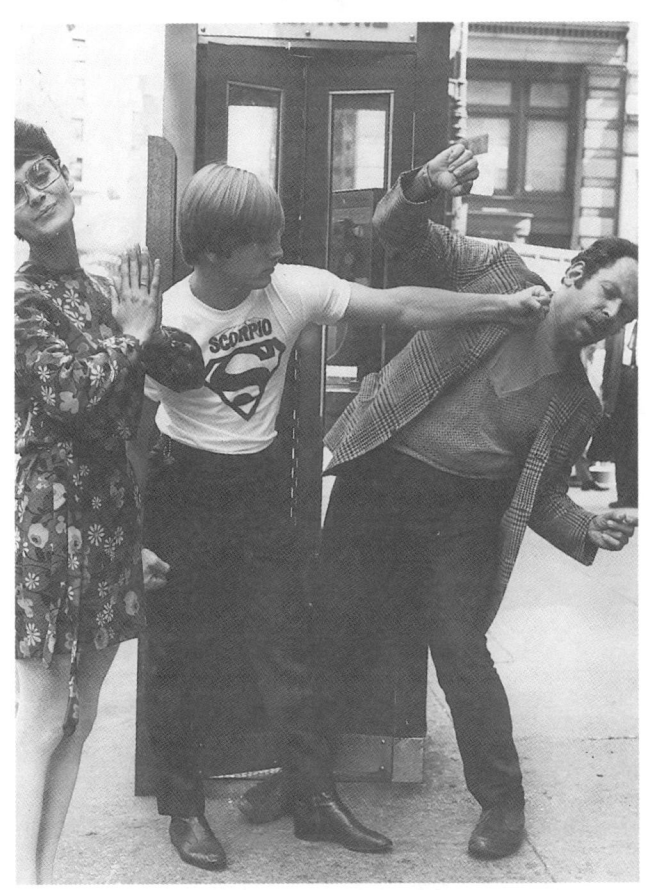

A modeling gig, 1968/Courtesy Joe Dallesandro

Photographed by Kenn Duncan/Courtesy Joe Dallesandro

With Cecil

television appearances

Miami Vice
"One Eyed Jack"
NBC-TV (November 2, 1984)
With JOE DALLESANDRO AS VINCENT DEMARCO.
Directed by Lee H. Katzin. 60 minute broadcast

Fortune Dane
ABC-TV (February 15, 1986-March 27, 1986)
With JOE DALLESANDRO AS "PERFECT" TOMMY NICAUTRI.
Various directors, including Charles Correll, John Patterson and Nicholas Sgarro.
60 minute broadcasts

Miami Vice
"Down For The Count"
NBC-TV
(Part 1-January 9, 1987/Part 2-January 16, 1987)
With JOE DALLESANDRO AS ALFREDO GIULINI.
Directed by Richard Compton. Two 60 minute broadcasts

Wiseguy
CBS-TV (1987)
With JOE DALLESANDRO AS PAUL "PAT THE CAT" PATRICE.
Four 60 minute broadcasts, listed below:

"New Blood"
(September 24, 1987)
Directed by Lyndon Chubbuck

"The Loose Cannon"
(October 1, 1987)
Directed by Larry Shaw

"A Deal's A Deal"
(October 29, 1987)
Directed by Charles Correll

"The Marriage of Heaven and Hell"
(November 5, 1987)
Directed by Zale Dalen

The Hitchhiker
"Fashion Exchange"
USA Network-Cable TV (1988)
With JOE DALLESANDRO AS JULIEN.
Directed by John Laing. 30 minute broadcast

The Hollywood Detective
USA Network-Cable TV
(October 25, 1989)
With JOE DALLESANDRO AS JERRY BRAZIL.
Directed by Kevin Connor. 88 minutes

Matlock
"The Informer"
NBC-TV
(Part 1-February 20, 1990/Part 2-February 27, 1990)
With JOE DALLESANDRO AS BOBBY BOYD.
Directed by Harvey Laidman. Two 60-minute broadcasts

With Penny Fuller, Carl Weathers and Daphne Ashbrook of **Fortune Dane**

renters', buyers' & screeners' guide

The Andy Warhol Museum
117 Sandusky Street
Pittsburgh, PA 15212-5890
412-237-8300, www.warhol.org/warhol
Regularly holds public screenings of Warhol/Morrissey features, including The Loves of Ondine and Lonesome Cowboys.

Arthouse Inc.
One Astor Place, Ste 9D
New York, NY 10003
212-979-5663, fx212-979-1683
arthouse@arthouseinc.com   www.arthouseinc.com
Offers for sale Jonas Mekas' documentary, Scenes From the Life of Andy Warhol, which includes a couple of silent shots of Joe hanging around Andy's Montauk estate in the mid-70s.

European Trash Cinema
P.O. Box 5367
Kingswood, TX 77325
Sells hard-to-find international video titles. Currently offers One Woman's Lover (Donna e Bello) and Born Winner (L'Ultima Volta).

Facets Multimedia, Inc.
1517 W Fullerton Avenue
Chicago, IL 60614
800-331-6197
Sale and rental of international collection of cult and foreign films. Flesh, Trash and Heat are available as rentals through their video-by-mail service.

Luminous Film & Video Wurks
P.O. Box 1047
Medford, NY 11763
516-289-1644, fx516-654-3637
LFVW@aol.com
Sells hard-to-find international video titles.

Currently offers The Climber (L'Ambizioso), Je T'Aime Moi Non Plus, Killer Nun (Suor Omicidio), Season for Assassins (Il Tempo Degli Assassini), The Streetwalker (La Marge).

Movies Unlimited
3015 Darnell Road
Philadelphia, PA 19115
800-4-Movies, 215-637-4444
www.moviesunlimited.com
One of the largest video sale resources in the world. Has most all American titles post-1984 available, as well as Seeds of Evil (The Gardener), The Hollywood Detective, and Superstar: The Life and Times of Andy Warhol (a documentary in which Joe appears in stills and film snippets).

TLA Video
1520 Locust Street, Ste 200
Philadelphia, PA 19102
800-333-852, fx215-790-1501
tlaone@ix.netcom.com
Premiere collection of gay and lesbian interest videos for sale. Offers AMG-The Fantasy Factory, a documentary with a snippet from Joe's AMG physique reel.

Video Search of Miami
P.O. Box 16-1917
Miami, FL 33116
888-279-9773 (toll free), fx305-598-5265
VSoM@aol.com   www.vsom.com
Sells hard-to-find international video titles. Currently offers Ambitious (L'Ambizioso), Je T'Aime (Je T'Aime Moi Non Plus), Safari Rally (6000 km di Paura), Street Walker (La Marge), Vacation for a Massacre (Vacanze Per Un Massacro).

©Francesco Scavullo. Reprinted with permission.

about the author

Michael Ferguson is a freelance writer who lives in Chicago. He served as editor of the ICM publication for the International Cinema Museum, and his work has appeared in *Cult Movies*, *Outré*, *Bikini*, the Chicago Psychotronic Film Society's *It's Only A Movie*, *Forrest J. Ackerman's Spacemen*, as well as on several websites. This is his first book.

Courtesy Joe Dallesandro

OTHER BOOKS FROM COMPANION PRESS

Quantity

_____ **THE BEST OF Gay Adult Video 1998**
Mickey Skee's Dirty Dozens
By Mickey Skee/204 pages/5-1/2x8-1/8
Over 100 b&w nude photos (including full-frontal)
$12.95 Softcover
ISBN# 1-889138-10-X

_____ **BAD BOYS On Video**
Interviews By Mickey Skee
224 pages/5-1/2x8-1/8
Over 100 b&w nude photos (including full-frontal)
$12.95 Softcover
1-889138-12-6 (Available Summer 1998)

_____ **The Films of KEN RYKER**
By Mickey Skee/152 pages/8-1/2 x 11
nearly 100 b&w nude photos (including full-frontal)
$18.95 Softcover
ISBN# 1-889138-08-8

_____ **The Films of KRISTEN BJORN**
By Jamoo/152 pages/8-1/2 x 11
100-plus b&w nude photos (including full-frontal
$18.95 Softcover
ISBN# 1-889138-00-2

_____ **SUPERSTARS—Gay Adult Video Guide**
By Jamoo/160 pages/5-1/2x8-1/8
nearly 100 nude photos (including full-frontal)
$12.95 Softcover
ISBN# 0-9625277-9-3

_____ **The X-Rated GAY VIDEO GUIDE**
By Sabin/448 pages/5-1/2x8-1/8
NO PHOTOS
$12.95 Softcover
ISBN# 1-889138-03-7

Quantity

_____ **The Complete VOYEUR VIDEO GUIDE**
By Steve Stewart/144 pages/5-1/2x8-1/8
nearly 100 b&w nude photos (including full-frontal)
$12.95 Softcover
ISBN# 1-889138-05-3

_____ **FULL-FRONTAL 2nd EDITION**
Male Nudity Video Guide
By Steve Stewart/144 pages
5-1/2x8-1/8/NO PHOTOS
$12.95 Softcover
1-889138-11-8

_____ **LITTLE JOE, SUPERSTAR**
The Films of Joe Dallesandro
By Michael Ferguson/216 pages/8-1/2 x 11
105 photos (including full-frontal)
$18.95 Softcover
1-889138-09-6

_____ **COMING-OF-AGE Movie & Video Guide**
A Guide To Sexuality In Mainstream Movies
By Don Lort/216 pages/8-1/2 x 11/
100-plus non-sexual photos
$18.95 Softcover
ISBN# 1-889138-02-9

_____ **CAMPY, VAMPY, TRAMPY Movie Sex Quotes**
By Steve Stewart/216 pages/4-1/4x6-5/8
$7.95 Softcover
ISBN# 0-9625277-6-9

_____ **PENIS PUNS, Jokes & One-Liners**
A Movie Quote Book
By Steve Stewart/124 pages/6 x 4-1/4
$5.95 Softcover
ISBN# 1-889138-07-X

SEE ORDER FORM ON REVERSE SIDE